MARIANNE WILLIAMSON

A RETURN TO LOVE
AND THE GIFT OF CHANGE

HarperOne
An Imprint of HarperCollinsPublishers

B&N ISBN: 978-1-4351-1960-4
ISBN: 978-0-06-199014-4

09 10 11 12 13   PHX/RRD   05 04 03 02 01

A Return to Love

Reflections on the Principles of *A COURSE IN MIRACLES*

Marianne Williamson

"Be not afraid, but let your world be lit by miracles."

—A Course in Miracles

HarperOne

An Imprint of HarperCollins*Publishers*

For both my fathers,
who art in Heaven.

CONTENTS

ACKNOWLEDGMENTS

This new edition of *A Return to Love* is possible because of the book's popularity since 1992. For that, my deepest thanks to Oprah Winfrey. Her enthusiasm and generosity have given the book, and me, an audience we would never otherwise have had.

Many thanks as well to my literary agent, Al Lowman. Because of him I started the book, and because of him I finished it. Andrea Cagan also did much to help bring this book to completion. Her contribution was enormous. Thanks to Carol Cohen, Adrian Zackheim, Mitchell Ivers, and all the others at HarperCollins who helped produce this new edition. For my friends Rich Cooper, Norma Ferarra, David Kessler, and Victoria Pearman, my gratitude is deep and abiding.

Thanks to every person who has attended my lectures since I began giving them.

Thanks to my parents for all they've given me, and to my daughter for bringing a sweetness to my life that soars way beyond words.

And most of all, thanks to all the many people who have read *A Return to Love* since it was first published and shared with me such powerful testimony of its value their lives. Their support for my efforts means more to me than I can express on this page.

FORWORD TO THE NEW EDITION

A Return of Love has had a life of its own, as does any book. An author is like a mother who brings a child into the world and then watches it live its own life story.

This particular book has had a wonderful life so far, and I have been priviledged to receive countless testimonials to its positive effect on readers. Because I am not the author of *A Course in Miracles* but merely an interpreter of its principles, I cannot take credit for the best things about *Return to Love*. The ideas in the Course had, and continue to have, a miraculous effect on my own life, and thus I understand the excitement that others feel upon coming across "miracles" for the first time.

I'm the older than I was when I wrote this book, and in some ways I am less innocent. I have tasted more of love's oppositions. Yet having seen as much as I have now seen of the world's resistance to the ways of love, I realize more deeply than ever the responsibility which each of us has to embrace it more fully and express it effectively. Hatred is the spiritual malignancy of our species and, like any other form of cancer, does its most terrible work not outwardly but within us. The fear behind it literally eats us alive, destroying minds, bodies, cultures, nations. External remedies can manage its effects, but only love has the power to undo it.

Undo it we must. From foreign wars to domestic catastrophes, our work is the work of casting fear from the world. We do this not only to serve ourselves but, most important, to serve our children. They shall inherit what we bequeath to them, and there is no greater gift to future generations than that we do the work God has asked us to do: love one another, that the world might be made right.

Fear unchecked grows exponentially. Love poured forth has the power to remove it. Thus is the power of God in our lives. If *A Return to Love* makes one iota of difference in anyone's ability to experience that power, then I am exceedingly glad I wrote it. I wish you miracles. I wish you love.

Marianne Williamson
January 1996

PREFACE

I grew up in a middle-class Jewish family, laced with the magical overtones of an eccentric father. When I was thirteen, in 1965, he took me to Saigon to show me what war was. The Vietnam War was beginning to rev up and he wanted me to see bullet holes firsthand. He didn't want the military-industrial complex to eat my brain and convince me war was okay.

My grandfather was very religious and sometimes I would go to synagogue with him on Saturday mornings. When the ark was opened during the service, he would bow and begin to cry. I would cry too, but I don't know whether I was crying out of a budding religious fervor, or simply because he was.

When I went to high school, I took my first philosophy class and decided God was a crutch I didn't need. What kind of God would let children starve, I argued, or people get cancer, or the Holocaust happen? The innocent faith of a child met the pseudointellectualism of a high school sophomore head on. I wrote a Dear John letter to God. I was depressed as I wrote it, but it was something I felt I had to do because I was too well-read now to believe in God.

During college, a lot of what I learned from professors was definitely extra-curricular. I left school to grow vegetables, but I don't remember ever growing any. There are a lot of things from those years I can't remember. Like a lot of people at that time—late sixties, early seventies—I was pretty wild. Every door marked "no" by conventional standards seemed to hold the key to some lascivious pleasure I had to have. Whatever sounded outrageous, I wanted to do. And usually, I did.

I didn't know what to do with my life, though I remember my parents kept begging me to do *something*. I went from relationship to relationship, job to job, city to city, looking for some sense of identity or purpose, some feeling that my life had finally kicked in. I knew I had talent, but I didn't know at what. I knew I had intelligence, but I was too frantic to apply it to my own circumstances. I went into therapy several times, but it rarely made an impact. I sank deeper and deeper into my own neurotic patterns, seeking relief in food, drugs, people, or whatever else I could find to distract me from myself. I was always trying to make something happen in my life, but nothing much happened except all the drama I created around things not happening.

There was some huge rock of self-loathing sitting in the middle of my stomach during those years, and it got worse with every phase I went through. As my pain deepened, so did my interest in philosophy: Eastern, Western, academic, esoteric. Kierkegaard, the I Ching, existentialism, radical death-of-God Christian theology, Buddhism, and more. I always sensed there was some mysterious cosmic order to things, but I could never figure out how it applied to my own life.

One day I was sitting around smoking marijuana with my brother, and he told me that everybody thought I was weird. "It's like you have some kind of virus," he said. I remember thinking I was going to shoot out of my body in that moment. I felt like an alien. I had often felt as though life was a private club and everybody had received the password except me. Now was one of those times. I felt other people knew a secret that I didn't know, but I didn't want to ask them about it because I didn't want them to know I didn't know.

By my mid-twenties, I was a total mess.

I believed other people were dying inside too, just like me, but they couldn't or wouldn't talk about it. I

 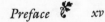

kept thinking there was something very important that no one was discussing. I didn't have the words myself, but I was sure that something was fundamentally off in the world. How could everybody think that this stupid game of "making it in the world"—which I was actually embarrassed I didn't know how to play—could be all there is to our being here?

One day in 1977, I saw a set of blue books with gold lettering sitting on someone's coffee table in New York City. I opened to the introduction. It read,

> "*This is* A Course in Miracles. *It is a required course. Only the time you take it is voluntary. Free will does not mean that you can establish the curriculum. It means only that you can elect what you want to take at a given time. The Course does not aim at teaching the meaning of love, for that is beyond what can be taught. It does aim, however, at removing the blocks to the awareness of love's presence, which is your natural inheritance.*"

I remember thinking that sounded rather intriguing, if not arrogant. Reading further, however, I noticed Christian terminology throughout the books. This made me nervous. Although I had studied Christian theology in school, I had kept it at an intellectual distance. Now I felt the threat of a more personal significance. I put the books back on the table.

It took another year before I picked them up again—another year, and another year's misery. Then I was ready. This time I was so depressed I didn't even notice the language. This time, I knew immediately that the Course had something very important to teach me. It used traditional Christian terms, but in decidedly nontraditional, nonreligious ways. I was struck, as most people are, by the profound authority of its voice. It answered questions I had begun to think were unanswerable. It talked about God in brilliant psychological terms, challenging my intelligence and never insulting it. It's a bit cliché to say this, but I felt like I had come home.

The Course seemed to have a basic message: *relax*. I was confused to hear that because I had always associated relaxing with resigning. I had been waiting for someone to explain to me how to fight the fight, or to fight the fight for me, and now this book suggested that I surrender the fight completely. I was surprised but so relieved. I had long suspected I wasn't made for worldly combat.

For me, this was not just another book. This was my personal teacher, my path out of hell. As I began reading the Course and following its Workbook exercises, I could feel almost immediately that the changes it produced inside of me were positive. I felt happy. I felt like I was beginning to calm down. I began to understand myself, to get some hook on why my relationships had been so painful, why I could never stay with anything, why I hated my body. Most importantly, I began to have some sense that I could change. Studying the Course unleashed huge amounts of hopeful energy inside me, energy that had been turning darker and more self-destructive every day.

The Course, a self-study program of spiritual psychotherapy contained in three books, claims no monopoly on God. It is a statement of universal spiritual themes. There's only one truth, spoken different ways, and the Course is just one path to it out of many. If it's your path, however, you know it. For me, the Course was a breakthrough experience intellectually, emotionally, and psychologically. It freed me from a terrible emotional pain.

I wanted that "awareness of love's presence" that I had read about, and over the next five years I studied the Course passionately. As my mother said at the time, I "read it like a menu." In 1983, I began sharing my understanding of the Course with a small gathering of people in Los Angeles. The group began to grow. Since then, my lecture audiences have grown significantly here and abroad. I have had the opportunity to see how relevant this material is to people throughout the world.

A Return to Love is based on what I have learned from *A Course in Miracles*. It is about some of the Course's basic principles as I understand them and relate them to various issues that affect our daily lives.

A Return to Love is about the practice of love, as a

strength and not a weakness, as a daily answer to the problems that confront us. How is love a practical solution? This book is written as a guide to the miraculous application of love as a balm on every wound. Whether our psychic pain is in the area of relationships, health, career, or elsewhere, love is a potent force, the cure, the Answer.

Americans are not that big on philosophy. We're very big on action, however, once we understand the reason for it. As we begin to understand more deeply why love is such a necessary element in the healing of the world, a shift will occur in how we live our lives within and without.

My prayer is that this book might help someone. I have written it with an open heart. I hope you'll read it with an open mind.

Marianne Williamson
Los Angeles, CA

INTRODUCTION

When we were born, we were programmed perfectly. We had a natural tendency to focus on love. Our imaginations were creative and flourishing, and we knew how to use them. We were connected to a world much richer than the one we connect to now, a world full of enchantment and a sense of the miraculous.

So what happened? Why is it that we reached a certain age, looked around, and the enchantment was gone?

Because we were taught to focus elsewhere. We were taught to think unnaturally. We were taught a very bad philosophy, a way of looking at the world that contradicts who we are.

We were taught to think thoughts like competition, struggle, sickness, finite resources, limitation, guilt, bad, death, scarcity, and loss. We began to think these things, and so we began to know them. We were taught that things like grades, being good enough, money, and doing things the right way, are more important than love. We were taught that we're separate from other people, that we have to compete to get ahead, that we're not quite good enough the way we are. We were taught to see the world the way that others had come to see it. It's as though, as soon as we got here, we were given a sleeping pill. The thinking of the world, which is not based on love, began pounding in our ears the moment we hit shore.

Love is what we were born with. Fear is what we have learned here. The spiritual journey is the relinquishment—or unlearning—of fear and the acceptance of love back into our hearts. Love is the essential existential fact. It is our ultimate reality and our purpose on earth. To be consciously aware of it, to experience love in ourselves and others, is the meaning of life.

Meaning doesn't lie in things. Meaning lies in us. When we attach value to things that aren't love—the money, the car, the house, the prestige—we are loving things that can't love us back. We are searching for meaning in the meaningless. Money, of itself, means nothing. Material things, of themselves, mean nothing. It's not that they're bad. It's that they're nothing.

We came here to co-create with God by extending

love. Life spent with any other purpose in mind is meaningless, contrary to our nature, and ultimately painful. It's as though we've been lost in a dark, parallel universe where things are loved more than people. We overvalue what we perceive with our physical senses, and undervalue what we know to be true in our hearts.

Love isn't seen with the physical eyes or heard with physical ears. The physical senses can't perceive it; it's perceived through another kind of vision. Metaphysicians call it the Third Eye, esoteric Christians call it the vision of the Holy Spirit, and others call it the Higher Self. Regardless of what it's called, love requires a different kind of "seeing" than we're used to—a different kind of knowing or thinking. Love is the intuitive knowledge of our hearts. It's a "world beyond" that we all secretly long for. An ancient memory of this love haunts all of us all the time, and beckons us to return.

Love isn't material. It's energy. It's the feeling in a room, a situation, a person. Money can't buy it. Sex doesn't guarantee it. It has nothing at all to do with the physical world, but it can be expressed nonetheless. We experience it as kindness, giving, mercy, compassion, peace, joy, acceptance, non-judgment, joining, and intimacy.

Fear is our shared lovelessness, our individual and collective hells. It's a world that seems to press on us from within and without, giving constant false testimony to the meaninglessness of love. When fear is expressed, we recognize it as anger, abuse, disease, pain, greed, addiction, selfishness, obsession, corruption, violence, and war.

Love is within us. It cannot be destroyed, but can only be hidden. The world we knew as children is still buried within our minds. I once read a delightful book called *The Mists of Avalon*. The mists of Avalon are a mythical allusion to the tales of King Arthur. Avalon is a magical island that is hidden behind huge impenetrable mists. Unless the mists part, there is no way to navigate your way to the island. But unless you believe the island is there, the mists won't part.

Avalon symbolizes a world beyond the world we see with our physical eyes. It represents a miraculous sense of things, the enchanted realm that we knew as children. Our childlike self is the deepest level of our being. It is who we really are and what is real doesn't go away. The truth doesn't stop being the truth just because we're not looking at it. Love merely becomes clouded over, or surrounded by mental mists.

Avalon is the world we knew when we were still connected to our softness, our innocence, our spirit. It's actually the same world we see now, but informed by love, interpreted gently, with hope and faith and a sense of wonder. It's easily retrieved, because perception is a choice. The mists part when we believe that Avalon is behind them.

And that's what a miracle is: a parting of the mists, a shift in perception, a return to love.

PART I

Principles

CHAPTER 1

Hell

"There is no place for hell in a world whose love-liness can yet be so intense and so inclusive it is but a step from there to Heaven."

Those passages with double quotation marks are quoted directly from A Course in Miracles. *Those passages with single quotation marks are paraphrased interpretations of that book. A complete listing of citations to* A Course in Miracles *appears beginning on p. 301.*

M.W.

1.   THE DARKNESS

"The journey into darkness has been long and cruel, and you have gone deep into it."

What happened to my generation is that we never grew up. The problem isn't that we're lost or apathetic, narcissistic or materialistic. The problem is we're terrified.

A lot of us know we have what it takes—the looks, the education, the talent, the credentials. But in certain areas, we're paralyzed. We're not being stopped by something on the outside, but by something on the inside. Our oppression is internal. The government isn't holding us back, or hunger or poverty. We're not afraid we'll get sent to Siberia. We're just afraid, period. Our fear is free-floating. We're afraid this isn't the right relationship or we're afraid it is. We're afraid they won't like us or we're afraid they will. We're afraid of failure or we're afraid of success. We're afraid of dying young or we're afraid of growing old. We're more afraid of life than we are of death.

You'd think we'd have some compassion for ourselves, bound up in emotional chains the way we are, but we don't. We're just disgusted with ourselves, because we think we should be better by now. Sometimes we make the mistake of thinking other people don't have as much fear as we do, which only makes us more afraid. Maybe they know something we don't know. Maybe we're missing a chromosome.

It's become popular these days to blame practically everything on our parents. We figure it's because of them that our self-esteem is so low. If only they'd been different, we'd be brimming with self-love. But if you take a close look at how our parents treated us, whatever abuse they gave us was often mild compared to the way we abuse ourselves today. It's true that your mother might have said repeatedly, "You'll never be able to do that, dear." But now you say to yourself, "You're a jerk. You never do it right. You blew it. I hate you." They might have been mean, but we're vicious.

Our generation has slipped into a barely camouflaged vortex of self-loathing. And we're always, even desperately, seeking a way out, through growth or through escape. Maybe this degree will do it, or this job, this seminar, this therapist, this relationship, this diet, or this project. But too often the medicine falls short of a cure, and the chains just keep getting thicker and tighter. The same soap operas develop with different people in different cities. We begin to realize that we ourselves are somehow the problem, but we don't know what to do about it. We're not powerful enough to overrule ourselves. We sabotage, abort everything: our careers, our relationships, even our children. We drink. We do drugs. We control. We obsess. We codepend. We overeat. We hide. We attack. The form of the dysfunction is irrelevant. We can find a lot of different ways to express how much we hate ourselves.

But express it we will. Emotional energy has got to go somewhere, and self-loathing is a powerful emotion. Turned inward, it becomes our personal hells: addiction, obsession, compulsion, depression, violent relationships, illness. Projected outward, it becomes our collective hells: violence, war, crime, oppression. But it's all the same thing: hell has many mansions, too.

I remember, years ago, having an image in my mind that frightened me terribly. I would see a sweet, innocent little girl in a perfect white organdy apron, pinned screaming with her back against a wall. A vicious, hysterical woman was repeatedly stabbing her through the heart with a knife. I suspected that both characters were me, that they lived as psychic forces inside my mind. With every passing year, I grew more scared of that woman with the knife. She was active in my system. She was totally out of control, and I felt like she wanted to kill me.

When I was most desperate, I looked for a lot of ways out of my personal hell. I read books about how our minds create our experience, how the brain is like a bio-computer that manufactures whatever we feed into it with our thoughts. "Think success and you'll get it," "Expect to fail and you will," I read. But no matter how much I worked at changing my thoughts, I kept going back to the painful ones. Temporary break-throughs would occur: I would work on having a more positive attitude, get myself together and meet a new man or get a new job. But I would always revert to the patterns of self-betrayal: I'd eventually turn into a bitch with the man, or screw up at the job. I would lose ten pounds, and then put them back on in five minutes, terrified by how it felt to look beautiful. The only thing more frightening than not getting male attention, was getting lots of it. The groove of sabotage ran deep and automatic. Sure, I could change my thoughts, but not permanently. And there's only one despair worse than "God, I blew it."—and that's, "God, I blew it *again*."

My painful thoughts were my demons. Demons are insidious. Through various therapeutic techniques, I'd become very smart about my own neuroses, but that didn't necessarily exorcise them. The garbage didn't go away; it just became more sophisticated. I used to tell a person what my weaknesses were, using such conscious language that they would think, "Well, obviously she knows what her patterns are, so she won't do *that* again."

But oh yes, I would. Acknowledging my patterns was just a way of diverting someone's attention. Then I'd go into a rampage or other outrageous behavior so quickly and smoothly that no one, least of all myself, could do anything to stop me before I'd ruined a situation completely. I would say the exact words that would make the man leave, or hit me, or make someone fire me, or worse. In those days, it never occurred to me to ask for a miracle.

For one thing, I wouldn't have known what a miracle was. I put them in the pseudo-mystical-religious garbage category. I didn't know, until reading *A Course in Miracles*, that a miracle is a reasonable thing to ask for. I didn't know that a miracle is just a shift in perception.

I once attended a twelve-step meeting where people were asking God to take away their desire to drink. I had never gone overboard with any one particular dysfunctional behavior. It wasn't drinking or drugs that was doing me in; it was my personality in general, that hysterical woman inside my head. My negativity was as destructive to me as alcohol is to the alcoholic. I was an artist at finding my own jugular. It was as though I was addicted to my own pain. Could I ask God to help me with that? It occurred to me that, just as with any other addictive behavior, maybe a power greater than myself could turn things around. Neither my intellect nor my willpower had been able to do that. Understanding what occurred when I was three years old hadn't been enough to free me. Problems I kept thinking would eventually go away, kept getting worse every year. I hadn't emotionally developed the way I should have, and I knew it. Somehow, somewhere, it was as though wires deep inside my brain had gotten crossed. Like a lot of other people in my generation and culture, I had gotten off track many years before, and in certain ways just never grew up. We've had the longest postadolescence in the history of the world. Like emotional stroke victims, we need to go back a few steps in order to go forward. We need someone to teach us the basics.

For me, no matter what hot water I had gotten into, I had always thought that I could get myself out of it. I was cute enough, or smart enough, or talented enough, or clever enough—and if nothing else worked, I could call my father and ask for money. But finally I got myself into so much trouble, that I knew I needed more help than I could muster up myself. At twelve-step meetings, I kept hearing it said that a power greater than I could do for me what I couldn't do for myself. There was nothing else to do and there was no one left to call. My fear finally became so great, that I wasn't too hip to say "God, please help me."

2. *THE LIGHT*

"The light is in you."

So I went through this grandiose, dramatic moment where I invited God into my life. It was terrifying at first, but then I kind of got off on the idea.

After that, nothing really felt the way I expected it to. I had thought that things would improve. It's as though my life was a house, and I thought God would give it a wonderful paint job—new shutters perhaps, a pretty portico, new roof. Instead, it felt as though, as soon as I gave the house to God, He hit it with a giant wrecking ball. "Sorry, honey," He seemed to say, "There were cracks in the foundation, not to mention all the rats in the bedroom. I thought we better just start all over."

I had read about people surrendering to God and then feeling this profound sense of peace descend like a mantle over their shoulders. I did get that feeling, but only for about a minute and a half. After that, I just felt like I'd been busted. This didn't turn me off to God so much as it made me respect His intelligence. It implied He understood the situation better than I would have expected. If I was God, I'd have busted me too. I felt more grateful than resentful. I was desperate for help.

A certain amount of desperation is usually necessary before we're ready for God. When it came to spiritual surrender, I didn't get serious, not really, until I was down on my knees completely. The mess got so thick that all the king's horses and all the king's men couldn't make Marianne function again. The hysterical woman inside me was in a maniacal rage, and the innocent child was pinned to the wall. I fell apart. I crossed the line between in-pain-but-still-able-to-function-normally, and the realm of the total basket case. I had what is commonly called a nervous breakdown.

Nervous breakdowns can be highly underrated

methods of spiritual transformation. They certainly get your attention. I have seen people have little mini-breakdowns year after year, each time stopping just short of getting the point. I think I was lucky to get mine over with in one fell swoop. The things I learned here, I will not forget. As painful as this experience was, I now see it as an important, perhaps necessary step in my breakthrough to a happier life.

For one thing, I was profoundly humbled. I saw very clearly that, 'of myself, I am nothing.' Until this happens, you keep trying all your old tricks, the ones that never did work but that you keep thinking might work this time. Once you've had enough and you can't do it anymore, you consider the possibility that there might be a better way. That's when your head cracks open and God comes in.

I felt during those years as though my skull had exploded. It seemed as though thousands of little pieces of it had shot into outer space. Very slowly, they began to come together again. But while my emotional brain was so exposed, it seemed to be rewired, like I'd had some kind of psychic surgery. I felt like I became a different person.

More people have felt their heads crack open in some way, than have admitted it to their friends. These days it's not an uncommon phenomenon. People are crashing into walls today—socially, biologically, psychologically and emotionally. But this isn't bad news. In a way, it's good. Until your knees finally hit the floor, you're just playing at life, and on some level you're scared because you know you're just playing. The moment of surrender is not when life is over. It's when it begins.

Not that that moment of eureka—that calling out to God—is it, and it's all Paradise from then on. You've simply started the climb. But you know you're not running around in circles at the bottom of the mountain anymore, never really getting anywhere, dreaming of the top and having no idea how to get there. For many people, things have to get very bad before there's a shift. When you truly bottom out, there comes an exhilarating release. You recognize there's a power in the universe bigger than you are, who can do for you what you can't do for yourself. All of a sudden, your last resort sounds like a very good idea.

How ironic. You spend your whole life resisting the notion that there's someone out there smarter than you are, and then all of a sudden you're so relieved to know it's true. All of a sudden, you're not too proud to ask for help.

That's what it means to surrender to God.

CHAPTER 2

God

"You are in God."

1.   GOD IS THE ROCK

"There is no time, no place, no state where God is absent."

There have been times in my life—and they still happen today, though they're more the exception now than the rule—when I have felt as though sadness would overwhelm me. Something didn't turn out the way I wanted it to, or I was in conflict with someone, or I was afraid of what might or might not happen in the future. Life in those moments can be difficult to bear, and the mind begins an endless search for its escape from pain.

What I learned from *A Course in Miracles* is that the change we're really looking for is inside our heads. Events are always in flux. One day people love you; the next day you're their target. One day a situation is running smoothly; the next day chaos reigns. One day you feel like you're an okay person; the next day you feel like you're an utter failure. These changes in life are always going to happen; they're part of the human experience. What we can change, however, is how we perceive them. And that shift in our perception is a miracle.

There's a biblical story where Jesus says we can build our house on sand or we can build it on rock. Our house is our emotional stability. When it is built on sand, then the winds and rain can tear it down. One disappointing phone call and we crumble; one storm and the house falls down.

When our house is built on rock, then it is sturdy and strong and the storms can't destroy it. We are not so vulnerable to life's passing dramas. Our stability rests on something more enduring than the current weather, something permanent and strong. We're depending on God.

I had never realized that depending on God meant depending on love. I had heard it said that God was love, but it had never kicked in for me exactly what that meant.

As I began to study *A Course in Miracles*, I discovered the following things:

> *God is the love within us.*
>
> *Whether we "follow Him," or think with love, is entirely up to us.*
>
> *When we choose to love, or to allow our minds to be one with God, then life is peaceful. When we turn away from love, the pain sets in.*

And whether we love, or close our hearts to love, is a mental choice we make, every moment of every day.

2.   LOVE IS GOD

"Love does not conquer all things, but it does set all things right."

Love taken seriously is a radical outlook, a major departure from the psychological orientation that rules the world. It is threatening not because it is a small idea, but because it is so huge.

For many people, God is a frightening concept. Asking God for help doesn't seem very comforting if we think of Him as something outside ourselves, or capricious or judgmental. But God is love. We were created in His image, or mind, which means that we are extensions of His love. This is why we are called the Sons of God.

We think we authored God, rather than realizing that He authored us. The Course says we have an 'authority problem.' Rather than accepting that we are the loving beings that He created, we have arrogantly thought that we could create ourselves, and then create God. Because *we* are angry and judgmental, we have projected those characteristics onto Him. We have made up a God in *our* image. But God remains who He is and always has been: the energy, the thought of unconditional love. He cannot think with anger or judgment; He is mercy and compassion and total acceptance. The problem is that we have forgotten this, and so we have forgotten who we ourselves are.

I began to realize that taking love seriously would be a complete transformation of my thinking. *A Course in Miracles* calls itself a 'mind training' in the relinquishment of a thought system based on fear, and the acceptance instead of a thought system based on love. Now, over a decade since starting the study of *A Course in Miracles*, my mind is hardly the touchstone of holy perception. I certainly don't pretend to consistently achieve a loving perspective of every situation in my own life. One thing I'm very clear about, however, is that when I do, life works beautifully. And when I don't, things stay stuck.

In order to love purely, we must surrender our old ways of thinking. For most of us, surrendering anything is difficult. We still think of surrender as failure, as something you do when you've lost the war. But spiritual surrender, although passive, is not weak. Actually, it is strong. It is a balance to our aggression. Although aggression is not bad—it is at the heart of creativity—it needs to be tempered by love in order to be an agent of harmony rather than violence. The mind that's separate from God has forgotten how to check in with love before it saunters out into the world. Without love, our actions are hysterical. Without love, we have no wisdom.

To surrender to God means to let go and just love. By affirming that love is our priority in a situation, we actualize the power of God. This is not metaphor; it's fact. We literally use our minds to co-create with Him. Through a mental decision—a conscious recognition of love's importance and our willingness to experience it—we "call on a higher power." We set aside our normal mental habit patterns and allow them to be superseded by a different, gentler mode of perception. That is what it means to let a power greater than we are direct our lives.

Once we get to the point where we realize that God is love, we understand that following God simply means following the dictates of love. The hurdle we have to face next is the question of whether or not love is such a wise thing to follow. The question is no longer "What is God?" The question we ask now is, "What is love?"

Love is energy. It's not something we can perceive with our physical senses, but people can usually tell you when they feel it and when they don't. Very few people feel enough love in their lives because the world has become a rather loveless place. We can hardly even imagine a world in which all of us were in love, all the time, with everyone. There would be no wars because we wouldn't fight. There would be no hunger because we would feed each other. There would be no environmental breakdown because we would love ourselves, our children and our planet too much to destroy it. There would be no prejudice, oppression or violence of any kind. There would be no sorrow. There would only be peace.

Although we may not realize it, most of us are violent people—not necessarily physically, but emotionally. We have been brought up in a world that does not put love first, and where love is absent, fear sets in. Fear is to love as darkness is to light. It's a terrible absence of what we need in order to survive. It's a place we go where all hell breaks loose.

When infants aren't held, they can become sick, even die. It's universally accepted that children need love, but at what age are people supposed to stop needing it? We never do. We need love in order to live happily, as much as we need oxygen in order to live at all.

3.   *ONLY LOVE IS REAL*

"God is not the author of fear. You are."

So the problem with the world is that we have strayed from God, or wandered away from love. According to *A Course in Miracles*, this separation from God first happened millions of years ago. But the important revelation, the crux of the Course, is that in reality it never happened at all.

The introduction to *A Course in Miracles* states:
> *"The Course can be summed up very simply:*
> *Nothing real can be threatened.*
> *Nothing unreal exists.*
> *Herein lies the peace of God."*

What that means is this:

1. Love is real. It's an eternal creation and nothing can destroy it.
2. Anything that isn't love is an illusion.
3. Remember this, and you'll be at peace.

A Course in Miracles says that only love is real: "The opposite of love is fear, but what is all-encompassing can have no opposite." When we think with love, we are literally co-creating with God. And when we're not thinking with love, since only love is real, then we're actually not thinking at all. We're hallucinating. And that's what this world is: a mass hallucination, where fear seems more real than love. Fear is an illusion. Our craziness, paranoia, anxiety and trauma are literally all *imagined*. That is not to say they don't exist for us as human beings. They do. But our fear is not our ultimate reality, and it does not replace the truth of who we really are. Our love, which is our real self, doesn't die, but merely goes underground.

The Course teaches that fear is literally a bad dream. It is as though the mind has been split in two; one part stays in touch with love, and the other part veers into fear. Fear manufactures a kind of parallel universe where the unreal seems real, and the real seems unreal.

Love casts out sin or fear the way light casts out darkness. The shift from fear to love is a miracle. It doesn't fix things on the earth plane; it addresses the real source of our problems, which is always on the level of consciousness. The only real problem is a lack of love. To address the world's problems on any other level is a temporary palliative—a fix but not a healing, a treatment of the symptom but not a cure.

Thoughts are like data programmed into a computer, registered on the screen of your life. If you don't like what you see on the screen, there's no point in going up to the screen and trying to erase it. Thought is Cause; experience is Effect. If you don't like the effects in your life, you have to change the nature of your thinking.

Love in your mind produces love in your life. This is the meaning of Heaven.

Fear in your mind produces fear in your life. This is the meaning of hell.

A shift in how we think about life produces a shift in how we experience it. To say, "God, deliver me from hell," means "God, Deliver me from my fearful thinking." The altar to God is the human mind. To "desecrate the altar" is to fill it with non-loving thoughts.

Adam and Eve were happy until she "ate of the knowledge of good and evil." What that means is that everything was perfect until they learned to close their hearts, to say, "I love you if you do this, but not if you do that," or, "I accept this part of you, but not that part." Closing our hearts destroys our peace because it's alien to our nature. It warps us and turns us into people we're not meant to be.

Freud defined neurosis as separation from self, and so it is. Our real self is the love within us. It's the "child of God." The fearful self is an impostor. The return to love is the great cosmic drama, the personal journey from pretense to self, from pain to inner peace.

So then it might go like this, or at least it did for me. I'd get myself into some terrible mess, and I'd remember that all I needed was a miracle, 'a shift in perception'. I'd pray, "God, please help me. Heal my mind. Wherever my thoughts have strayed from love—if I've been controlling, manipulative, greedy, ambitious for myself—whatever it is, I'm willing to see this differently. Amen."

So, the universe would hear that, and "Ding!," I'd get my miracle. Relationship transformed, situation healed. But then I'd go back to the same kind of fearful thinking that had gotten me down on my knees to begin with, and I'd repeat the pattern. I'd get myself into some emotional car crash, once again end up on my knees, once again ask God to help me, and once again be returned to sanity and peace.

Finally, after a lot of repetition of those embattled scenarios, I said to myself, "Marianne. Next time you're down on your knees, why don't you just *stay* there?" Why don't we stay in the realm of the answer, rather than always returning to the realm of the problem? Why not seek some level of awareness where we don't *create* these problems for ourselves all the time? Let's not just ask for a new job, a new relationship, or a new body. Let's ask for a new world. Let's ask for a new life.

When I was down on my knees completely, and I

knew what it meant to feel sincerely humbled, I almost expected to feel God's anger or contempt. Instead, it was as though I heard a gentle voice say, "Can we start now?" Until that point, I was hiding from my love, and so resisting my own life. The return to love is not the end of life's adventure, but the beginning. It's the return to who you really are.

CHAPTER 3
You

*"The Thought God holds of you is like a star,
unchangeable in an eternal sky."*

1.   THE PERFECT YOU

"Again—nothing you do or think or wish or make is necessary to establish your worth."

You are a child of God. You were created in a blinding flash of creativity, a primal thought when God extended Himself in love. Everything you've added on since is useless.

When Michelangelo was asked how he created a piece of sculpture, he answered that the statue already existed within the marble. God Himself had created the Pieta, David, Moses. Michelangelo's job, as he saw it, was to get rid of the excess marble that surrounded God's creation.

So it is with you. The perfect you isn't something you need to create, because God already created it. The perfect you is the love within you. Your job is to allow the Holy Spirit to remove the fearful thinking that surrounds your perfect self, just as excess marble surrounded Michelangelo's perfect statue.

To remember that you are part of God, that you are loved and lovable, is not arrogant. It's humble. To think you are anything else is arrogant, because it implies you're something other than a creation of God.

Love is changeless and therefore so are you. Nothing that you have ever done or will ever do can mar your perfection in the eyes of God. You're deserving in His eyes because of what you are, not because of what you do. What you do or don't do is not what determines your essential value—your growth perhaps, but not your value. That's why God is totally approving and accepting of you, exactly as you are. What's not to like? You were not created in sin; you were created in love.

2.   *THE DIVINE MIND*

> *"God has lit your mind Himself, and keeps your mind lit by His Light because His Light is what your mind is."*

Psychologist Carl Jung posited the notion of the "collective unconscious," an innate mental structure encompassing the universal thought forms of all humanity. His idea was that if you went deeply enough into your mind, and deeply enough into mine, there is a level we all share. The Course goes one step further; if you go deeply enough into your mind, and deeply enough into mine, we have the *same mind*. The concept of a divine, or "Christ" mind, is the idea that, at our core, we are not just identical, but actually the same being. "There is only one begotten Son" doesn't mean that someone else was it, and we're not. It means we're all it. There's only one of us here.

We're like the spokes on a wheel, all radiating out from the same center. If you define us according to our position on the rim, we seem separate and distinct from one another. But if you define us according to our starting point, our source—the center of the wheel—we're a shared identity. If you dig deep enough into your mind, and deep enough into mine, the picture is the same: at the bottom of it all, what we are is love.

The word Christ is a psychological term. No religion has a monopoly on the truth. Christ refers to the common thread of divine love that is the core and essence of every human mind.

The love in one of us is the love in all of us. 'There's actually no place where God stops and you start,' and no place where you stop and I start. Love is energy, an infinite continuum. Your mind extends into mine and into everyone else's. It doesn't stay enclosed within your body.

A Course in Miracles likens us to 'sunbeams' thinking we're separate from the sun, or waves thinking we're separate from the ocean. Just as a sunbeam can't separate itself from the sun, and a wave can't separate itself from the ocean, we can't separate ourselves from one another. We are all part of a vast sea of love, one indivisible divine mind. This truth of who we really are doesn't change; we just forget it. We identify with the notion of a small, separate self, instead of the idea of a reality we share with everyone.

You aren't who you think you are. Aren't you glad? You're not your grades, or your credentials, or your resumes, or your house. We aren't those things at all. We are holy beings, individual cells in the body of Christ. *A Course in Miracles* reminds us that the sun continues to shine and the ocean continues to swell, oblivious to the fact that a fraction of their identity has forgotten what it is. We are who God created us to be. We are all one, we are love itself. "Accepting the Christ" is merely a shift in self-perception. We awaken from the dream that we are finite, isolated creatures, and recognize that we are glorious, infinitely creative spirits. 'We awaken from the dream that we are weak, and accept that the power of the universe is within us.'

I realized, many years ago, that I must be very powerful if I could mess up everything I touched, everywhere I went, with such amazing consistency. I figured there must be a way to apply the same mental power, then embedded in neurosis, in a more positive way. A lot of today's most common psychological orientation is to analyze the darkness in order to reach the light, thinking that if we focus on our neuroses—their origins and dynamics—then we will move beyond them. Eastern religions tell us that if we go for God, all that is not authentically ourselves will drop. Go for the light and darkness will disappear. Focus on Christ means focus on the goodness and power that lie latent within us, in order to invoke them into realization and expression. We get in life that which we focus on. Continual focus on darkness leads us, as individuals and as a society, further into darkness. Focus on the light brings us into the light.

"I accept the Christ within" means, "I accept the beauty within me as who I really am. I am not my weakness. I am not my anger. I am not my small-mindedness. I am much, much more. And I am willing to be reminded of who I really am."

3.   *THE EGO*

"The ego is quite literally a fearful thought."

As children, we were taught to be "good" boys and girls, which of course implies we were not that already. We were taught we're good if we clean up our room, or we're good if we make good grades. Very few of us were taught that we're *essentially* good. Very few of us were given a sense of unconditional approval, a feeling that we're precious because of what we *are*, not what we *do*. And that's not because we were raised by monsters. We were raised by people who were raised the same way we were. Sometimes, in fact, it was the people who loved us the most who felt it was their responsibility to train us to struggle.

Why? Because the world as it is, is tough, and they wanted us to make good. We had to become as crazy as the world is, or we would never fit in here. We had to achieve, make the grade, get into Harvard. What's strange is that we didn't learn discipline from that perspective, so much as a weird displacement of our sense of power away from ourselves and onto external sources. What we lost was a sense of our own power. And what we learned was fear, fear that we weren't good enough, just the way we are.

Fear does not promote learning. It warps us. It stunts us. It makes us neurotic. And by the time we were teenagers, most of us were severely cracked. Our love, our hearts, our real "self" were constantly invalidated by people who didn't love us and by people who did. In the absence of love, we began slowly but surely to fall apart.

Years ago, I told myself not to worry about a devil. I remember thinking that there's no force of evil out stalking the planet. That, I told myself, is all in my mind. Then I realized this is not good news. Since every thought creates experience, there's no worse place it could possibly be. While it's true there isn't an actual devil out there grabbing for our souls, there is a tendency in our minds, which can be amazingly strong, to perceive without love.

Having been taught since we were children that we are separate, finite beings, we have a very hard time when it comes to love. Love feels like a void that threatens to overwhelm us, and that's because, in a certain sense, it is and it does. It overwhelms our small self, our lonely sense of separateness. Since that sense of separateness is who we think we are, we feel like we'll die without it. What's dying is the frightened mind, so the love inside us can get a chance to breathe.

In Course terminology, our entire network of fearful perceptions, all stemming from that first false belief in our separation from God and one another, is called the ego. The word ego is used differently here than the way in which it is often used in modern psychology. It is being used as the ancient Greeks used it—as the notion of a small, separated self. It is a false belief about ourselves, a lie about who and what we really are. Even though that lie is our neurosis, and living that lie is a terrible anxiety, it's amazing how resistant we are to healing the split.

Thought separated from love is a profound miscreation. It's our own power turned against ourselves. The moment the mind first deviated from love—when 'the Son of God forgot to laugh'—an entire illusionary world came into being. *A Course in Miracles* calls this moment our "detour into fear," or "separation from God."

The ego has a pseudo-life of its own, and like all life forms, fights hard for its survival. As uncomfortable as our life might be, as painful or even desperate at times, the life we're living is the life we know, and we cling to the old rather than try something new. Most of us are so sick of ourselves, in one way or another. It's unbelievable how tenaciously we cling to what we've prayed to be released from. The ego is like a virus in the computer that attacks the core system. It seems to show us a dark parallel universe, a realm of fear and pain that doesn't actually exist but certainly seems to. Lucifer was the most beautiful angel in Heaven before he fell. The ego is our self-love turned into self-hatred.

The ego is like a gravitational force field, built up over eons of fearful thinking, which draws us away from the love in our hearts. The ego is our mental power turned against ourselves. It is clever, like we are, and smooth-talking, like we are, and manipulative, like we are. Remember all the talk about a silver-tongued devil? The ego doesn't come up to us and say, "Hi, I'm your self-loathing." It's not stupid, because we're not. Rather, it says things like, "Hi, I'm your adult, mature, rational self. I'll help you look out for number one." Then it proceeds to counsel us to look out for ourselves, at the expense of others. It teaches us selfishness, greed, judgment, and small-mindedness. But remember, there's only one of us here: What we give to others, we give to ourselves. What we withhold from others, we withhold from ourselves. In any moment when we choose fear instead of love, we deny ourselves the experience of Paradise. To the extent that we abandon love, to that extent we will feel it has abandoned us.

4.   HOLY SPIRIT

"The Holy Spirit is the call to awaken and be glad."

The power of the mind is itself neutral. It is the power given to us freely by God. 'We have the free will to think whatever we want to think, but no thoughts are neutral. There is no such thing as an idle thought. All thought creates form on some level.' Nothing can deprive us of our own creativity. We are personally responsible for what direction we apply it in.

Taking responsibility for our lives, then, means taking responsibility for our thoughts. And praying to God to "save" our lives, means praying for Him to save us from our own negative thoughts.

Since only God exists, and everything else is an illusion, then the effects of lovelessness are only happening within the ego's hallucination. The word sin means loveless perception. It is an archery term. It means "you missed the mark." So God isn't angry at our sins because they're not really happening. He doesn't see sins, but only errors in perception. He doesn't want to punish us, but to heal us. The way He heals us is through a force of conciousness called the Holy Spirit.

The Course teaches that the Holy Spirit was created in the moment when the first fearful thought was thought. As perfect love, God corrects all mistakes the moment they occur. He couldn't force us back to love, because love doesn't force. It does, however, create alternatives. The Holy Spirit is God's alternative to fear.

The Holy Spirit was God's answer to the ego. He is God's "eternal communication link with His separated Sons," a bridge back to gentle thoughts, "the great Transformer of Perception." Often the Holy Spirit is referred to as the "Comforter." God can't force His way back into our thinking, because that would be violating our free will. But the Holy Spirit is a force of consciousness within us that "delivers us from Hell," or fear, whenever we consciously ask Him to, working with us on the Causal level, transforming our thoughts from fear to love. We cannot call on him in vain. Having been created by God, He's built into the computer. He comes to us in many forms, from a conversation with a friend to a serious spiritual path; from a lyric in a song to an excellent therapist. He is the inexorable drive toward wholeness that exists within, no matter how disoriented or crazy we get. Something within us always longs to go home, and He is that something.

The Holy Spirit guides us to a different perception of reality: one that is based on love. His correction of our perception is called the Atonement. He reminds us that, in every situation, the love you've given is real, and the love you have received is real. Nothing else exists. Anything other than love is an illusion. In order to escape the illusion and find inner peace, remember that only love in a situation is real. Everything else is a mistake and does not exist. It must be forgotten. We must consciously be willing to let it go.

The only thing lacking in any situation is our own awareness of love. In asking the Holy Spirit to help us, we are expressing our willingness to perceive a situation differently. We give up our own interpretations and opinions, and ask that they be replaced by His. When in pain, we pray, "Dear God, I am willing to see this differently." Surrendering a situation to God means surrendering to Him our *thoughts* about it. What we give to God, He gives back to us renewed through the vision of the Holy Spirit. Some people think that if we surrender to God, we're giving up personal responsibility. But the opposite is true. We're taking the ultimate responsibility for a situation by being responsible for our thoughts about it. We're responsible enough to know that, when left to our own mental devices, we will instinctively respond from fear. We're responsible enough to ask for help.

Sometimes people think that calling on God means inviting a force into our lives that will make everything rosy. The truth is, it means inviting everything into our lives that will force us to grow—and growth can be messy. The purpose of life is to grow into our perfection. Once we call on God, everything that could anger us is on the way. Why? Because the place where we go into anger instead of love, is our wall. Any situation that pushes our buttons is a situation where we don't yet have the capacity to be unconditionally loving. It's the

Holy Spirit's job to draw our attention to that, and help us move beyond that point.

Our comfort zones are the limited areas in which we find it *easy* to love. It's the Holy Spirit's job not to respect those comfort zones, but to bust them. We're not at the mountaintop until *any* zone is comfortable. Love isn't love until it's unconditional. We're not experiencing who we really are until we experience our perfect love.

In order to insure our progress toward the goal of enlightenment, 'the Holy Spirit has a highly individualized curriculum for everyone.' Every encounter, every circumstance can be used by Him for His purposes. He translates between our perfect cosmic self and our worldly insanity. He enters into the illusion and leads us beyond it. He uses love to create more love, and He responds to 'fear as a call for love.'

The Holocaust was not God's will, nor is AIDS. Both of them are products of fear. When we invite the Holy Spirit into these situations, however, He uses them as reasons and opportunities for us to grow into the very level of deep love through which they are eradicated from the earth. They challenge us to love more deeply than we have ever loved before.

If we really desire a moral answer to the Holocaust, we do everything in our power to create a world in which it could never happen again. As any thinking person knows, Hitler did not act alone. He could never have done what he did without the help of thousands of people who, although they did not share his evil vision, did not have the moral fiber to say no to it. What would the Holy Spirit have us do now? Although we cannot guarantee that a Hitler will never again be born, we can in fact create a world in which, even if a Hitler appeared, there would be so much love that hardly anyone would listen or conspire with him.

The spiritual path, then, is simply the journey of living our lives. Everyone is on a spiritual path; most people just don't know it. The Holy Spirit is a force in our minds that knows us in our perfectly loving, natural state—which we've forgotten—but enters into the world of fear and illusion with us, and uses our experiences here to remind us who we are. He does this by showing us the possibility of a loving purpose in everything we think and do. He revolutionizes our sense of why we are on the earth. He teaches us to see love as our only function. Everything we do in our lives will be used, or interpreted, by the ego or the Holy Spirit. The ego uses everything to lead us further into anxiety. The Holy Spirit uses everything to lead us into inner peace.

5.   ENLIGHTENED BEINGS

> *"Enlightenment is but a recognition, not a change at all."*

There are people who have lived on the earth, and perhaps there are people living here now, whose minds have been completely healed by the Holy Spirit. They have accepted the Atonement. In all religions, there are stories of saints or prophets who worked miracles. That is because, when the mind returns to God, it becomes a vessel for His power. The power of God transcends the laws of this world. Saints and prophets, by accepting the Atonement, have actualized the Christ within them. They have been purified of fearful thoughts and only love remains within their minds. These purified beings are called the Enlightened ones. Light means understanding. The enlightened "understand."

Enlightened people don't have anything we don't have. They have perfect love inside, and so do we. The difference is that they don't have anything *else*. Enlightened beings—'Jesus and others— exist in a state that is only potential in the rest of us.' The Christ-mind is merely the perspective of unconditional love. You and I have the Christ-mind in us as much as Jesus does. The difference between him and us is that we are tempted to deny it. He's beyond that. His every thought and action stems from love. The unconditional love, or Christ within him, is 'the truth that sets us free,' because it's the perspective that saves us from our own fearful thoughts.

Jesus and other enlightened masters are our evolutionary elder brothers. According to the laws of evolution, a species develops in a certain direction until that development is no longer well adapted for survival. At that point, a mutation occurs. Although the mutation doesn't represent the majority of the species, it represents the line of evolution better adapted for the species' survival. The descendants of the mutation are then the ones to survive.

Our species is in trouble because we fight too much. We fight ourselves, each other, our planet, and God. Our fear-ridden ways are threatening our survival. A thoroughly loving person is like an evolutionary mutation, manifesting a being that puts love first and thus creates the context in which miracles occur. Ultimately, that is the only *smart* thing to do. It is the only orientation in life which will support our survival.

The mutations, the enlightened ones, show the rest of us our evolutionary potential. They point the way. There is a difference between a wayshower and a crutch. Sometimes people claim they don't need a crutch like Jesus. But he's not a crutch; he's a teacher. If you want to be a writer, you read the classics. If you want to make great music, you listen to music composed by great musicians who have gone before. If you're studying to be a painter, it's a good idea to study the great masters. If Picasso came into your room while you were learning to draw and said, "Hi, I have a couple of hours. . .would you like some hints?" would you say *no*?

So it is with spiritual masters: Jesus, Buddha, or any other enlightened being. They were geniuses in the way they used their minds and hearts, just as Beethoven was a genius with music, or Shakespeare a genius with words. Why not learn from them, follow their lead, study what they were doing right?

A Course in Miracles uses traditional Christian terminology, but it uses it in very non-traditional ways. Words like Christ, Holy Spirit, salvation, Jesus, etc., are used for their psychological rather than religious significance. As a student and teacher of *A Course in Miracles*, I have learned much about the resistance that many people have to Christian terms. As a Jew, I thought it was only other Jews who would have a problem with the word Jesus. But I was wrong. It's not just Jews who get nervous at the mention of his name. Say the word Jesus to a group of moderate Christians, and there is likely to be as much resistance to the topic as there is in anyone else.

I understand why. As it says in the Course, "some bitter idols have been made of him who would be only brother to the world." So many Christian terms have been used to create and perpetuate guilt, that many thinking people have decided to reject them entirely. In many cases, in fact, the problem is worse for Christians than it is for Jews. Jewish children are usually taught nothing at all about Christian terms. For many Christian children, on the other hand, these words were charged with guilt, punishment, and fear of hell.

Words are just words, and new ones can always be found to replace ones that offend. In the case of Jesus, however, the problem isn't as simple as just coming up with another word. Jesus is his name. There's no point in pretending that his name is Herbert. By automatically rejecting Jesus, based on what some traditional Christians have done with and in his name, many people have thrown out the baby with the bath water. In relation to *A Course in Miracles* and other esoteric presentations of Christic philosophy, they have rejected the material offhand based on its language. They have fallen into a mental trap which in Alcoholics Anonymous is called "contempt prior to investigation."

Years ago, I was attending a dinner party in New York City. The topic of conversation at the table was a novel that had recently been published. Someone asked me if I had read it. I hadn't, but I had read the book review in the *New York Times*. I lied and said, "Yes." I was so appalled at myself. I hadn't read the book, but I had enough information to pretend, for a moment, that I had. I was willing to let someone else's opinion stand in for my own.

Not long after that, I thought of that incident when I was deciding whether or not to read a book—namely, *A Course in Miracles*—that dealt in any way with Jesus. I hadn't learned anything about him as a child. I had simply been told "We don't read that, dear." But Jews are also known for encouraging intellectual achievement in their children. I had been taught—although you would never have known it the night of that party—to read, and to think for myself—and so I did. To me, *A Course in Miracles* does not push Jesus. 'Although the books come from him, it is made very clear that you can be an advanced student of the Course and not relate personally to him at all.'

The Course understands our resistances but it doesn't cater to them. It is time for a huge revolution in our understanding of Christic philosophy, and most particularly in our understanding of Jesus. The Christian religion has no monopoly on the Christ, or on Jesus himself. In every generation, we must rediscover truth for ourselves.

Who is Jesus? He is a personal symbol of the Holy Spirit. Having been totally healed by the Holy Spirit, He has become one with Him. He's not the only face the Holy Spirit takes. He is *a* face. He is definitely a top of the mountain experience, but that's not to say he's the only one up there.

Jesus lived within this world of fear, and perceived only love. Every action, every word, every thought was guided by the Holy Spirit instead of the ego. He was a thoroughly purified being. To think about him is to think about, and so to call forth, the perfect love inside ourselves.

Jesus reached total actualization of the Christ mind, and was then given by God the power to help the rest of us reach that place within ourselves. As he says in the Course, "I am in charge of the process of Atonement." Sharing God's vision of things, he has *become* that vision. He sees each one of us as God sees us—innocent and perfect, loving and lovable—and he teaches us to see ourselves that way. That is how he leads us out of hell and into Heaven. To see with his eyes is to atone for our errors in perception. That is the miracle he works in our lives, the mystical light that bursts forth within our souls. Our minds were created as altars to God's Son. He represents God's Son. To worship Him is to worship the potential for perfect love which lies within us all.

Fairy tales are mystical allusions to the power of the inner self, handed down from generation to generation. They are stories of transformation. Tales like Snow White and Sleeping Beauty are metaphors for the relationship between the ego and the divine mind. The wicked stepmother, which is the ego, can put the Sleeping Beauty or Christ within us to sleep, but she can never destroy it. What is created by God is indestructible. The most destructive thing she can do is to cast a spell over us, to put the beauty to sleep. And so she does. But the love inside us doesn't die; it just falls asleep for a very long time. In every fairy tale, the Prince arrives. His kiss reminds us who we are, and why we came here. Prince Charming is the Holy Spirit, and He comes, in various guises and in various suits of clothes, to awaken us with His love. Just when it seems all hope is lost, when it seems as though evil has triumphed at last, our Saviour appears and takes us in his arms. He has many faces, and one of them is Jesus. He is not an idol, or a crutch. He is our elder brother. He is a gift.

CHAPTER 4

Surrender

"For in God's hands we rest untroubled..."

1.   *FAITH*

"There is no problem in any situation that faith will not solve."

What if we truly believed there is a God—a beneficent order to things, a force that's holding things together without our conscious control? What if we could see, in our daily lives, the working of that force? What if we believed it loved us somehow, and cared for us, and protected us? What if we believed we could afford to relax?

The physical body is at work every moment, an array of mechanisms with a brilliance of design and efficiency our human efforts have never begun to match. Our hearts beat, our lungs breathe, our ears hear, our hair grows. And we don't have to make them work—they just do. Planets revolve around the sun, seeds become flowers, embryos become babies, and with no help from us. Their movement is built into a natural system. You and I are integral parts of that system, too.

We can let our lives be directed by the same force that makes flowers grow—or we can do it ourselves.

To trust in the force that moves the universe is faith. Faith isn't blind, it's visionary. Faith is believing that the universe is on our side, and that the universe knows what it's doing. Faith is a psychological awareness of an unfolding force for good, constantly at work in all dimensions. Our attempts to direct this force only interferes with it. Our willingness to relax into it allows it to work on our behalf. Without faith, we're frantically trying to control what it is not our business to control, and fix what it is not in our power to fix. What we're trying to control is much better off without us, and what we're trying to fix can't be fixed by us anyway. Without faith, we're wasting time.

There are objective, discernible laws of physical phenomena. Take gravity, for instance, or the law of thermodynamics. You don't exactly have faith in the law of gravity, so much as you just know that it is.

There are objective, discernible laws of non-physical phenomena, as well. These two sets of laws—those which rule both the external and internal worlds—are parallel.

Externally, the universe supports our physical survival. Photosynthesis in plants and plankton in the ocean produce the oxygen that we need in order to breathe. It is important to respect the laws that rule the physical universe because violation of these laws threatens our survival. When we pollute the oceans or destroy plant life, we are destroying our support system and so are destroying ourselves.

Internally, the universe supports our survival as well—emotionally and psychologically. The internal equivalent to oxygen, what we need in order to survive, is love. Human relationships exist to produce love. When we pollute our relationships with unloving thoughts, or destroy or abort them with unloving attitudes, we are threatening our emotional survival.

So the laws of the universe merely describe the way things are. These laws aren't invented; they're discovered. They are not dependent on our faith. Faith in them merely shows we understand what they are. Violation of these laws doesn't bespeak a lack of goodness; just a lack of intelligence. We respect the laws of nature in order to survive. And what is the highest internal law? That we love one another. Because if we don't, we will all die. As surely as a lack of oxygen will kill us, so will a lack of love.

2.   RESISTANCE

"Faithlessness is not lack of faith but faith in nothing."

A Course in Miracles tells us that 'there is no such thing as a faithless person.' Faith is an aspect of consciousness. We either have faith in fear or we have faith in love, faith in the power of the world or faith in the power of God.

We've basically been taught that it's our job as responsible adults to be active, to be masculine in nature—to go out and get the job, to take control of our lives, to take the bull by the horns. We've been taught that that's our power. We think we're powerful because of what we've achieved rather than because of what we are. So we're caught in a Catch-22: we feel powerless to achieve until we already have.

If somebody comes along and suggests that we go with the flow, maybe lighten up a little, we really feel hysterical. After all, we're total underachievers as is, as far as we can see. The last thing we can imagine doing is becoming any more passive than we already are.

Passive energy has its own kind of strength. Personal power results from a balance of masculine and feminine forces. Passive energy without active energy becomes lazy, but active energy without passive energy becomes tyrannous. An overdose of male, aggressive energy is macho, controlling, unbalanced, and unnatural. The problem is that aggressive energy is what we've all been taught to respect. We've been taught that life was made for quarterbacks so we exalt our masculine consciousness, which, when untempered by the feminine, is hard. Therefore, so are we—all of us, men and women. We've created a fight mentality. We're always fighting for something: for the job, the money, the relationship, to get out of the relationship, to lose weight, to get sober, to get them to understand, to get them to stay, to get them to leave, and on and on. We never put away our swords.

The feminine, surrendered place in us is passive. It doesn't *do* anything. The spiritualization process—in men as well as women—is a feminization process, a quieting of the mind. It is the cultivation of personal magnetism.

If you have a pile of iron shavings and you want to arrange them in beautiful patterns, you can do one of two things. You can use your fingers and try to arrange the tiny pieces of iron into beautiful, gossamer lines—or you can buy a magnet. The magnet will attract the iron shavings. It symbolizes our feminine consciounessness, which exerts its power through attraction rather than activity.

This attractive, receptive, feminine aspect of our consciousness is the space of mental surrender. In Taoist philosophy, "yin" is the feminine principle, representing the forces of the earth, while "yang" is the masculine principle, representing spirit. When God is referred to as "He," then all mankind becomes "She." This isn't a man-woman issue. Reference to God as masculine principle in no way impinges on feminist conviction. Our feminine self is just as important as our masculine.

The right relationship between male and female principle is one in which the feminine surrenders to the masculine. Surrender is not weakness or loss. It is a powerful nonresistance. Through openness and receptivity on the part of human consciousness, spirit is allowed to infuse our lives, to give them meaning and direction. In Christic philosophical terms, Mary symbolizes the feminine within us, which is impregnated by God. The female allows this process and is fulfilled by surrendering into it. This is not weakness on her part; it is strength. The Christ on earth is fathered by God, and mothered by our humanness. Through a mystical connection between the human and divine, we give birth to our higher Self.

3.   GIVING UP RESULTS

"You will never lose your way for God leads you."

When we surrender to God, we surrender to something bigger than ourselves—to a universe that knows what it's doing. When we stop trying to control events, they fall into a natural order, an order that works. We're at rest while a power much greater than our own takes over, and it does a much better job than we could have done. We learn to trust that the power that holds galaxies together can handle the circumstances of our relatively little lives.

Surrender means, by definition, giving up attachment to results. When we surrender to God, we let go of our attachment to how things happen on the outside and we become more concerned with what happens on the inside.

The experience of love is a choice we make, a mental decision to see love as the only real purpose and value in any situation. Until we make that choice, we keep striving for results that we think would make us happy. But we've all gotten things that we thought would make us happy, only to find that they didn't. This external searching– looking to anything other than love to complete us and to be the source of our happiness—is the meaning of idolatry. Money, sex, power, or any other worldly satisfaction offers just temporary relief for minor existential pain.

"God" means love, and "will" means thought. God's will, then, is loving thought. If God is the source of all good, then the love within us is the source of all good. When we love, we are automatically placing ourselves within an attitudinal and behavioral context that leads to an unfoldment of events at the highest level of good for everyone involved. We don't always know what that unfoldment would look like, but we don't need to. God will do His part if we do ours. Our only job in every situation is to merely let go of our resistance to love. What happens then is up to Him. We've surrendered control. We're letting Him lead. We have faith He knows how.

There's a myth that some people are more faithful than others. A truer statement is that in some areas, some of us are more surrendered than others. We surrender to God first, of course, the things we don't really care that much about anyway. Some of us don't mind giving up our attachment to career goals, but there's no way we're going to surrender our romantic relationships, or vice versa. Everything we don't care that much about—fine—God can have it. But if it's really, really important, we think we better handle it ourselves. The truth is, of course, that the more important it is to us, the more important it is to surrender. That which is surrendered is taken care of best. To place something in the hands of God is to give it over, mentally, to the protection and care of the beneficence of the universe. To keep it ourselves means to constantly grab and clutch and manipulate. We keep opening the oven to see if the bread is baking, which only ensures that it never gets a chance to.

Where we have an attachment to results, we tend to have a hard time giving up control. But how can we know what result to try to achieve in a situation when we don't know what's going to happen tomorrow? What do we ask for? Instead of, "Dear God, please let us fall in love, or please give me this job," we say, "Dear God, my desire, my priority is inner peace. I want the experience of love. I don't know what would bring that to me. I leave the results of this situation in your hands. I trust your will. May your will be done. Amen."

I used to feel I couldn't afford to relax because God had more important things to think about than my life. I finally realized that God is not capricious, but is rather an impersonal love for all life. My life is no more or less precious to Him than is anyone else's. To surrender to

God is to accept the fact that He loves us and provides for us, because he loves and provides for all life. Surrender doesn't obstruct our power; it enhances it. God is merely the love within us, so returning to Him is a return to ourselves.

4.   THE SURRENDERED LIFE

> *"Holy Child of God, when will you learn that only holiness can content you and give you peace?"*

To relax, to feel the love in your heart and keep to that as your focus in every situation—that's the meaning of spiritual surrender. It changes us. We become deeper, more attractive people.

In Zen Buddhism, there's a concept called "zen mind," or "beginner's mind." They say that the mind should be like an empty rice bowl. If it's already full, then the universe can't fill it. If it's empty, it has room to receive. This means that when we think we have things already figured out, we're not teachable. Genuine insight can't dawn on a mind that's not open to receive it. Surrender is a process of emptying the mind.

In the Christic tradition, this is the meaning of "becoming as a little child." Little children don't think they know what things mean. In fact, they know they don't know. They ask someone older and wiser to explain things to them. We're like children who don't know, but think we do.

The wise person doesn't pretend to know what it's impossible to know. "I don't know" can be an empowering statement. When we go into a situation not knowing, there is something inside us which *does*. With our conscious mind, 'we step back in order that a higher power within us can step forward and lead the way.'

We need less posturing and more genuine charisma. Charisma was originally a religious term, meaning "of the spirit," or "inspired." It's about letting God's light shine through us. It's about a sparkle in people that money can't buy. It's an invisible energy with visible effects. To let go, to just love, is not to fade into the wallpaper. Quite the contrary, it's when we truly become bright. We're letting our own light shine.

We are meant to be this way. We are meant to shine. Look at small children. They're all so unique before they start *trying* to be, because they demonstrate the power of genuine humility. This is also the explanation of "beginner's luck." When we go into a situation not knowing the rules, we don't pretend to know how to figure anything out, and we don't know yet what there is to be afraid of. This releases the mind to create from its own higher power. Situations shift gear and lights go on simply because our minds have opened up to receive love. We have gotten out of our own way.

Love is a win-mode, a successful and attractive vibration. We think that success is difficult, and so, for us, it is. Success in life doesn't have to involve negative tension. We don't have to be struggling all the time. If you think about it, "taking the bull by the horns" would be a very dangerous thing to do. In fact, ambitious tension actually limits our ability to succeed because it keeps us in a state of contraction, emotionally and physically. It seems to give us energy but doesn't really, like the white sugar of mental health; there's a short high, followed by a crash. The cultivation of mental rest, or surrender, is like eating healthy food. It doesn't give us an immediate rush, but over time it provides a lot more energy.

This doesn't require sitting in a lotus position all day. We still get excited, but more gently. Many people associate a spiritual life with a grade B movie, but God doesn't get rid of all the drama in our lives. He just gets rid of the *cheap* drama. There is no higher drama than true personal growth. Nothing could be more genuinely dramatic than boys becoming real men and girls becoming real women.

Something amazing happens when we surrender and just love. We melt into another world, a realm of power already within us. The world changes when we change. The world softens when we soften. The world loves us when we choose to love the world.

Surrender means the decision to stop fighting the world, and to start loving it instead. It is a gentle liberation from pain. But liberation isn't about breaking out of anything; 'it's a gentle melting into who we really are.' We let down our armor, and discover the strength of our Christ self. *A Course in Miracles* tells us that although 'we think that without the ego, all would be chaos, the opposite is true. Without the ego, all would be love.'

We are simply asked to shift focus and to take on a more gentle perception. That's all God needs. Just one sincere surrendered moment, when love matters more than anything, and we know that nothing else really matters at all. What He gives us in return for our openness to Him, is an outpouring of His power from deep within us. We are given His power to share with the world, to heal all wounds, to awaken all hearts.

CHAPTER 5

Miracles

"Your holiness reverses all the laws of the world.
It is beyond every restriction of time, space,
distance, and limits of any kind."

1.   *FORGIVENESS*

"Before the glorious radiance of the kingdom, guilt melts away, and transformed into kindness will nevermore be what it was."

"Miracles occur naturally as expressions of love." They reflect a shift in how we think, releasing the power of the mind to the processes of healing and correction.

This healing takes many forms. Sometimes a miracle is a change in material conditions, such as physical healing. At other times, it is a psychological or emotional change. It is a shift not so much in an objective situation—although that often occurs—as it is a shift in how we *perceive* a situation. What changes, primarily, is how we hold an experience in our minds—how we experience the experience.

The world of the human storyline, of all our concentration on behavior and all the things that occur outside us, is a world of illusion. It's a veil in front of a more real world, a collective dream. A miracle is not a rearrangement of the figures in our dream. A miracle is our awakening from it.

In asking for miracles, we are seeking a practical goal: a return to inner peace. We're not asking for something outside us to change, but for something inside us to change. We're looking for a softer orientation to life.

Old Newtonian physics claimed that things have an objective reality separate from our perception of them. Quantum physics, and particularly Heisenberg's Uncertainty Principle, reveal that, as our perception of an object changes, the object itself literally changes. The science of religion is actually the science of consciousness, because ultimately all creation is expressed through the mind. Thus, as *A Course in Miracles* says, our greatest tool for changing the world is our capacity to 'change our mind about the world.'

Because thought is the creative level of things, changing our minds is the ultimate personal empowerment. Although it is a human decision to choose love instead of fear, the radical shift that this produces in every dimension of our lives is a gift from God. Miracles are an 'intercession on behalf of our holiness,' from a thought system beyond our own. In the presence of love, the laws that govern the normal state of affairs are transcended. Thought that is no longer limited, brings experience that is no longer limited.

We are heir to the laws that govern the world we believe in. If we think of ourselves as beings of this world, then the laws of scarcity and death, which rule this world, will rule us. If we think of ourselves as children of God, whose real home lies in a realm of awareness beyond this world, then we will find we are "under no laws but God's."

Our self-perception determines our behavior. If we think we're small, limited, inadequate creatures, then we tend to behave that way, and the energy we radiate reflects those thoughts no matter what we do. If we think we're magnificent creatures with an infinite abundance of love and power to give, then we tend to behave that way. Once again, the energy around us reflects our state of awareness.

'Miracles themselves are not to be consciously directed.' They occur as involuntary effects of a loving personality, an invisible force that emanates from someone whose conscious intention is to give and receive love. As we relinquish the fears that block the love within us, we become God's instruments. We become His miracle workers.

God, as love, is constantly expanding, flourishing and creating new patterns for the expression and attainment of joy. When our minds, through focus on love, are allowed to be open vessels through which God expresses, our lives become the canvases for the expression of that joy. That's the meaning of our lives. We are here as physical representations of a divine principle. To say that we're on the earth to serve God, means that we're on the earth to love.

We weren't just randomly thrown onto a sea of rocks. We have a mission—to save the world through the power of love. The world needs healing desperately, like a bird with a broken wing. People know this, and millions have prayed.

God heard us. He sent help. He sent you.

To become a miracle worker means to take part in a spiritual underground that's revitalizing the world, participating in a revolution of the world's values at the deepest possible level. That doesn't mean you announce this to anyone. A member of the French underground didn't walk up to a German officer occupying Paris and say, "Hi, I'm Jacques. French Resistance." Similarly, you don't tell people who would have no idea what you're talking about, "I'm changed. I'm working for God now. He sent me to heal things. The world's about to shift big time." Miracle workers learn to keep their own counsel. Something that's important to know about spiritual wisdom is that, when spoken at the wrong time, in the wrong place, or to the wrong person, the one who speaks sounds more like a fool than a wise one.

The Course tells us of God's plan for the salvation of the world, called 'the plan of the teachers of God.' The plan calls for God's teachers to heal the world through the power of love. This teaching has very little to do with verbal communication, and everything to do with a quality of human energy. "To teach is to demonstrate." A teacher of God is anyone who chooses to be one. "They come from all over the world. They come from all religions and from no religion. They are the ones who have answered." The adage that "many are called but few are chosen" means that 'everyone is called, but few care to listen.' God's call is universal, going out to every mind in every moment. Not everyone, however, chooses to heed the call of his own heart. As all of us are only too aware, the loud and frantic voices of the outer world easily drown out the small still loving voice within.

Our job as a teacher of God, should we choose to accept it, is to constantly seek a greater capacity for love and forgiveness within ourselves. We do this through a "selective remembering," a conscious decision to remember only loving thoughts and let go of any fearful ones. This is the meaning of forgiveness. Forgiveness is a major cornerstone of *A Course in Miracles* philosophy. Like many of the traditional terms used in the Course, it is used in a very nontraditional way.

Traditionally, we think of forgiveness as something we are to do when we see guilt in someone. In the Course, however, we're taught that it's our function to remember that there *is* no guilt in anyone, because only love is real. It is our function to see through the illusion of guilt, to the innocence that lies beyond. "To forgive is merely to remember only the loving thoughts you gave in the past, and those that were given you. All the rest must be forgotten." We are asked to extend our perception beyond the errors that our physical perceptions reveal to us—what someone did, what someone said—to the holiness within them that only our heart reveals. Actually, then, there is nothing to forgive. The traditional notion of forgiveness—what *The Song of Prayer* calls "forgiveness-to-destroy"—is then an act of judgment. It is the arrogance of someone who sees themselves as better than someone else, or perhaps equally as sinful, which is still a misperception and the arrogance of the ego.

Since all minds are connected, then the correction of anyone's perception is on some level a healing of the entire racial mind. The practice of forgiveness is our most important contribution to the healing of the world. Angry people cannot create a peaceful planet. It amuses me to think how angry I used to get when people wouldn't sign my peace petitions.

Forgiveness is a full time job, and sometimes very difficult. Few of us always succeed, yet making the effort is our most noble calling. It is the world's only real chance to begin again. A radical forgiveness is a complete letting go of the past, in any personal relationship, as well as in any collective drama.

2.   *LIVING IN THE PRESENT*

> *"All your past except its beauty is gone, and nothing is left but a blessing."*

God exists in eternity. The only point where eternity meets time is in the present. "The present is the only time there is." A miracle is a shift in thinking from what we might have done in the past or should be doing in the future, to what we feel free to do right here, right now. A miracle is a release from internal bondage. Our capacity for brilliance is equal to our capacity to forget the past and forget the future. That's why little children are brilliant. They don't remember the past, and they don't relate to the future. Be us as little children, that the world might finally grow up.

One of the exercises in the Course Workbook reads, "The past is over. It can touch me not." Forgiving the past is an important step in allowing ourselves the experience of miracles. The only meaning of anything in our past is that it got us here, and should be honored as such. All that is real in our past is the love we gave and the love we received. Everything else is an illusion. The past is merely a thought we have. It is literally all in our minds. The Course teaches, "Give the past to Him Who can change your mind about it for you." To surrender the past to the Holy Spirit is to ask that only loving, helpful thoughts about it remain in our minds, and all the rest be let go.

What we are left with then is the present, the only time where miracles happen. 'We place the past and the future as well into the hands of God.' The biblical statement that "time shall be no more" means that we will one day live fully in the present, without obsessing about past or future.

The universe provides us with a clean slate in every

moment; God's creation holds nothing against us. Our problem is that we don't believe this. Let us ask forgiveness, not of 'God who has never condemned us,' but of ourselves, for all we think we did and did not do. Let us give ourselves permission to begin again.

We all encounter situations in our lives where we wish we hadn't done something we did, or wish we had done something we didn't. They're those moments in our lives, be they yesterday or several years ago, that make us cringe to think about. One of the most freeing techniques provided us in *A Course in Miracles* is a prayer on page 83 of the Text, in which we instruct the universe to undo our errors:

> *"...the first step in the undoing is to recognize that you actively decided wrongly, but can as actively decide otherwise. Be very firm with yourself in this, and keep yourself fully aware that the undoing process, which does not come from you, is nevertheless within you because God placed it there. Your part is merely to return your thinking to the point at which the error was made, and give it over to the Atonement in peace. Say this to yourself as sincerely as you can, remembering that the Holy Spirit will respond fully to your slightest invitation:*

> *I must have decided wrongly, because I am not at peace.*

> *I made the decision myself, but I can also decide*
>   *otherwise.*
> *I want to decide otherwise, because I want to be*
>   *at peace.*
> *I do not feel guilty, because the Holy Spirit will*
>   *undo all consequences of my wrong decision*
>   *if I will let Him.*
> *I choose to let Him, by allowing Him to decide*
>   *for God for me.*

And that's it! It's a course in *miracles*, not a course in moving the furniture. 'Miracles reverse physical laws. Time and space are under His command.'

As for the future, the Course points out that there is no way for us to know what's going to happen tomorrow, or the next day, or five years from now. Only the ego speculates about tomorrow. In Heaven, 'we place our future in the hands of God.' The Holy Spirit returns our minds to total faith and trust, that should we live with fully open hearts today, tomorrow will take care of itself. As Jesus said in the Sermon on the Mount, "Be ye not anxious for tomorrow, for tomorrow shall be anxious for itself."

'The ego bases its perception of reality on what has happened in the past, carries those perceptions into the present and thus creates a future like the past.' If we felt that we were lacking in our past, our thoughts about the future are based on those perceptions. We then enter the present in an effort to compensate for the past. Since that perception is our core belief, we recreate its conditions in the future. "Past, present and future are not continuous, unless you force continuity upon them." In the present, we have the opportunity to break the continuity of the past and future by asking the Holy Spirit to intervene. This is the miracle. We want a new life, a new beginning. We desire a life untainted by any darkness of the past, and being 'entitled to miracles,' we are entitled to that full release. This is what it means to say that Jesus washes us clean of our sins. He completely removes all loveless thoughts. We relinquish any thoughts of judgment, of anyone or anything, that hold us to the past. We relinquish any thoughts of attachment that keep us grasping at the future.

The world of the ego is a world of constant changes, ups and downs, darkness and light. Heaven is a realm of constant peace because it is an awareness of a reality that lies beyond change. "And Heaven will not change, for birth into the holy present is salvation from change."

The world that the Holy Spirit reveals to us is a world that lies beyond this world, a world revealed to us through a different perception. We die to one world in order to be born into another. "To be born again is to let the past go, and look without condemnation upon the present." The world of time is not the real world, and the world of eternity is our real home. We are on our way there. We are pregnant with possibilities.

3.   *RESURRECTION*

"Your resurrection is your awakening."

The purpose of our lives is to give birth to the best which is within us.

The Christ comes as a little child because the symbol of the newborn infant is the symbol of someone whose innocence is unmarred by past history or guilt. The Christ child within us has no history. It is the symbol of a person who is given the chance to begin again. The only way to heal the wounds of the past, ultimately, is to forgive them and let them go. The miracle worker sees that his purpose in life is to be used in the service of the forgiveness of mankind—to awaken us from our collective sleep.

The Course tells us: "The Bible says that a deep sleep fell upon Adam, and nowhere is there reference to his waking up." So far, there has been no "comprehensive reawakening or rebirth." We can all contribute to a global rebirth to the extent that we allow ourselves to be awakened from our own personal dream of separation and guilt, to release our own past and accept a new life in the present. It is only through our own personal awakening that the world can be awakened. We cannot give what we don't have.

We're all assigned a piece of the garden, a corner of the universe that is ours to transform. Our corner of the universe is our own life—our relationships, our homes, our work, our current circumstances—exactly as they are. Every situation we find ourselves in is an opportunity, perfectly planned by the Holy Spirit, to teach love instead of fear. Whatever energy system we find ourselves a part of, it's our job to heal it—to purify the thought forms by purifying our own. It's never really a circumstance that needs to change—it's *we* who need to change. The prayer isn't for God to change our lives, but rather for Him to change us.

That's the greatest miracle, and ultimately the only one: that you awaken from the dream of separation and become a different kind of person. People are constantly concerning themselves with what they *do*: have I achieved enough, written the greatest screenplay, formed the most powerful company? But the world will not be saved by another great novel, great movie, or great business venture. It will only be saved by the appearance of great people.

A glass vase is meant to hold water. If more water is poured into the vase than its volume can contain, then the vase will shatter. So it is with our personalities. The power of God, particularly at this time, is pouring into us at rapid pace and high velocity. If our vessel, our vehicle—our human channel—is not prepared properly through devotion and deep reverence for life, then the very power that is meant to save us begins to destroy us. Our creativity, rather than making us personally powerful, then makes us hysterical. That is why creative power—God within us—is experienced as a double-edged sword: if received with grace, it blesses us; if received without grace, it drives us insane. This is one of the reasons why so many creative people have turned to a destructive use of drugs: to actually dull the experience of the reception of God's power rather than enhance it. God's power coming into us, in a culture that had no name for that power or acknowledgment of genuine spiritual experience, so frightened us that we ran to drugs or alcohol to avoid feeling what was really happening. It was only when we were stoned that we had the courage to claim our own experience.

"Miracles are everyone's right," says *A Course in Miracles*, "but purification is necessary first." Impurities—mental or chemical—pollute the system and desecrate the altar within. Our vehicle then can't handle the experience of God. The waters of spirit rush into us, but the vase begins to crack. It's not the flow of power we have to work on—God's love is already pouring in as fast as we can handle it—but the preparedness with which we receive it.

A Course in Miracles likens us to people in a very bright room who have their fingers in front of their eyes, complaining that it's dark in here. The light has come but we don't see it. We don't realize that the present is always a chance to begin again, a light-filled moment. We respond to light as if it were darkness, and so the light turns to dark. Sometimes it is only in retrospect that we can see that we were given another chance at life, a new relationship or whatever, but because we were too busy reacting to the past, we missed the opportunity at something radically new.

When we're truly honest with ourselves, our problem is not that opportunities for success haven't appeared. God is always expanding our possibilities. We are given plenty of opportunities, but we tend to undermine them. Our conflicted energies sabotage everything. To ask for another relationship, or another job, is not particularly helpful if we're going to show up in the new situation exactly as we showed up in the last one. Until we're healed of our internal demons, our fearful mental habits, we will turn every situation into the same painful drama as the one before. Everything we do is infused with the energy with which we do it. If we're frantic, life will be frantic. If we're peaceful, life will be peaceful. And so our goal in any situation becomes inner peace. Our internal state determines our experience of our lives; our experiences do not determine our internal state.

The term crucifixion means the energy pattern of fear. It represents the limited, negative thinking of the ego, and how it always seeks to limit, contradict or invalidate love. The term resurrection means the energy pattern of love, which transcends fear by replacing it. A miracle worker's function is forgiveness. In performing our function, we become channels for resurrection.

God and man are the ultimate creative team. God is like electricity. A house can be wired for it, but if there aren't any light fixtures, what good does that do? If

God is seen as electricity, then we are His lamps. It doesn't matter the size of the lamp, or its shape, or design. All that matters is that it gets plugged in. It doesn't matter who we are, or what our gifts are. All that matters is that we are willing to be used in His service. Our willingness, our conviction, give us a miraculous power. The servants of God bear the imprint of their Master.

Lamps without electricity cast no light, and electricity without lamps casts no light either. Together, however, they cast out all darkness.

4.   COSMIC ADULTHOOD

"Child of God, you were created to create the good, the beautiful and the holy."

As we become purer channels for God's light, we develop an appetite for the sweetness that is possible in this world. A miracle worker is not geared toward fighting the world that is, but toward creating the world that could be.

Just treating the symptom of a problem isn't really treating it. Take nuclear bombs, for example. If we all work hard, sign enough petitions and elect new officials, then we can ban the bomb. But if we don't get rid of the hatred in our hearts, what good will that do, ultimately? Our children or our children's children will manufacture a destructive force more powerful than the bomb, if they are still carrying within them enough fear and conflict.

Everything in the physical universe becomes part of the journey into fear, or the journey back to love, depending on how it's used by the mind. What we devote to love, is used for love's purposes. So we work within the worldly illusion, politically, socially, environmentally, etc., but we recognize that the real transformation of the world comes not from what we're doing, but from the consciousness with which we're doing it. We're actually just buying time while the real transformation of global energies has a chance to kick in.

The miracle worker's purpose is spiritually grand, not personally grandiose. The high cosmic drama is not *your* career, *your* money, or any of your worldly experiences. Your career is certainly important, as is your money, your talent, your energy, and your personal relationships. But they're important only to the extent that they are devoted to God to use for His purposes. When we outgrow our immature preoccupation with the small self, we transcend our selfishness and become cosmically mature.

Until we find that cosmic maturity, we're childish. We're worrying about our car payments, our career advancements, our plastic surgery, our petty hurts, while political situations careen towards disaster and the hole in the ozone looks worse every day. Childishness is when we're so preoccupied with things that ultimately don't matter, that we lose our essential connection with things that do.

There's a difference between childish and childlike. Childlike implies spirituality, as in tenderness, and a profound not-knowing that makes us open to new impressions. Childlike is when see ourselves as children in the arms of God. We learn to step back and let Him lead the way.

God isn't separate from us, because He's the love inside our minds. Every problem, inside and out, is due to separation from love on someone's part. Thirty-five thousand people a day die of hunger on earth, and there's no dearth of food. The question is not, "What kind of God would let children starve?" but rather, "What kind of people let children starve?" A miracle worker returns the world to God by making a conscious change to a more loving way of life. Waiting with cynical resignation for the world's collapse makes us part of the problem, not the answer. We must consciously recognize that, for God, "there is no order of difficulty in miracles." Love heals all wounds. No problem is too small for God's attention, or too big for Him to handle.

Every system in the world—socially, politically, economically, biologically—is beginning to crumble under the weight of our own cruelty. Without miracles, it could be argued that the gig is up, that it's already too late to save the world. Many people are convinced that the world is headed for an inevitable major collapse. Any thinking person knows that the world is in many ways moving in a downward spiral, and an object continues to move in whatever direction it's currently headed. Only the application of a stronger counterforce can change its direction. Miracles are that counterforce. When love reaches a critical mass, when enough people become miracle-minded, the world will experience a radical shift.

This is the eleventh hour. The Course tells us that it's not up to us what we learn, but only whether we learn through joy or through pain. We *will* learn to love one another, but whether we learn it painfully or peacefully is entirely up to us. If we continue in our dark ways and we manifest nuclear war, then even if there are only five people left on the planet at the end of the conflagration, those five people will have gotten the point. They would surely look at one another and say, "Let's try to get along." But we can bypass the scenario of a nuclear Armageddon if we so desire. Most of us have already suffered our own personal Armageddons. There's no need to go through the whole thing again collectively. We can get the point later, or we can get the point now. Knowing that we have a choice is a genuinely adult understanding of the world.

After Dorothy had gone through her whole dramatic journey to Oz, the good witch told her that all she had had to do was click her heels together three times and say, "I want to go home," "I want to go home," "I want to go home." There had been no need for the long traipse down the yellow brick road. Dorothy, who I'm sure was outraged, said, "Why didn't you tell me that?" The witch replied: "You wouldn't have believed me!"

In ancient Greek tragedies, there's a common device called "Deus ex machina." The plot builds up to a disastrous climax, and just when it looks as though all hope is lost, a god appears and saves the day. That's an important piece of archetypal information. At the last moment, when things look the worst, God *does* tend to appear. Not because he has a sadistic sense of humor, waiting until we're totally desperate before showing us his muscle. He takes so long because it's not until then that we bother to think about Him. All this time, we thought we were waiting for Him. Little did we know, He was waiting for us.

5.   *REBIRTH*

> *"This is what is meant by 'The meek shall inherit the earth': They will literally take it over because of their strength."*

It is time to fulfill our purpose, to live on the earth and think only the thoughts of Heaven. 'Thus shall Heaven and Earth become as one. They will no longer exist as two separate states.'

There are times when miraculous thinking is not easy, because our mental habit patterns are permeated with fear. When that's the case—when our anger, jealousy or hurt seem stuck to our hearts and we can't let them go—how do we work miracles then? By asking the Holy Spirit to help us.

The Course tells us that we can do many things, but one thing we can never do is call on the Holy Spirit in vain. We are told that 'we don't ask God for too much; in fact, we ask for too little.' Whenever we feel lost, or insane, or afraid, all we have to do is ask for His help. The help might not come in the form we expected, or even thought we desired, but it will come, and we will recognize it by how we feel. In spite of everything, we will feel at peace.

We think there are different categories of life, such as money, health, relationships, and then, for some of us, another category called "spiritual life." But only the ego categorizes. There is really only one drama going on in life: our walk away from God, and our walk back. We simply reenact the one drama in different ways.

The Course says 'we think we have many different problems, but we only have one.' Denying love is the only problem, and embracing it is the only answer. Love heals all of our relationships—to money, the body, work, sex, death, ourselves, and one another. Through the miraculous power of pure love, we let go our past history in any area and begin again.

If we treat miraculous principles like toys, they will be like toys in our lives. But if we treat them like the power of the universe, then such will they be for us. The past is over. It doesn't matter who we are, where we came from, what Mommy said, what Daddy did, what mistakes we made, what diseases we have, or how depressed we feel. The future can be reprogrammed in this moment. We don't need another seminar, another degree, another lifetime, or anyone's approval in order for this to happen. All we have to do is ask for a miracle and allow it to happen, not resist it. There can be a new beginning, a life unlike the past. Our relationships shall be made new. Our careers shall be made new. Our bodies shall be made new. Our planet shall be made new. So shall the will of God be done, on earth as it is in Heaven. Not later, but now. Not elsewhere, but here. Not through pain, but through peace. So be it. Amen.

PART II

Practice

CHAPTER 6

Relationships

"The Holy Spirit's temple is not a body, but a relationship."

1.   THE HOLY ENCOUNTER

"When you meet anyone, remember it is a holy encounter. As you see him, you will see yourself. As you treat him, you will treat yourself. As you think of him, you will think of yourself. Never forget this, for in him you will find yourself or lose yourself."

Before I read *A Course in Miracles*, I studied many other spiritual and philosophical writings. It felt as though they led me up a huge flight of stairs to a giant cathedral inside my mind, but once I reached the top of the stairs, the door to the church was locked. The Course gave me the key that opened the door. The key, very simply, is other people.

Heaven, according to the Course, is neither a condition nor a place, but rather the "awareness of perfect oneness." Since the Father and the Son are one, then to love one is to love the other. The love of God is not outside us. There is a line in a song from the play *Les*

Miserables that says, "To love another person is to see the face of God." The "face of Christ" is the innocence and love behind the masks we all wear, and seeing that face, touching it and loving it in ourselves and others, is the experience of God. It is our divine humanness. It is the high we all seek.

In every relationship, in every moment, we teach either love or fear. "To teach is to demonstrate." As we demonstrate love towards others, we learn that we are lovable and we learn how to love more deeply. As we demonstrate fear or negativity, we learn self-condemnation and we learn to feel more frightened of life. We will always learn what we have chosen to teach. "Ideas leave not their source," which is why we are always a part of God, and why our ideas are always a part of us. If I choose to bless another person, I will always end up feeling more blessed. If I project guilt onto another person, I will always end up feeling more guilty.

Relationships exist to hasten our walk to God. When surrendered to the Holy Spirit, when He is in charge of our perceptions, our encounters become holy encounters with the perfect Son of God. *A Course in Miracles* says that everyone we meet will either be our crucifier or our savior, depending on what we choose to be to them. Focusing on their guilt drives the nails of self-loathing more deeply into our own skin. Focusing on their innocence sets us free. Since 'no thoughts are neutral,' every relationship takes us deeper into Heaven or deeper into Hell.

2. FORGIVENESS IN RELATIONSHIPS

*"Forgiveness takes away what stands between
your brother and yourself."*

A Course in Miracles prides itself on being a practical
Course with a practical goal: the attainment of inner
peace. Forgiveness is the key to inner peace because it is
the mental technique by which our thoughts are transformed from fear to love. Our perceptions of other
people often become a battleground between the ego's
desire to judge and the Holy Spirit's desire to accept
people as they are. The ego is the great fault-finder. It
seeks out the faults in ourselves and others. The Holy
Spirit seeks out our innocence. He sees all of us as we
really are, and since we are the perfect creations of God,
He loves what He sees. The places in our personality
where we tend to deviate from love are not our faults,
but our wounds. God doesn't want to punish us, but to
heal us. And that is how He wishes us to view the
wounds in other people.

Forgiveness is "selective remembering"—a conscious decision to focus on love and let the rest go. But
the ego is relentless—it is "capable of suspiciousness at
best and viciousness at worst." It presents the most subtle and insidious arguments for casting other people out
of our hearts. The cornerstone of the ego's teaching is:
"The Son of God is guilty." The cornerstone of the
Holy Spirit's teaching is: "The Son of God is innocent."

The miracle worker consciously invites the Holy Spirit to enter into every relationship and deliver us from the temptation to judge and find fault. We ask Him to save us from our tendency to condemn. We ask Him to reveal to us the innocence within others, that we might see it within ourselves.

"Dear God, I surrender this relationship to you," means, "Dear God, let me see this person through your eyes." In accepting the Atonement, we are asking to see as God sees, think as God thinks, love as God loves. We are asking for help in seeing someone's innocence.

I was once vacationing in Europe with my family. Although my mother and I were both making noble efforts at getting along well with each other, we weren't succeeding. Old patterns of attack and defense were continuously cropping up between us. She wanted a more conservative daughter, and I wanted a more enlightened mother. I kept opening the Course for help and inspiration but much to my chagrin, I seemed to open the book to the same section each time I picked it up. I would read, "Think honestly what you have thought that God would not have thought, and what you have not thought that God would have you think." In other words, where were my thoughts not aligned with God's? It was driving me crazy. I wanted support for my defensive feelings. The last thing I wanted to be told was that the only error was an error in my own thinking.

Finally, glancing across St. Mark's Square in Venice,

I looked closely at my mother and said to myself, "It's true—God's not looking at her and thinking, 'Sophie Ann is such a bitch.'" As long as I chose to see her that way, as long as I was not willing to give up my focus on her errors, I could not be at peace because I was not sharing God's perception. As soon as I saw this, I released my tense fixation on what I perceived to be her guilt. From that point forward, the situation began to shift. Miraculously, she was nicer to me, and I was nicer to her.

It's easy to forgive people who have never done anything to make us angry. People who do make us angry, however, are our most important teachers. They indicate the limits to our capacity for forgiveness. "Holding grievances is an attack on God's plan for salvation." The decision to let go our grievances against other people is the decision to see ourselves as we truly are, because any darkness we let blind us to another's perfection also blinds us to our own.

It can be very hard to let go of your perception of someone's guilt when you know that by every standard of ethics, morality, or integrity, you're right to find fault with them. But the Course asks, "Do you prefer that you be right or happy?" If you're judging a brother, you're wrong even if you're right. There have been times when I have had a very hard time giving up my judgment of someone, mentally protesting, "But I'm *right*." I felt as though giving up my judgment amounted to condoning their behavior. I felt, "Well, *somebody's* got to uphold principle in this world. If we just forgive things all the time, then all standards of excellence will disintegrate!"

But God doesn't need us to police the universe. Shaking our finger at someone doesn't help them change. If anything, our perception of someone's guilt only keeps them stuck in it. When we are shaking a finger at someone, figuratively or literally, we are not more apt to correct their wrongful behavior. Treating someone with compassion and forgiveness is much more likely to elicit a healed response. People are less likely to be defensive, and more likely to be open to correction. Most of us are aware on some level when we're off. We'd be doing things differently if we knew how. We don't need attack at this point; we need help. Forgiveness forges a new context, one in which someone can more easily change.

Forgiveness is the choice to see people as they are *now*. When we are angry at people, we are angry because of something they said or did before this moment. But what people said or did is not who they are. Relationships are reborn as we let go perceptions of our brother's past. 'By bringing the past into the present, we create a future just like the past.' By letting the past go, we make room for miracles.

An attack on a brother is a reminder of his guilty past. In choosing to affirm a brother's guilt, we are choosing to experience more of it. The future is programmed in the present. To let the past go is to remember that in the present, my brother is innocent. It is an act of gracious generosity to accept a person based on what we know to be the truth about them, regardless of whether or not they are in touch with that truth themselves.

Only love is real. Nothing else actually exists. If a person behaves unlovingly, then, that means that, regardless of their negativity—anger or whatever—their behavior was derived from fear and doesn't actually exist. They're hallucinating. You forgive them, then, because there's nothing to forgive. Forgiveness is a discernment between what is real and what is not real.

When people behave unlovingly, they have forgotten who they are. They have fallen asleep to the Christ within them. The job of the miracle worker is to remain awake. We choose not to fall asleep and dream of our brother's guilt. In this way we are given the power to awaken him.

A prime example of a miracle worker is Pollyanna. The ego knows this, which is why she is constantly invalidated in this culture. She walked into a situation where everyone had been in a nasty mood for years. She chose not to see the nastiness. She had faith in what lay beyond it. She extended her perception beyond what her physical senses revealed to her, to what her heart knew to be true about every human being. It didn't matter how anyone behaved. Pollyanna had faith in the love she knew existed behind anyone's fear, and thus she invoked their love into expression. She exercised the power of forgiveness. Within a short time, everyone was nice and everyone was happy! Whenever someone says to me, "Marianne, you're being a Pollyanna," I think to myself, "If only I were that powerful."

3.   GIVING UP JUDGMENT

"Judgment is not an attribute of God."

A Course in Miracles tells us that whenever we are contemplating attacking someone, it is as though we are holding a sword above their head. The sword, however, doesn't fall on them but on us. Since all thought is thought about ourselves, then to condemn another is to condemn ourselves.

How do we escape judgment? Largely through a reinterpretation of what we're judging. *A Course in Miracles* describes the difference between a sin and an error. 'A sin would mean we did something so bad that God is angry at us.' But since we can't do anything that changes our essential nature, God has nothing to be angry at. Only love is real. Nothing else exists. 'The Son of God cannot sin. We can make mistakes,' to be sure, and we obviously do. But God's attitude toward error is a desire to heal us. Because we ourselves are angry and punishing, we have concocted the idea of an angry, punishing God. We are created in God's image, however, and not the other way around. As extensions of God, we are ourselves the spirit of compassion, and in our right minds, we don't seek to judge but to heal. We do this through forgiveness. When someone has behaved unlovingly—when they yell at us, or lie about us, or steal from us—they have lost touch with their essence. They have forgotten who they are. But everything that someone does, says the Course, is either 'love or a call for love.' If someone treats us with love, then of course love is the appropriate response. If they treat us with fear, we are to see their behavior as a call for love.

The American prison system illustrates the philosophical and practical difference between the choice to perceive sin or to perceive error. We see criminals as guilty and seek to punish them. But whatever we do to others, we are doing to ourselves. Statistics painfully prove that our prisons are schools for crime; a vast number of crimes are committed by people who have already spent time in prison. In punishing others, we end up punishing ourselves. Does that mean we're to forgive a rapist, tell him we know he just had a bad day and send him home? Of course not. We're to ask for a miracle. A miracle here would be a shift from perceiving prisons as houses of punishment to perceiving them as houses of rehabilitation. When we consciously change their purpose from fear to love, we release infinite possibilities of healing.

Forgiveness is like the martial arts of consciousness. In Aikido and other martial arts, we sidestep our attacker's force rather than resisting it. The energy of the attack then boomerangs back in the direction of the attacker. Our power lies in remaining nonreactive. Forgiveness works in the same way. When we attack back, and defense is a form of attack, we initiate a war that no one can win. Since lovelessness is not real, we're not at the effect of it in ourselves or others. The problem, of course, is that we think we are. In seeking a miracle, we don't take part in life's battles, but rather we are asking to be lifted above them. The Holy Spirit reminds us that the battle is not real.

"Vengeance is mine, sayeth the Lord," means, "Relinquish the idea of vengeance." God balances all wrong, but not through attack, judgment or punishment. Contrary to how it feels when we're lost in the emotions that tempt us to judge, there's no such thing as righteous anger. When I was a little girl, I would fight with my brother or sister, and when my mother came home she would be annoyed at us for arguing. One of us would always say, "They did it first." It actually doesn't matter who "did it first." Whether you're attacking first or attacking back, you're an instrument of attack and not of love.

Several years ago I was at a cocktail party where I got into a very heated debate about American foreign policy. Later that night, I had a kind of waking dream. A gentleman appeared to me and said, "Excuse me, Miss Williamson, but we thought we should tell you: In the cosmic roll call, you are considered a hawk, not a dove."

I was incensed. "No way," I said indignantly. "I'm totally for peace. I'm a dove all the way."

"I'm afraid not," he said. "I'm looking on our charts, and it says very clearly right here: Marianne Williamson, warmonger. You're at war with Ronald Reagan, Caspar Weinberger, the CIA, in fact the entire American defense establishment. No, I'm sorry. You're definitely a hawk."

I saw, of course, that he was right. I had just as many missiles in my head as Ronald Reagan had in his. I thought it was wrong for him to judge communists, but I thought it was okay for me to judge him. Why? Because I was *right*, of course!

I spent years as an angry left-winger before I realized that an angry generation can't bring peace. Everything we do is infused with the energy with which we do it. As Gandhi said, "We must *be* the change." What the ego doesn't want us to see is that the guns we need to get rid of first are the guns in our own heads.

4.   *THE CHOICE TO LOVE*

> *"The ego is the choice for guilt; the Holy Spirit the choice for guiltlessness."*

The ego always emphasizes what someone has done wrong. The Holy Spirit always emphasizes what they've done right. The Course likens the ego to a scavenger dog that seeks out every scrap of evidence for our brother's guilt and lays it at its master's feet. The Holy Spirit, similarly, sends out its own messengers to seek evidence of our brother's innocence. The important thing is that we decide what we want to see before we see it. We receive what we request. "Projection makes perception." We can find—and in fact, we *will* find—whatever it is we're looking for in life. The Course says that we think we will understand a person enough to know whether or not they are lovable, but that unless we love them, we can never understand them. The spiritual path involves taking conscious responsibility for what we choose to perceive—our brother's guilt or innocence. We see a brother's innocence when it's all we *want* to see. People are not perfect—that is, they do not yet express externally their internal perfection. Whether we choose to focus on the guilt in their personality, or the innocence in their soul, is up to us.

What we think of as people's guilt is their fear. All negativity derives from fear. When someone is angry, they are afraid. When someone is rude, they are afraid. When someone is manipulative, they are afraid. When someone is cruel, they are afraid. There is no fear that love does not dissolve. There is no negativity that forgiveness does not transform.

Darkness is merely the absence of light, and fear is merely the absence of love. We can't get rid of darkness by hitting it with a baseball bat, because there is nothing to hit. If we want to be rid of darkness, we must turn on a light. Similarly, if we want to be rid of fear, we cannot fight it but must replace it with love.

The choice to love is not always easy. The ego puts up terrible resistance to giving up fear-laden responses. This is where the Holy Spirit comes in. It's not our job to change our own perceptions, but to remember to ask Him to change them for us.

Let's say your husband has left you for another woman. You can't change other people, and you can't ask God to change them, either. You can, however, ask to see this situation differently. You can ask for peace. You can ask the Holy Spirit to change your perceptions. The miracle is that, as you release judgment of your husband and the other woman, the pain in your gut begins to subside.

The ego might say in that situation that you'll never be at peace until your husband comes back. But peace isn't determined by circumstances outside us. Peace stems from forgiveness. Pain doesn't stem from the love we're denied by others, but rather from the love that we deny them. In a case like that, it feels as though we're hurt by what someone else did. But what really has occurred is that someone else's closed heart has tempted us to close our own, and it is our own denial of love that hurts us. That's why the miracle is a shift in our own thinking: the willingness to keep our own heart open, regardless of what's going on outside us.

A miracle is always available in any situation, because no one can decide for us how to interpret our own experience. 'There are only two emotions: love and fear.' We can interpret fear as a call for love. Miracle workers, says the Course, are generous out of self-interest. We give someone a break so we can stay in peace ourselves.

The ego says that we can project our anger onto another person and not feel it ourselves, but since all minds are continuous, whatever we project onto another we continue to feel. Getting angry at someone else might make us feel better for a while, but ultimately all the fear and guilt comes back at us. If we judge another person, then they'll judge us back—and even if they don't, *we'll feel like they did!*

Living in this world has taught us to instinctively respond from an unnatural space, always jumping to anger, or paranoia, or defensiveness, or some other form of fear. Unnatural thinking feels natural to us, and natural thinking feels unnatural.

A Course in Miracles is not about pouring pink paint over our anger and pretending it doesn't exist. What is psychologically unsound is spiritually unsound. Denial or suppression of emotions is unsound. You don't say, "I'm not angry, really I'm not. I'm on page 140 of *A Course in Miracles* and I don't get angry anymore," when inside you're seething. The Holy Spirit tells us, "Don't try to purify yourself before coming to me. I am the purifier." I was once on my way to giving a lecture on the Course, and I thought about a woman I knew who I was feeling annoyed at. Very quickly, I tried to hide the thought, as though it wasn't holy enough for me to be thinking at such a time. Then it seemed as though a voice in my head said, "Hey, I'm your friend. Remember?" The Holy Spirit wasn't judging me for my anger; He was there to help me move past it.

We mustn't forget what the Holy Spirit is for. We don't deny we're upset, but at the same time we own up to the fact that all our feelings stem from our own loveless thinking, and we're willing to have that lovelessness healed. Growth is never about focusing on someone else's lessons, but only on our own. We aren't victims of the world outside us. As hard as it is to believe sometimes, we're always responsible for how we see things. There would be no savior if there were no need for one. Of course things happen in this world that make it almost impossible to love—cruel, horrible things—but the Holy Spirit is within us to do the impossible. He does for us what we can't do for ourselves. He will lend us His strength, and when His mind is joined with ours, ego thinking is cast out.

But we must be aware of our ego feelings in order to release them. "He cannot shine away what you keep hidden, for you have not offered it to Him and he cannot take it from you." It would be violating our free will for the Holy Spirit to change our mental patterns unasked. But when we ask Him to change them, He will. When we're angry, or upset for any reason, we're asked to say, "I'm angry but I'm willing not to be. I'm willing to see this situation differently." We ask the Holy Spirit to enter into the situation and show it to us from a different perspective.

Once I was having porcelain fingernails applied, and my manicurist's friend came into the room. I couldn't tolerate her personality. From the moment this woman opened her mouth, I felt like someone was running fingernails over a blackboard. Since my hands weren't free, I couldn't leave the room, and since the manicurist was someone who came to my lectures, I felt ashamed of my own reaction. I prayed and asked God for help. His response was dramatic. Within moments, the "obnoxious" woman began talking about her childhood, and particularly her relationship with her father. As she began to describe her upbringing, it became perfectly clear to me how she would have grown up with little self-esteem, and an inordinate need to develop grandiose personality characteristics, which in her mind would denote strength. Her defenses didn't work, of course. Coming from fear, they merely put people off. Suddenly, the same behavior that had so irritated me five minutes before, now elicited in me a deep compassion. The Holy Spirit had pointed me to the information that would melt my heart. Now I saw her differently. That was the miracle: Her behavior hadn't changed, but *I* had.

5.   LEVELS OF TEACHING

> *"Therefore, the plan includes very specific con-*
> *tacts to be made for every teacher of God."*

Relationships are assignments. They are part of a vast plan for our enlightenment, the Holy Spirit's blueprint by which each individual soul is led to greater awareness and expanded love. Relationships are the Holy Spirit's laboratories in which He brings together people who have the maximal opportunity for mutual growth. He appraises who can learn most from whom at any given time, and then assigns them to each other. Like a giant universal computer, He knows exactly what combination of energies, in exactly what context, would do the most to further God's plan for salvation. No meetings are accidental. "Those who are to meet will meet, because together they have the potential for a holy relationship."

The Course says that there are 'three levels of teaching' in relationship. The first level is what we think of as a casual encounter, such as two strangers meeting in an elevator or students who "happen" to walk home from school together. The second level is a "more sustained relationship, in which, for a time, two people enter into a fairly intense teaching-learning situation and then appear to separate." The third level of teaching is a relationship which, once formed, lasts all our lives. At this level, "each person is given a chosen learning partner who presents him with unlimited opportunities for learning."

Even at the first level of teaching, the people in the elevator might smile at one another or the students might become friends. It is mostly in casual encounters that we are given a chance to practice the fine art of chiseling away the hard edges of our personalities. Whatever personal weaknesses are evident in our casual interactions will inevitably appear magnified in more intense relationships. If we're crabby with the bank teller, it will be harder to be gentle with the people we love the most.

At the second level of teaching, people are brought together for more intense work. During their time together, they will go through whatever experiences provide them with their next lessons to be learned. When physical proximity no longer supports the highest level of teaching and learning between them, the assignment will call for physical separation. What then appears to be the end of the relationship however, is not really an end. Relationships are eternal. They are of the mind, not the body, since people are energy, not physical substance. Bodies joining may or may not denote real joining, since joining is of the mind. People who have slept in the same bed for twenty-five years may not be truly joined, and people who are many miles apart may not be separate at all.

Often we see a couple who has separated or divorced and look with sadness at the "failure" of their relationship. But if both people learned what they were meant to learn, then that relationship was a success.

Now it may be time for physical separation so that more can be learned in other ways. That not only means learning elsewhere, from other people; it also means learning the lessons of pure love that come from having to release the form of an existing relationship.

Third-level, life-long relationships are generally few because "their existence implies that those involved have reached a stage simultaneously in which the teaching-learning balance is actually perfect." That doesn't mean, however, that we necessarily recognize our third-level assignments; in fact, generally we don't. We may even feel hostility toward these particular people. Someone with whom we have a lifetime's worth of lessons to learn is someone whose presence in our lives forces us to grow. Sometimes it represents someone with whom we participate lovingly all our lives, and sometimes it represents someone who we experience as a thorn in our side for years, or even forever. Just because someone has a lot to teach us, doesn't mean we like them. People who have the most to teach us are often the ones who reflect back to us the limits to our own capacity to love, those who consciously or unconsciously challenge our fearful positions. They show us our walls. Our walls are our wounds—the places where we feel we can't love any more, can't connect any more deeply, can't forgive past a certain point. We are in each other's lives in order to help us see where we most need healing, and in order to help us heal.

6.   THE SPECIAL RELATIONSHIP

*"The special love relationship is the ego's chief
weapon for keeping you from Heaven."*

We can all relate to the desire to find Mr. or Ms. Right.
It's almost a cultural obsession. But according to *A
Course in Miracles*, the search for the perfect person to
"fix" us is one of our biggest psychic wounds, and one
of the ego's most powerful delusions. It represents a
notion that *A Course in Miracles* calls the "special relationship." Although the word "special" normally
implies something wonderful, from a Course perspective, special means different, therefore separate, which is
characteristic of ego rather than spirit. A special relationship is a relationship based on fear.

'God created only one begotten Son' and He loves
all of us as one. To Him, no one is different or special
because no one is actually separate from anyone else.
Since our peace lies in loving as God loves, we must
strive to love everyone. Our desire to find one "special
person," one part of the Sonship who will complete us,
is hurtful because it is delusional. It means we're seeking
salvation in separation rather than in oneness. The only
love that completes us is the love of God, and the love
of God is the love of everyone. That doesn't mean that
the form of our relationships is the same with everyone,
but it means that we are seeking the same content in
every relationship: a quality of brotherly love and friendship that goes beyond the changes of form and bodies.

Just as the 'Holy Spirit was God's answer to the separation, the special relationship was then the ego's answer to the creation of the Holy Spirit.' After the separation, we began to feel a huge gaping hole within us, and most of us still feel it. The only antidote for this is the Atonement, or return to God, because the pain we feel is actually our own denial of love. The ego, however, tells us differently. It argues that the love we need must come from someone else, and that there's one special person out there who can fill up that hole. Since the desire for that person actually stems from our belief that we're separate from God, then the desire itself symbolizes the separation and the guilt we feel because of it. Our search then carries the energy of the separation. It becomes about guilt. This is why so much anger is often aroused in our closest relationships. We're projecting onto someone else the rage we feel against ourselves for cutting off our own love.

Often when we think we are "in love" with a person, as *A Course in Miracles* indicates, we're actually anything but. The special relationship is based not on love but on guilt. The special relationship is the ego's seductive pull away from God. It is a major form of idolatry, or temptation to think that something other than God can complete us and give us peace. The ego tells us that there is some special person out there who will make all the pain go away. We don't really believe that, of course, but then on the other hand we really do. Our culture has bred the idea into us, through books, songs, movies, advertising, and more importantly, the conspiracy of other egos. It is the job of the Holy Spirit to transform the energy of special love from treachery to holiness.

The special relationship makes other people—their behavior, their choices, their opinions of us—too important. It makes us think we need another person, when in fact we are complete and whole as we are. Special love is a "blind" love, seeking to heal the wrong wound. It addresses the gap between ourselves and God, which doesn't actually exist but which we think does. By addressing this gap as real, and displacing its source onto other people, we actually manufacture the experience we seek to rectify.

Under the Holy Spirit's guidance, we come together to share joy. Under the ego's direction, we come together to share desperation. Negativity, however, cannot really be shared because it is an illusion. "A special relationship is a kind of union from which union is excluded."

A relationship is not meant to be the joining at the hip of two emotional invalids. The purpose of a relationship is not for two incomplete people to become one, but rather for two complete people to join together for the greater glory of God.

The special relationship is a device by which the ego separates rather than joins us. Based on a belief in internal emptiness, it is always asking, "What can I get?", whereas the Holy Spirit asks, "What can I give?" The ego seeks to use other people to fulfill our needs as we define them. Certain voices go on endlessly these days about whether or not "our needs are being met" in a relationship. But when we try to use a relationship to serve our own purposes, we falter because we are reinforcing our illusion of need. Under the ego's guidance we're always looking for something, yet always sabotaging what we've found.

One of my girlfriends called me one day and said she had had a date with someone she really liked. The next week, she called and said he had broken a date with her in order to go out of town. She didn't like him after all. "I won't take that from anyone," she told me. "I'm ready for a *relationship*."

"No you're not ready for a relationship," I told her. "Not if another person isn't allowed to make a mistake, you're not."

The ego had told her to reject the man because she was ready for a relationship, but what it was really doing was to make sure she wouldn't have one. The ego isn't looking for someone to love; it's looking for someone to attack. Its dictate in love is "Seek, and do not find." It looks for a reflection of itself, another mask that hides the face of Christ. In the special relationship, I'm afraid to show you the real truth about myself—my fears, my weaknesses— because I'm afraid that if you see them, you'll leave. I'm assuming you're as judgmental as I am. And I'm also not really jumping up and down wanting to see your weak spots either because it makes me nervous to think I'm involved with someone who has them. The whole setup mitigates against authenticity and therefore against real growth. A special relationship perpetuates the self-punishing masquerade in which we all seek desperately to attract love through being someone we're not. Although we're seeking love, we're actually fostering our own self-hatred and lack of self-esteem.

What's our miracle here? It's a shift from thoughts of specialness to thoughts of holiness. Our mental patterns in regard to relationships are so fraught with fear—attack and defensiveness, guilt and selfishness, however prettily disguised—that many times we are brought to our knees. As always, that's a good place to be. We pray for God to guide our thoughts and feelings. 'You can place any relationship under the Holy Spirit's care and be sure that it will not result in pain.'

7.   THE HOLY RELATIONSHIP

"The holy relationship is the old unholy relationship transformed and seen anew."

If the special relationship is the ego's response to the creation of the Holy Spirit, the holy relationship is the Holy Spirit's response back. The 'holy relationship is the old, special relationship transformed.' In the special relationship, the ego guides our thinking and we meet in fear, mask to mask. In the holy relationship, the Holy

Spirit has changed our minds about the purpose of love and we meet heart to heart.

A Course in Miracles describes the difference between an unholy and a holy alliance:

> *"For an unholy relationship is based on differences, where each one thinks the other has what he has not. They come together, each to complete himself and rob the other. They stay until they think that there is nothing left to steal, and then move on. And so they wander through a world of strangers, unlike themselves, living with their bodies perhaps under a common roof that shelters neither; in the same room and yet a world apart.*
>
> *A holy relationship starts from a different premise. Each one has looked within and seen no lack. Accepting his completion, he would extend it by joining with another, whole as himself."*

The purpose of a special relationship is to teach us to hate ourselves, while the purpose of a holy relationship is to heal us of our self-loathing. In the special relationship, we are always trying to hide our weaknesses. In the holy relationship, it's understood that we all have unhealed places, and that healing is the purpose of our being with another person. We don't try to hide our weaknesses, but rather we understand that the relationship is a context for healing through mutual forgiveness. Adam and Eve were naked in the garden of Eden but not embarrassed. That doesn't mean they were physically naked. It means they were emotionally naked, totally real and honest, yet they were not embarrassed because they felt accepted completely for who they were.

The Course presents an image of the special relationship as a picture set in a frame. The ego is more interested in the frame—the idea of the perfect person who will "fix" everything—than we are in the picture, which is the person himself. The frame is baroque, and decorated with rubies and diamonds. But the Course says the rubies are our blood and the diamonds are our tears. That is the essence of specialness. It is not love but exploitation. What we call love is often hate or at best, robbery. Although we may not know it consciously, our search is often for someone who has what we think we don't have, and once we get it from them we'll be ready to move on. In a holy relationship, we're interested in the picture itself. All we want by way of a frame is a light support that does just enough to keep the picture in place. We're not interested in our brother for what he can do for us. We're interested in our brother, period.

The holy relationship is, above all else, a friendship between two brothers. We are not put here to audition one another, put someone on trial, or use other people to gratify our own ego needs. We are not here to fix, change or belittle another person. We are here to support, forgive and heal one another. I was once counseling a couple who were in the process of messily completing their relationship. The man had moved on to date someone else and the woman was angry. During our session she said to him about the new girlfriend, "You only like her because she tells you how *wonderful* you are all the time!" He looked at her very seriously and quietly said, "Yeah, I think that has something to do with it."

How do we find a holy relationship? Not by asking God to change our partners, but by asking God to change our minds. We don't run away from someone we're attracted to because we're afraid of specialness. Anytime there's a potential for love, there's a potential for specialness. I often ask audiences, "What's the first thing we should do when we're attracted to someone?" and they reply in pep-rally fashion, "*pray!*" The prayer goes something like this: "Dear God, you know, and I know, that I have more potential for neurosis in this area than in any other. Please take my attraction, my thoughts and feelings about this person and use them for your purposes. Let this relationship unfold according to your will, Amen."

Spiritual progress is like a detoxification. Things have to come up in order to be released. Once we have asked to be healed, then our unhealed places are forced to the surface. A relationship that is used by the Holy Spirit becomes a place where our blocks to love are not suppressed or denied, but rather brought into our conscious awareness. We never get crazy like we do around the people we're really attracted to. Then we can see our dysfunctions clearly, and when we're ready, ask God to show us another way.

As temples of healing, relationships are like a trip to the divine physician's office. How can a doctor help us unless we show him our wounds? Our fearful places have to be revealed before they can be healed. *A Course in Miracles* teaches that 'darkness is to be brought to light, and not the other way around.' If a relationship allows us to merely avoid our unhealed places, then we're hiding there, not growing. The universe will not support that.

The ego thinks of a perfect relationship as one in which everybody shows a perfect face. But this is not necessarily so, because a show of strength is not always honest. It is not always a genuine expression of who we are. If I pretend to have it together in some area where I really don't, I am fostering an illusion about myself. I would only be doing this out of fear—fear that if you saw the truth about me, I would be rejected.

God's idea of a "good relationship" and the ego's idea of one are completely different. To the ego, a good relationship is one in which another person basically behaves the way we want them to and never presses our buttons, never violates our comfort zones. But if a relationship exists to support our growth, then in many ways it exists to do just those things; force us out of our limited tolerance and inability to love unconditionally. We're not aligned with the Holy Spirit until people can behave in any way they choose to, and our own inner peace isn't shaken. There have been times in my life where my thought about a relationship was, "This is terrible," but upon further reflection I realized God would probably be saying, "Oh, this is good." Marianne gets to see, in other words, her own neuroses more clearly.

A girlfriend once told me she had broken up with her boyfriend.

"Why?" I asked.

"Because he didn't call me for five days."

I didn't say anything.

"He knows I need verbal reassurance on a daily basis," she continued. "So I set my limits. Don't you think that's good?"

"No," I said. "I think it's childish." I paused. "Have you considered accepting him as he is?"

"Well, thanks for the support," she said.

I responded, "You're welcome."

I knew she thought of support as agreement from others that her boyfriend was guilty. Support for the belief in guilt is extremely easy to find. But real support is when we help one another see beyond someone's errors, to drop our judgments and see the love that lies beyond.

Our neuroses in relationships usually stem from our having an agenda for another person, or for the relationship itself. It's not our job to try to make a relationship into something we think it should be. If someone

doesn't behave like a great romantic partner, then perhaps they're not meant to be that for us. That doesn't
make them wrong. Not every relationship is meant to
be the ultimate romance: if the train doesn't stop at
your station, it's not your train. The ego seeks to use a
relationship to fill our needs as we define them; the
Holy Spirit asks that the relationship be used by God to
serve His purposes. And His purpose is always that we
might learn how to love others more purely. We love
purely when we release other people to be who they
are. The ego seeks intimacy through control and guilt.
The Holy Spirit seeks intimacy through acceptance and
release.

In the holy relationship, we don't seek to change
someone, but rather to see how beautiful they already
are. Our prayer becomes "Dear God, take the scales
from in front of my eyes. Help me to see my brother's
beauty." It is our failure to accept people exactly as they
are that gives us pain in a relationship.

Our ego is merely our fear. We all have egos, that
doesn't make us bad people. Our egos are not where
we are bad but where we are wounded. The Course
says that we are 'all afraid on some level that if people
saw who we really are, they would recoil in horror.'
That is why we invent the mask, to hide our true selves.
But the true self— the Christ within us—is that which
is most beautiful. We must reveal ourselves at the deepest level in order to find out how lovable we really are.
When we dig deeply enough into our real nature, we

do not find darkness. We find endless light. That is what the ego doesn't want us to see; that our safety actually lies in letting *down* our mask. But we cannot do this when we're constantly afraid of being judged. The holy relationship is a context where we feel safe enough to be ourselves, knowing that our darkness will not be judged but forgiven. In this way we are healed, and freed to move on into the light of our true being. We are motivated to grow. A holy relationship is this: "a common state of mind, where both give errors gladly to correction, that both may happily be healed as one."

8.   ROMANTIC LOVE

"There is no love but God's."

'There are no different categories of love. There isn't one kind of love between a mother and a child, another between lovers, and another between friends. The love that is real is the love that lies at the heart of all relationships. That is the love of God and it doesn't change with form or circumstance.'

A girlfriend of mine remarked to me recently, "Your relationship with your baby must be showing you a whole new kind of love." "No, it's not," I replied. "But it's showing me a new depth of tenderness, which is teaching me more about what love is."

People ask, "Why can't I find a deep, intimate romance?" The question is understandable, because people are lonely. An intimate romantic love, however, is like taking graduate work toward a Ph.D. in the ways of love, and many of us are hardly out of elementary school. When we're not in a relationship, the ego makes it seem as though all the pain would go away if we were. If the relationship lasts, however, it will actually bring much of our existential pain to the surface. That's part of its purpose. It will demand all of our skills at compassion, acceptance, release, forgiveness, and self-lessness. We might tend to forget the challenges involved in a relationship when we're not in one, but we remember them clearly enough once we are.

Relationships don't necessarily take the pain away. The only thing that "takes the pain away" is a healing of the things that cause the pain. It isn't the absence of other people in our lives that causes us the pain, but rather what we do with them when they're there. Pure love asks for nothing but peace for a brother, knowing that only in that way can we be at peace ourselves. How many times have I had to ask myself, "Do I want him to be at peace, or do I want him to call?" Pure love of another person is the restoration of our heartline. The ego, therefore, is marshaled against it. It will do everything it can to block the experience of love in any form. When two people come together in God, the walls that appear to separate us disappear. The beloved doesn't seem to be a mere mortal. They seem for a while to be something else, something more. The truth is, they *are* something more. No one is anything less than the perfect Son of God, and when we fall in love, we have an instant when we see the total truth about someone. They *are* perfect. That's not just our imagination.

But the craziness sets in quickly. As soon as the light appears, the ego begins its powerful drive to shut it out. All of a sudden, the perfection we glanced on the spiritual planes becomes projected onto the physical. Instead of realizing that spiritual perfection and physical, material imperfection exist simultaneously, we start looking for material, physical perfection. We think someone's spiritual perfection isn't enough. They have to have perfect clothes as well. They have to be hip. They have to dazzle. And so no one gets to be a human being anymore. We idealize one another, and when someone doesn't live up to the ideal, we're disappointed.

Rejecting another human being simply because they are human, has become a collective neurosis. People ask, "When will my soul mate get here?" But praying for the right person is useless if we're not ready to receive him. Our soul mates are human beings, just like we are, going through the normal processes of growth. No one is ever "finished." The top of one mountain is always the bottom of another, and even if someone meets us when we feel "on top" of things, the chances are good that very soon we'll be going through something that challenges us. It is our commitment to growth that makes this inevitable. But the ego doesn't like the look of people when they're "going through things." It's unattractive. As in every other area, the problem in relationships is rarely that we haven't had wonderful opportunities or met wonderful people. The problem is, we haven't known how to take the greatest advantage of the opportunities we've had. Sometimes we didn't recognize at the time how wonderful those people were. Love is all around us. The ego is the block to our awareness of love's presence. The idea that there is a perfect person who just hasn't arrived yet is a major block.

Our vulnerability to the myth of "Mr. Right" stems from our glorification of romantic love. The ego uses romantic love for its "special" purposes, leading us to jeopardize our relationships by overvaluing their romantic content. The difference between a friendship and a romance can be illustrated with the image of a long-stemmed rose. The stem is the friendship; the blossom the romance. Because the ego is sensation-oriented, our focus automatically goes to the blossom. But all the nourishment that the blossom needs in order to live, reaches it through the stem. The stem might look boring in comparison, but if you take the blossom off the stem it will not last for long. I shared that image in a lecture once, and a woman then added a lovely thought: A long-term romance is like a rose bush. In any given season, a blossom might fall off. But if the plant is well nourished, then the season will come around again, and new blossoms appear. The disappearance of romantic fervor doesn't necessarily spell the end of a wonderful relationship, except to the ego. The Spirit can see the seeds of rebirth in any pattern of decline.

A Course in Miracles says it is 'not our job to seek for love, but to seek for all the barriers we hold against its coming.' Thinking that there is some special person out there who is going to save us is a barrier to pure love. It is a large gun in the ego's arsenal. It is a way the ego tries to keep us away from love, although it doesn't want us to see that. We seek desperately for love, but it is that same desperation that leads us to destroy it once it gets here. Thinking that one special person is going to save us tempts us to load an awful lot of emotional pressure on whoever comes along that we think might fit the bill.

We don't have to remind God that we'd like wonderful relationships. He's already clear about that. *A Course in Miracles* teaches us that a desire is a prayer. The most enlightened prayer isn't "Dear God, send me someone wonderful," but, "Dear God, help me realize that I am someone wonderful." Years ago I would pray for a wonderful man to come and take my desperation away. Ultimately I said to myself, "Why don't you try to deal with that before he gets here?" I can't imagine any man saying to a friend, "Gee, I met a fabulous desperate woman last night!" Looking for Mr. Right leads to desperation because there is no Mr. Right. There is no Mr. Right because there is no Mr. Wrong. There is whoever is in front of us, and the perfect lessons to be learned from that person.

If your heart's desire is for an intimate partner, the Holy Spirit might send someone who isn't the ultimate intimate partner for you, but rather something better: someone with whom you are given the opportunity to work through the places in yourself that need to be healed before you're *ready* for the deepest intimacy. The belief in special love leads us to discount anything we don't see as "ultimate relationship" material. I've overlooked some diamonds that way, failing to take advantage of situations that would have only served to speed up my growth. We sometimes fail to work on ourselves in the relationships that are right in front of us, thinking that "real life" begins when *they* get here. This is just a ploy of the ego once again, making sure that we'll seek but not find. The problem with not taking relationships seriously if they don't feel like "Mr. Right" is this: Every once in a while, Mr. Right gets here—he sometimes even appears as Mr. Wrong transformed— but we blow it because we're not in practice. He's here, but we're not ready. We haven't been working on ourselves. We were waiting for Mr. Right.

A Course in Miracles says that one day we will realize that nothing occurs outside our minds. How a person seems to show up for us is intimately connected to how we choose to show up for them. I have learned that my most productive responses in relationships come not from my focus on the particulars about another person, but rather from my commitment to playing my own role in the relationship on as high a level as I'm capable. Love is a participatory emotion. In a holy relationship, we take an active role in creating the context in which the interaction can unfold most constructively. We actively create the conditions of interest, rather than passively waiting around to see whether or not we're interested.

No one is always gorgeous. No one is always sexy. But love is a decision. Waiting to see whether someone is good enough is childish, and it is bound to make the other person feel on some level as though they're auditioning for the part. In that space, we feel nervous, and when we're nervous, we're not at our best. The ego is looking for someone attractive enough to support. The mature and miracle-minded among us support people in being attractive. Part of working on ourselves, in order to be ready for a profound relationship, is learning how to support another person in being the best that they can be. Partners are meant to have a priestly role in each other's lives. They are meant to help each other access the highest parts within themselves.

I've been with men who never seemed to think I was good enough. I've also been with men who were smart enough to say, "You look beautiful tonight" often enough for it to bolster my self-esteem and help me show up for life in a more beautiful way. None of us are really objectively attractive or unattractive. There is no such thing. There are people who manifest the potential for sparkle that we all share, and those who don't. Those who do are usually people who somewhere along the line, either from parents or lovers, were told verbally or nonverbally, "You're wonderful and beautiful." Love is to people what water is to plants.

Examining the past can help clarify many of our problems, but healing doesn't occur in the past. It occurs in the present. There is practically a mania these days for blaming the events of our childhood for our current despair. What the ego doesn't want us to see is that our pain doesn't come from the love we weren't given in the past, but from the love we ourselves aren't giving in the present. Salvation is only found in the present. Every moment we have a chance to change our past and our future by reprogramming the present. Such a view is blasphemy to the ego and we are judged harshly for espousing it. Although we might have learned the ways of lovelessness from our parents, perpetuating their patterns by denying them love now is hardly the way out of the problem. We don't get to the light through endless investigation of the darkness. After a certain point, the discussion always becomes circular. The only way to the light is through entering the light.

"My parents didn't tell me I was beautiful. Poor me." is not a miracle-minded thought. Rather, it supports a feeling of victimization. The miracle-minded attitude here would be, "My parents didn't tell me I was beautiful. The value of knowing this is that now I'm clearer about why I don't have an easy time letting anyone else tell me that, and I understand why I haven't developed the habit of saying it to others. I can develop the habit now. The choice to give what I haven't received is always an available option." A man mentioned to me recently that when he was a child, his father never gave him presents. I suggested that a healing would come from his sending his father lots of presents now.

I used to worry too much about whether or not I was supported, and not enough about whether or not I was actively supporting others. Romantically, I realized that I needed to help a man feel more like a man, rather than spend my time worrying about whether or not he *was* enough of a man. We help another person access their highest by accessing our own. Growth comes from focus on our own lessons, not on someone else's. *A Course in Miracles* teaches that "only what you have not given can be lacking in any situation." I spent years waiting for a man to make me "feel like a real woman." Only when I realized that my feminine energy was not a man's gift to me, but rather my gift to myself and to him, did the men around me start to demonstrate the more masculine energy I craved.

The fairy tale called "The Frog Prince" reveals the deep psychological connection between our attitudes toward people and their capacity for transformation. In the story, a princess kisses a frog and he becomes a prince. What this signifies is the miraculous power of love to create a context in which people naturally blossom into their highest potential. Neither nagging, trying to get people to change, criticizing, or fixing can do that. The Course says we think we're going to understand people in order to figure out whether or not they're worthy of our love, but that actually, until we love them, we can never understand them. What is not loved is not understood. We hold ourselves separate from people and wait for them to earn our love. But people deserve our love because of what God created them to be. As long as we're waiting for them to be anything better, we will constantly be disappointed. When we choose to join with them, through approval and unconditional love, the miracle kicks in for both parties. This is the primary key, the ultimate miracle, in relationships.

9. RELINQUISHING FEAR

"Perfect love casts out fear."

A good relationship isn't always crystals and rainbows. It's a birth process, often painful, often messy. When my daughter was first born, she was covered with blood and everything else. There was a lot to go through before the Gerber baby finally appeared.

A "spiritual relationship" isn't necessarily one in which two people are smiling all the time. Spiritual means to me, above all else, authentic. At my New Year's Eve service last year, I said that we were together not for mindless but for mindful celebration. That would include some grief and acknowledgement of disappointments in the past year, which would have to be processed and forgiven before we could honestly celebrate the stroke of midnight and the mark of a new beginning.

And so it is that, in relationships as well, we're brought together for real work. Real work can only occur in the presence of rigorous honesty. We all long for that, but we are afraid of honestly communicating with another person because we think they'll leave us if they see who we really are.

A couple from my lectures once came to me for counseling. Earlier that day, the man had told the woman he was breaking off their relationship. She was shocked and hurt and asked him if he would come with her to see me in order to help her work through the loss. As the two of them sat across from me on my couch, I assured Bob that I wasn't there to try to get them back together, but to join with them in asking for peace.

I remembered a similar situation I had been in myself once, and how brilliantly my therapist had handled it. I said exactly the things that she had said. I said to him, "Bob, why are you so angry at Deborah?"

"I'm not angry at her," he said.

"Well, you sure sound angry," I told him.

"I know that it's not my job to fix Deborah," he said. "I don't want to change her; I just want out."

"Oh, I bet you think that's so spiritual," I said.

He looked surprised. I think he thought he'd been a good *A Course in Miracles* student.

"You haven't suspended judgment of Deborah," I said. "You've withheld vital information from her, data without which she couldn't function effectively within the relationship. Why don't you tell her why you're so angry?"

Once again he repeated, "I'm not angry."

"Well," I said. "You're an actor. Just pretend you are. Go on Bob, we're safe here. Let her have it."

And boy, once he got started, did he let it out. He told her that she had no concept of how to live with another person. She just did everything however she wanted to do it, and if he wanted to come along, well that was just great. I don't remember exactly what else he had to say, but there was a lot of communication that came gushing out once he allowed it to. When he was finished, Deborah, obviously moved, said quietly and sincerely, "I never knew that. Thank you for telling me."

They left my office and did not break up. Their relationship, they later told me, was reborn in that session. The anger that Bob was feeling was pent up energy that came from the fact that he had felt it "unspiritual" to share his honest feelings with Deborah as they went along.

It's far better to communicate than to suppress our feelings. Anger is often a result of a series of uncommunicated feelings building up inside of us and ultimately exploding. In a holy relationship, we consider it part of our commitment to stay current in the honest expression of our feelings, and to support our partner in doing the same. So much is then communicated as we go along that the chances of anger building up inside either of us is lessened.

Until then, we must deal with what's real. If anger comes up, it must be accepted. If we think our partner won't love us if we get angry, then we stop being honest and the relationship is doomed for sure. I've suggested to couples that they agree not to break up a relationship because of a fight. It's very important to have a safe space for fighting. I say that because fighting isn't always fighting. Once I was having a "dramatic discussion" with a friend. A mutual friend of ours spoke up and said, "I can't stand the way you guys are always fighting." "We're not fighting," I said. "We're Jewish." He thought we were fighting; we thought we were having a passionate conversation.

Anger is a hot topic for spiritual seekers. Many people, for instance, have an issue with Jesus's anger with the money-changers. If Jesus was so pure, they ask, then how could he have gotten angry? But no Jew or Italian would have a problem with that scene. The removal of ego is not the removal of personality. What we call Jesus's anger was energy. An outburst of emotion doesn't have to be so quickly labeled anger. It's a release of energy and doesn't have to be thought of as a negative or "unspiritual" emotion.

Just because someone isn't expressing their rage, by the way, doesn't mean they don't have any. Rage turned outward is called rage. Rage turned inward is called ulcers and cancer and things like that. The unhealthiest thing you can do with anger is to deny you have it. The miraculous perspective is not to pretend you're not angry, but rather to say, "I'm angry but I'm willing not to be. Dear God, please show me what it is I'm not seeing." There is a way of sharing our anger with people, without expressing it as an attack. Instead of saying, for instance, "You made me feel this or that," you say, "This is how I'm feeling. I'm not saying *you made me feel* this way, or that you're to blame. I'm simply sharing this as part of my healing, in order to release this feeling and move beyond it." In this way, you're taking responsibility for your feelings, and what could have been seen as an argument—or even avoided as unpleasant—can become an important part of the healing power of relationships. We're then not adversaries in the conversation, but partners. Real relationships demand honest communication, and no matter how painful, no matter how frightening. *A Course in Miracles* says that miracles arise from total communication given and received.

When you ask God to heal your life, He shines a very bright light on everything you need to look at. You end up seeing things about yourself that maybe you'd rather not see. We have a lot of armor that has accumulated in front of our hearts—a lot of fear self-righteously masquerading as something else. As anyone who has ever been in serious psychotherapy is well aware, the process of personal growth isn't always easy. We must face our own ugliness. We often must become painfully aware of the unworkability of a pattern before we're willing to give it up. It often seems, in fact, that our lives get worse rather than better when we begin to work deeply on ourselves. Life doesn't actually get worse; it's just that we feel our own transgressions more because we're no longer anesthetized by unconsciousness. We're no longer distanced, through denial or dissociation, from our own experience. We're starting to see the truth about the games we play.

This process can be so painful that we are tempted to go backwards. It takes courage—this is often called the path of the spiritual warrior—to endure the sharp pains of self-discovery rather than choose to take the dull pain of unconsciousness that would last the rest of our lives. I laugh whenever anyone suggests that *A Course in Miracles* has us taking an easy way out. It's a lot of things, but it's *not* easy. We have to look the ego straight in the eye before we have the power to relinquish it.

The ego isn't a monster. It's just the *idea* of a monster. We all have demons and dragons within us, but we also have the dashing prince. I've never read a fairy tale where the dragons triumphed over the prince. And I've never really tried to outgrow a pattern and not had the experience of God's grace given me when I sincerely and humbly asked. "You take the good with the bad," my father used to tell us when we were children. The more we learn about the light within us, the easier it ultimately becomes to forgive ourselves for the fact that we're not perfect yet. If we were perfect, we wouldn't have been born. It's our mission to become perfect, however, and looking at where we're not is an important part of the process. We become perfected personalities by accepting the spiritual perfection which already exsists within us.

There is a story about Leonardo da Vinci that has always moved me. Early in his career, he was painting a picture of Christ and found a profoundly beautiful young male to model for his portrait of Jesus. Many years later, Leonardo was painting a picture that included Judas. He walked through the streets of Florence looking for the perfect person to play the great betrayer. Finally he found someone dark-looking enough, evil-seeming enough to do the job. He went up to the man to approach him to do the modeling. The man looked at him and said, "You don't remember me, but I know you. Years ago, I was the model for your picture of Jesus."

In the movie *Star Wars*, Darth Vader turns out to have been a nice guy after all, a long time ago. And Lucifer was the most beautiful angel in Heaven before he fell. The ego is simply where a glitch occurred, where the wires got crossed, where love became blocked. As many times as I've expressed negativity instead of love in my life, there's one thing I'm very sure of: I would have done better if I had known how. I would have expressed with love if I had felt at that moment that I could have, and still had my needs met.

Until we fully appreciate that the ego is the impostor within us, we often feel embarrassed to admit to ourselves, not to mention anyone else, the games we play. Instead of feeling compassion for ourselves, and remembering that our neuroses are our wounds, we tend to be too ashamed to look at them. We think we're bad. 'We think that if we, or anyone else God forbid, were to see the real truth about us, we would all recoil in horror.' The truth, rather, is that if we, or anyone else, were to see the real truth about us, we would all be dazzled by the light. In looking deeply into ourselves, however, we first have to face what *A Course in Miracles* calls the 'ring of fear.' Before the Prince can save the damsel in distress, he has to slay the dragons that surround her castle. So do we all. Those dragons are our demons, our wounds, our egos, our brilliant ways of denying love to ourselves and others. The ego's patterns have to be rooted out, detoxed from our system, before the pure love within us can have a chance to come forth.

A spiritual teacher from India once pointed out that there is no such thing as a gray sky. The sky is always blue. Sometimes, however, gray clouds come and cover the blue sky. We then think the sky is gray. It is the same with our minds. We're always perfect. We can't not be. Our fearful patterns, our dysfunctional habits, take hold within our minds and cover our perfection. Temporarily. That is all. We are still perfect sons of God. There has never been a storm that hasn't passed. Gray clouds never last forever. The blue sky does.

So what are we to do with our fear, our anger, the clouds that cover the love inside us? Relinquish them to the Holy Spirit. He transforms them through love, and never through an attack on another person. It is attack, not the anger itself, which is destructive. Yelling into pillows has become popular in certain circles, and for good reason. Getting the energy up and out is often a good way to shed the physical tension that makes it so difficult to pray when you need it most. Our anger stands in front of our love. Letting it out is part of the process of relinquishing it. The last thing you want to do—ever—is to buy into the insidious delusion that spiritual lives and spiritual relationships are always quiet, or always blissful.

10.   WORKING ON OURSELVES

"Only what you have not given can be lacking in any situation."

Relationships are meaningful because they are opportunities to expand our hearts and become more deeply loving. The Holy Spirit is the medium of miracles, a guide to a different way of viewing ourselves in relation to other people. I watch my baby as she extends her love to everyone she meets. She hasn't learned yet that anyone is unsafe. Nothing stands between her natural impulse to love and her expression of that love. She smiles with the tenderness of her true feelings. One day I will have to teach her that not every expression of love is appropriate. But locking your door is vastly different from locking your heart. The greatest challenge of parenthood will be to support her in keeping an open heart while living in such a fearful world.

We can't really give to our children what we don't have ourselves. In that sense, my greatest gift to my daughter is that I continue to work on myself. Children learn more through imitation than through any other form of instruction. Our greatest opportunity to positively affect another person's life is to accept God's love into our own.

That is one of the primary principles of miracles in relationships: We are to look to ourselves—our own lessons, thoughts and behavior—in order to find peace with another person. "The sole responsibility of the miracleworker is to accept the Atonement for himself." The ego will always tempt us to think that the breakdown of a relationship has to do with what *they* did wrong, or what *they're* not seeing, or what *they* need to learn. The focus must remain on ourselves. We're affected by other peoples' lovelessness only to the extent to which we judge them for it. Otherwise we are invulnerable to the ego, as the Son of God is meant to be.

Sometimes people will say to me, "But Marianne, I think ninety percent of this is their stuff." "Fine," I say. "Then we have ten percent to investigate and learn from." That ten percent that is "your" part is what you need to look at and learn from. It is what you will carry with you into the next scenario. The ego knows this, which is why it tries to put the focus on the other person. The ego's purpose is to make us continually self-destruct without knowing that we're doing it. It's hard enough cleaning up your own act. Trying to clean up someone else's is just an ego trick to keep you from applying yourself to your own lessons. In order to learn the most from relationships, you have to focus on your own issues.

These days it's very common to hear people complain that their issue is that they choose the "wrong" people. The ego is very sly here. It's trying to convince us that we're taking responsibility for the problem, when in fact we're only doing that to a very small degree. Because our description of the problem still makes someone guilty, it can only lead into further darkness, not light. "I continue to choose people who can't commit" is not a miracle-minded perception. A more enlightened question might be, "How committable am I, really? How prepared am I in the deepest recesses of my being to give and receive love in an intimate, committed way?" Or, "How can I forgive those who could not go past a certain wall of fear when dealing with me? How can I forgive myself for the ways in which I contributed to or participated in their fear?"

Sometimes it seems as though you're hooked: You feel obsessed or compulsive about another person. When this is the case, it's a pretty good bet that on some level you're not letting them off the hook. In spite of the temptation to look outside yourself for the source as well as the answer to a problem, you hold to miracle-minded thought by looking inside yourself for both. The price you pay for not taking responsibility for your own pain is the failure to realize that you can change your conditions by changing your thoughts. Regardless of who initiated a painful interaction, or how much of the error still lies in someone else's thinking, the Holy Spirit always provides you with complete escape from pain through forgiveness on your part. The other person doesn't have to consciously join you in the change. 'Whoever is saner at the time,' says *A Course in Miracles*, 'is to invite the Holy Spirit into a situation.' It doesn't matter whether or not another person shares our willingness to let God enter. Everything you need in life already exists inside your head.

I once had a crush on a gay man. It might have been unreasonable, but I couldn't get him out of my mind. I asked for a miracle, and the following thoughts occurred to me: "You know, Marianne, you're obsessed, you're so unreleased about this because you're not releasing *him*. Accept him as he is. Release him to be where he wants to be, doing whatever he wants to do with whomever he wants to do it. It's what *you're* not giving that is lacking here. It's what *you're* doing to *him* that's causing you pain. Emotionally, your ego is trying to control him, which is why you're feeling controlled by your emotions." I got it. I released him in my mind, and then I felt released.

11.   CLOSED HEARTS

> *"No one can doubt the ego's skill in building up false cases."*

I once knew a man who came on very strong at the beginning of relationships, but couldn't seem to help closing his heart as soon as a woman had opened hers. I have heard that kind of behavior referred to as an "addiction to the attraction phase" in relationships. This man did not maliciously go around hurting women. He sincerely wanted to be in a genuine, committed relationship. What he lacked were the spiritual skills that would enable him to settle down in one place long enough to build anything solid with an equal partner. As soon as he saw human faults and weaknesses in a woman, he would run. The narcissistic personality is looking for perfection, which is a way of making sure that love never has a chance to blossom. The initial high can be so heady, so tantalizing, that the real work of growth which needs to follow the initial attraction phase can seem too dull, too hard to commit to. As soon as the other person is seen to be a real human being, the ego is repelled and wants to find somewhere else to play.

At the end of a relationship with someone like this, we feel as though we've taken cocaine. We had a fast and very exciting ride, and it felt at the time like something meaningful was happening. Then we crashed and realized that nothing meaningful had happened at all. It was all made up. Now all we have is a headache, and we can see that this kind of thing isn't good, isn't healthy, and we don't want to do it again.

But there's a reason why we're attracted to relationships such as this. We were drawn to the illusion of meaning. Sometimes someone who has nothing to offer in a real relationship can come on like they're offering the world. They are so dissociated from their own feelings that they have become highly skilled performers, unconsciously playing whatever part our fantasies prescribe. But the responsibility for our pain still remains our own. If we hadn't been looking for a cheap thrill, we wouldn't have been vulnerable to the lie.

How could we have been so stupid? That's the question we always ask ourselves at the end of these experiences. But once we've had enough of them, we admit to ourselves that we weren't really stupid at all. We suspected this was a drug. The problem was, we wanted it. We saw exactly what the game was with this person, usually within the first fifteen minutes, yet we were so attracted to the high, we were willing to pretend we didn't see it, for just a night, or a week, or however long it lasted. The fact that someone said to us, "You are so fabulous. You're such a wonderful woman. This is such a great date. How lucky a guy is to get to date you," when he's only known you for an hour, is a blinking red light to any thinking woman. The problem is, the depth of our wounds can be so great—we can be so hungry to hear those words, because deep down we suspect that they're untrue—that hearing them can cause us to put aside all rational considerations. When we're starved, we're desperate.

Women say to me sometimes, "Marianne, why do I always meet emotionally abusive men?" My answer is usually the following: "The problem is not that you met him—the problem is that you gave him your number." The problem, in other words, is not that we attract a certain kind of person, but rather that we are attracted *to* a certain kind of person. Someone who is distant emotionally might remind us, for instance, of one or both of our parents. "His energy is distant and subtly disapproving—I must be home." The problem, then, is not just that we are offered pain, but that we are *comfortable* with that pain. It's what we have always known.

The flip side of our dangerous attractions to people who have nothing to offer us is our tendency to feel bored by people who do. Nothing that is alien to our system can enter into us and stay there for long. This is true whether we're talking about something taken into our bodies or into our minds. If I swallow a piece of aluminum foil, my body will regurgitate until the offending object is expelled. If I'm being asked to swallow an idea that doesn't "agree" with me, then my psychological system will go through the same process of regurgitation in order to expel the offending material.

If I'm convinced that I'm not good enough, I will have a difficult time accepting someone into my life who thinks I am. It's the Groucho Marx syndrome of not wanting to like anyone who would want me in their club. The only way that I can accept someone's finding me wonderful, is if I find myself wonderful. But to the ego, self-acceptance is death.

This is why we're attracted to people who don't want us. We know they're not into it from the gate. We pretend to be surprised later when we find ourselves betrayed and they leave after an intense but fairly short stay. They fit perfectly into our ego's plan: I will not be loved. The reason that nice, available people seem boring to us is because they bust us. The ego equates emotional danger with excitement, and claims that the nice, available person isn't dangerous enough. The irony is that the opposite is true: available people are the ones who *are* dangerous, because they confront us with the possibility of real intimacy. They might actually hang around long enough to get to know us. They could melt our defenses, not through violence but through love. This is what the ego doesn't want us to see. Available people are frightening. They threaten the ego's citadel. The reason we're not attracted to them is because we're not available ourselves.

12.   HEALING OUR WOUNDS

"Healing is the way in which separation is overcome."

Our barriers to love are rarely consciously chosen. They are our efforts to protect the places where the heart is bruised. Somewhere, sometime, we felt as though an open heart caused us pain or humiliation. We loved with the openness of a child, and someone didn't care, or laughed, or even punished us for the effort. In a quick moment, perhaps a fraction of a second, we made a decision to protect ourselves from ever feeling that pain again. We would never again allow ourselves to be so vulnerable. We built emotional defenses. We tried to build a fortress across our heart, to protect us from any cold assault. The only problem is, according to the Course, that we create what we defend against.

There was a time in my life when I felt I should stop opening up so much to people who didn't honor my heart as I wished it to be honored. I was angry at people who I felt had hurt me, but I denied the anger instead of getting in touch with it and releasing it to God. This is a common trap for Course students. If anger isn't brought up into conscious awareness, it has no place to go. It either turns into an attack on self or an inappropriate unconscious attack on others.

So not recognizing the full extent of my anger, and thinking that the lesson to be learned was merely that I shouldn't reveal so much of my honest feelings, I then went into relationships with two strikes against me: I was closed—read that as cold—and armed with hidden emotional knives coming from my unconscious anger. Contrary to whatever front I might have been able to lead with, that's not exactly a delightful package. Between the coldness and the anger, I could turn off the saintliest men. This, of course, only increased my anger and distrust.

I was once talking to a very wise therapist. I made some comment like, "Well, a lot of women my age are finding it very hard to find really loving, committable, available men." Her answer rang through my head like church bells. "When a woman says that to me," she said, "what we usually find when we look closely enough is a contempt for men."

Contempt for men. Contempt for men. The words resounded through my skull. I don't know if that was the issue for every woman she spoke to, but I knew she had hit the nail on the head in my case. I had often thought about the idea in the Course that we think we are angry at what our brother did to us, but that really we are angry because of what we've done to him. I had vaguely known that that was true, but it took a lot of uncovering to see what it was I was *doing* to these guys who I just *knew* were doing all these horrible things to me! The Course speaks of "shadow figures" we bring with us from our past. It tells us that we tend to see no one as they are now. We keep blaming someone in the present for something someone else did in the past.

Some poor man would tell me, "Darling, I'm not able to come back Sunday night like I'd planned. I've got to keep working on this project. I might not be back until Tuesday." Well, he might as well have just told me that my cat was dead and the dog was dying. The problem wasn't that the man wasn't coming home for a few days more. The problem was how it made me feel inside to hear him say that. Such a dark despair would run across my heart, I can't begin to tell you. I wasn't relating to that man, or this circumstance. I was remembering all the times I had ever felt as though I didn't matter, I wasn't attractive, Daddy didn't want to hold me, or someone else didn't want to have sex anymore.

From a Course perspective, this situation was coming up now in order for me to feel that feeling, and know that it had nothing to do with the present. I asked for a miracle: 'I am willing to see this differently. I am willing to remember who I am.' God's answer to my pain was not going to be—contrary to what my ego kept insisting was the only way out of this grief—a man who was going to tell me sixty times a day, "You're fabulous, you're wonderful, I love you, I want you," and then show me just how desirable I really was, maybe twice, preferably three times a day. The healing, in fact, was bound to come ultimately from men who would not—because no one can, really— tolerate my neediness, or the guilt I would try to project onto them in order to get my needs met. Or what I thought my needs were. My real need, of course, was to realize that

I didn't need a man to fill what only felt like these insatiable emotional needs. The needs themselves were not real, but merely a reflection of the fact that I thought of myself as less than perfect. Salvation would only come through my relinquishing the thought that I wasn't good enough. By defending myself against being abandoned, I continued to recreate the conditions in which it was bound to occur.

Why can't men commit? I can only answer for some of them that I've known, but in those cases, and in the cases of many women I've observed, men haven't committed because the women have been armored against it. Our armor is our darkness—the dark of the heart, the dark of the pain, the dark of the moment when we make that wicked comment or that unfair request.

Our defenses reflect our wounds. But no person can heal those wounds. They can give us love, innocently and sincerely, but if we're already convinced that people can't be trusted—if that's the decision we've already made—then our mind will construe whatever someone's behavior is, as evidence that our previously drawn conclusion was correct. The Course tells us we decide what we want to see before we see it. If we want to focus on someone's lack of respect for our feelings, we can certainly find it, given the fact that I don't know of many enlightened masters available for dating in the major cities of America today. But a lot of people are making greater efforts than we give them credit for, and are working against some formidable odds when our egos have convinced us that men or women are jerks, or don't like us, or always leave, or that there just aren't any good ones out there.

13.   CHANGING OUR MIND

"The fundamental change will occur with the change of mind in the thinker."

The goal of spiritual practice is full recovery, and the only thing you need to recover from is a fractured sense of self. If you don't already believe it yourself, another person cannot convince you you're okay. If they act as though you are, you will either not believe them, or become so dependent on their reinforcement that you proceed through your dependency to change their mind. Either way, you stay convinced that you're not okay. The only exercise in the Workbook of *A Course in Miracles* that is repeated several times is "I am as God created me." As I have mentioned earlier, the Course says that your only real problem is that you have forgotten who you are.

You awaken to your own perfection through your desire to see the perfection in someone else. Sometimes this is not easy. When I feel the old familiar darkness starting to descend around me, when a man, for instance, makes a comment that I know intellectually is probably innocent enough, but which makes me feel that I am abandoned or uncared for or rejected, I've been through enough in my life to know that the evil does not lie in what he just said. He is not the enemy. The enemy is this feeling, which in the past has led me to attack or defend enough to make him feel exactly what I'm feeling he's feeling but he really isn't. I can choose to see this differently. This is my wall. This is where we must be very conscious and call on God. Ask for a miracle: "Dear God, please help me. This is it. Right here. There is where the sword enters my heart. This is where I blow it every time."

The moment when the pain is greatest is a wonderful opportunity. The ego would prefer that we never look too directly into the pain. When in crisis, there's a good opportunity we might have a slip and ask Heaven for help. The ego would prefer that we not go into crisis. The ego prefers that a mild river of misery run through the background of our lives, never bad enough to make us question whether our own choices are creating the pain. When the pain is here, that is when we have a chance to "rout Satan and remove him forever." A man once said to me, "You know, Marianne, you can work on this stuff with your therapist, *A Course in Miracles*, your editor, the relationships lecturer, and all of your girlfriends, but none of them provide you with the opportunity that you have by working it out with me." What he meant of course, is with them I could describe the pain, but with him I could feel it. And in that moment, if I didn't take the childish, narcissistic cop-out and leave, but remained to face the fear and move through it, then the purpose of the relationship could be fulfilled. When our darkness is brought to light and forgiven, then we can move on.

We heal through noticing, and prayer. Awareness alone does not heal us. If analysis by itself could heal our wounds, we would all be healed by now. Our neuroses have become deeply embedded into our psyches, like a tumor that wraps itself around a vital organ.

The process of miraculous change is twofold:

1. I see my error or dysfunctional pattern.
2. I ask God to take it from me.

The first principle without the second is impotent. As they say in Alcoholics Anonymous, "your best thinking got you here." You're the problem but you're not the answer.

The second principle isn't enough to change us, either. The Holy Spirit can't take from us what we won't release to Him. He won't work without our consent. He cannot remove our character defects without our willingness, because that would be violating our free will. We chose those patterns, however mistakenly, and He will not force us to give them up.

In asking God to heal you, you are committing to the choice to be healed. This means the choice to change. The ego's resistance to this is intense. It wants us to think that an old dog doesn't change. "I'm angry because I'm an alcoholic," for instance, might describe your anger, but it doesn't justify it. The only advantage of knowing that you're angry, is so that you can make a choice to be otherwise. You can spend years in therapy, but until the choice is made to *do it differently*, you just keep going around in circles. Of course it feels unnatural to be gentle when you've been harsh for many years, but that's no excuse for not trying.

A Course in Miracles says that the most effective way to teach a child is not by saying 'Don't do that,' but 'Do this.' We don't reach the light through endless analysis of the dark. We reach the light by choosing the light. Light means understanding. Through understanding, we are healed.

If the purpose of a relationship is for people to be healed, and healing can only occur when our wounds are revealed, then the ego confronts us with a terrible Catch-22. If I don't show myself, there can be no growth. Without growth, there will ultimately be boredom, which is death for the relationship. But if I do reveal myself honestly, then I might appear unattractive and my partner will leave.

The ego's narcissism has us waiting for the perfect person to appear. The Holy Spirit knows that the search for perfection in another is just a smokescreen that hides our need to develop the perfect within ourselves. And if there is a perfect person out there—which there isn't—would they date *you*? When we give up the childish obsession with scanning the planet for Mr. or Ms. Right, we can begin to develop the skills of compassionate relationship. We stop judging people and start relating to them instead. We recognize, first and foremost, that we're not in a relationship to focus on how well the other person is learning their lessons, but rather to focus on learning our own.

The ego defends against love, not fear. Pain in relationships can be a perversely comfortable pain, in that it is one we know. We're used to it. I once heard a tape by Ram Dass, an American spiritual teacher, in which he told of seeing a newspaper article about an abused baby being taken away from his mother. As a police matron tried to take the baby, he kept struggling to remain in his mother's arms. Although his mother was the one who beat him, she was the one he knew. He was used to her. He wanted to remain in familiar territory.

This story illustrates our relationship to our own egos. The ego is our pain, but it is what we know, and we resist moving out of it. The effort it takes to grow out of painful patterns often feels more uncomfortable than remaining within them. Personal growth can be painful, because it can make us feel ashamed and humiliated to face our own darkness. But the goal of personal growth is the journey out of dark emotional patterns that cause us pain, to those that create peace. *Psychotherapy: Purpose, Process and Practice* says that at their peak, religion and psychotherapy become one. They both represent the relationship between thought and experience, and are used by the Holy Spirit to celebrate one of the most glorious human potentials: our capacity to change.

There is a tendency these days to analyze our neuroses ad infinitum, yet use the analysis itself to justify rather than heal the wound. After a certain point, having seen why a pattern developed ("My father was emotionally unavailable," or "My mother abused me") and the effect it has had on our personalities ("I don't know how to let a man get close to me," or "I now have a hard time trusting any authority figure"), actual change occurs because of a decision on our part: the decision to heal, the decision to change. It ultimately doesn't matter so much why I become angry or defensive. What matters is that I decide I want to be healed, and I ask God to help me.

Like an actor reading lines from a script, I can choose a new response to life, a new reading. Some people at this point would yell, "Denial!" But what we are denying is the impostor within us. Just because we have an honest feeling, that doesn't mean it's who we honestly are. My angry self is *not* the real me. Does it have to be acknowledged? Yes, but only in order to go beyond it. Once I've seen my anger, I'm ready, as they say in AA, to "act as if" I can do it differently. Because I can. Our ego has made up a fictional character that we now think of as our personality. But we are constantly creating that personality, and if we choose, we are constantly recreating it.

I was once talking to a friend and he made some comment about how he was afraid that, if we got closely involved, one of us might get hurt. "Which one of us are you concerned for?" I asked. He answered, "You."

I felt an anticipatory rejection. I was angry and I told him so.

"That's what I mean," he said. "You obviously take things so personally that I don't think I could stand it for long."

I knew that this was a moment I had repeated in various ways with various people, and I had asked for healing many times. I was open. I asked him, "Tell me honestly: How could I have done it differently? What else could I have said?"

"You could have just smiled and said, 'Don't flatter yourself.'"

I was so excited. I was like an eager actress working with a great director. "Oh that's so great," I said. "Let's go back and do that scene one more time. Say what you said again."

"You know, Marianne, I just have this awful feeling that if we really got together, one of us would get hurt."

"Which one of us are you afraid for?" I asked.

"You."

I looked at him and smiled. "Don't flatter yourself."

He laughed and I howled with excitement. This had been no small awakening. It was a genuine empowerment, a reprogramming of my emotional computer in an area where I had unconsciously gone for an unworkable response pattern every time. I now established a new groove, a new set of possibilities. Initially I had chosen the way of anger. Now I chose the way of love. I did not have to be the wounded animal. I could choose to identify with my own strength, which was in fact the more natural role for me to play. I could choose to see others through a generous, trusting nature. My brother was not here to attack me. He was here to love me. It was completely up to me whether to trust that, and love him back.

In accepting the Atonement, the correction of our perceptions, we are returned to who we really are. Our true, purely loving self can never be uncreated. All illusions will be undone. Although experiences such as childhood trauma can lead us to deviate from our true nature, the truth itself is held in trust for us by the Holy Spirit until we choose to return.

14.   PRACTICING FORGIVENESS

"Forgiveness is the only sane response."

To the ego, love is a crime. It seeks to convince us that forgiveness is a dangerous position that entails an unfair sacrifice on our part. The ego claims that forgiveness can lead us into situations where we become someone's doormat. 'To the ego, love is weakness. To the Holy Spirit, love is strength.'

I was dating someone several years ago when the

Olympic games were playing in Los Angeles. The opening ceremonies were a marvelous theatrical presentation and it was very difficult to get tickets. Because he was involved in the media, Mike was given, at the last minute, one pass that would enable him to go.

I was very excited for him. Everyone in town knew it was going to be a wonderful event. We decided that I would watch the ceremonies on T.V. and we would meet afterwards. At the conclusion of the broadcast, I started getting dressed and figured that it might be an hour or so before I heard from him, since the traffic around the stadium was bound to be horrendous.

An hour passed and then another. Well, he's in T.V., I thought, so maybe something came up. Another hour and then another. Midnight came and went. I took off my clothes and make-up. It was 2 A.M., then 3. At times I fell asleep, at times I lay in the dark and stared at the ceiling, at times I was livid, and at other times I was scared he was lying in a ditch somewhere. I started calling his house. No answer. I'd call again. No answer. Finally, hardly having slept at all, I called at around 6 A.M. and he answered the phone.

"Hello," he said.

"Mike?" I said. "This is Marianne."

"Oh, hi."

"Are you all right?"

"Yeah, why?"

"We had a date yesterday. Did you forget?"

"Oh, right," he said. "I had a kind of late night."

I don't know what I said to get off the phone, but I know how I felt and it wasn't wonderful. I had been stood up and I felt the kind of blow to my self-esteem that starts in your gut and shoots emotional black ink through all your veins. Dazed, I somehow fell asleep. When I woke up, I had a whole new take on the situation. I just knew that he was going to wake up feeling sorry for how he had acted. He was going to show up at my door any minute, carrying a dozen roses and saying, "Hi, babe, can I take you to brunch?" The scenario in my head called for my being oh-so- gracious: "Of course you can, darling" would come out of my mouth in a girlish melody. The problem is, he never came. Not only did he not come. He never called.

I was in a dark zone. Now what would *A Course in Miracles* say about that? I knew I needed a miracle. But all I could come up with were two choices for ways to deal with this, both of which I had tried before in similar situations, and neither one felt good or got me what I wanted.

My first choice was to get very angry and let him know it. "Who do you think you are to treat me like that, you son-of-a-bitch?" The problem with that choice was that it would completely invalidate my position. "Marianne's a nice girl, but her temper just doesn't cut it. She's hysterical when she doesn't get her way."

The only other choice I could imagine was to forgive him and let it go. But that didn't feel good either.

"It's okay you stood me up, Mike. I don't care. It doesn't matter." Unconditional love I could understand, but not unconditional dating. I didn't know what to do. I asked for a miracle. I considered the possibility of another possibility. I gave the situation to God and remembered that I need do nothing.

From a Course perspective, the first thing I had to deal with was my own judgment. As long as I was not at peace, my behavior would carry the energy of my conflict. Conflicted behavior cannot bring peace. It can only produce more conflict. First I had to deal with my own perceptions. The rest would follow.

So I came up with an exercise; I would repeat constantly, out loud when I could and silently when other people were present: "I forgive you Mike, and I release you to the Holy Spirit. I forgive you Mike, and I release you to the Holy Spirit. I forgive you Mike, and I release you to the Holy Spirit."

Since Mike didn't call the day after our early morning phone call or the day after, or the day after that, I had a lot of negative feelings to try to dissipate. My forgiveness chant—a kind of mantra, or repeated affirmation of spiritual wisdom—worked like a healing balm on my emotional turmoil. It deterred my temptation to focus on Mike's behavior, and kept me focused on my own feelings instead. My goal was inner peace, and I knew I couldn't have that as long as I perceived him as guilty.

In case you're wondering, it took him two weeks to call. The constant repetition of "I forgive you Mike, and I release you to the Holy Spirit," this willingness to forgive someone, had worked on my brain like a pleasurable drug. I didn't care whether I heard from him again or not.

So one day I'm in my house, the phone rings, and I hear Mike's familiar voice. "Marianne?"

Before I could even think about it consciously, a real warmth and love filled up my chest. "Mike? Hi! It's so good to hear from you!" And it was. It felt wonderful to hear his voice.

"How are you doing? I've missed you." (Can you *believe* he said that?!?)

I don't know if I said I'd missed him, too. His line was so ridiculous, I probably didn't say anything. But I do remember this: He said, "Well, when can I see you?"

I said, "When would you like to?"

"How about tonight?"

At that moment, words came out of my mouth that startled me as much as they must have startled him. I said with a lot of love and kindness, "Mike, I really care for you and that's not going to change. I'm still your friend no matter what. But when it comes to dating, we don't seem to do the same dance. So if you want to have lunch sometime, please call. But as far as a date is concerned, I need to pass."

We both mumbled a few more pleasantries and then got off the phone. I was worried that I had rejected a brother, but just as that worry came into my mind, I saw an internal image of lots of champagne bottles with their corks popping off in the middle of Heaven. I hadn't rejected a brother. I had simply accepted myself in a whole new way. He had a win—a lesson learned and a friendship if he wanted it—and I had a win. Forgiveness hadn't turned me into a doormat. It had taught me how to own my yes and own my no, without anger, with dignity and with love.

15.   COMMUNICATING LOVE

"To communicate is to join and to attack is to separate."

The Holy Spirit accepts people unconditionally. To the ego, this is an outrageous thought, because unconditional love is the death of the ego. How will people grow if we all go around just accepting each other as we are all the time? Accepting people as they are has the miraculous effect of helping them improve. Acceptance doesn't prohibit growth; rather, it fosters it.

People who are always telling us what's wrong with us don't help us so much as they paralyze us with shame and guilt. People who accept us help us to feel good about ourselves, to relax, to find our way. Accepting another person doesn't mean we never share constructive suggestions. But like everything else, our behavior is not so much the issue as the energy that it carries. If I'm criticizing someone in order to change them, that's my ego talking. If I've prayed and asked

God to heal me of my judgment, however, and then I'm still led to communicate something, the style of my sharing will be one of love instead of fear. It won't carry the energy of attack, but rather of support. Behavioral change is not enough. Covering an attack with sugary icing, with a sweet tone of voice or therapeutic jargon, is not a miracle. A miracle is an authentic switch from fear to love. When we speak from the ego, we will call up the ego in others. When we speak from the Holy Spirit, we will call up their love. A brother who is in error, says the Course, calls for teaching, not attack.

The following section in the Course is a powerful guide to right-minded communication in relationships.

> *"Errors are of the ego, and correction of errors lies in the relinquishment of the ego. When you correct a brother, you are telling him that he is wrong. He may be making no sense at the time, and it is certain that, if he is speaking from the ego, he will not be making sense. But your task is still to tell him he is right. You do not tell him this verbally, if he is speaking foolishly. He needs correction at another level, because his error is at another level. He is still right, because he is a Son of God."*

Miracles are created in an invisible realm. The Holy Spirit improves our style. He teaches us how to communicate from love instead of attack. Often people will say, "Well, I told *them*. I really communicated!" But communication is a two-way street. It only occurs if one person speaks, and the other one can hear them. We've all been in conversations where two people spoke and no one heard a thing. We've also had conversations where no one said anything and both people understood everything perfectly. In order to truly communicate, we must take responsibility for the heart space that exists between us and another. It is that heart space, or the absence of it, which will determine whether communication is miraculous or fearful. Sometimes, of course, that means keeping our mouths shut. Silence can be a powerfully loving communication. There have been times when I was wrong, and I knew I was wrong, and I knew they knew I was wrong, and I loved them for having the graciousness not to say anything. It gave me a chance to recoup with dignity.

When we do speak, the key to communication is not what we say, but rather the attitude that lies behind what we say. Since there is only one mind, all of us are telepathically communicating all the time. Every moment, we are choosing to join or to separate, and the person to whom we're speaking feels what we have chosen regardless of our words. The choice to join is the key to communication because it is the key to communion. The point is not to seek our goal in a communication, but to find a pure ground of being from which to mount our message. We don't seek joining through our words; we accept the thought that we are joined with the other person before we speak. That acceptance is itself a miracle.

The teacher of God is a finely-tuned intuitional instrument. *A Course in Miracles* says we're to listen to our brother, first and foremost. If we're supposed to speak, He'll let us know. Jesus once sent His disciples out into the countryside and told them to teach the gospel. "What shall we say?" they asked Him. His answer was, "I'll tell you when you get there." We're not to try to figure out what to say to a brother. It is merely our job to ask the Holy Spirit to purify our perceptions of the other person. From that place within, and only from that place, will we find the power of words and the power of silence, which bring the peace of God.

16.   COMMITMENT

"Whom God hath brought together, the ego cannot put asunder."

A Course in Miracles says we are to have total commitment in all of our relationships, and they will never compete with one another. Commitment in a relationship means commitment to the process of mutual understanding and forgiveness—no matter how many conversations it takes, nor how uncomfortable those conversations might sometimes be.

When we physically separate from someone we've been involved with, that doesn't mean the relationship is over. Relationships are eternal. The "separation" is another chapter in the relationship. Often, letting go of the old form of the relationship becomes a lesson in pure love much deeper than any that would have been learned had the couple stayed together. At the so-called end of relationships, I have sometimes felt like I was falling in love with the person more deeply than I had been before. What I've discovered for myself is that the Holy Spirit sometimes pulls out all the stops at that moment, simply because it takes all the love we're capable of to let a person go. "I love you so much that I can release you to be where you need to be, to go where you need to go." This moment in a relationship is not about an ending. It's about the ultimate fulfillment of the purpose in any relationship: that we find the meaning of pure love.

Sometimes the lesson to be learned in a relationship is how to hang in there and try to work things out. Other times, the lesson to be learned is how to exit a situation that doesn't serve. No one can determine for another person what principle applies in what circumstance. It is ultimately our connection to the Holy Spirit, our own intuitional guidance, that alone can lead us to the higher unfoldment of events through the deepest understanding.

I have said in many lectures, "Never abandon a person when you're leaving." What does that mean? It means that it's important for us to honor the eternal nature of relationships. When relationships change form, their content need not be diminished. The ego says, "Look, it's over with them. It didn't work out.

We're no longer together. What was, was. I'm with someone new now." The "ex" becomes a second-rate citizen. Often the new mate feels justified in saying, "Why are you talking to *them*? *We're* together now." Woe to the person who doesn't support the healing between a man or woman and their ex. Ultimately you discover that how the person treated the last one is exactly how they'll treat you. We feel jealousy, the need to hold on to what we've got, because in this area, as in every other, the ego says that there's only so much love to go around, that another person's good takes away from our own. The ego is a belief in finite resources, but love is infinite. Whenever love is added to any part of the system, there is an increase to every part. Love only gives rise to more love. If my husband or boyfriend heals with his past relationships, it only increases his capacity to love me from a healed and whole place. The last woman in his life is not my competition. She is my sister.

A man I once knew came over to my house for dinner. We had been dating a short time, and I asked him what he had been doing all day. He told me he had been working on a script with his last girlfriend, who was still his writing partner. He told me that they had gotten into a pretty sticky conversation about their relationship. She was still hurt, having a hard time letting go, the same stuff we all know. I asked him how they had left it. He said she was pretty upset. I put down the food I was preparing, looked him in the eye and said,

"Go call her." The thought of that woman being on the other side of town somewhere, enduring that horrible anxiety while we sat down to a romantic dinner, was hard for me to bear. I had been in her place. How totally unethical it would have been for me not to support that woman in her feelings.

"You don't mind?" he said.

"Not at all," I told him. "Dinner can wait."

Our needs are not separate. If we contribute to another person's pain, it will always come back to haunt us. If we do what we can to help them, someone will always come around to do the same for us. It's not enough to sit idly by while others hurt, using the catch-all phrase "It's not my responsibility" or "It would be codependent of me to get involved" as an excuse for a selfish stance. A woman once said to me after a situation in which I felt betrayed, "I never intended to hurt you." I said, "But you never intended to love me, either." Love is not neutral. It takes a stand. It is a commitment to the attainment of the conditions of peace for everyone involved in a situation.

17. *FAITH IN RELATIONSHIPS*

"Faith is the acknowledgement of union."

Often we long for another person because, in an invisible, intangible realm, we're still communicating, still connecting, still seeking resolution. People will say,

"You're being neurotic. It's time to let go." But there was a time when widows wore weeds for a year; grief was understood, acknowledged, validated. It's not neurotic to grieve a relationship; what's neurotic is when we don't. On some level, no matter how disassociated from our feelings we might be, every relationship brings hope—hope that this might be a safe place, a haven, a rest after all our battles.

When a relationship doesn't work out, for whatever reason, our disappointment is natural. Every intense encounter represents a deep and complicated karmic connection. An ending relationship is much like a death, and in many cases the sadness is even greater. When someone has died, there has often been completion and understanding that doesn't occur when both people are alive but have separated without higher awareness. Perhaps the one we love is simply on the other side of town now, sleeping with someone else, yet they are really universes away since the resolution we so crave has not occurred. There's no need to pretend this isn't a knife to the heart. It is, and there's nothing to do but cry the tears that gush forth like blood from a wound.

'Now is the time for faith.' Let us be softened by our tears. When emotional knives hit the heart, walls crumble that didn't belong there to begin with. We can learn then. We can learn what is illusion and what is real. We can learn that idols can never ever be trusted, and we can learn about a love that never, ever leaves.

There are many conflicts in relationships that try

our faith. One of them is betrayal. Betrayal is a word that we don't really understand until it's happened to us. There's an unparalleled pain when a friend is the one who's holding the knife.

In the Course, Jesus says that although, according to the thinking of the world, he was betrayed, he didn't choose that perception for himself. In other words, he knew that he couldn't really be betrayed, because what isn't love isn't real. So when we are attacked, when the medicine is so bitter that it takes all our power not to crumble as we take it, what do we do then? Where is our solace?

Someone once told me that the way peacock feathers are made is from peacocks eating thorns. What a beautiful image, that the harsh things we have to digest can contribute to our beauty. But not always. Only when we open up enough to really take in the horror, oddly enough. Resistance and defense only make the error more real, and increase our pain.

If Jesus had yelled from the cross, "I hate all you guys," it would have been a completely different story. There would have been no resurrection. What created the space for his triumph was his defenselessness, his holding to love despite what others were doing to him. The body can be destroyed, but truth cannot be. Truth will always reassert itself, given a symbolic three days. Three days represents the time it takes between the crucifixion and the resurrection, between an open-hearted response to hurt and the experience of rebirth that will always follow.

How often I've said to myself and others, "This is just the three days. Hold on. Hold on." When our friends have turned against us, or we have been cheated or lied about, the temptation is so strong to defend, attack back. But the Course says that "in our defenselessness, our safety lies." It is one more place where our power comes from saying, "I will step back and let Him lead the way." The Christ within us can handle any assault because it is not affected by lovelessness. Only our belief that we are affected by fear can make it affect us. Defense is a way of agreeing with the attacker in the power of his attack, and so making it real in our experience.

It takes great courage and personal strength to hold on to our center during times of great hurt. It takes wisdom to understand that our reactiveness only fans the flames of false drama. Love creates a mystical shield around us, protecting us from chaos. When we are in the midst of loss, or betrayal, or crisis of any kind, there is power in the words, "Be still and know I am." Truth can never be destroyed. There is no loss except in time, says the Course, and time does not exist.

18.   MARRIAGE

"You undertook, together, to invite the Holy Spirit into your relationship."

Marriage, like everything else, can be used by either the ego or the Holy Spirit. Its content is never predetermined. It is a living organism that reflects the continuous choices of the individuals involved.

Very little is sacred anymore in this world, but one thing must be treated with reverence or else the moral fabric of the world disintegrates: an agreement between two people. An enlightened marriage is a commitment to participate in the process of mutual growth and forgiveness, sharing a common goal of service to God.

A man once told me that his relationship with his ex-wife worked beautifully for the first year they were together. At that time they were both actively involved in an organization dedicated to personal growth. Once they left the organization, however, the marriage fell apart. This doesn't indicate that the marriage had nothing going for it anyway. Rather, it reveals the importance of a context bigger than the personal concerns of one or even both parties.

Why is marriage a more profound commitment than other forms of relationship, such as a couple who are living together? Because it is an agreement that, while a whole lot of shaking and screaming might go on, no one's going to leave the room. We are both safe to go through whatever emotion is called forth from deep within us—and whenever we are truthful, there are times when we are upset—but it is safe to do that here. No one is leaving.

The commitment of marriage is publicly declared. When guests are present at a wedding and the ceremony is a religious one, a ritual is performed in which collective prayers form a circle of light and protection around the relationship.

A marriage is God's gift to a man and woman. It is a gift that should then be given back to Him. A man's wife is literally God's gift to Him. A woman's husband is God's gift to her. But God only gives gifts that are meant for everyone. So it is that a marriage is meant to be a blessing on the world, because it is a context in which two people might become more than they would have been alone. The entire world is blessed by the presence of healed people. One of the Course's Workbook exercises reads, "When I am healed, I am not healed alone."

A partner's support and forgiveness enable us to stand forth more magnificently in the world. *A Course in Miracles* tells us that love is not meant to be exclusive, but inclusive. Several years ago there was a popular song that included the refrain, "You and me against the world." If any man every said that to me, I'd tell him I was switching sides. We don't get married to escape the world; we get married to heal it together.

Under the Holy Spirit's guidance, a married couple commit to the creation of a context in which their individual resources—material, emotional and spiritual—are placed in each other's service. As we give, so shall we receive. Service does not mean self-sacrifice. It means giving the needs of another person the same priority as our own. The ego claims that one person wins at the expense of another. The Holy Spirit enters into any situation bringing a win for everyone involved. In marriage we have a wonderful opportunity to see through the illusion of separate needs. The married couple is not to think only in terms of what's good for him or her, but rather what is good for them. This is one of the many ways in which marriage can be part of the healing of the Son of God.

As with anything else, the key to a successful marriage is the conscious awareness of God. The marriage is surrendered to Him to be used for His purposes. The saying that the family that prays together stays together, is true. The enlightened marriage includes the presence of a mystical third. The Holy Spirit is asked to guide perceptions, thoughts, feelings and actions in order that in this, as in all things, God's will might be done on earth as it is in Heaven.

19.   FORGIVING OUR PARENTS, OUR FRIENDS, OURSELVES

"The holiest of all spots on earth is where an ancient hatred has become a present love."

There is no coming to consciousness without forgiving our parents. Whether we like it or not, our mother is our primary image of an adult woman, and our father is our primary image of an adult man. If we hold grievances against our mother, then if we are a man, we will not be able to escape the projection of guilt onto other adult women who come into our lives; and if we are a woman, we will not be able to escape self-condemnation as we grow into our womanhood. If we hold grievances against our father, then if we are a woman, we will not be able to escape projection of guilt onto other adult men who come into our lives; and if we are a man, we will not be able to escape self-condemnation as we grow into our manhood.

That's it. At a certain point, we forgive because we *decide* to forgive. Healing occurs in the present, not the past. We are not held back by the love we didn't receive in the past, but by the love we're not extending in the present. Either God has the power to renew our lives, or He doesn't. Could God be looking at any of us and saying, "I'd love to give you a joyful life, but your mother was so terrible, my hands are tied"?

There is a lot of talk today about people growing up in dysfunctional homes. Who *didn't* grow up in a dysfunctional home! This world is dysfunctional! But there is nothing we have been through, or seen, or done, that cannot be used to make our lives more valuable now. We can grow from any experience, and we can transcend any experience. This kind of talk is blasphemy to the ego, which respects pain, glorifies pain, worships pain, and creates pain. Pain is its centerpiece. It sees forgiveness as its enemy.

Forgiveness remains the only path that leads out of hell. Whether we're forgiving our parents, someone else, or ourselves, the laws of mind remain the same: As we love, we shall be released from pain, and as we deny love, we shall remain in pain. Every moment, we're either extending love or projecting fear, and every thought takes us nearer to Heaven or hell. What will it take to make us remember that 'the ark is entered two by two,' that there is no getting into Heaven without taking someone with you?

Practice and commitment are the keys to love. What I've seen for myself, and witnessed others grapple with also, is not an argument with the power of love. I can see the truth of all these principles. But I have also seen how often I would resist the experience of love, when holding on to a grievance seems more important than letting it go. An entire world has been built on fear. Fear's system will not be dismantled in a moment. We can work on ourselves every moment that we live. The world is healed one loving thought at a time. Mother Theresa said that there are no great deeds—just small deeds done with great love.

Each of us have different fears, and different manifestations of fear, but all of us are saved by the same technique: the call to God to save our lives by salvaging our minds. "Lead us not into temptation, but deliver us from evil, for Love is the Kingdom, and Love is the glory, and Love is the power, forever and ever."

CHAPTER 7

Work

"I am only here to be truly helpful.
I am here to represent Him who sent me.
I do not have to worry about what to say or what
to do, because He Who sent me will direct me.
I am content to be wherever He wishes, knowing
He goes there with me.
I will be healed as I let Him teach me to heal."

1. SURRENDERING OUR CAREERS

"Seeing your strengths exactly as they are, and equally aware of where they can be best applied, for what, to whom and when, He chooses and accepts your part for you."

Success means we go to sleep at night knowing that our talents and abilities were used in a way that served others. We're compensated by grateful looks in people's eyes, whatever material abundance supports us in performing joyfully and at high energy, and the magnificent feeling that we did our bit today to save the world.

The Atonement means putting love first. In everything. In business as well as everything else. You're in business to spread love. Your screenplay should spread love. Your hair salon should spread love. Your agency should spread love. Your life should spread love. The key to a successful career is realizing that it's not separate from the rest of your life, but is rather an extension of your most basic self. And your most basic self is love.

Knowing who you are and why you came here—that you are a child of God and that you came here to heal and be healed—is more important than knowing what you want to do. What you want to do is not the important question. The question to ask is, "When I do *anything*, how should I do it?" And the answer is, "Kindly." People don't normally associate business with kindness, because business has come to be regarded as simply a tool for making money. Miracle-workers are not in business only to make money; they're in business to inject love into the world.

Each of us has a particular part to play in "God's plan for salvation." The Holy Spirit's job is to reveal to us our function and to help us perform it. 'The Holy Spirit asks us if it's reasonable to assume that He would assign us a task, and then not provide us with the means of its accomplishment.'

Once again, we're not deciding for ourselves what part to play in life, but rather asking that it be revealed to us where He would have us go and what He would have us do. We surrender our careers to Him. During World War II, the Allied generals oversaw all troop activity from a central headquarters, from which they issued orders. The commanders on various fronts didn't necessarily know how their movements fit into an over-all military scheme: they just knew they did, because they knew there was a general intelligence behind the issuing of their orders. So it is with us. We might not know how or where our talents would best be put to use, but the Holy Spirit does. *A Course in Miracles* teaches us to 'avoid self-initiated plans, and to instead surrender our plans to God.'

Some people have said, "But I'm afraid to surrender my career to God. I'm a musician—what if He wants me to be an accountant?" My answer to that is, why would He? Wouldn't He rather have someone who understands numbers do that job?

If you're talented at music, that talent is of God. If something makes your heart sing, that's God's way of telling you it's a contribution He wants you to make. Sharing our gifts is what makes us happy. We're most powerful, and God's power is most apparent on the earth when we're happy.

A Course in Miracles says that the 'only real pleasure comes from doing God's will.' The crux of salvation in any area is a shift in our sense of purpose. Relationships, careers, bodies—all these areas of our lives are reborn in spirit when we dedicate them to God's purposes, asking that they be used as instruments through which the world is healed.

That shift is a miracle. As always, we consciously ask for it. "Dear God, please give my life some sense of purpose. Use me as an instrument of your peace. Use my talents and abilities to spread love. I surrender my job to you. Help me to remember that my real job is to love the world back to health. Thank you very much. Amen."

2.   *GOD'S WILL*

> *"Where would you have me go?*
> *What would you have me do?*
> *What would you have me say, and to whom?"*

People ask themselves, "Do I want to serve God, or do I want to be happy?" Since certain organized religions have represented the spiritual life as a life of sacrifice and austerity, it can be hard for some people to imagine that a life lived close to God is a life full of joy. *A Course in Miracles* says the 'only real pleasure comes from doing God's will.'

God does not demand sacrifice. The life of sacrifice is the life we live *before* we find a higher sense of identity and purpose: the sacrifice of the memory of how magnificent we really are, and what an important job we came here to do. And that's a lot to sacrifice, because when we can't remember why we're going somewhere, we have a hard time acting on full throttle once we get there. Love gives energy and direction. It's spiritual fuel.

Any career, when given to the Holy Spirit, can be used as part of the plan of the restoration of the world. No job is too big or too small for God to use. You have the unlimited power of the universe within you and so does everyone else. It's nothing to take personal credit for, nor anything to feel guilty about. Our real power emanates from a force that's in us but not of us. 'Be humble before God,' says the Course, 'yet great in him.' Remembering this keeps us connected to our innocence, and as long as we have that, the power will keep pouring through us. Forget it, and the faucet could be turned off at any moment. Stop blessing the universe, and the universe will seem to stop blessing you. Whatever your activity, just ask that it be used to bless the world.

I remember one day complaining to my girlfriend June how unhappy I was, and she said, "Marianne, I don't mean to be hard on you, but do you ever do anything for anyone else?" That comment felt like a brick to my forehead, although I did very little about it at the time. After I went through my period of very deep depression several years later, however, human suffering became a much more personally significant subject. I thought that if other people suffered a fraction as much as I had, then my heart burst for them and I wanted to be of help. God seemed to say to me then, "People suffer deeply, and there have been people suffering around you all your life. You just didn't notice. You were shopping."

I used to worry, as do many people, about what I was supposed to do with my life. I never seemed to be able to stick with any one thing very long or make money or find any real satisfaction in my work. I felt paralyzed. I remember once asking God to reveal to me what He wanted me to know in order that I might change. I got down on my knees and worked myself into a grandiose meditative state. I saw visual images of a glorious sky and a group of angels marching through the clouds to bring me His answer. A couple of cherubs held up a scroll that they then began to unfold. My heart started racing as I awaited God's message, which I was sure would be extremely important. Slowly the letters on the scroll began to form words: "Marianne, you're a spoiled brat."

The reason I was paralyzed was because I had lost touch with the sole memory of why I came to earth. Telling me I was a spoiled brat was the perfect information, the key to unlock my energies. The problem was my selfishness. Like actors who have spent so much time learning how to act that they didn't learn how to live, and so end up making lousy actors because they ultimately have nothing authentic to reveal about life, we sometimes lose our personal power by forgetting why we have it. We study up on how to run businesses, not stopping to think about *why* we're in business except to make money. This is not a spiritually powerful beam, and the universe will tolerate it less and less as the nineties unfold.

3.   *PERSONAL POWER*

   "All power is of God."

Don't ask God to send you a brilliant career, but rather ask Him to show you the brilliance within you. It is the recognition of our brilliance that releases it into expression. Stable, meaningful external effects don't occur until we've experienced an internal stirring. Once an internal stirring has occurred, external effects cannot fail to happen. We're all capable of an internal stirring, and are in fact coded for it. It is our potential for greatness. Achievement doesn't come from what we do, but from who we are. Our worldly power results from our personal power. Our career is an extension of our personality.

People who profoundly achieve aren't necessarily people who do so much; they're people around whom things get done. Mahatma Gandhi and President Kennedy were both examples of this. Their greatest achievements lay in all the energy they stirred in other people, the invisible forces thay unleashed around them. By touching their own depths, they touched the depths within others.

That kind of charisma, the power to effect what happens on the earth from an invisible realm within, is the natural right and function of the Son of God. The word "charisma" was originally a religious term. It means "of the spirit." The new frontiers are internal ones. The real stretch is always within us. Instead of expanding our ability or willingness to go out and get anything, we expand our ability to receive what is already here for us.

Personal power emanates from someone who takes life seriously. The universe takes us a seriously as we take it. There is no greater seriousness than the full appreciation of the power and importance of love. Miracles flow from the recognition that love is the purpose of our careers.

A Course in Miracles discusses a traditional Christian concept called "the gifts of the Holy Spirit." This idea is that, when our lives are given to the Holy Spirit to use for His purposes, new talents emerge within us. We don't get our lives together and then give them to God, but rather we give our lives to God and then things start coming together. As our hearts open, our talents and gifts begin to blossom. Many people have told me that once they're successful and have made a lot of money, they will use that success to help the world. But that's a delay technique by which the ego tries to keep us from showing up fully in our own lives. Even if we don't yet consider ourselves successful, we can devote our work now to being used in the service of the healing of the world. From that point of power our careers will take off.

No matter what we do, we can make it our ministry. No matter what form our job or activity takes, the content is the same as everyone else's: we are here to minister to human hearts. If we talk to anyone, or see anyone, or even think of anyone, then we have the opportunity to bring more love into the universe. From a waitress to the head of a movie studio, from an elevator operator to the president of a nation, there is no one whose job is unimportant to God.

When you know this, when you fully live up to the

opportunity to heal, you achieve an energy that pushes you forward in worldly endeavors. Love makes you more attractive. That means you attract, like a magnet. You don't just attract people; you attract various circumstances that reflect back to you the power of your devotion. Your personal power is not something that is going to reveal itself at some later date. Your power is a result of your decision to reveal it. You are powerful in whatever moment you choose to be. The choice to be used as an instrument of love, right here, right now, is a choice for personal empowerment.

A Course in Miracles tells us that all of the children of God have power—yet no one has "special" power. 'All of us are special,' and yet none of us are special. No one has any more potential than anyone else for spreading the love and light of God. Many of our traditional notions of success rely on our talking ourselves into the belief that we're special and we have something special to offer. The truth is, none of us are special because special people would be different and separate from others. The oneness of Christ makes this impossible. The belief in specialness, therefore, is delusional and thus breeds fear.

What a Beethoven, Shakespeare or Picasso has done is not *create* something, so much as they have accessed that place within themselves from which they could *express* that which has been created by God. Their genius then, is actually expression and not creation. That's why great art strikes us with the shock of recognition, the wish that *we* had said that. The soul thrills at the reminder of what we all already know.

The Course says that 'one day, all the gifts of God will be shared equally by everyone.' We all have the potential for greatness, but it gets plowed out of us early. Fear entered when someone told us there's a first prize, second prize and third prize, that some efforts deserve an A, and some get a C. After a while, part of us becomes afraid to even try. The only thing we have to give to the world is our own grasp on it. The ego argues that this is not enough. It leads us to cover up our simple truth, to try to invent a better one. But the ego isn't protecting us here, although, as always, it pretends to. It isn't guarding against our making fools of ourselves; it is guarding against our experience of who we really are, the brilliance of expressing it, and the joy that the expression brings to ourselves and others.

I love the story of the little girl who showed her teacher a picture she painted of a tree. The tree was purple. The teacher said, "Sweetheart, I've never seen a purple tree, now have I?"

"Oh?" said the little girl. "That's too bad."

We can't fake authenticity. We think we need to create ourselves, always doing a paste-up job on our personalities. That is because we're trying to be special rather than real. We're pathetically trying to conform with all the other people trying to do the same.

A tulip doesn't strive to impress anyone. It doesn't struggle to be different than a rose. It doesn't have to.

It *is* different. And there's room in the garden for every flower. You didn't have to struggle to make your face different than anyone else's on earth. It just is. You *are* unique because you were created that way. Look at little children in kindergarten. They're all different without trying to be. As long as they're unselfconsciously being themselves, they can't help but shine. It's only later, when children are taught to compete, to strive to be better than others, that their natural light becomes distorted.

The natural light of God within us all is what the Course refers to as our grandeur. The ego's efforts to embellish our natural state is what the Course refers to as grandiosity. "It is easy to distinguish gandeur from grandiosity," says the Course, "because love is returned and pride is not." The ego interferes with the clear expression of our power by trying to get us to add something to it. This is actually a ploy by which it thwarts our capacity to express who we really are, and accept full recognition from others in return.

Once again, separation is the ego's goal. I used to always be on an emotional roller-coaster ride, feeling I was better than other people, and then feeling I was worse. "I'm better, no I'm not as good, I'm better, no I'm not as good." They're the same mistake. The truth is, we're just like everybody else. Knowing this—that we're no better or worse than anyone else because we're all essentially the same—is a thought lacking in luster only until we fully appreciate what kind of club we belong to. Humanity is a group of infinitely powerful creatures. 'Our power, however, is in us but not of us.' It is God's spirit inside of us that enlightens and enlivens our lives. Of ourselves we're really no big deal.

This thought has helped me in my career. I walk onto a stage and sometimes speak to more than a thousand people at a time. I can't imagine dealing with the pressure of having to convince myself that I have something special to offer. I don't try to. I don't have to impress anyone, and if I'm not thinking that I have to, there's nothing to do but relax. I walk out on stage without feeling the need to make people think I'm special, because I know I'm not. I just talk to friends, casually and with enthusiasm. That's it. There isn't anything else. Everything else is just an illusion. The Son of God doesn't have to embellish who he is.

We're tempted to think that we're more impressive when we put on airs. We're not, of course; we're rather pathetic when we do that. The Course states, "Grandiosity is always a cover for despair." The light of Christ shines most brightly within us when we relax and let it be, allowing it to shine away our grandiose delusions. But we're afraid to let down our masks. What is really happening here, unconsciously, is not that we are defending against our smallness. The ego is actually, in those moments, defending against God.

As I interpret the Course, 'our deepest fear is not that we are inadequate. Our deepest fear is that we are powerful beyond measure. It is our light, not our darkness, that most frightens us.' We ask ourselves, Who am I to be brilliant, gorgeous, talented, fabulous? Actually, who are you *not* to be? You are a child of God. Your playing small doesn't serve the world. There's nothing enlightened about shrinking so that other people won't feel insecure around you. We are all meant to shine, as children do. We were born to make manifest the glory of God that is within us. It's not just in some of us; it's in everyone. And as we let our own light shine, we unconsciously give other people permission to do the same. As we're liberated from our own fear, our presence automatically liberates others.

A miracle worker is an artist of the soul. There's no higher art than living a good life. An artist informs the world of what's available behind the masks we all wear. That's what we're all here to do. The reason so many of us are obsessed with becoming stars is because we're not yet starring in our own lives. The cosmic spotlight isn't pointed *at* you; it radiates from *within* you. I used to feel like I was waiting for someone to discover me, to "produce" me, like Lana Turner at the drugstore. Ultimately I realized that the person I was waiting for was myself. If we wait for the world's permission to shine, we will never receive it. The ego doesn't give that permission. Only God does, and He has already done so. He has sent you here as His personal representative and is asking you to channel His love into the world. Are you waiting for a more important job? There isn't one.

There is a plan for each of us, and each of us is precious. As we open our hearts more and more, we're moved in the directions in which we're supposed to go. Our gifts well up inside of us and extend of their own accord. We accomplish effortlessly.

How could Leonardo da Vinci not have painted? How could Shakespeare not have written? In *Letters to a Young Poet*, Rilke tells a young writer to write only if he *has* to. We are to do what there is a deep psychological and emotional imperative for us to do. That's our point of power, the source of our brilliance. Our power is not rationally or willfully called forth. It's a divine dispensation, an act of grace.

4.   MONEY

"Joy has no cost."

Do what you love. Do what makes your heart sing. And *never do it for the money*. Don't go to work to make money; go to work to spread joy. Seek ye first the kingdom of Heaven, and the Masaratti will get here when it's supposed to.

God doesn't have a poverty consciousness. He doesn't want you to have a boring life or a boring career. He doesn't have anything against the things of this world. 'Money isn't evil; it's just nothing.' Like anything else, it can be used for holy or unholy purposes.

I once had a small bookstore. A man came in one

day and told me that he was going to teach me how to make money. "Every person that walks in that door," he said, "is a potential sale. And that's what you should silently say to yourself whenever a customer walks into the store: Potential sale, potential sale."

His advice sounded exploitative to me. He was advising me to view other people as pawns in my own scheme. I prayed and received these words: "Your store is a church." Church, esoterically, means the gathering of souls. It's not an outer plane but rather an inner plane phenomenon. People don't come into your place of business so that you can *get* anything. They're sent so that you can give them love.

After I said the prayer and got the feeling that my store was a church, I understood that my only job was to love the people who came there. I actually did that: every time I saw a customer walk in, I would silently bless them in some way or another. Not everyone bought a book every time they came in, but people began to consider me their bookseller. Customers were attracted to a peaceful feeling in the air. People might not know where it comes from, but they can feel it when love is being sent in their direction.

I'm amazed when I walk into stores and the sales people are rude, as if they're doing you some kind of favor letting you be there. A rude attitude is destructive to the emotional fabric of the world. Where I grew up, we left a store with that kind of energy because it doesn't feel good to be there.

When our goal is making money, creativity becomes distorted. If I saw money as the ultimate goal of my teaching career, then I would have to think more about what people wanted to hear and less about what I feel it's important to say. My energy would become tainted with efforts to get people to come back, to sell them on my lectures, to get them to bring their friends. But if the purpose of my career is to channel God's love, then I'm only there to open my heart, open my brain and open my mouth.

When we're working solely for money, our motivation is getting rather than giving. The miraculous transformation here is a shift from a sales mentality to a service mentality. Until we make this switch, we're operating from ego and concentrating on the things of this world rather than on love. This idolatry casts us into alien emotional territory, where we are always afraid. We're afraid of either failure or success. If we're closer to success, we'll fear success. If we're closer to failure, we'll fear failure. The issue isn't success or failure. The issue is the presence of fear, and its inevitability wherever love is absent.

Like everything else, money is either holy or unholy, depending on the purposes ascribed to it by the mind. We tend to do with money what we do with sex: we desire it but we judge the desire. It is the judgment that then distorts the desire, turning it into an ugly expression. Because we are ashamed to admit that we want these things, we have insidious ways of pretending that we don't—such as condemning our desires even as we act them out. The loss of purity is in us, then—not in money or in sex. They are both just canvasses onto which we project our guilt.

Just as the fearful mind is the source of promiscuity and sex is merely the vehicle through which it is expressed, so money is not the source of greed. The mind is the source of greed, and money is one of the places where it expresses itself. Both money and sex can be used for holy as well as unholy purposes. Like nuclear energy, the problem isn't the energy, but how it is applied.

Our judgment of wealth is actually an ego ploy to make sure we never have any. I was once driving around a very wealthy neighborhood in Houston and I thought, "These people work for huge multi-national corporations that oppress people throughout the Third World." Then I stopped myself: How do *I* know what all those people do for a living, and how do I know what they do with their money? My judgmental attitude, masquerading as political consciousness, was actually my ego's way of trying to make sure that *I* would never have any money. What we mentally refuse to permit others, we refuse ourselves. What we bless in others, we draw to us.

When I was younger, I cherished the belief that, by being poor, I was somehow showing my camaraderie with the impoverished. Behind that thought, I see now, was my fear that I would fail if I tried to make money. I ultimately realized that poor people didn't need my sympathy so much as they needed cash. There's nothing pure or spiritual about poverty. We often see impoverished people who are very holy, but it isn't the poverty that creates the holiness. I've known some extremely spiritual wealthy people, and I've known some poor people who were anything but.

The Bible says it's harder for a rich man to get into Heaven than it is for a camel to walk through the eye of a needle. That's because the *attachment* to money is a huge temptation to deviate from love. But the moral imperative is not to block the reception of money into our lives. The challenge is to spiritualize our relationship to it, by seeing that its only purpose is to heal the world. In an enlightened society, rich people will not necessarily have less money. Poor people, however, will have much more. The problem, contrary to the ego's perception, is not just the distribution of wealth, but the consciousness around it. Money is not scarce. It is not a finite resource. We are not poor because the rich are rich. We are poor because we do not work with love.

It behooves us to remember that our money is God's money, and we want to have whatever He wants us to have in order to do with it whatever He wants us to do. God wants us to have whatever material support contributes to our greatest happiness. The ego tries to convince us that God demands sacrifice, and that the life of service would be a life of poverty. This is not the case. 'Our purpose on this earth is to be happy,' and it is the Holy Spirit's function to help us achieve that. He leads us to whatever material abundance supports us in standing forth joyously within the world, without binding us further to it.

There's much work to be done for the healing of the world, and some of it costs money. Often the Holy Spirit sends us money so that we can perform tasks He wants accomplished on His behalf. A responsible attitude towards money is one in which we're open to whatever comes, and trusting that it always will.

In asking for miracles, we ask the Holy Spirit to remove the obstacles to our reception of money. These obstacles take the form of thoughts, such as: money is impure, or having money means we're greedy; rich people are bad, or I shouldn't make more money than my parents did. Having money means that we have more money with which to employ other people and heal the world. There's nothing beautiful about what happens to a society when money stops circulating.

One of the principles to remember about money is how important it is to pay for services rendered. If we begrudge someone else the right to make a living, we are begrudging ourselves the same. What we give, we will receive, and what we withhold will be withheld from us. And the universe doesn't register the difference between stealing from a huge corporation, or stealing from a nice little old lady.

The universe will always support our integrity.

Sometimes our debts are so big or confusing, that even though we have the best of intentions, the burden and the guilt may be so overwhelming, that we just go on automatic, push the bills to the back of the drawer and try to forget them. Or change our phone number. The universe will not support that. A big person is not someone who never falls down. A big person is someone who, when they fall, does what it takes to get up again. As always, the issue is to ask for a miracle. There's no debtor's prison in this country. Once again, according to the Course, "Miracles are everyone's right but purification is necessary first." Purity of heart creates breakthroughs. If you owe back bills, no matter how much, write a letter to the company or individual, own the issue, apologize if appropriate, and let them know that you are setting up a payment plan, effective immediately. Send them something with the letter. Don't set yourself up for failure. If you can't afford to send fifteen dollars a month, that's okay. Send five dollars, if that's all you can. But make sure you send it and send it regularly and on time. It doesn't matter if the bill is fifty thousand dollars. The Course says "there is no order of difficulty in miracles." No matter what the shape of a problem, its form or its size, a miracle can handle it. Miracles mean that at any moment we can begin again. No matter what the problem, as long as we return our minds to a graceful position now, the universe will always help us clean up the mess and start over. To repent means to think again. In every area, the universe will support us to the extent that we support it.

Most of us have a lot "on" money—anything from an inappropriate need for it to an inappropriate judgment of it. Many of us received strong messages about money during our childhoods. We were taught, verbally or nonverbally, that it is overly important, or unspiritual, or hard to get, or the root of all evil. Many of us are afraid that people won't like us if we don't make money, or afraid that they won't like us if we do. Money is an area where we need, individually and collectively, a radical healing of our mental habits.

We pray. Dear God, "I surrender to you all my thoughts about money, I surrender to you my debts, I surrender to you my wealth. Open my mind to receive abundantly. Channel your abundance through me in a way that serves the world. Amen."

5.   *MINISTRY*

> *"And that one Voice appoints your function and relays it to you, giving you the strength to understand it, do what it entails, and to succeed in everything you do that is related to it."*

There's no more potent way to thank God for your gifts, or to increase them, than by sharing them. You will be given as much power in the world as you are willing to use on His behalf.

Think of your career as your ministry. Make your work an expression of love, in service to mankind. Within the worldly illusion, we all have different jobs. Some of us are artists, some of us are business people, some of us are scientists. But in the real world that lies beyond all this, we all have the same job: to minister to human hearts. All of us are here as ministers of God.

A few years ago I went back to Houston for a special reunion of my high school drama department. Our teacher was retiring, and ex- students of his from all over the country came to pay their respects. At the dinner, a lot of attention was given to the fact that many of Mr. Pickett's students had gone on to become successful actors. But many of his students had gone on to become successful people, period. By teaching us the truth about acting, he taught us the truth about life. Once you know; 1. Leave your personal problems at the stage door; 2. Treat the material with honesty, dignity and without embellishment; 3. Show up fully no matter how many people are in the audience, then you know everything you need to know in order to have a powerful professional career. To know the real truth about anything is to know the truth about everything. In learning the principles of ministry, we learn the principles of success, regardless of what form our ministry takes.

One of the things I've realized is that I've really only had one career. I've had many jobs, but they all had one basic element in common: me. The form of my work had mainly to do with where I was at that time in my life, and every form taught me something essential to my "career development.

As ministers of God, we let our careers be an expression of our own depth, of what really *matters* to us. Knowing that we are acting on behalf of a higher purpose than our own self-aggrandizement gives us the joy we're all seeking. Whatever we do, whatever our job, it can be a vessel through which we teach the message of salvation: that the Son of God is innocent, and we are all Sons of God. Kindness to Him transforms the world. We don't necessarily teach this verbally, but rather non-verbally. The problem most people have is that they're more concerned with the mode of their expression than with what they're seeking to express. That's because they don't *know* what they want to express. This generation, this culture, is full of people who want desperately to write a story, but for all the wrong reasons. I meet people who want to be in the spotlight, but have no idea what they would say if it was pointed at them. This is a fraudulent posture. It means we want the record contract more than the satisfaction of making music. The highest prize we can receive for creative work is the joy of being creative. Creative effort spent for any other reason than the joy of being in that light-filled place, love, God, whatever we want to call it, is lacking in integrity. It diminishes us. It reduces inspiration to mere sales.

A few years ago I visited Kauai. My friend and I

took a ride on a boat along the Napali coastline. The boat was one of a fleet owned by a man known as Captain Zodiac. Zodiac is the word for the incredible land formations that meet the sea there. This man loved the coastline so passionately that he took the word for his own name. One day someone said to him, "You know a lot about this coastline and its history. A lot of people would love to see what you see here, and know what you know. Why don't you take people out on your boat and give them a tour?"

Captain Zodiac's rides are a great service to tourists on Kauai. They spread joy. They lift the cultural vibration. And the boat rides became quite a business. Captain Zodiac now has lots of boats, and he's very successful. His business formed around his love.

The issue is whether we're working for money, or working for love. What we need to investigate is which one is the more abundant attitude. As with Captain Zodiac, and contrary to the ego's arguments, love is actually good business.

Any job can become a ministry, as long as it is dedicated to love. Your career can be an empty canvas for God to write on. Whatever your talents or abilities, He can use them. Our ministry becomes a joyous experience for ourselves and others as we let a mysterious force direct us. We simply follow instructions. We are allowing God's spirit to move through us, using our gifts and resources however He sees fit, to do His work in the world. This is the key to a successful career.

Success is not unnatural; it is the most natural thing in the world because it is the natural result of man's co-creation with God. In *A Movable Feast*, Hemingway writes about writing. He describes the difference between his writing a story, and a story writing itself. When he finds himself writing the story, he knows it's time to stop for the day. Our life is meant to be a story that mysteriously writes itself, and our work is the creative fruit of our lives.

"God, please use me" is the most powerful affirmation we can say for an abundant career. It is the miracle worker's prayer. Everybody wants a great job. Accept that it's already been given to you. The fact that you're alive means a function has been assigned to you: open your heart to everyone and everything. That way you're a vessel of God. Don't worry about what to say or what to do. He'll let you know.

I used to think I was lazy. I was always tired. Actually, I was just blocked until I discovered the purpose of my life. When our energy is applied in the direction of co-creating with God, of a willingness to supply love where there was none before, new energy bursts forth from deep inside us.

The world never gives you permission to shine. Only love does that. I remember being a cocktail waitress and walking into work one night thinking, "Oh, I get it! They think this is a bar!" As *A Course in Miracles* student, I now saw it differently. "This isn't a bar, and I'm not a waitress. That's just an illusion. Every business is a front for a church, and I'm here to purify the thought forms, to minister to the children of God." We can take our own lives seriously, regardless of whether or not anyone else does. No job really has any more potential impact on the planet than any other. We're always impacting the world in which we live, through our presence, our energy, our interactions with others. The question is, what kind of impact are we having?

I once knew a woman who wanted to be an actress, but wasn't getting work. In the meantime, she was working as a personal assistant to a professional writer. He adored her work and wanted her to travel with him all around the country, doing book tours, setting up lectures and helping him in various ways. Although she told me that she found working with him very exhilarating, she didn't want to leave Los Angeles because she felt she needed to be available in case there were acting jobs here that she might audition for.

"Nothing would be better for your acting career," I told my friend, "than that you would start starring in your own life." The reason many people want to be actors is not because they are truly called to the art, but rather because they want so desperately to create something beautiful in their own lives. Show up! Be enthusiastic! Put some energy into the life you're living now! How will anyone ever be impressed by your starlike quality if you're waiting to cultivate that quality until you become a star?

How would a miracle worker decide whether to go

on the trip or stay in Los Angeles? We make decisions by asking that the 'Holy Spirit decide for us.' There are always so many factors in life that we can't know. 'We make no decisions by ourselves,' but ask how we might be most helpful in carrying out His plan. The moral authority that this attitude gives us creates a starlike quality. It is our humility, our desire to be of service, that makes us stars. Not our arrogance.

An ego thought that tempts a lot of people is the insistence that "I don't do windows." There's an old Zen tradition of disciples spending years dusting the altars of their masters as part of their preparation and training. The apprentice learns from being in the presence of the master, from serving him, and in time will surpass him. As the I Ching says, the universe fills up the modest and cuts down the proud. In modesty, we allow things to blossom. We're not ashamed to admit we're still in process. The ego emphasizes the goal rather than the process by which we achieve it. This is actually the ego's way of sabotaging us. We become proud and hardened, and thereby less attractive. There is nothing likable about false pride. It doesn't help us get work, or to get more successful.

Our job is to tend to our own growth as people, our grace and integrity and humility. We need no other goal. The core of our being then grows into a substantial power, externally as well as internally. Our ministry becomes a direct line of creation, from God through us to all mankind.

6. NEW HEARTS, NEW JOBS

> *"Child of God, you were created to create the good, the beautiful and the holy. Do not forget this."*

The ego says, "Your value is based on your credentials. You need a Ph.D. or its equivalent before you can get a good job." But some of the best and brightest of our generation were educated more by life than by school. There's a mass of talent in our society who have been everywhere and done everything, but have few credentials to show for it. Our achievements have been mainly internal.

Our ministries—our new careers—will reflect these internal achievements. They will express a new integration of mind and heart. They will express the consciousness of people contributing their individual resources to a general healing tide. These careers will be created as individual reflections of our unique talents. We will not "find" these jobs; we will create them. There are no ads in the "Help Wanted" section of newspapers for world saviors or miracle-workers. New forms of employment are emerging in response to new energies.

Carl Jung advised people to look closely into whatever fairy tales or myths particularly attracted them as children. When I was a child, I was enchanted by a fairy tale called "The Girl in the Patchwork Dress." In this story, the crown prince of a kingdom is going around the country looking for a bride. In one town, a huge ball is being held so that the Prince can have a chance to meet all the young ladies who live there. One girl wanted very much to go to the ball but she didn't have enough money to buy the material she would need in order to make a beautiful ball gown. So she did what she could. She picked up scraps of material from other girls' worktables, and put together a patchwork dress.

On the night of the ball, she entered the party and grew embarrassed when she saw how beautiful all the other girls' dresses were. Feeling ashamed, she hid in a closet. The prince came to the party, danced with all the girls there, and at a certain point, he had had enough. He was bored and he was going home. But as he was leaving, he noticed a piece of cloth sticking out of a closet door. He ordered his guards to open the door, where they discovered the girl in the patchwork dress. The prince danced with her, found her more interesting than any of the other girls, and he married her.

When I thought of that story as an adult, I knew why it had meant so much to me as a child. It revealed a significant archetype in my own life. I would ultimately taste a little bit of just about everything life had to offer. This would never earn me a degree in anything, but it would earn me a kind of overview. That vision of things would become the basis for my career. A lot of people among us are like the girl in the patchwork dress. We have a little bit of this, and a little bit of that. But you can't get a Ph.D. in having been everywhere and done everything. Put it all together, and we don't have a degree, but we're interesting people with interesting stories to tell. The patchwork dress symbolizes the consciousness of a generalist, one who synthesizes, while the other beautiful gowns symbolize the consciousness of a specialist. Both the generalist and the specialist are important viewpoints in the functioning of a healthy society.

Ultimately, it is not our credentials but our commitment to a higher purpose that creates our effectiveness in the world. Our resumes are important only if we think they are. I was eating dinner one night with a girlfriend of mine who is an excellent writer and a published author. I mentioned to another friend at the table, a man in publishing, that I thought Barbara should write a monthly column in one of the major women's magazines, called "The Healing Perspective" or "News from the Heartland" or something like that. Every month she could write some interesting piece about how an emotional breakthrough from fear to love had a healing impact in some personal or societal condition. I felt the column would give people hope.

But our friend in publishing took a different perspective. "Barbara couldn't do that," he said. "No magazine would publish it. She's not a Ph.D. She's not an authority. They won't see her as an established voice."

I wanted to turn to Barbara and place an invisible shield of cotton over her ears. I didn't want her to listen to his words. I didn't want her to believe his limited thinking. I didn't want her to close her mind to miracles.

I remember years ago, drinking a cup of coffee late one night as I had done many times before. "How can you do that?" a friend asked. "Won't that keep you up all night?" As of that night, coffee kept me up all night. I had never before, ever, made the conscious connection between coffee and caffeine and sleeplessness, and so, in my experience, there had never been one. Neither need there be an automatic connection between a lack of credentials and a lack of opportunity.

The desire to serve God creates the means by which we do so. Our power doesn't lie in our resume or our connections. Our power doesn't lie in what we've done or even in what we're doing. Our power lies in our clarity about why we're on the earth. We'll be important players if we think that way. And the important players of the coming years will be the people who see themselves as here to contribute to the healing of the world. Everything else is trivial in comparison. Where you went to school is no big deal, or even whether you went to school at all. God can use the flimsiest resume. He can use the smallest gifts. Whatever our gift is to God, however humble it may seem, He can turn it into a mighty work on His behalf. Our greatest gift to Him is our devotion. From that point of power, doors open. Careers blossom. We heal, and the world around us heals.

7.   GOALS

"God is the only goal I have today."

Goal-setting has become very popular in recent years. It is a process of focusing the mind on a desired result. This is actually just another way of trying to get the world to do what we want it to do. It is not spiritual surrender.

A Course in Miracles discusses a difference between "magic and miracles." Magic is when we focus the mind on a desired manifestation, giving our shopping list to God and telling Him what we want Him to do for us. Miracles are when we ask God what we can do for Him.

Miracles shift us from a "get" to a "give" mentality. The desire to get something reflects a core belief that we don't have enough already. As long as we believe there is scarcity inside us, we'll continue to manufacture scarcity around us because that is our basic thought. No matter what we get, it will never be enough.

When our desire is to give instead of get, our core belief is that we have so much abundance, we can afford to give it away. The subconscious mind takes its clue from our core beliefs, and brilliantly manufactures situations that reflect them. Our willingness to give directs the universe to give to us.

The miracle worker's goal in every circumstance is peace of mind. *A Course in Miracles* tells us that 'we don't know what would make us happy; we just think we do.' All of us have gotten things we thought would make us happy and they didn't. If we write affirmations for a brown Mercedes Benz, the power of the subconscious mind is such that we will probably get it. The point is, we won't necessarily be happy once we do. The miracle-minded perception would be to make happiness itself our goal and to relinquish the thought that we know what that would look like. We never know what's going to happen in a month, or a year from now. If we got what we wanted now, then perhaps we would be worse off for it later on.

Let's say you're going in for a job interview. You want the job very much, and someone might have suggested to you that you should affirm you'll be getting the job, making that your goal. But a miracle worker makes peace our only goal. What that does is to direct the mind to focus on all the factors that contribute to our peace, and leave everything else out of our conscious consideration. The mind, like the physical eye, is inundated with so many impressions at one time, that a built-in censor mechanism brings focus to our perception. It chooses what we'll notice and what we won't.

Making our goal anything other than peace is emotionally self-destructive. If our goal is to get the job, then that's fine if we do, but if we don't get the job, we'll feel depressed. If we make peace our goal, then if we get the job, that's great, but if we don't, we're still peaceful.

The Course tells us it's important to set a goal at the beginning of a situation, or it will seem to unfold chaotically. If our goal is peace, we're programmed for emotional stability no matter what happens. The mind will have been directed to see the situation from a peaceful perspective. If we didn't get the job we wanted, it won't matter so much. We will truly understand that there's something better coming up soon, or that this wasn't really the perfect job for us anyway. We will have faith in God. The miracle is that we will really *feel* our faith. It won't just be positive goo thrown over our pain. Our emotions flow from our thoughts, and not the other way around.

Another problem with setting specific goals is that they can be limiting. Perhaps we're asking for something good, when God's will was that we be given something great. Our looking over God's shoulder only interferes with His capacity to make us happy. Once we truly understand that God's will is that we be happy, we no longer feel the need to ask for anything other than that God's will be done.

Once when I was lecturing in New York, a young man stood up and asked me about affirmations. At that time, "Hill Street Blues" was a popular T.V. show. He said, "I've been writing down fifty times before I go to sleep at night, 'I have a regular part on Hill Street Blues, I have a regular part on Hill Street Blues.' Are you telling me I shouldn't do that?"

I said, "You can write those affirmations fifty times before you go to bed at night, and chances are good you'll pull in a part on Hill Street Blues because the mind is very powerful. But for all you know, a year will pass, an important director will be wanting you for the lead in a major feature film, but they won't be able to get you because you're under contract for a little part in Hill Street Blues!"

The issue underlying our need to tell God what to do is our lack of trust. We're afraid to leave things in God's hands because we don't know what He'll do with them. We're afraid He'll lose our file. If we're going to set any goal, let us set the goal of being healed of the belief that God is fear instead of love. Let us remember from the Course that "our happiness and our function are one." If God is our goal, that's the same thing as saying that happiness is our goal. There's no need to believe that God can't figure out the details or provide the ways to make it happen.

8.   GOD'S PLAN

"Only God's plan for salvation will work."

Sometimes we carry an attitude at work because we think the job is beneath us, or we resent the fact that other people are the boss and we're not. We're in a hurry to get to the top of the heap. We don't realize that, as we spread love, we climb naturally. Maybe not most quickly, but remember the story of the tortoise and the hare. The tortoise, although he walked slowly and steadily, reached the goal before the quick-footed hare.

"May God's will be done" is the same thing as saying, "May I become the best that I'm capable of being." As we grow in personal stature, we grow into a more responsible energy. People will *want* to hire us, to work with us. Our progress will occur easily. Our success will be an effortless accomplishment. Things will just *happen*. You can have a great resume, but if you have a rotten personality, the going will get rough for you somewhere down the line. A good resume can get you an important interview, but you won't get the job unless they like you.

Much of today's psychological orientation is brittle. It's brittle because everyone is trying so hard, and we're all trying so hard because we think we have to. The way of surrender is like letting God be the sculptor, and letting ourselves be the clay. In the sculpting classes I took in high school, we had to spray the clay with water each day or it would get too dry to work with. That's how we have to be for God: malleable, like moist clay. If we're rigidly attached to getting something, including getting things to work out the way we think they should work out, we are not relaxed. We then have very little room for spontaneous insights.

We never really know why we're going someplace. I have made what I thought were professional contacts that turned out to be personal contacts, and vice versa. In God's world, there's only one work going on, and that's the preparation of His teachers, those who demonstrate love. According to the Course, the Holy

Spirit uses any situation given to Him as a lesson in love for everyone involved. But we have to be willing to give up our attachment to a particular outcome in a given situation. We might see a certain project as a vehicle for making money, for instance, and then feel disappointed if it doesn't. We feel confused because we thought we were following the Holy Spirit's guidance in making the effort. But it could be that the real purpose of that particular project was not to make money at all. We do not always know at the time why the Holy Spirit directs us as He does. The miracle worker's function is merely to follow instructions in a desire to serve God. Our compensation, materially and emotionally, will arrive in God's own time and way.

One of the reasons we're always trying to control the results in life is because we think the universe, when left to its own devices, is chaotic. But God is the ultimate order. He is the principle of constantly expanding love in action, in all dimensions, for all life. His power is thoroughly impersonal. He doesn't like some people more than others. He works like a computer. Trusting God is like trusting gravity.

These are important points to remember:

1. God's plan works.
2. Yours doesn't.

As stated by the Course, "I need add nothing to His plan. But to receive it, I must be willing not to substitute my own in place of it. And that is all. Add more, and you will merely take away the little that is asked." It's not our job to figure out how to accomplish God's purposes on earth. That's not help; it's interference. It is merely our job to so deeply align our hearts and minds with His spirit within us, that our lives then become involuntary instruments of His will. Insights occur. Situations shift gear. Our efforts to consciously control the unfolding of good does not produce good so much as it brings forth a slightly less tainted brand of human wilfullness.

I have heard it said that living out of our vision is more powerful than living out of our circumstance. Holding on to a vision invokes the circumstances by which the vision is achieved. Vision is content; material circumstances mere form. I have a friend who is running for political office. Having been in politics for many years, his tendency is to think that his political success depends on his being a good politician. But part of the decay of our social order has come about because we are governed by so many people who are politicians rather than leaders. Lyndon Johnson was a great politician but not much of a leader. John Kennedy was a great leader but not much of a politician. The strength of a positive vision for America, through its inspirational effects on all the people who want desperately to see our nation healed, will do more to get someone elected than any amount of conventional politicking. It will touch our hearts.

I told my friend that the key to a successful campaign would be to surrender the campaign to the Holy Spirit and ask that it be used as an instrument of His peace. My friend said that sounded great, but he needed to figure out how to do that. I told him he didn't have to figure out anything. "All you have to do is to be willing," I told him, "and the Holy Spirit will enter where He is invited. You'll be brilliant. You'll be charismatic. Don't try to figure out your message; just ask God what He would have you say. Step back and let Him lead the way."

A silent prayer before every speech and every political appearance would help bring his energies in line with truth. Once I accompanied him to a political rally, and in the car on the way, he shared with me some understandable judgments of certain people who would be there. "Pray that your perceptions be healed," I said to him as we walked into the building. "Your goal is to lead us into a compassionate society, but you can't give what you don't have. Start by being compassionate towards the people at this rally. As your mind is healed, its effect on others will be automatic. You won't even have to think about what to say. The perfect words will come right out, because love will guide your mind." That's what it would mean to let God run his campaign.

And so it is with any business. Before the meeting, or the interview or the session, or whatever, try saying this prayer:

"Dear God, I surrender this situation to you. May it be used for your purposes. I ask only that my heart be open to give love and to receive love. May all the results unfold according to your will. Amen." Whatever you do, do it for God.

We are strong enough to do any job He asks us to do. Don't be concerned about your own readiness, says the Course, but be consistently aware of His. It is not you doing the work, but the spirit who is within you. Forgetting this causes fear. *A Course in Miracles* says that the presence of fear is a sure sign we're trusting in our own strength. "If you are trusting in your own strength, you have every reason to be apprehensive, anxious and fearful." Of ourselves, none of us have the capacity to work miracles. With 'the power that is in us but not of us,' however, there is nothing we can not do.

9. SALES TO SERVICE

"Love would always give increase."

When we are motivated by the desire to sell, we are only looking out for ourselves. When we are motivated by the desire to serve, we are looking out for others. Miracles shift us from a sales to a service mentality. Since in the realm of consciousness we only get to keep what we give away, a service mentality is a far more abundant attitude."

The thought system that dominates our culture is laced with selfish values, and relinquishing those values is a lot easier said than done. The journey to a pure heart can be highly disorienting. For years we may have worked for power, money and prestige. Now all of a sudden we've learned that those are just the values of a dying world. We don't know where to search for motivation anymore. If we're not working in order to get rich, then why are we working at all? What are we supposed to do all day? Just sit home and watch TV?

Not at all, but thinking so is a temporary phase many people go through—when the values of the old world no longer have a hold on us, but the values of the new don't yet grab your soul. They will. There comes a time, not too long into the journey to God, when the realization that the world could work beautifully if we would give it the chance, begins to excite us. It becomes our new motivation. The news isn't how bad things are. The news is how good they could be. And our own activity could be part of the unfolding of Heaven on earth. There is no more powerful motivation than to feel we're being used in the creation of a world where love has healed all wounds.

We are no longer ambitious for ourselves, but are rather inspired by the vision of a healed world. Inspiration rearranges our energies. It sources within us a new power and direction. We no longer feel like we're trying to carry a football to the finish line, clutching it to our chest and surrounded by hostile forces. We feel instead as though angels are pushing us from behind and making straight our path as we go.

Purity of heart will not make us poor. The exaltation of poverty as a spiritual virtue is of the ego, not the spirit. A person acting from a motivation of contribution and service rises to such a level of moral authority, that worldly success is a natural result.

Give all your gifts away in service to the world. If you want to paint, don't wait for a grant. Paint a wall in your town that looks drab and uninviting. You never know who's going to see that wall. Whatever it is you want to do, give it away in service to your community. At my lectures in Los Angeles, I grew so tired of hearing actors moan about not getting jobs. "Go to hospitals, to retirement homes, to mental institutions," I said. "There was acting before there were acting jobs. If you want to act, *act*." Some people who heard me formed a group called the Miracle Players, and they did just that.

"I don't want to do it because I can't make a living doing it," is a very weak beam to send into the universe. I lectured on *A Course in Miracles* for at least two years before it became the source of my income. When I started lecturing, I had no idea it would become my profession. Some things you do for no other reason than because they're the right thing to do. "I'll do this because it serves, even if I'm not paid," is a very high beam. It says to the universe that you must be very serious. And when you get serious about the universe, the universe gets serious about you.

I never felt the need to advertise much for my lectures. I figured if they were of genuine interest to people, then people would hear about them. That's not to say that advertising is bad, as long as the motivation for advertising is to inform people as opposed to manipulating them. Arnold Patent wrote that if you genuinely have something to say, there is someone who genuinely needs to hear it. We don't have to invent an audience so much as we have to hone the message we plan to give them once they get here. Serving three people is as important as serving three hundred. Once we're clear about how to deal with a small following, a large following will develop automatically, if that would serve the world. Our power lies in our clarity about the role our work can play in the creation of a more beautiful world. The miracle is to think of our career as our contribution, however small, to the healing of the universe.

The ego's world is based on finite resources, but God's world is not. In God's world, which is the real world, the more we give, the more we have. Our having a piece of the world's pie doesn't mean there's less for anyone else, and someone else having a piece of the pie doesn't mean there's less for us. So we needn't compete, in business or anywhere else. Our generosity towards others is key to our positive experience of the world. There's enough room for everyone to be beautiful. There's enough room for everyone to be successful. There's enough room for everyone to be rich. It is only our thinking that blocks that possibility from happening.

The people who have achieved more than you, in any area, are only a half step ahead of you in time. Bless them and praise their gifts, and bless and praise your own. The world would be less rich without their contributions, and it would be less rich without yours. There's more than room for everyone; in fact, there's a need for everyone.

As we are healed, the world is healed. Doing anything for a purpose other than love means reliving the split from God, perpetuating and maintaining that split. Every person is a cell in the body of human consciousness. At the moment, it is as though the body of Christ is suffering from cancer. In cancer, a normal working cell decides that it no longer wants to function in contribution to the whole. Instead of being part of the support system of the blood or the liver, the cell goes off and builds its own kingdom. That's a malignancy, which threatens to destroy the organism.

So it is with the body of humanity. Everyone's gone off to do their own thing: *my* career, *my* store, *my* money. We've lost sight of our essential interrelatedness, and this forgetfulness threatens to destroy us. The "my" mentality is the ego. It is the belief in separation. It is the cosmic disease. Taking what we have and devoting it to the restoration of the whole is our salvation and the salvation of the world. Our devotion then becomes our work, and our work becomes our devotion.

CHAPTER 8

The Body

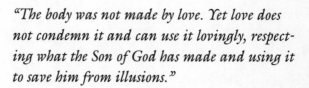

"The body was not made by love. Yet love does not condemn it and can use it lovingly, respecting what the Son of God has made and using it to save him from illusions."

1.   THE BODY'S PURPOSE

"Let the body have healing as its purpose."

In the world of bodies, we are all separate. In the world of spirit, we are all one. Citing the Course, we heal the separation between the two by shifting our awareness from 'body identification' to 'spirit identification.' This heals the body as well as the mind.

We think we're separate because we have bodies, when in truth, we have bodies because we think we're separate. The Course says that the body is "a tiny fence around a little part of a glorious and complete idea." But that doesn't mean the body is bad. Like everything else within the world of form, the mind ascribes to it either fearful or loving purposes. The ego's use of the body is to maintain the illusion of separation: 'The ego uses the body for attack, pleasure and pride.' The Holy Spirit's use of the body is to heal that illusion: "In this sense, the body does become a temple to God; His voice abides in it by directing the use to which it is put."

The body's holiness lies in its potential for communication. When given to the Holy Spirit, the body becomes "a beautiful lesson in communion which has value until communion is." The 'Holy Spirit asks us to give Him our hands, our feet, our voices, in order that He might use them as instruments for saving the world.' To see the body as a means by which the world is transformed, and not an end in itself, is a healthy perception of the body. To see the body as an end instead of a means, to ascribe to it selfish or unloving purposes, is to put a burden on the body that the body was never meant to carry. This is sick thinking, which produces sickness in the body.

Living on this earth, we have learned to see ourselves as bodies. An individual body is physically small and vulnerable in relation to the rest of the universe, and so, since we think we are bodies, we experience ourselves as small and vulnerable. Living within the realization that we are much more than bodies, that we are spirits within the mind of God, expands the level of our awareness and places us outside the limitations of ordinary physical law. This correction of our perception, this Atonement, is our healing. It is not the body that gets sick, but the mind. As shown in the Course, health or sickness of the body "depends entirely on how the mind perceives it, and the purpose that the mind would use it for." It is not the body but the mind that is in need of healing, and the only healing is a return to love.

Our bodies are merely blank canvases onto which we project our thoughts. Disease is loveless thinking materialized. This doesn't mean that people who have contracted a disease thought lovelessly, while the rest of us didn't. Great saints have contracted terminal illnesses. The lovelessness that manufactures disease is systemic; it is laced throughout racial consciousness. Which soul manifests illness is based on many factors.

Let's say an innocent child dies of environmentally-based cancer. How was lovelessness the problem here? The loveless thinking was not necessarily in the child, but in many of us who, over the years, lived without reverence for the environment, allowing it to be polluted by toxic chemicals. The child's physical sickness resulted, indirectly, from the sickness in someone else's mind. Our loving thoughts affect people and situations we never even dream of, and so do our mistakes. Since our minds do not stop at our brain casings—since there is no place where one mind stops and another starts—then our love touches everyone, and so does our fear.

A healthy perception of our bodies is one in which we surrender them to the Holy Spirit and ask that they be used as instruments through which love is expressed into the world. The Course states, "The body is merely part of your experience in the physical world.... [It] is nothing more than a framework for developing abilities, which is quite apart from what they are used for." *A Course in Miracles* says that "health is the result of

relinquishing all attempts to use the body lovelessly."
The use of the body for any other purpose than the
extension of love is diseased thinking. It is at odds with
our natural knowingness and the conflict it engenders is
reflected in our physical as well as our mental states.

2. HEALTH AND HEALING

"The body is not the source of its own health."

A friend of mine told me that we're not punished *for*
our sins, but *by* our sins. Sickness is not a sign of God's
judgment on us, but of our judgment on ourselves. If
we were to think that God created our sickness, how
could we turn to Him for healing? As we've already
established, God is all that is good. He creates only
love, therefore he did not create sickness. Sickness is an
illusion and does not actually exist. It is part of our
worldly dream, our self-created nightmare. Our prayer
to God is that He awaken us from the dream.

When any of us awaken, the entire world is brought
closer to Heaven. In asking for healing, we are not just
asking for our own health, but rather we are asking that
the idea of sickness be removed from the mind of God's
Son. As shown in *A Course in Miracles,* "If the mind
can heal the body, but the body cannot heal the mind,
then the mind must be stronger than the body." Forgiveness is the ultimate preventative medicine as well as
the greatest healer. We heal the body by remembering

that it is not who we really are. We are spirits and not bodies, we are eternally healthy and we are incapable of sickness. These are merely statements of the truth about ourselves, and it is always truth that sets us free.

Illness is a sign of separation from God, and healing is a sign that we have returned to Him. The return to God is merely the return to love. In his book *Quantum Healing*, Dr. Deepak Chopra tells a powerful story about the connection between love and physical healing:

> *An Ohio University study of heart disease in the 1970s was conducted by feeding quite toxic, high-cholesterol diets to rabbits in order to block their arteries, duplicating the effect that such a diet has on human arteries. Consistent results began to appear in all the rabbit groups except for one, which strangely displayed 60 percent fewer symptoms. Nothing in the rabbits' physiology could account for their high tolerance to the diet, until it was discovered by accident that the student who was in charge of feeding these particular rabbits liked to fondle and pet them. He would hold each rabbit lovingly for a few minutes before feeding it; astonishingly, this alone seemed to enable the animals to overcome the toxic diet. Repeat experiments, in which one group of rabbits was treated neutrally while the others were loved, came up with similar results.*

Once again, the mechanism that causes such immunity is quite unknown—it is baffling to think that evolution has built into the rabbit mind an immune response that needs to be triggered by human cuddling.

Studies have shown that cancer patients who attend support groups live, on the average, twice as long after diagnosis as those who don't. What is this "psycho-immunological factor" which, by now, science knows exists, but doesn't know how to identify? That factor is love, or God.

God is of no practical value if we perceive Him merely as a free-floating concept, divorced from the power of physical expression. It is only when He is expressed on the earth, His love channeled through human beings as in the case of the student cuddling the rabbits, or support groups where the space is created for increased compassion and understanding, that He is allowed to penetrate the veil of human darkness.

Over the last several years I have counseled many people diagnosed with cancer, AIDS and other life-challenging illnesses. In 1987, I asked my friend Louise Hay if she would help me start a nonprofit organization dedicated to helping people in physical crisis, to be called The Los Angeles Center for Living. In 1989, The Manhattan Center for Living opened in New York City. The Centers' mission statement is that we provide free nonmedical support services to people dealing with life-challenging illness and grief. On both coasts, we have seen the miracles that occur when people invoke the power of love in the midst of disease and grief.

"Do not look to the god of sickness for healing but only to the God of love," says the Course, "for healing is the acknowledgement of Him." In the traditional Western medical model, a healer's job is to attack disease. But if the consciousness of attack is the ultimate problem, how could it be the ultimate answer? A miracle worker's job is not to attack illness, but rather to stimulate the natural forces of healing. We turn our eyes away from sickness to the love that lies beyond it. No sickness can diminish our capacity to love.

Does that mean that it is a mistake to take medicine? Absolutely not. *A Course in Miracles* reminds us that the Holy Spirit enters into our lives at our present level of consciousness. Many of us believe that the doctor in the white coat can heal us with that pill he's giving us. Therefore, says the Course, we should take the pill. But the healing doesn't come from the pill. It comes from our belief.

Cancer studies have shown that rates of recovery in patients choosing traditional medical treatment, versus those taking a more holistic route, are roughly equal. This makes perfect sense, because in neither case is the recovery a result of the form of cure. It is the patient's mental and emotional interaction with his treatment that activates its healing power.

I have led support groups for people dealing with

life-challenging illness, where during the entire session, disease was mentioned only in passing. We attend groups not to grow closer to our disease, but rather to grow closer to the power for healing which lies within us. Many of the issues that confront us when we are ill are the same issues that confronted us in one way or another when we were still healthy, but we didn't deal with them until now. Life goes on when we are ill. It is merely intensified. We tend to handle illness basically the way we handle everything else in life. We must avoid the temptation to see illness as a block to our capacity to find God, and instead use it as a springboard from which we soar into His arms.

3.   *HEALTHY THINKING*

> *"Healing, then, is a way of approaching knowledge by thinking in accordance with the laws of God."*

There is a healing force within each of us, a kind of divine physician seated within our minds and in communication with every cell of our being. This force is the intelligence that drives the immune system. Its presence is obvious to us whenever we cut a finger or break a leg.

What is this "divine intelligence" and how is it activated? 'The Atonement releases the mind to its full creative power.' "Jesus saves" means "love heals the mind." How did Jesus heal the leper? By forgiving him. He stood in the midst of illusion and yet saw only the truth as God created it. He healed through corrected perception. When he stood in front of a leper, he didn't see leprosy. He extended his perception beyond what the physical senses revealed, to reality as seen through the vision of the Holy Spirit. Within the leper is the Son of God, perfect, unalterable, changeless. The spirit is eternally healthy. The spirit cannot get sick and the spirit cannot die.

Jesus sees only as God sees. He accepted the Atonement for himself. Jesus did not *believe* in leprosy. Since all minds are connected, in his presence the leper no longer believed in it either. And so the leper was healed.

In *A Course in Miracles*, Jesus, who is the personal symbol of the Holy Spirit, says, "Your mind and mine can unite in shining your ego away." Asking the Holy Spirit to heal us when we are sick means asking him to heal the thoughts within us which give rise to sickness.

Several years ago, when I had just begun lecturing on *A Course in Miracles*, I had a series of three car accidents in which I was rear-ended on the freeway. In every case, I had surrendered the experience immediately, remembering that I was not subject to the effect of worldly danger, and was not harmed or hurt in any way.

A week or so after the last accident, I developed a cold and a serious sore throat. On a Friday afternoon, with a lecture to give about the Course the next morning, I was feeling terrible. I had a date for drinks after work with my girlfriend Sarah. Since I felt so bad I wanted to cancel the date and go home to bed, but when I called Sarah's office I was told that she had already left for the day. I had no choice but to go to the café, and on my way driving there, I turned my attention to healing my throat. I wished desperately for access to a doctor, because I knew that an antibiotic called Erythromycin had always healed this throat problem for me in the past. Since I was new in Los Angeles, I didn't know any doctors yet. I turned to the Course. How did this happen, I asked myself. Where did my thinking deviate from truth? Where was my wrong-minded perception? I received the answer as soon as I asked, and it struck me like a bolt of lightning. Although I had applied principle in relation to the accident itself, I had "given into temptation" right afterwards. In what way? After three accidents, everyone I knew had come up to ask me if I was all right. They put their hands on me, rubbed my neck and back gently, inquired as to whether I'd seen a doctor, and oozed gentleness all over me. *The attention felt good. Being sick made people love me more.* Instead of responding with a full tilt, "I'm fine," the "I'm fine" came out a little more timidly, lest they'd stop rubbing my neck. I had bought into—entered into agreement with—the idea of my physical vulnerability in order to receive the payoff of love and attention.

I paid a high price for my "sin," i.e. loveless perception. My perception was wrong-minded in the sense that I saw myself as a body rather than a spirit, which is a loveless rather than loving self-identification. Choosing to believe I was vulnerable, even for an instant, made me so. Thus my sore throat.

Great, I thought. I got it! "God," I said. "I totally understand how this happened. I return my mind to the point of my error, and I atone. I go back. I ask that my perception be healed, and I ask to be released from the effects of my wrong-minded thinking. Amen." I closed my eyes at a red light while I said the prayer, and fully expected to be free of my sore throat when I opened them again.

The prayer over, I opened my eyes. My throat still hurt. This wasn't supposed to happen. Now more depressed than ever, I went into the cafe where I was to meet my friend and took a seat at the bar. I noticed as I entered that there was a man at the other end of the bar, looking at me in a flirtatious kind of way. He was anything but my type. I looked at him as though to say, "One more look my direction, buddy, and you're dead."

"Can I help you?" asked the bartender.

"Yes," I whispered hoarsely. "I want some brandy, some honey and some milk."

The man at the other end of the bar watched as the bartender returned with the items I'd requested. "What are you trying to do?" he asked.

I did not want to speak to this man. I wanted him

The Body 🌸 235

to go away. But once the Course has gotten into your system, you never again have guilt-free bitchy thoughts. "He's your brother, Marianne," I said to myself. "He's an innocent child of God. *Be nice.*"

I softened. "I'm trying to make a hot toddy," I said. "I have a very bad sore throat."

"Well first of all, that's not the way to make a hot toddy," he said, "and secondly, that's not what you want anyway. You probably need some penicillin."

"That's true, I do," I said, "Erythromycin would cure this but I just moved to L.A. and I don't know any doctors who would prescribe it to me."

The man got up and walked over to where I was sitting. He put a credit card on the bar and beckoned the bartender. "Come on, let's go next door," he said to me. "I can get you some Erythromycin."

I looked at him like he was crazy, but I also noticed that the credit card said "Dr." on it. "What's next door?" I asked.

"A Thrifty drugstore."

And so it was. We walked next door to Thrifty and my new friend the doctor prescribed the medicine I wanted. After throwing one pill into my mouth, I became ecstatic.

"You don't understand," I said to him, practically jumping up and down. "*This is a miracle!* I prayed for healing, and I corrected my thoughts but the Holy Spirit couldn't give me an instantaneous healing because I'm not advanced enough yet to receive it—it would be too threatening to my belief system—so He had to enter at the level of my understanding, and you were there, but if I hadn't opened my heart to you I would never have been able to receive the miracle because I wouldn't have been open!"

He handed me his business card. "Young lady, here's my number," he said. "I'm a psychiatrist and I haven't prescribed an antibiotic in twenty-five years. But trust me, you should give me a call."

As I told the good doctor, I asked that my misperceptions be healed—I accepted the Atonement—but the healing could still only enter at the level of my receptivity. The Course tells us that the Holy Spirit steps aside in the presence of fear. Most of us, were we to have a broken leg healed instantly upon hearing the word Jesus, would find the healing more depressing than the wound. That's because, if such a thing is possible, the entire world is something other than we think it is. Giving up our limited understanding of the world, which we experience as a kind of pseudo- control, is more of a threat to us than a broken leg. Some people, says *A Course in Miracles*, would rather die than change their minds. The Holy Spirit finds ways to express His power through vehicles we can accept. Medicine is such a vehicle.

There is a saying in Alcoholics Anonymous that "Every problem comes bearing its own solution." Crisis comes bearing its solution in that it takes us to our knees, our most humble thinking. If we had been there to begin with—if we had placed the power of God before our own, putting love before all personal ambitions—then our problems would not have developed.

An epidemic such as AIDS is a collective heartbreak, pulling millions of people into its painful vortex. But this also means that it brings millions of people to their knees. As soon as enough of us get there, as soon as love reaches a critical mass or, as the Course says, enough people become miracle-minded, there will be a sudden breakthrough in consciousness—a rapture, an instantaneous healing. It will be as though millions of us are stopped at that red light, recognizing our lovelessness and asking that we be healed. When the cure for AIDS is finally found, we will give prizes to a few scientists, but many of us will know that millions and millions of prayers helped it happen.

4.   *SAVING THE MIND, SAVING THE BODY*

"Only salvation can be said to cure."

The experience of illness is a call to a genuinely religious life. In that sense, it is for many people one of the best things that ever happened to them.

One of the problems with illness is that it strongly tempts us to obsess about the body at the very time when we need most to concentrate on spirit. It takes spiritual discipline to turn that around. Spiritual practice is mental and emotional exercise, not unlike physical exercise in the way it works. Through spiritual work we are seeking to rebuild our mental musculature. We achieve so little, says *A Course in Miracles*, because we have undisciplined minds. Training our minds to think from a loving, faithful perspective is the greatest boost we can give to our immune systems, and one of the greatest challenges we can pose to our minds.

Changing our lives can be difficult. For a person who has been diagnosed with a physical ailment, the call to change is imperative. Where we used to eat unhealthy foods, we must now eat healthy ones. Where we used to smoke, drink, or get too little sleep, we must now change those habits. And where our minds used to run instinctively in the directions of fear, paranoia and attack, we must now do everything possible to train our minds to think differently.

The body-mind connection might be new to Western science, but it is not new to Eastern medicine, or to the fields of religion and philosophy. The body has an intelligence of its own. As Deepak Chopra writes in *Quantum Healing*, "Life itself is intelligence riding everywhere on chemicals. We mustn't make the mistake of thinking that the rider and the horse are the same." In the traditional Western model of healing, we are trying to get the horse to move in a new direction, without considering having a conversation with the horse's driver. A spiritual, holistic notion of healing includes treatment not only of the body, but of the mind and spirit as well. As Chopra writes, "We have ultimately arrived at a dramatic shift in world view. For the first time in the history of science, mind has a visible scaffold to stand upon. Before this, science declared that we are physical machines that somehow learned to think. Now it dawns that we are thoughts that have learned to create a physical machine."

Love changes the way we think about our disease. Illness comes from separation, says *A Course in Miracles*, and healing comes from joining. Of course people hate their cancer, or hate their AIDS, but the last thing a sick person needs is something else to hate about themselves. Healing results from a transformed perception of our relationship to illness, one in which we respond to the problem with love instead of fear. When a child presents a cut finger to his or her mother, the woman doesn't say, "Bad cut." Rather, she kisses the finger, showers it with love in an unconscious, instinctive activation of the healing process. Why should we think differently about critical illness? Cancer and AIDS and other serious illnesses are physical manifestations of a psychic scream, and their message is not "Hate me," but "Love me."

If I'm yelling, the person in front of me can react in one of two ways. He can yell back, screaming at me to shut up, but this will tend to make me scream more. Or he can tell me that he cares what my feelings are and he loves me and is sorry that I'm feeling this way, which will tend to quiet me down. Those are our two choices with critical illness. Attacking disease is not a cure.

Attacking a disease only makes it yell louder. Healing comes from entering into a conversation with our illness, seeking to understand what it's trying to tell us. The physician seeks to understand the chemical alphabet through which illness speaks. The metaphysician seeks to understand what the illness is trying to say.

Lucifer is seen to have been the most beautiful angel in Heaven before he "fell." In *Star Wars*, Darth Vader turns out to have been a nice guy at an earlier time. Disease is love turned into fear—our own energy, meant to sustain us, turned against ourselves. Energy cannot be destroyed. Our job is not to kill disease, but to turn its energy back in the direction it came from— to turn fear back into love.

Visualization has become a popular technique for the treatment of critical illnesses. People often visualize a PAC man, or soldier with a machine gun, setting out to destroy the threatening cells or virus. But we can take a more loving approach. Underneath Darth Vader's ugly mask lay a real man with a real heart. AIDS, for instance, can be thought of as "Angels-In-Darth Vader-Suits."

Here are some enlightened visualizations: Imagine the AIDS virus as Darth Vader, and then unzip his suit to allow an angel to emerge. See the cancer cell or AIDS virus in all its wounded horror, and then see a golden light, or angel, or Jesus, enveloping the cell and transforming it from darkness into light. As we said before, a scream responds best to love. That is when it calms down. That is when it stops.

I have used an interesting letter-writing technique in my work, where people write a letter to AIDS or cancer or whatever illness they might have, and tell it everything they feel. The letter begins,
for instance:

> Dear Cancer,
> These are my honest feelings.
> . . . . .
> . . . . .
> Signed,
> Ed

And then we wrote a letter back, to Ed from AIDS.

> Dear Ed,
> These are my honest feelings.
> . . . . .
> . . . . .
> Signed,
> AIDS

The following letters were written in one of my AIDS workshops:

> Dear AIDS,
> I used to hate you. I was confused and afraid to accept the idea of death and sickness.

I believed the newsprint and TV, doctors, and
all of that fear that others tried to lay into
me on a daily basis. However, today I find
I'm not dead three and a half years later,
and even with all these medical problems,
I'm more alive today than ever. I'm a
grown-up thanks to your appearance in
my life. You've given me a reason to live
and I love you for it. My friends are sick or
dead but I'm not them. I'm me. And I
do not feel threatened or afraid of
something that was once an enemy and has
now become my strength.

Steve

Dear Steve,
   If I was, as they say, out to get you, don't
you think you'd be dead by now? I'm
not able to kill, harm, or make you sick.
I have no brain, brute strength or great harm-
ing force. I'm just a virus. You give me the
power you should give to God. I take what
I can because I don't want to die any more
than you do. Yes, I live off your fears. But
I die from your peace of mind, serenity,
honesty, faith and desire to live.
   Sincerely,

The AIDS virus

Dear AIDS,

I am so afraid of dying young. I am so afraid of going to the hospital and having all these needles and things stuck in me. I am so afraid of pain. Why do you have to do this to me and my friends? What did we ever do to make you mad at us and want to hurt us? If there is something you are trying to tell us, can't you tell us in a different way? I miss my friends. Why did you have to kill them? Why did you have to cause them such physical pain? Sometimes I'm so angry at you but right now I'm not angry. I'm just sad. I'm confused. I don't know what to do to calm you down. So far you've left me alone, but why, and for how long? John is such a gentle person. Why must he suffer? If it's love you want, we can love you. If you have any doubts, look at the love surrounding this disease. Please answer soon. Tell us what you want. I feel like we don't have much time but I'm willing to listen and learn. Thank you.

Carl

Dear Carl,

I don't understand this any better than you do. I don't mean you and your loved ones any harm. I'm just trying to exist, just like you, doing it in the best way I know how. Unfortunately, it ends up hurting people. I just want love, just like you do. I'm crying out but no one seems to hear me. Maybe if we try listening to each other and talking to each other, we can find a way to exist in peace without hurting each other. Right now, I feel like you only want to destroy me rather than dealing with whatever it is inside of you that brought me here. Please don't hate me and try to destroy me. Love me.

Let's talk and listen to each other and try to live in peace. Thanks.

AIDS

Dear HIV,

A little over eleven years ago you blew into town. Everything has changed since that time. Many people have left because of you. I really miss them a lot. There has been so much pain and suffering because of you. On a conscious level, no one wanted you. I myself have been personally dealing with you too long already. Back in '87 and '88, you almost took me out. I just thought you might like to know that it is 1991 now and I'm still around and so are you. Isn't it about time we stop this bullshit and become friends? Let's put the past behind us and grow forward together. I have tried to love you as best I can, but sometimes I really have difficulty doing so. Please, let's be friends and make up.

Love always,

Paul

Dear Paul,
  Okay.
  Love,

HIV

Dear AIDS,

I'm really pissed off! Why do I have to worry about you and death when I'm only 26? I want to know I'll be alive for my ten-year class reunion, but no—it's a big maybe. I'm also sick of worrying that every cold I get or sleep pattern that's different is a sign of the end coming. I'm tired of worrying about others finding out. Get out of my body. I don't want you here! That's all.

Russ

Dear Russ,

Both you and I don't know how we came to be, but we're here together. I would be glad to go, but that door is not open to me. Hey, I've given you a perspective on life and death most people your age never think about! Work with me, we'll get through this.

AIDS

Dear AIDS,

I, like lots of other people, have been through so much pain and so many changes, both physically and mentally. Now, yes, there is a great part inside me who is very angry and sad. It feels like a big nightmare. Yes, I must have done something to cause this disease. But what a wound to be punished like this. I must say, I do not like all the pain I've gone through with this crazy disease, and I don't like the suffering it has put me through mentally. But I pray daily.

Peter

Dear Peter,

I'm in your body and yes I am a virus and yes I have caused you a great deal of discomfort. But I do assure you that the power of your mind does make a difference. You know if it did not, you would not be here. Yes, I have altered your life in some ways, but in some ways positively. Your mind is much more powerful than I am.

AIDS

Dear AIDS,

I hate the uncertainty. But I feel thankful for the kick in the butt this was in my life, and to those around me. You made me find the strength I always had, and made me see the love those around me could show. You made us all learn to appreciate every day and the strength I was capable of. I know I keep saying strength, but it's true, AIDS gave me strength. This is because when you find out your biggest fear in life comes true and you can still move on, fear no longer has any strength. Thank you for helping me stop beating up on myself and hating what I wasn't, and making me love what I am.

Andrew

Dear Andrew,

You're welcome.

AIDS

Dear AIDS virus,

Go to Hell. You took a shining star from my family. I miss him and loved him and I never told him. Why do you invade us in our prime? Why do you strike with such vengeance? I hate the pain and agony you cause, but somehow you brought out the best in Leo and the best in his family.

Inez

Dear Inez,

I didn't bring out the worst or best. I just am. And how you live with me is up to each of you.

AIDS

I suggest to every person dealing with a serious illness in themselves or others, that they consider starting a journal in which they "communicate" with their illness. Seeing sickness as our own love that needs to be reclaimed, is a more positive approach to healing than is seeing the sickness as something hideous we must get rid of. Energy cannot be destroyed. It can, however, be miraculously transformed. That miracle emerges from our own thoughts, our own decision to let go our belief in fear and danger, and to embrace instead, a view of the world that is based on hope and love. There is certainly nothing to lose, no risk in trying. "The Atonement is so gentle you need but whisper to it and all its power will rush to your assistance and support." God does His part when we do ours.

5.   THE BODY IN RELATIONSHIPS

"The body does not separate you from your
brother, and if you think it does you are insane."

Our real identity lies not in our body, but in our spirit. "The Christ in you inhabits not a body," says the Course. Neither is another person's body who they really are, either. The body is an illusionary wall that appears to separate us, the ego's chief device in trying to convince us that we are separate from each other and separate from God.

The Course calls the body "the central figure in the

dreaming of the world." The human storyline, where bodies talk and move and suffer and die, forms a veil of unreality in front of God's creation. It hides "the face of Christ." My brother might lie, but he is not that lie. My brothers might fight, but they remain joined in love.

"Minds are joined," says the Course, but "bodies are not." The body of itself is nothing. It cannot forgive, it cannot see, and it cannot communicate. "If you choose to see the body you behold a world of separation, unrelated things, and happenings that make no sense at all."

"When you equate yourself with a body, you will always experience depression," says the Course. Equating another person with a body will bring up the same anxiety. One of the ways the body can be used to manufacture depression is through loveless sex. Our sexual impulses become canvases onto which we extend our love or project our fear. When sex is of the Holy Spirit, it is a deepening of communication. When it is of the ego, it is a substitute for communication. The Holy Spirit uses sex to heal us; the ego uses it to wound us. Sometimes we have thought that sex with another person would cement the bond between us, and instead it turned out to manufacture more illusion and anxiety than there was before. It is only when sex is a vehicle for spiritual communion that it is truly loving, that it joins us to another person. Then it is a sacred act.

Holiness means the presence of a loving purpose, and in that sense, the body and its accouterments can be a holy expression. Many spiritual seekers have felt the need to eschew all body-related things. But that can actually be as ego-centered as an overattachment to the physical. Anything used to spread joy and communicate love is a part of God's plan for salvation.

When I was about twenty years old, I had my first date with a man in a suit. I had never before been picked up at my house by a man wearing anything but bluejeans. When I opened the door and saw a hand-some man in a suit and a beautiful overcoat, my first thought was that maybe he was in the mafia!

I went on the date and struggled for the entire evening with my conflicts about his wardrobe. I couldn't tell this man, of course, that I was turned off by his gor-geous clothes! He was an Italian, and my first exposure to a European man's sensibilities towards women. Years later I would remember what this man taught me.

We started dating, and I had never known someone to make such a fuss over me. He treated our nights out like major events. Did I wish to see a play or a movie? Did I want to go to this restaurant, or that? What should he wear? I was so surprised by what a big deal it was to him, whether he wore the blue shirt or the white. At first it annoyed me, coming as I was from a sixties mentality that viewed all such considerations as irrelevant. But I ultimately saw that the central issue for him was that he wished to make me happy. His dressing up was a way to please me, a way of communicating how much he cared.

Many years after that relationship, I was walking through a clothing store with a boyfriend. He was looking at two jackets, and couldn't decide which one to buy. When I indicated which I liked, he acted almost as though I was his mother—he would prove to me that my opinion wouldn't dictate his decision. I said to him, "That's the difference between you and me. If I were buying clothes, your liking something would make me more prone to buy it. What's the point of being in a relationship with you if it doesn't motivate me to try to please you, to make your life more pleasurable, to sweeten things for you?"

That's the only purpose for make-up, or clothes, or anything else in the world of form. Their point is not to seduce another person, but to add light to the world in the form of beauty and pleasure. The meaning in things is how much we use them to contribute happiness to the world. Clothes and other personal effects are no different than any other art form. If we perceive them lovingly, they can lift the vibrations and increase the energy in the world around us.

This is not narcissism or vanity. Our *not* caring whether the boyfriend or husband, girlfriend or wife really likes the outfit—that's the narcissism. I have had boyfriends who were as adamant that they preferred me without make-up, as others have been that they wanted me always to wear it. The change for me has had nothing to do with what kind of men I dated, but with a shift from "I don't care what he wants," to "I care very much what makes him happy." The first part of the sexual revolution entailed women breaking from the oppressive patterns of subservience to men. The second part entails our recognition that there is no point in developing individuality except to then surrender it to a higher identity. And the highest identity is our relationship with others. A life lived for oneself alone is not liberation, but merely another form of bondage. Since we are not bodies, we do not exist in isolation. Living as though we do can only lead to pain.

6.   VANITY, WEIGHT AND AGE

"The eyes of the body see only form."

What is vanity? What is the ego-oriented, neurotic obsession with weight, hair, looks, and sex appeal that drives Americans to spend billions of dollars a year on products they can't afford and don't really need, and young women to fall into dangerous disease patterns in their efforts to be thin? These things are inevitable results of a cultural orientation that leaves out the reality of spirit. Concentration on the body as an end rather than a means in our perception, breeds fear. Fear that we're not good enough or attractive enough. Fear that they won't like us. Fear that we'll lose out in life. There is no way to escape this painful maelstrom without replacing body identification with the memory that we aren't bodies at all, that who we are is the love inside us, and it is that love alone that determines our value. When our minds are filled with light, there is no room for darkness. When we understand who and what we really are, there is no room for pain and confusion.

When I was in my twenties, I had a problem with weight—not enough of a problem to be called fat, but enough to keep me miserable. There was a problematic ten to fifteen pounds that I could never shake. Anytime I went on a diet, I ended up gaining weight. This makes sense psychologically, because if someone tells us not to think about the Eiffel Tower, we'll think about it all the time. Telling myself not to think about food only made me more obsessed about it. Deprivation is a lousy way to lose weight. I used to pray about my problem and would receive the following guidance: "Eat anything you want." That sounded thoroughly insane to me. "But if I tell myself to do that," I thought, "then I'll start eating and I'll never stop." To that my internal guidance responded, "Yes, you will do that at first. You will have to compensate for all the pressure you've been putting on yourself for years. And then you will have had enough. Then you will return to your natural rhythms. Then you will heal."

So I let go. I met a woman who had lost a huge amount of weight and told me she had asked God to do it for her. "I didn't ask that I lose weight," she said. "I just asked that he take the monkey off my back. I didn't even care if I was fat. I told Him that if He wanted me to be fat, to make me comfortable with it. I just wanted out of this Hell."

I decided that it didn't matter how much I

weighed. I couldn't take the horror of the obsession anymore. Becoming a student of *A Course in Miracles*, I began to realize that how much I weighed didn't matter. All that mattered was love. If I could train my mind to concentrate more on that, then my problems would disappear by themselves. In the Eastern religions it is often said, "Go for God, and all that is not authentically you will drop." As I got more involved with practicing the Course, I stopped thinking so much about my weight. That was all. And one day I looked in the mirror and saw that it was gone.

What I realized was that my weight had nothing to do with my body, but with my mind. I was terrified of people, and had unconsciously manufactured a wall around myself to protect me from them. I was terrified, however, because of the love that I myself was not giving. My ego's purpose for the weight was to keep me separate, and until I gave up that purpose, I would never be able to give up the extra pounds. My subconscious mind was merely following instructions. As I began to put my energy into reaching across the wall, when I allowed the Christ to enter my mind, the wall miraculously disappeared.

After learning in the Course that the body isn't important, I couldn't understand why we should exercise or eat well. What I learned was that, when I exercise, I actually think less about my body than when I don't. When I don't exercise, I can't help thinking about heavy thighs and a thick waist. Similarly, the point of healthy food is that it supports us in existing the most lightly and energetically within the body. It is heavier, unhealthy food that ties us to the body. We take care of the body as a way of taking better care of the spirit.

As we exist today, an aging body reflects the heaviness of our pained and worried thoughts. As we begin to travel more lightly within the body, and our minds give up our constant preoccupation with body thoughts, aging becomes a different experience. I read somewhere that the Virgin Mary never aged, although she lived into her fifties. I can see why. If we were to achieve a state in which only love and caring filled our minds, and neither past nor future lay as burdens on our shoulders, aging would become a youthing process. Spiritually, we should be getting younger the older we get, since the only purpose of time is that we learn to more consistently relinquish our attachment to form. Then the body springs into perfect life, a healthy instrument and a thing of joy.

Part of our cultural neurosis has been an abhorrence of age. Like anything else, age will only transform when we have first accepted it as it is. Many of us think age is so terrible, so unappealing, so unsexy, when actually those are just thoughts we have. Walking down the street in Paris, French women in their fifties and sixties exude a mature sexuality. Here, we tend to hold the thought that women that age are "over the hill."

Let's change our minds. Let's remember that the longer we live, the more we know, and the more we know, the more beautiful we are. We can actively create a new context for the experience of aging by shifting our outlook towards older people in our society. The ego, after all, claims that a diminished body is a diminished person. We are a cold and uncaring culture in our treatment of older Americans. In China, elders are respected and revered, which is a large part of why the Chinese live so long as healthy, productive citizens. We have a thought in America that youth is better, and so it is. Not because that is an objective truth, but only because it is a thought we carry and manifest as our collective experience.

No matter what the illness or addiction or distorted physical expression, its cause is in the mind, and only there can it be healed. The greatest power we're given, says the Course, is the power to change our mind. Our physical condition does not determine our emotional condition. The experience of peace comes only from the mind. "Peace of mind," says *A Course in Miracles*, "is clearly an internal matter."

7.   *THE MEANING OF HEALING*

"Forget not that the healing of God's Son is all the world is for."

When we think of healing, we usually think of physical healing, but *A Course in Miracles* defines health as "inner peace." There are people experiencing critical illness who are at peace, and people in perfect physical health who are emotionally tortured.

In his book *Teach Only Love*, Jerry Jampolsky sets forth his principles of attitudinal healing. He teaches that peace is possible regardless of physical circumstances. In surrendering our illness to God, we surrender the experience in its entirety, knowing that anything can be used by the Holy Spirit to bring more love into our awareness.

Many people have spoken of their illnesses as a "wake-up call." That means wake up and experience life—wake up and bless each morning, wake up and appreciate friends and family. I have heard people with critical illnesses say that their lives only really began when they were diagnosed. Why is that? Because whenever we are diagnosed with a critical illness, much of our superficial personal baggage is dropped in the first five minutes. Why do I act so arrogantly? Why I am pretending to be so tough? Why am I judging so many people? Why am I not appreciating all the love and beauty that surrounds me? Why am I avoiding the simplest and most important element of my being, the love in my heart?

Dropping our illusions is a healing in itself. Within each of us there is a core—our essence, our true being. That is the place of God who is within us. Finding that essence is our return to God. It is the purpose of our lives, and even our most painful experiences can serve that purpose.

A Return to Love

Over the years, I have officiated at many funerals and memorial services. Some of the most impressive sights I have ever seen have been the grieving faces of people confronting a naked truth that cannot be denied or shoved away. When someone we love is no longer with us, our sadness opens us to new opportunities for growth. Tears can be a great softener.

I recently officiated at a funeral for a young man who had died of AIDS. He was loved deeply by his friends, and many people cried during the service. Towards the end of the funeral, several of his closest friends stood up to sing a song that they had often sung with him. Many of them could barely keep from breaking down as they sang. The pure heartbreak reflected in their faces was so stunning to see; I kept thinking as I watched, that those among them who were actors had probably never given such an honest performance.

Another time, I officiated at the funeral of a young woman who had been brutally murdered. She was married and the mother of a three-year-old baby. I will never forget the look on her husband's face as he sat listening to me in the church. I said to him, "Michael, you will never be the same, we all know that. You have two choices: You will become harder or you will become softer. You will conclude from this that no one, including God, is ever to be trusted again, or you will allow your heartbreak to so soften you—you will allow your tears to so melt the walls that surround your heart—that you will become a man of rare depth and sensitivity."

The Body 🌿 259

Then I spoke to the women in the room. "This little boy has lost his mother. This child no longer has a woman's arms around him. Do not let this go uncorrected. Commit now within your hearts to visit him, to visit his father, to take up the slack as best you can, to become women of mature substance as of this moment. Take this responsibility seriously, that in this one thing, at least, the personal growth brought on by this darkness might be a way in which it is cast out."

Oddly enough, I had to leave that funeral to go across town where I was performing a marriage ceremony. As I gave the service, I noticed a similarity between the eyes of the groom and the eyes of the young man who had just buried his wife. Of course the groom was not grieving, but joyous. What looked the same was the pure unadulterated love in his eyes, with no artificial ingredients placed on top. Just listening, and nakedness, and openness, and love.

Healing is a return to love. Illness and death are often painful lessons in how much we love, but they are lessons nonetheless. Sometimes it takes the knife that emotionally pierces our heart, to pierce the walls that lie in front of it.

One night in Los Angeles, during the meditation period following my lecture, I noticed two of my friends crying in the back of the church. They were in deep sorrow over the impending death of a mutual friend who had AIDS. It hurt me to see them in so much pain. Suffering, I've found, gives you X-ray vision into the suffering of others.

"Can't this burden be lifted?" I asked God. We'd all seen so much sorrow, so much pain and death from this disease by then. "Isn't this enough? Can't it all be over?"

What occurred to me next was striking. I was reminded of my own "dark night of the soul" almost a decade before. Hadn't I changed from my pain, in deep and ultimately positive ways? If my soul had used that experience as a path to greater awareness of myself, how did I know that these other people weren't doing the same? It isn't my task to judge—to help, in any and every way possible, yes, but not to doubt the ultimate wisdom of all things. The greatest gift we can give to a person in pain is to hold in our own minds the thought that there is a light beyond this darkness. What goes on externally is only the tip of the iceberg in any situation. The lessons, the real changes, the opportunities to grow—these are things the body's eyes can't see. They remain beneath the spiritual water line, but they are there. And they represent a much more vast picture of the soul's journey than what we can see from the perspective of our physical senses. Growth is not always about getting what we think we want. Always, it's about becoming the men and women we have the potential to be. Loving, pure, honest, clear.

A longer life is not necessarily a better life. A healthy life is not determined by physical condition. Life is merely the presence of love, and death is merely its absence. Physical death is not real death at all. We're big enough now to realize that there's life beyond the physical. As we find that life, we grow into ourselves, as sons of men and as Sons of God.

8.   DEATH AND REINCARNATION

"There is no death. The Son of God is free."

A Course in Miracles says that birth is not a beginning but a continuation, and death is not an end but a continuation. Life goes on forever. It always was and always will be. Physical incarnation is just one form that life can take.

A Course in Miracles mentions the Great Rays, a concept also found in other metaphysical teachings. The Great Rays are lines of energy that emanate from within each of us, on subtler levels than our physical senses yet perceive. Our physical senses reflect our current belief system, and as our belief system expands, so will our senses. There will come a time when we will physically perceive the Great Rays. Some people, such as those who see auras, are already beginning to. Buddha and Jesus and other enlightened masters are often pictured with halos around their heads or lines of light radiating from their hearts.

These lines of light and energy are our life force. The body is merely a temporary encasement. Because we do not yet realize this, we think that the death of the body is the death of the person. It is not. There was a time when people thought that the earth was flat, and so ships that reached the horizon were believed to have fallen off the face of the earth. There will come a time when our present perception of death will seem as quaint and ignorant and old-fashioned as that. The spirit does not die when the body dies. Physical death is like taking off a suit of clothes.

To the ego, reality is only what we can perceive physically. But many things that we know to exist cannot be seen with the naked eye—neither atoms nor protons nor viruses nor cells. Scientists are now beginning to recognize a oneness that lies beyond all perceived reality. This oneness is God, and our beingness lies within it.

Physical incarnation is a classroom experience, and souls come to the class to learn what they need to learn. It's much like tuning in to a channel on a television. Let's say we're all tuned to Channel 4. When someone dies, they're no longer on Channel 4, but that doesn't mean they're not broadcasting. They're now on channel 7 or 8. Cable systems exist regardless of whether or not we have the cable equipment with which to receive them. It is only the arrogance of the ego that would have us believe that what we can't physically perceive must not exist.

People have reported seeing a light exiting through the top of the head of a dying person. Many people have also spoken of their "near-death experiences," where the physical body is let go temporarily. I once met a young woman who had been in a major plane crash. She lost over half the blood in her body and her legs were almost completely severed. In describing her experience to me, she said, "I died and then came back. It felt seductive, very warm, like a wonderful motherly love. But I knew I had a choice. I thought of my father, and I knew my death would be unbearable for him, so I fought and came back.

"I never cry at funerals anymore," she said. I can cry for the people who are left here, but I know from my experience that the people who died are in a wonderful place."

Once the Great Rays are registered by our physical senses, the body will seem to be a mere shadow in front of our true selves. When we hear that someone has died, it will merely mean that a shadow has been removed. Death will no longer be perceived as the end of a relationship. When Jesus said, 'Death shall be the last enemy,' he meant that 'it shall be the last thing we perceive as an enemy.' The problem is not really death, but what we think death is. We will all die. Some of us will take the 9:30, and some of us will be on the 10:07, but we are all headed out. Accepting a healing of our thoughts about what that means is a cornerstone in our transformation from body to spirit orientation.

Life is like a book that never ends. Chapters close, but not the book itself. The end of one physical incarnation is like the end of a chapter, on some level setting up the beginning of another. I once heard a friend say, "My relationship with my father has only improved since his death."

A Course in Miracles says that communication does not stop with the destruction of the physical body. True communication rests on more than what is said or heard physically. When someone has died, we must speak with them differently than we did before, but in staying open to the possibility of an eternal life force, we direct our minds to develop the capacity for a transphysical conversation.

Letter-writing can help foster such communication. First we write a letter to the person who has died, and then we write another letter back, from them to us. What is the point of such exercises? They expand the mind to accept greater possibilities than the ego normally allows us to consider. People in my grief support groups have often told me that they had had a dream about someone who had died. When the "dead" person had shown up in the dream, the dreamer would say "You can't be here. You're dead." At that point, the person would say, "Oh," and the dream would end. It had been denied permission to continue.

Writing the letters, or having any other kind of conversation or experience that broadens our openness to the possibility of life beyond death, stretches our self-imposed mental boundaries. Our dreams and other emotional experiences then become freed from the bondage of our refusal to believe. Sometimes when someone has died we say, "This isn't happening. It feels unreal. I feel like they're still here." That's because they are. Although the ego voices of the world will say, "It's just your imagination," the truth is that it is death itself that is "just our imagination." The truth as God created it is that death does not exist, and deep in our hearts we know that this is true.

What about reincarnation? The following is from the chapter on reincarnation in the Teacher's Manual of the Course:

> *"In the ultimate sense, reincarnation is impossible. There is no past or future, and the idea of birth into a body has no meaning either once or many times. Reincarnation cannot, then, be true in any real sense.... If [the concept] is used to strengthen the recognition of the eternal nature of life, it is helpful indeed.... Like many other beliefs, it can be bitterly misused. At least, such misuse offers preoccupation and perhaps pride in the past. At worst, it induces inertia in the present.... There is always some risk in seeing the present in terms of the past. There is always some good in any thought which strengthens the idea that life and the body are not the same."*

Technically then, reincarnation doesn't exist in quite the way we think of it simply because there is no linear time. If we have past lives, or future lives, then they're all happening at once. Still, it's helpful to be reminded that we have a life separate from the experience of any one physical lifetime. *A Course in Miracles* has no doctrine. An advanced student of the Course may or may not believe in reincarnation. 'The only meaningful question is whether a concept is helpful.' We are told to ask our own Internal Teacher for guidance in our thinking about any idea and its use in our lives.

In the enlightened world, we will still drop the body. But death will be experienced very differently. It is written in "The Song of Prayer," an extension of *A Course in Miracles*:

> *"This is what death should be; a quiet choice, made joyfully and with a sense of peace, because the body has been kindly used to help the Son of God along the way he goes to God. We thank the body, then, for all the service it has given us. But we are thankful, too, the need is done to walk the world of limits, and to reach the Christ in hidden form and clearly seen at most in lovely flashes. Now we can behold Him without blinders, in the light that we have learned to look upon again.*
>
> *We call it death, but it is liberty. It does not come in forms that seem to be thrust down in pain upon unwilling flesh, but as a gentle welcome to release. If there has been true healing, this can be the form in which death comes when it is time to rest a while from labor gladly done and gladly ended. Now we go in peace to freer air and gen-*

*tler climate, where it is not hard to see the gifts
we gave were saved for us. For Christ is clearer
now; His vision more sustained in us; His voice,
the word of God, more certainly our own.*

*This gentle passage to a higher prayer, a kind
forgiveness of the ways of earth, can only be
received with thankfulness."*

I once read of an ancient Japanese religion that cel-
ebrated when people died, and mourned when they
were born. It was understood that birth meant the forc-
ing of an infinite spirit into a finite focus, while death
meant the release of all limits and the freedom to live
the full range of possibilities that God in His mercy
offers us.

Life is much more than the life of the body; it is an
infinite expanse of energy, a continuum of love in
countless dimensions, a psychological and spiritual
experience independent of physical form. We have been
alive forever. We will be alive forever more. But the life
of the body is an important classroom. It is our opportunity to deliver the world from Hell. "Dear God, may
your will be done, on earth as it is in Heaven."

CHAPTER 9

Heaven

"Heaven is here. There is nowhere else. Heaven is now. There is no other time."

1. THE DECISION TO BE HAPPY

"Heaven is a decision I must make."

'God's will is that we be happy' now. In asking that God's will be done, we are instructing our minds to focus on the beauty in life, to see all the reasons to celebrate instead of mourn.

Usually we figure out what we think would make us happy, and then try to make those things happen. But happiness isn't circumstance-dependent. There are people who have every reason in the world to be happy who aren't. There are people with genuine problems who are. The key to happiness is the decision to be happy.

There has been a lot of talk in the last few years about "allowing our feelings." It's an important concept, but one that can be used by the ego for its own purposes. Most of the time, when we hear someone say "feel your feelings," they mean feel the negative ones: "Feel your pain," "feel your anger," "feel your shame."

But we need support in feeling our positive feelings just as much as we need support in feeling our negative ones. It is the experience of genuine emotion of any kind that the ego resists. We need support and permission to feel our love, to feel our satisfaction and to feel our happiness.

The ego does hidden battle against happiness. I remember when I was in college, walking around with books of Russian poetry under my arm, cultivating what I felt was a sophisticated, cynical frown worthy of my intellectual prowess. I felt it indicated that I understood the human condition. Ultimately I realized that my cynicism revealed very little understanding of the human condition, because the most important facet of that condition is that we are always at choice. We can always choose to perceive things differently.

There is an old cliche, "You can see the glass half empty, or you can see it half full." You can focus on what's wrong in your life, or you can focus on what's right. But whatever you focus on, you're going to get more of. Creation is an extension of thought. Think lack, and you get lack. Think abundance, and you get more.

"But when I'm going on like everything's great, I'm not being honest with myself," I can hear the voices say. But the negative self is not our honest self; rather, it is the impostor. We need to be in touch with our negative feelings, but only in order to release them and feel the love which lies beneath them.

It's not so difficult to feel positive feelings or think positive thoughts. The problem is that we resist them. They make us feel guilty. To the ego, there is no greater crime than claiming our natural inheritance. If I'm rich, says the ego, someone else will be poor. If I become successful, someone's feelings might get hurt. Who am I to have it all? I'll be a threat and people won't like me anymore. These are some of the arguments the ego spews into our consciousness. The Course admonishes us to beware the danger of a hidden belief. A hidden belief that many of us hold is that there is something wrong with being too happy.

The ego's religious dogma hasn't helped. Suffering has been glorified. People have focused on the crucifixion more than the resurrection. But crucifixion without the resurrection is a meaningless symbol. Crucifixion is the energy pattern of fear, the manifestation of a closed heart. Resurrection is the reversal of that pattern, brought about by a shift in thought from fear to love.

Look at the crucifixion, says *A Course in Miracles*, but do not dwell upon it. "Blessed are those who have faith who cannot see," says Jesus. It's easy to have faith when things are going well. But there are times in everyone's life when we have to fly on instruments, just like a pilot making a landing in low visibility. He knows the land is there, but he can't see it. He must trust his instruments to navigate for him. And so it is with us, when things aren't what we'd like them to be. We know that life is always in process, and always on its way to greater good. We just can't see that. During those times, we rely on our spiritual radar to navigate for us. We trust there's a happy ending. By our faith, through our trust, we invoke its proof.

Resurrection is actively called forth. It represents the decision to see light in the midst of darkness. In the Talmud, the Jewish book of wisdom, the Jew is told how to behave in the midst of dark times. "During the time of the darkest night," says the Talmud, "act as if the morning has already come."

God provides the answer to every problem the moment it occurs. Time, as we've already seen, is just a thought. It is the physical reflection of our faith or faithlessness. If we think it's going to take time for a wound to heal, it will. If we accept God's will as already accomplished, we experience the healing of all wounds immediately. As cited in the Course, "Only infinite patience produces immediate results." The universe is created to support us in every way. God is constantly expressing His infinite care for us. The only problem is, we don't agree with Him. We don't love ourselves as He loves us, and so we block our experience of the miracles to which we're entitled.

The world has taught us we are less than perfect. In fact, we have been taught that it's arrogant to think we're deserving of total happiness. This is the point where we're stuck. If anything comes into our lives—love, success, happiness—which seems like it would be suited to a "deserving" person, our subconscious mind

concludes it can't possibly be for us. And so we sabotage. Few people have wronged us like we've wronged
ourselves. No one has snatched the candy away from us
like we've thrown it away from ourselves. We have been
unable to accept joy because it doesn't match who we
think we are.

In contrast to the ego's meager appraisal of our
worth, stands truth as God created it. There is no light
more bright than the light that shines within us.
Whether or not we see that light is irrelevant. It's there
because God placed it there.

It is not only our right, but in a way, our responsibility to be happy. God doesn't provide any of us with
happiness that is only meant for us alone. When God
sends us happiness, he does so in order that we might
then stand up more fully in the world on His behalf.

Happiness is a sign that we have accepted God's
will. It's a lot easier to frown than to smile. It's easy to
be cynical. In fact, it's an excuse for not helping the
world. Whenever people say to me, "Marianne, I'm so
depressed about world hunger," I say to them, "Do
you give five dollars a month to one of the organiza-
tions that feed the hungry?" The reason I ask is that I
have noticed that people who participate in the solution
to problems, don't seem to find themselves as
depressed about those problems as do people standing
on the sidelines doing nothing. Hope is born of participation in hopeful solutions. We are happy to the extent
that we choose to notice and to create the reasons for

happiness. Optimism and happiness are the results of spiritual work.

A Course in Miracles states, "Love waits on welcome, not on time." Heaven merely awaits our acceptance. It is not something we'll experience "later." "Later" is just a thought. "Be of good cheer," said Jesus "for I have overcome the world." He realized, and so can we all, that the world has no power before the power of God. It is not real. It is only an illusion. God has created love as the only reality, the only power. And so it is.

2.   *OUR CAPACITY FOR BRILLIANCE*

"You can stretch out your hand and reach to Heaven."

In the eyes of God, we're all perfect and we have unlimited capacity to express brilliantly. I say unlimited capacity rather than unlimited potential, because potential can be a dangerous concept. We can use it to tyrannize ourselves, to live in the future instead of in the present, to set ourselves up for despair by constantly measuring ourselves against what we think we could be rather than what we are. Until we're perfect masters, it is by definition impossible to live up to our potential. Our potential always remains something we're only capable of living later.

Potential is a concept that can bind us to personal powerlessness. Focus on human potential remains impotent without a focus on human capacity. Capacity is expressed in the present. It is immediate. The key to it lies not in what we have inside of us, but rather in what we are willing to own that we have inside of us. There is no point in waiting until we are perfect in what we do, or enlightened masters, or Ph.D.s in life, before opening ourselves to what we're capable of doing now. Of course, we're not as good today as we'll be tomorrow, but how will we ever get to tomorrow's promise without making some sort of move today? I remember spending years of my life so upset about the life choices I felt I had available, that I never moved. I was paralyzed by all the possibilities. I couldn't figure out which road would lead me to the fulfillment of my 'potential"; this glorious neurotic myth that lay always just in front of anything I could manifest now. So I was always too scared to move. And fear, of course, is the great betrayer of Self. The difference between those people "living their potential" and those who don't, is not the amount of potential itself, but the amount of permission they give themselves to live in the present.

We are the adult generation. We have adult bodies, adult responsibilities, and adult careers. What many of us lack is an adult context for our lives, one in which we give ourselves permission to shine, to blossom fully, to show up powerfully in the present without fearing that we're not good enough. Waiting for a powerful future is a way of making sure it never gets here. An adolescent dreams of what will be. An adult takes joy in today.

I once had a therapist who told me that my problem was that I wanted to move directly from point A to point x,y and z. She pointed out that I seemed incapable of moving from point A to point B, of putting one foot in front of another. It's much easier to dream about point Z than to actually move to point B. It's easier to practice our Oscar acceptance speech, than to get up and go to acting class.

We're often afraid to do anything unless we know we can do it extremely well. But we get to Carnegie Hall by practicing. I remember how freeing it was several years ago to read in an interview with Joan Baez that some of Bob Dylan's early songs weren't so wonderful. We have this image of genius springing fully grown out of Zeus's forehead. I once asked someone to lecture for me while I was out of town, and he answered that he felt he couldn't lecture as well as I. "Of course you can't!" I said. "I've been doing it for years! But how will you ever *get* great at it unless you start doing it?" I think the reason people don't have hobbies today as much as they did in past generations, is because we can't bear to do anything we're not fabulous at. Several years ago I started taking piano lessons again, after having played for many years as a child. Chopin, I'm not, but there was so much therapeutic value in just playing. I saw very clearly that you don't have to be a virtuoso at everything you do, in order to be a virtuoso at life. Virtuosity in life means singing out—not necessarily singing well.

Most of us feel on some level like race horses champing at the bit, pressing at the gate, hoping and praying for someone to open the door and let us run out. We feel so much pent up energy, so much locked up talent. We know in our hearts that we were born to do great things, and we have a deep-seated dread of wasting our lives. But the only person who can free us is ourselves. Most of us know that. We realize that the locked door is our own fear. But we have learned by now, that on some level our terror of moving forward is so great that it would take a miracle to free us.

The ego would have us born with great potential, and die with great potential. In between, there is ever-increasing suffering. A miracle frees us to live fully in the present, to release our power and to claim our glory. The Son of God is risen to Heaven when he releases the past, releases the future, and thus releases himself to be who he is today. 'Hell is what the ego makes of the present.' Heaven is another take on the altogether.

3.   *SPIRITUAL PRACTICE*

   "An untrained mind can accomplish nothing."

Love takes more than crystals and rainbows, it takes discipline and practice. It's not just a sweet sentiment from a Hallmark card. It is a radical commitment to a different way of being, a mental response to life that is completely at odds with the thinking of the world. Heaven is a conscious choice to defy the ego's voice. The more time we spend with the Holy Spirit, the greater our capacity is to focus on love. *A Course in Miracles* tells us that five minutes spent with Him in the morning (doing the Workbook or any other serious practice of prayer or meditation) guarantees that He will be in charge of our thought forms throughout the day. What that means is that we take responsibility for making what in Alcoholics Anonymous is called "conscious contact" with Him. Just as we go to the gym to build up our physical musculature, so we meditate and pray to build up our mental musculature. The Course says we achieve so little because we have undisciplined minds: we instinctively go into paranoid or judgmental, fearful reactions instead of loving ones. The Course says we are 'far too indulgent of mind-wandering.' Meditation disciplines the mind..

When we meditate, our brains literally emit different brain waves. We receive information at a deeper level than we do during normal waking consciousness. *A Course in Miracles* says that its Workbook is the crux of the Course, because the 'exercises train our minds to think along the lines the text sets forth. It's not *what* we think that transforms us, but *how* we think.' The principles of miracles become "mental habits" in our "problem-solving repertoire."

Spiritual growth is not about becoming more metaphysically complicated, but rather it is about growing simpler, as these very basic principles begin to permeate more and more deeply into our thought system. Meditation is time spent with God in silence and quiet listening. It is the time during which the Holy Spirit has a chance to enter into our minds and perform His divine alchemy. What changes because of this is not just what we do, but who we are.

In the Workbook of *A Course in Miracles*, which is a 365-day set of psychological exercises, we are given a very specific curriculum for relinquishing a thought system based on fear and accepting instead a thought system based on love. Each day, we are given a specific thought to focus on, eyes closed, for a specific amount of time. We're even told in the introduction that we don't have to like the exercises and we might even be hostile to them, but we should just *do* them. Our attitude doesn't affect their efficacy in any way. If I'm lifting weights at the gym, I can either love the experience or hate it, but it doesn't really matter. All that affects my body is whether or not I lift the weights. So it is with meditation. Also, as with physical exercise, the effects of meditation are cumulative. When we go to the gym and work out for an hour, we don't really see any change in our bodies at the end of the hour. If we go every day for thirty days, however, then we do see a change. So it is with meditation. And sometimes, we're not the ones who can see the change as much as others can. We might not even be aware of how much the quality of our energy, the invisible emanations of our minds, affect our environment and the people within it. But others do. And they respond accordingly.

Spiritual practice supports the development of personal power. Spiritually powerful people are not necessarily people who do so much, as they are people around whom things get done. Gandhi caused the British to leave India, but he wasn't a man who ran around a lot. Powerful forces swirled around him. President Kennedy is another example. Legislatively, he achieved relatively little, but he unleashed invisible forces within others that altered the consciousness of at least one American generation. At the highest level of our being, we don't *do* anything. We are at rest when the power of God works through us. Meditation is a profound relaxation. The ego's frantic voice, its vain imaginings, are burned away.

We all have within us a direct radio line to the voice for God. The problem is, the radio is full of static. In our quiet times we spend with God, the static melts away. We learn to hear the small still voice for God. In Heaven, that is the only voice we hear. That is why we are happy there.

4.   *SEEING THE LIGHT*

> *"Child or light, you know not that the light is in you."*

Only the light within us is real. We are not afraid of the dark within ourselves, so much as we are afraid of the light. The dark is familiar. It's what we know. "Yet neither oblivion nor hell is as unacceptable to you as Heaven." The light, the thought that we might indeed be good enough, is such a threat to the ego that it takes out its very big guns to defend against it.

Someone I know remarked to me about a mutual friend, "He has a mean-spirited soul." "No, he doesn't," I replied. "He has a mean-spirited personality. His soul is one of the brightest I've ever seen. His mean-spiritedness is simply a defense against the light. If he were to let in his light and choose to really express all his love, it would overwhelm his ego. His meanness is his armor, his protection against the light."

Our defense against light is always some form of guilt that we project onto ourselves or others. God can love us infinitely, the universe can support us unendingly, but until we agree with God's kind appraisal of us and the universe's merciful behavior, we will do everything in our power to keep the miracles we're entitled to at bay. Why the self-hatred? As we've already seen, the ego is our mind's endless need to attack itself. And how do we escape this? Through the acceptance of God's will as our own. God's will is that we be happy. God's will is that we forgive ourselves. God's will is that we find our place in Heaven now.

It is not our arrogance but our humility which teaches us that who we are is good enough, and what we have to say is valid. It is our own self-hatred that makes it difficult for us to consistently support and nurture other people, because supporting others amounts to supporting ourselves. When I speak publicly, there is a palpably different feeling between audiences who want me to win, and those who are sitting back signalling, "Oh yeah? *Show* me." The former is a context in which I am invited to shine, and the latter is one in which I am challenged to shine. Isn't life challenging enough? Is human kindness so lightweight?

When we know that love is an infinite resource—that there is enough abundance of every kind for everyone and that only what we give to others we get to keep—then we stop denigrating other people, and start blessing them instead. Several years ago I was living in a house with a teenage girl. One day I came home and she was sitting on her bed with five or six girlfriends, surrounding a poster of Christie Brinkley. As hard as it is to believe this, these girls were struggling to make a case for the fact that Christie Brinkley wasn't really all that beautiful, or if she was, she probably wasn't all that smart. I gently pointed out to them that what was really going on was that each of them wanted very much to look just like her, but were defending against it because they thought it was impossible. "It's okay for you to want to be beautiful, too." I said. "In fact, it's good, and in your own ways you can be. The way to do that is to bless her beauty, praise it, permit it to be so you can permit your own. Christie Brinkley being beautiful doesn't mean that you don't get to be. There's enough beauty to go around. It's just an idea. Anyone can have it. As you bless what she has, you multiply your chances of having it too."

A person who succeeds in any area is only creating more of a possibility for others to do the same. Holding on to the thought of finite resources is a way of holding on to hell.

We must learn to think only divine thoughts. Angels are the thoughts of God, and in Heaven, humans think like angels. Angels light the way. Angels do not begrudge anyone anything, angels do not tear down, angels do not compete, angels do not constrict their hearts, angels do not fear. That's why they sing and that's how they fly. We, of course, are only angels in disguise.

5.   *THE END OF THE WORLD*

> *"The end of the world is not its destruction, but its translation into Heaven."*

The end of the world as we know it wouldn't be such a horrible thing, if you think of all the ways in which the world is full of pain and suffering. In the "end days," we will not escape the horrors of the world through vehicles that soar into outer space, but through vehicles that soar into inner space. Those vehicles are our healed minds, guided by the Holy Spirit.

What does Heaven look like? Most of us have only had tiny glimpses, but those glimpses were enough to keep us always hoping to go back. The Course says there's an "ancient melody" we all remember, always beckoning, always calling us to return. Heaven is our home. It's where we came from. It's our natural state.

We've all had Heavenly moments on earth, usually at our mother's breast or at someone else's. There is a feeling of inner peace that comes from total relinquishment of judgment. We don't feel the need to change others, and we don't feel the need to be different than we are. We can see, for whatever reason, the total beauty of another person, and we feel that they can see the beauty in us as well.

The world sees the special relationship, whether romantic or otherwise, as the only valid context for such an experience. That is our primary neurosis, our most painful delusion. We keep looking to the body for love, but it is not there. We 'embark upon an endless search for what we cannot find'—one person, one circumstance that holds the key to Heaven. But Heaven is within us. It has nothing ultimately to do with the thoughts of someone else, and everything to do with what we choose to think ourselves, not just about one person, but about all people. So forgiveness of mankind, of everyone in every circumstance, is our ticket to Heaven, our only way home.

Our goal is God. Nothing short of that goal will bring us joy. And it is joy to which we are entitled. Although we're relatively aware of the transformative power of pain, we know very little about the transformative power of joy because we know so little about joy at all.

Talk of joy is not simplistic. No one is saying that it's easy; we're just affirming that it's our goal. As we've already seen, there is no getting to Heaven without acknowledging hell—not its ultimate reality, but its reality for us while we remain in this illusion. This illusion is very powerful indeed. *A Course in Miracles* is not proposing emotional denial and suppression of darkness as a way to light. It is a psychotherapeutic process by which darkness is brought to light—not the other way around. In the enlightened world, psychotherapy, guided by the Holy Spirit, will certainly have a place. According to the Course, "No one can escape from illusions unless he looks at them, for not looking is the way they are protected." The way to Heaven is fraught with demons on the side of the road, just as the fairy tale castle is surrounded by dragons.

A Course in Miracles says, "What is healing but the removal of all that stands in the way of knowledge? How else can one dispel illusions except by looking at them directly, without protecting them?" The work toward enlightenment often entails a painful and not very pretty arousal of the worst of which we're capable, made plain to both ourselves and others, in order that we might consciously choose to release our personal darkness. But without a commitment to light, a conscious intent to go for Heaven, we remain enamored of darkness, too tempted by its complexities.

The temptation to 'analyze darkness as a way to light' is illustrated in some traditional psychotherapeutic models. When used by the ego, psychotherapy is a tool for endless ego investigation: assignment of blame and focus on the past. When used by the Holy Spirit, it is a search for light. It is a sacred interaction in which two people together, consciously or unconsciously, invite the Holy Spirit to enter into their relationship, and to transform painful perceptions into loving knowledge. The only reason we all need therapy so much is because we've lost an essential connection to the meaning of friendship. Real relationship of any kind is a form of psychotherapy, as is true religion. The Holy Spirit's psychotherapists, professional or otherwise, ask only to accept the Atonement for themselves, that their own healed perceptions might help enlighten others.

In the world to come, couples will use psychotherapy more and more frequently, not as crisis counseling, but as maintenance procedure. There was a time when most people saw therapy as something you did only if you were "crazy." Now we see it as a valuable tool for staying sane. So it is that couples will come to see the value in a constant and consistent, formal evaluation of their thoughts and feelings as they walk two by two into the arms of God.

Just outside of Heaven's gate, there's a lot of action—all within an illusion, of course, but an illusion that must be transformed from within. The only meaning of any event within the world of form is that it stimulates within us an impulse to reach for the gate, or turn our back on Heaven. As we stand before the gate, uncertain of which way to go, impelled to love and yet so trained to fear, we need to realize the sacred responsibility that has been placed in our hands. "And so you walk toward Heaven or toward hell, but not alone." We choose for everyone, for many years to come.

The decisions we make today, individually and collectively, will determine whether the planet goes to hell or goes to Heaven. One thing, however, is sure: we are the transitional generation. The critical choices lie in our hands. Future generations will know who we were. They will think of us often. They will curse us, or they will bless us.

6.   *HEAVEN'S GATE*

"Think not the way to Heaven's gate is difficult at all."

We are poised at Heaven's gate. In our minds, we left there millions of years ago. Today we are returning home.

We are a Prodigal Son generation. We left home and now there's an excitement in the air because we're back. We did everything to violate love, of ourselves and others, before a life of wholesomeness began to attract us. That's not our shame but our strength. There are certain doors we don't have to go through because a false moralism said not to, but because we opened them already and we know they lead nowhere. Oddly enough, this gives us a kind of moral authority. We speak from experience. We've done the dark side. We're ready to move on. We're attracted to the light. When Bhagwan Shree Rajneesh was asked by his disciples, "Why does it say in Scripture, 'God loves a sinner'?" his answer was, "They tend to be more interesting people."

We're an interesting generation; we just don't see that about ourselves. When I first realized what a decisive time this is, that the decisions made on this planet in the next twenty years will determine whether or not mankind survives much longer, I was afraid for the world. The fate of the world is left up to us? Not us, I thought. Anyone but us. We're spoiled brats, morally bankrupt. But when I looked more closely, what I saw surprised me. We're not bad. We're wounded. And our wounds are simply our opportunities to heal.

Outside Heaven's gate, healing is the buzzword, and it is shaping our desires. There is a holy return in the air today, despite the pain, despite the conflicts. Enough people have taken on its mandate, consciously or unconsciously, to have already caused the feeling of a cautious excitement, a hope for Heaven. In every area, there are at least vague intimations of greater responsibilities.

Before we awaken, the 'Holy Spirit transforms our bitter dreams into happy ones.' Here are some reflections on a few happy dreams that could possibly bring the whole world a little closer to Heaven.

There has to be a mass, collective forgiveness of what went before in order for our culture to have a chance to heal itself and begin again. Some of the best and the brightest that America has to offer are dropping through the cracks because they can't shake their pasts. How sad for America that anyone who has had too much sex or drugs in their past, for instance, is too scared to enter politics for fear of being crucified for their personal histories. The important thing about our past is not what happened, but what we have done with what happened. Anything can contribute to our being a more compassionate person now, if we choose.

The meaningful question is never what we did yesterday, but what we have learned from it and are doing today. No one can counsel a recovering alcoholic like another recovering person, who has been on the road to recovery longer. No one can counsel a person in grief like someone who has grieved. No one can help with anything like someone who has been through the pain themselves.

I never had much interest in Richard Nixon until I saw him on television a few years after he left the White House. This man, I thought, has suffered complete humiliation, which he can blame on no one but himself. The only way that any person could survive such a crushing experience would be if he got on his knees and threw himself into the arms of God. Watching him on the screen, I felt that he had done just that. I saw a softness in his face that we had never seen before. *Now* this man is interesting, I said to myself. He seems to have tasted the fires of purification. Now he has more to offer us than ever. Now I would trust him to speak to me from a more genuine place.

Just outside the gate, we're never afraid to apologize. How wonderful it would be for America if we were to make amends, in our hearts and to the world, for the violation of our own most sacred principles in dealing with nations such as Vietnam. We are a great country, and like all nations, we have made our mistakes. Our greatness lies not in our military might but in our holding to sacred, internal truths. A big nation, like a big individual, admits when it has made mistakes, atones for its errors, and asks God and man for a chance to begin again. This would not make us look weak to the rest of the world. It would make us look humble and honest, two traits without which there is not greatness.

And wouldn't it be wonderful—Abraham Lincoln paved the way—if we could just make one huge, simple apology to all black Americans? "On behalf of our ancestors, we apologize for bringing you here as slaves from your native home. We recognize the pain that this terrible violation has caused generations of good people. Please forgive us. Let us begin again." And then, the least we can do is build a lasting memorial to the American slaves. White Americans have more of an internal need to do this than blacks. Afro-Americans will find it much easier to forgive us when we have asked for forgiveness. All of these things, of course, apply as well to the American Indians. Until this Atonement, there will be little room for a miraculous healing of our racial tensions.

The parades for our soldiers coming home from the Persian Gulf conflict, for me, represented in part an attempt to rectify our harsh treatment of Vietnam veterans. I just wish there were parades for our teachers, our scientists and our other national treasures.

Speaking of national treasures, children are our most important resources. For a fraction of the cost of keeping one criminal in jail for a year, we could provide a child from an underprivileged background a plethora of personal and educational opportunities that would occlude the propensity to hopeless despair. The temptation to experience drugs, delinquency and other paths to a criminal behavior would then be greatly diminished. There is no amount of money, time or energy too great to spend on our children. They are our angels, our future. In failing them, we are failing ourselves.

Just outside the gate, there is so much to do, as we allow the motivation for a transformed world to energize our souls and make manifest our convictions. We must have faith in God and faith in ourselves. Whatever He wills, He can let us know, and whatever He wants done, He can show us how to do it. In every community, there is work to be done. In every nation, there are wounds to heal. In every heart, there is the power to do it.

7.   *CHRISTMAS*

"The sign of Christmas is a star, a light in the darkness."

Christmas is a symbol of change. The meaning of Christmas is the birth of a new self, mothered by our humanness and fathered by God. Mary symbolizes the feminine within us all, who is impregnated by spirit. Her function is to say yes, I will, I receive, I will not abort this process, I accept with humility my holy function. The child born from this mystical conception is the Christ within us all.

The angels awakened Mary in the middle of the night and told her to meet them on the roof. "The middle of the night" symbolizes our darkness, our confusion, our despair. "Come onto the roof" means turn off the television, sober up, read better books, meditate, and pray. The angels are the thoughts of God. We can only hear them in a pure mental atmosphere.

Most of us have heard the angels beckon us to the rooftop already. Otherwise, we would not be reading books like this one. What happens at this point is that we are given the opportunity, the challenge, to accept God's spirit, to allow His seed into our mystical body. We shall be His safety and protection. We shall, if we agree to, allow our hearts to be a womb for the Christ child, a haven in which He can grow in fullness and prepare for earthly birth. God has chosen that His Son be born through each of us.

"There is no room here," said the innkeeper to Joseph. The "inn" is our intellect. There is little if any room there for the things of spirit. But that doesn't matter because God doesn't need it. All he needs is a little space in the manger, just a little willingness on our part in order for Him to be born on earth. There, "surrounded by animals," at one with our natural human self, we give birth to the One who rules the universe.

Shepherds in the field see the "star of Christmas" before anyone else. Shepherds are those who tend the flocks, who care, who protect and heal the children of the earth. Of course they see the sign of hope first, because they are the ones providing it. They have made of their lives fertile ground of miracles. They see the star and they follow the star. They are led to the scene of Jesus in the arms of man.

And worldly kings gather to pay homage to Him. That is because the power of the world is nothing before the 'power of innocence. The lion lies down with the lamb;' our strength is in harmony with our innocence. Our gentleness and our power are not at odds.

"Long lay the world in sin and error pining, till He appeared and the soul felt its worth," goes the Christmas carol. With the birth of Christ, not just once a year but in every moment, we allow ourselves to take on the mantle of divine Sonship, to be more than we were the moment before. We expand our self-awareness and self-identity. The 'son of man recognizes himself, and in so doing becomes the Son of God.'

And thus is the world redeemed, brought back, healed and made whole. The dream of death is over when we receive the vision of real life. Jesus in our hearts is merely the truth that is etched upon it, the "alpha and the omega," where we began and where we will return to. Even if he takes another name, even if he takes another face, He is in essence the truth of who we are. Our joined lives form the mystical body of Christ. To reclaim our place within this body is to return home. We once again find the right relationship to God, to each other, and to ourselves.

8.   EASTER

> *"The resurrection's whole compelling power lies in the fact it represents what you want to be."*

Christmas and Easter are attitudinal bookends for an enlightened worldview. With an enlightened view of Christmas, we understand that it is within our power, through God, to give birth to a divine Self. With an enlightened view of Easter, we understand that this Self is the power of the universe, before which death itself has no real power.

'Resurrection is the symbol of joy.' It is the great

"aha!"—the sign of total understanding that we are not at the effect of lovelessness, in ourselves and others. The acceptance of the resurrection is the realization of the fact that we need wait no longer to see ourselves as healed and whole.

I was sitting around talking with my girlfriend Barbara. She had recently experienced a kind of emotional triple-header: her father lay dying, she broke up with a boyfriend of seven years, and then she fell into a rather passionate liaison with a classic "Peter Pan." As we discussed the principles of resurrection and our desire for Heaven, she remarked to me, "I guess I just have to trust that God has a plan, and that things will get better when they're supposed to."

In a desire to understand the principles of *A Course in Miracles* as deeply as possible, I pointed out to her that, theoretically, since there is no time, this has nothing to do with God saving us "later." The message of resurrection is that the crucifixion never occurred, except in our minds. Christ-consciousness is not that the wounds of her father's death will heal, or that her break-up with the boyfriend would grow more comfortable in time, or that her affair would one day turn into a friendship. Christ-consciousness is the understanding that Heaven is here now: her father will not die when he dies, the change of form in the long-term relationship means absolutely nothing because the love itself is changeless, and Peter Pan's departure means nothing because the bond that unites them is eternal.

Her sadness rests not on fact, but on fiction. It is her interpretation of events, and the events themselves, that keeps her heart in chains. Heaven is the transformation of these events within her mind. The physical world then follows. 'The resurrection is our awakening from the dream, our return to right-mindedness, and thus our deliverance from Hell.'

And so she gladdened. Barbara and I laughed like little children as we allowed ourselves to scan our lives, the relationships, the circumstances, the events that make up our crosses to bear. We recognized how avidly we drill the nails into our own hands and feet, holding on to earthly interpretation of things when a choice to do otherwise would release us and make us happy. We prayed for a more consistent ability to remember that only love is real. We saw, if even for a few minutes, the needlessness of our despair. We saw in that time a glimpse of Heaven and we prayed for the ability to experience more of it.

From *A Course in Miracles*:

> "The journey to the cross should be the last 'useless journey.' Do not dwell upon it, but dismiss it as accomplished. If you can accept it as your own last useless journey, you are also free to join my resurrection. Until you do so, your life is indeed wasted. It merely re-enacts the separation, the loss of power, the futile attempts of the ego at reparation, and finally the crucifixion of the

body, or death. Such repetitions are endless until they are voluntarily given up. Do not make the pathetic error of "clinging to the old rugged cross." The only message of the crucifixion is that you can overcome the cross. Until then you are free to crucify yourself as often as you choose. This is not the gospel I intended to offer you. We have another journey to undertake, and if you will read these lessons carefully they will help prepare you to undertake it."

At the end of the Workbook, we are told "This course is a beginning, not an end." A spiritual path is not home; it is a road home. Home is within us, and every moment we are choosing to rest there, or to fight the experience. Our real terror, says the Course, is of redemption.

But there is within us One who knows the truth, who has been given by God the job of outwitting our ego, outsmarting our self-hatred. The Christ does not attack our ego; He transcends it. And 'He is within us every moment, in every circumstance. He is to our left and to our right, before us and behind us,' above us and beneath us. 'He responds fully to our slightest invitation.'

With our prayers we invite Him in, He who is already there. With prayer, we speak to God. With miracles, He responds. The endless chain of communication between loved and lover, between God and man, is the most beautiful song, the sweetest poem. It is the highest art and the most passionate love.

Dear God,

> *I give this day to you, the fruit of my labor and the desires of my heart. In your hands I place all questions, on your shoulders I place all burdens. I pray for my brothers and for myself. May we return to love. May our minds be healed. May we all be blessed. May we find our way home, from the pain to peace, from fear to love, from hell to Heaven.*
> *Thy Kingdom come, thy will be done, on earth as it is in Heaven.*
> *For Thine is the Kingdom, and the Power, and the Glory.*
> *Forever and ever.*
> *Amen.*

ENDNOTES

The following citations refer to themes espoused in the book as gleaned from *A Course in Miracles* by the Foundation for Inner Peace. The first page number is from *A Return to Love*—the last page number in the citation is from *A Course in Miracles*.

Sources with the letter "M" preceding them are from *A Course in Miracles: Manual for Teachers*. Those preceded by a "W" are taken from *A Course in Miracles: Workbook*. Those without a letter before them are from *A Course in Miracles* text.

p. 115   pp. 333–337
p. 118   p. 267f
p. 121   pp. W-159, 444, W-225
p. 125   pp. 315, M-51
p. 129   p. 343
p. 130   pp. 113f, 12
p. 134   p. 289
p. 137   pp. W-159, 367
p. 138   p. 343
p. 139   p. 22
p. 141   p. 358
p. 142   p. 145
p. 146   p. 134
p. 148   pp. 330, 32
p. 149   p. 216
p. 150   pp. 99, W-162
p. 152   p. 96
p. 154   *Psychotherapy: Purpose, Process
                and Practice*, p. 5
p. 157   pp. 593, 226
p. 162   p. 142
p. 163   pp. 263, 155
p. 165   pp. 332, 292
p. 168   pp. 373, 338
p. 169   p. 86
p. 171   pp. W-277, W-284, 511, 339
p. 173   p. W-254
p. 174   p. 522
p. 176   p. 404

Chapter 7

Chapter 8

Chapter 9

The Gift of
CHANGE

Spiritual Guidance for Living Your Best Life

MARIANNE WILLIAMSON

HarperOne
An Imprint of HarperCollins*Publishers*

For my mother

Contents

Acknowledgments

Writing a book can take over your life for a while. To those who supported me while I wrote this one, I am deeply grateful: To Bob Barnett, whose steady hand has steered my literary career for years. I profoundly appreciate his sage and invaluable counsel, both on this book and on previous ones. I consider myself extremely fortunate to have his guidance in my life.

To Steve Hanselman, for welcoming me back to Harper-Collins and for making me feel like I belong there. I hope this book is worthy of his confidence and faith.

To Mickey Maudlin, for taking as much care with my nervous author's psyche as with my words. To Terri Leonard, Claudia Boutote, Jennifer Johns, Priscilla Stuckey, Lisa Spindler, and Jim Warner, thank you for your professional excellence and generous support.

To Andrea Cagan, for being the muse who once again came through for me, using her editorial and emotional genius to get me back on the literary track.

To Nancy Peske, whose editorial assistance was completely invaluable. I cannot overestimate her talents or her help to me. Whatever is good in this book is partly because of her. Whatever is not so good, is all because of me.

To Oprah Winfrey, for creating my national audience to begin with and for continuing to support my work. She has made a world of difference in my life, as she has in the lives of millions of others. In my heart I thank her constantly.

To Chalanda Sai Ma, for her light in my veins.

To Victoria Pearman, Diane Meyer Simon, Stacie Maier, Christen Brown, Suzannah Galland, Alyse Martinelli, Bonnie Raitt, Joycelyn Thompson, and Anne Lamott—for love and sisterhood.

To Richard Cooper, for reading my book, my mind, and my heart.

To Tammy Vogsland, Casey Palmer, Matthew Albracht, Marci Stassi, Mary Holloway, Andy Stewart, Debra Carter, Kristina Roenbeck, Maryvette, Helen Sushynska, and John Marusich, for their unique contributions to my life.

To my mother, for everything she is and has been and always will be for me.

And to my darling Emma, for filling my heart with a love that so matters. You are my biggest blessing.

To all of the above, my deep and abiding thanks. Particularly this time, I could not have done it without you.

Behold, I tell you a mystery: We shall not all sleep, but we shall all be changed—in a moment, in the twinkling of an eye, at the last trumpet. For the trumpet will sound, and the dead will be raised incorruptible, and we shall be changed.

—1 Corinthians 15:51–52, NKJV

The Challenge to Grow

*T*he times in which we live are difficult, more difficult than a lot of people seem willing to admit. There is an abiding sense of collective anxiety, understandable but not always easy to talk about.

When things aren't going well for you in your personal life, perhaps you call a friend or family member or go to a therapist or support group to process your pain. Yet when your feelings of upset are based on larger social realities, it's hard to know how to talk about them and to whom. When you're afraid because you don't know where your next paycheck is going to come from, it's easy to articulate; when you're worried about whether the human race is going to survive the next century, it feels odd to mention it at lunch.

And so, I think, there is a collective depression among us, not so much dealt with as glossed over and suppressed. Each of us, as individual actors in a larger drama, carries an imprint of a larger despair. We are coping with intense amounts of chaos and fear, both personally and together. We are all being challenged, in one form or another, to recreate our lives.

On the level of everyday conversation, we conspire with each other to pretend that things are basically okay, not because we think they are but because we have no way of talking together about these deeper layers of experience. If I tell you what happened in my personal life today, I might also mention how I am feeling about it, and both are considered relevant. But when it comes to our collective experience, public dialogue allows for little discussion of events of equally personal magnitude. "We accidentally bombed a school today, and fifty children died." How do we *feel* about that? Uh-oh, we don't go there. . . .

So we continue to talk mainly about other things, at a time when the news of the day is as critical as at any time in the history of the world. Not dealing with our internal depths, we emphasize external superficialities. Reports on the horrors of war appear intermittently between reports on box office receipts for the latest blockbuster movie and a Hollywood actress's vintage Valentino. I see the same behavior in myself, as I jump from writing about things that demand I dig deep to obsessively checking my e-mails for something light and fun to distract me. It's like avoidance behavior in therapy—wanting to share the gossip but not wanting to deal with the real, more painful issues. Of course we want to avoid the pain. But by doing so, we inevitably cause more of it.

That is where we are today. We are acting out our anger and fear because we are not facing the depth of our pain. And keeping the conversation shallow seems a prerequisite for keeping the pain at bay. Those who would engage in a deeper conversation are systematically barred from the mainstream: from newspapers and magazines, from TV, and especially from political power.

One night I was watching a news broadcast about the latest videotape purportedly sent by Osama bin Laden to an Arab television network. The focus of the American news story was not on bin Laden's message but rather on the technology by which

Americans had verified the recording. His message was too horri-fying; it was as though we were trying to emotionally distance ourselves from it by having a beautiful news reporter discuss the technology of the tape rather than its contents.

Visiting a medical office one day recently, I asked my doctor, a member of the "greatest generation," how he had been feeling lately.

"Fine," he said. "How about you?"

"I'm okay," I said. "But I feel like everybody is freaking out on the inside these days; we're just not talking about it. I think the state of the world has us more on edge than we're admitting."

"I think that's true," he sighed. "Things would get bad before, but you always had a sense they would ultimately be okay. Now I don't necessarily feel that way . . ." His voice trailed off, his sadness obvious. As unhappy as he was with the state of the world, he seemed grateful I had brought it up. The fact that we go about our lives as though the survival of the world is not at stake is not the sign of a stiff upper lip. It is the sign, rather, of a society not yet able or willing to hold a conversation about its deepest pain.

We are being challenged by world events, by the tides of his-tory, to develop a more mature consciousness. Yet we cannot do that without facing what hurts. Life is not a piece of tragic fic-tion, in which at the end of the reading we all get up and go out for drinks. All of us are actors in a great unfolding drama, and until we dig deep, there will be no great performances. How each of us carries out our role will affect the end of the play.

Who we ourselves become, how we grow and change and face the challenges of our own lives, is intimately and causally con-nected to how the world will change over the next few years. For the world is a projection of our individual psyches, collected on a global screen; it is hurt or healed by every thought we think. To whatever extent I refuse to face the deeper issues that hold me back, to that extent the world will be held back. And to whatever extent I find the miraculous key to the transformation of my own life, to that extent I will help change the world. That is what this book is about: becoming the change that will change the world.

Yet we seem to have great resistance to looking at our lives, and our world, with emotional honesty. And I think we are avoiding more than pain. We are avoiding the sense of hopelessness we *think* we will feel when confronted by the enormity of the forces that obstruct us. Yet, in fact, it's when we face the darkness squarely in the eye—in ourselves and in the world—that we begin at last to see the light. And that is the alchemy of personal transformation. In the midst of the deepest, darkest night, when we feel most humbled by life, the faint shadow of our wings begins to appear. Only when we have faced the limits of what we can do, does it begin to dawn on us the limitlessness of what God can do. It is the depth of the darkness now confronting our world that will reveal to us the magic of who we truly are. We are spirit, and thus we are more than the world. When we remember that, the world itself will bow to our remembrance.

Returning to Love

In 1978 I became a student of a self-study program of spiritual psychotherapy called *A Course in Miracles;* in 1992 I wrote a book of reflections on its principles called *A Return to Love.* Claiming no monopoly whatsoever on spiritual insight, the Course is a psychological mind training based on universal spiritual themes. It teaches people how to dismantle a thought system based on fear and replace it with a thought system based on love. Its goal is attaining inner peace through practicing forgiveness. You will notice it referred to throughout this book, and many of its teachings will be reflected in what I write. When there is no specific reference for quoted material or concepts from *A Course in Miracles* (published by the Foundation for Inner Peace), I have added an asterisk to mark *A Course in Miracles* principle.

Although the Course uses traditional Christian terminology, it is not a Christian doctrine. Its terms are used in a psychological context, with universal meaning for any student of spiritual principles, regardless of whether they have a Christian orientation.

Spiritual principles do not change, but we do. As we mature through the years, we access more deeply information we had only abstractly understood before. Twenty years ago, I saw the guidance of the Course as key to changing one's personal life; today, I see its guidance as key to changing the world. More than anything else, I see how deeply the two are connected.

That is why I have written this book. It is, once more and hopefully in a deeper way, my reflections on some of the principles in *A Course in Miracles*.

Looking back at *A Return to Love* several years after writing it, I was struck by the example I used of how hard it can be to try to forgive someone. I told a story about a man who stood me up for a date to the Olympics in Los Angeles and how I struggled to work through my anger and resentment. I'm incredulous now that I ever thought someone standing me up for a date was a profound example of the ego's cruelty. In the words of Bob Seger, "Wish I didn't know now what I didn't know then." It's pretty easy to espouse forgiveness when nobody's ever really hurt you too deeply.

Life was more innocent for all of us not so long ago. Today the world seems filled with such sorrow and danger; it's not so easy anymore to simply spout off metaphysical principles and expect everything to be okay by morning. These are times that challenge our spiritual assumptions, as the power of darkness seems to be taunting us, demanding, "So where's all that love you believe in *now?*"

The answer is that love is inside us, just waiting to be unleashed. The darkness is an invitation to light, calling forth the spirit in all of us. Every problem implies a question: Are you ready to embody what you say you believe? Can you reach within yourself for enough clarity, strength, forgiveness, serenity, love, patience, and faith to turn this around? That's the spiritual meaning of every situation: not what happens to us, but what we *do* with what happens to us and who we decide to become because of what happens to us. The only real failure is the failure to grow from what we go through.

The Challenge to Grow

Whether we like it or not, life today is different in ways we never expected. The speed of change today is faster than the human psyche seems able to handle, and it's increasingly difficult to reconcile the rhythms of our personal lives with the rapidity of a twenty-four-hour news cycle.

Dramatic endings and beginnings seem more prevalent than usual. Birth, death, divorce, relocation, aging, career change—not to mention the fact that the world itself seems so irrevocably altered—all seem to hail some kind of sea change. Things we thought stable and secure seem less so, and things we thought distant possibilities have come strangely close. Many people feel right now like we're jumping out of our skin. It's gone way past uncomfortable into a haunting sense that we might be living a lie.

It's not that our relationships lack integrity or our careers don't truly jive with our deepest soul purpose. It's deeper than that—some sense that reality is like a layer of cellophane separating us from a truly magical existence. We feel some loss of meaning like a sickness we can't shake. We would love to burst out, as though we've been crouching in a small box for a long time. We ache to spread our arms and legs and backs, to throw our heads back, to laugh with glee at the feel of sunshine on our faces. We can't remember when we last did that. Or when we did, it was like taking a vacation, visiting a tourist attraction. The most marvelous things about life don't seem to make up the fabric of our normal existence anymore. Or maybe they never did. We're not sure.

Most of us live with a deep, subconscious longing for another kind of world. We sing about it, write poetry about it, watch movies about it, create myths about it. We continue to imagine it though we never quite seem to find it. Our secret desire is to penetrate the veil between the world we live in and a world of something much more real. One thing we know for sure: *this* world can't be it.

Many of us are ready to make a break for freedom, to find that better world beyond the veil and no longer buy into the absurdity of a pain-laden world that takes itself so seriously. The question is, How do we do that? If the world we live in isn't as real as it's cracked up to be, and the world we want is on the other side of the veil, then where does that leave us?

Who among us doesn't feel displaced at times, in a world that's supposedly our home yet is so completely at odds with the love in our hearts? And how do we make the world more aligned with who we are, instead of always having to struggle to align ourselves with the world?

Perhaps we are living in a magic hour, like that between night and day. I think we stand between two historic ages, when a critical mass of the human race is trying to detach from its obedience to fear-based thought systems. We want to cross over to someplace new.

When we look at the innocence of children, as they love and learn, we wonder: So why can't people remain like that? Why must babies grow up to face fear and danger? Why can't we do what it takes to protect their innocence and love? You're not the only one feeling so concerned; the world is on a self-destructive course, and our children and their children's children are pleading with us to change things.

The times in which we live call for fundamental change, not merely incremental change. Millions of people feel called in their souls to the task of global transformation, wanting to be its agents in a monumental shift from a world of fear to a world of love. We can feel the time is now, and we know we're the ones to do it. The only problem is, we don't exactly know how.

How can we best participate in a task so huge and idealistic? We sense new energy rising up everywhere, calling us toward more enlightened ways of seeing, living, thinking, and being. Books arrayed in bookstores proclaim a better way to love, to lead, to live. Seminars and support groups keep us working on ways to improve ourselves, practicing spiritual disciplines and religious rituals. We get involved in causes and politics, licking envelopes, sending money. But somehow, still, we don't seem to be hitting the sweet spot, the miraculous key to turning the world around.

We can't avoid the news, the war, the terror alerts, the fear. We're doing what we can to change the world in our own small way, but new ideas and more compassionate forces seem overwhelmed by their opposites. A few things seem to be getting better, but many things seem to be getting much worse. Just when love seemed to be the hot new topic, hatred sounded its clarion call. And the entire world could not but hear.

The Eternal Compass

The most important thing to remember during times of great change is to fix our eyes anew on the things that don't change.

Eternal things become our compass during times of rapid transition, binding us emotionally to a steady and firm course. They remind us that we, as children of God, are still at the center of divine purpose in the world. They give us the strength to make positive changes, wisdom to endure negative changes, and the capacity to become people in whose presence the world moves toward healing. Perhaps we're alive during these fast-moving times in which "the center does not hold" in order to become the center that does. I've noticed in myself that if something small and ultimately meaningless has gone wrong—I can't find the file I left on top of my desk, my daughter failed to do what I asked her to do before going to a friend's house—I can easily get rattled. But if someone calls to inform me of a serious difficulty—someone has been in an accident, or a child is in trouble—I notice a profound stillness come over me as I focus on the problem.

In the former case, my temptation to become frantic does not attract solutions, but rather hinders them. There is nothing in my personal energy that invites help from others, nor do I have the clarity to think through what I need to do next. In the latter case, however, all of my energy goes toward a higher level of problem-solving: my heart is in service to others, and my mind is focused and clear. When I am at the effect of the problem, I become part of the problem. When I am centered within myself, I become part of the solution. And that phenomenon, multiplied many times over, is the force that will save the world.

When things in the world are troubling, our need is not to join in the chaos, but to cleave to the peace within.

The only way to gain power in a world that is moving too fast is to learn to slow down. And the only way to spread one's influence wide is to learn to go deep. The world we want for ourselves and our children will not emerge from electronic speed but rather from a spiritual stillness that takes root in our souls. Then, and only then, will we create a world that reflects the heart instead of shattering it.

The time is past for tweaking this or that external circumstance. No superficial change will fix things. What we need is more than behavioral change and more than psychological change; we need nothing less than for an otherworldly light to enter our hearts and make us whole. The answer lies not in the future or in another place. No change in time or space but rather a change in our perception holds the key to a world made new. And the new world is closer than we think. We find it when we settle deeply into the hidden, more loving dimensions of any moment, allowing life to be what it wants to be and letting ourselves be who we were created to be. In what *A Course in Miracles* calls a Holy Instant, we're delivered by love from the fear that grips the world.

Each of us is connected to a cosmic umbilical cord, receiving spiritual nourishment from God each moment. Yet in slavish dedication to the dictates of a fear-based ego, we resist the elixir of divine sustenance, preferring instead to drink the poison of the world. It's so amazing that we do this, given the extraordinary pain that underlies so much of daily living. Yet the mental confusion created by our dominant thought forms is so intense, and we are so trained by the world to do fear's bidding, that deliverance comes at most in flashes. Fortunately, there are more of those flashes than usual today. While darkness seems to be all around us, an understanding of a deeper nature is emerging to light our way.

That light—a kind of contemporary, secular star of Bethlehem—indicates newness on the horizon and beckons us to follow it to the birth of something fantastic. The wonders of the external world are as nothing compared to what's happening inside us. This is not an end time but a new beginning. What is being born is a new kind of human, played out dramatically in each of our lives. Freed from the limitations of the ego, free to see and hear and touch the magic we've been missing all our lives, we're becoming at last who we really are.

Toward the end of his life, the literary giant George Bernard Shaw was asked what person in history he would most like to have been. His response was that he would most like to have been the George Bernard Shaw he might have been and never became.

A New Beginning

It is an article of faith that God always has a plan. No matter what craziness humanity has fallen into, He has always delivered us ultimately to the peace that lies beyond.

Today, we can stand in the midst of the great illusions of the world and by our very presence dispel them. As we cross the bridge to a more loving orientation—as we learn the lessons of

spiritual transformation and apply them in our personal lives—
we will become agents of change on a tremendous scale. By
learning the lessons of change, internally and externally, each of
us can participate in the great collective process in which the
people of the world, riding a wave of enlightened understanding,
see the human race on a destructive course and turn it around in
time.

To some this might feel like the period of a Great End, perhaps even at times an Armageddon, but in fact this is the time of
a Great Beginning. It is time to die to who we used to be and to
become instead who we are capable of being. That is the gift that
awaits us now: the chance to become who we really are.

And that is the miracle: the gift of change.

CHAPTER ONE

Crossing the Bridge

Life as we knew it is passing away, and something new is emerging to take its place.

All of us are playing a part in a larger transformative process, as each of us is being forced to confront whatever it is we do, or even think, that keeps love at bay. For as we block love's power to change our own lives, we block its power to change the world.

Humanity is moving forward now, though in some ways we are doing so kicking and screaming. Nature seems to be saying to all of us, "Okay, it's time. No more playing around. Become the person you were meant to be."

We would like to, but it's hard. The problems of the world today seem larger than they have ever been before, making it easy to succumb to cynicism, fear, hopelessness, and despair. Until, that is, we remember who we are.

For who we really are is a power bigger than all our problems, both personal and collective. And when we have remembered who we are, our problems—which are literally nothing other than manifestations of our forgetfulness—will disappear.

Well *that* would be a miracle, you might say. And that is precisely the point.

THIS BOOK IS ABOUT LEARNING who we are, that we might become agents of miraculous change. As we release the fear-based thoughts we've been taught to think by a frightened and frightening world, we see God's truth revealed: that who we are at our core is love itself. And miracles occur naturally as expressions of love.*

It is said in Alcoholics Anonymous that every problem comes bearing its own solution. And the gift being borne by our current challenges is the opportunity to make a large leap forward in the actualization of our own potential. The only way the world can make a quantum leap, from conflict and fear to peace and love, is if that same quantum leap occurs within us. Then and only then will we become the men and women capable of solving the problems that plague us. As we leap into the zone of our most authentic selves, we enter a realm of infinite possibility.

Until we enter that zone, we are blocked, for God cannot do for us what He cannot do through us. To say He has the solutions to our problems is to say He has a plan for the changes each of us needs to go through in order to become the people *through whom* He can bring forth those solutions. The most important factor in determining what will happen in our world is what you decide to let happen within you. Every circumstance—no matter how painful—is a gauntlet thrown down by the universe, challenging us to become who we are capable of being. Our task, for our own sakes and for the sake of the entire world, is to do so.

Yet for us to become who we most deeply want to be, we must look at who we are now—even when what we see doesn't please us. This moment is driving us to face every issue we've ever avoided facing, compelling us to get to some rock-bottom, essential truth about ourselves whether we like what we see there or not.

*An asterisk indicates quoted material or concepts from *A Course in Miracles.*

And until we make that breakthrough in ourselves, there will be no fundamental breakthrough in the world. The world we see reflects the people we've become, and if we do not like what we see in the world, we must face what we don't like within ourselves. Having done so, we will move through our personal darkness to the light that lies beyond. We will embrace the light and extend the light.

And as we change, the world will change with us.

From Fear to Love

We spend so much time on unimportant things—things with no ultimate meaning—yet for reasons no one seems to fully understand, such nonessentials stand at the center of our worldly existence. They have no connection to our souls whatsoever, yet they have attached themselves to our material functioning. Like spiritual parasites, they eat away our life force and deny us our joy. The only way to rid ourselves of their pernicious effects is to walk away . . . not from things that need to get done, but from thoughts that need to die.

Crossing the bridge to a better world begins with crossing a bridge inside our minds, from the addictive mental patterns of fear and separation, to enlightened perceptions of unity and love. We're in the habit of thinking fearfully, and it takes spiritual discipline to turn that around in a world where love is more suspect than fear.

To achieve a miraculous experience of life, we must embrace a more spiritual perspective. Otherwise, we will die one day without ever having known the real joy of living. That joy emerges from the experience of our true being—when we detach from other people's projections onto us, when we allow ourselves permission to dream our greatest dreams, when we're willing to forgive ourselves and others, when we're willing to remember that we were born with one purpose: to love and be loved.

Anyone who looks at the state of the world today is aware that something radically new is called for—in who we are as a species and in our relationship to each other and our relationship to the earth itself. Yet the psychological fundamentals that hold this dysfunctional world in place are like sacred cows: we are afraid to touch them, for fear something bad will happen to us if we do. In fact, something bad will happen to us if we do *not.* It is time to change. It is time to do what we know in our hearts we were born to do.

We are here to participate in a glorious subversion of the world's dominant, fear-based thought forms.

There are only two core emotions: love and fear. And love is to fear as light is to darkness: in the presence of one, the other disappears. As we shift our perceptions from fear to love—sometimes in cases where it's not so hard and ultimately in cases where it takes spiritual mastery to do so—we become miracle workers in the truest sense. For when our minds are surrendered to love, they are surrendered to a higher power. And from that, all miracles follow.

Miracles

A miracle is a shift in perception from fear to love. It is a divine intercession from a thought system beyond our own, rearranging our perceptions and thus rearranging our world.*

The miracle is beyond what the mortal mind can understand. God's guidance doesn't come as a blueprint that the rational mind can follow, but rather as spiritual illumination, creating psychological breakthroughs that our mortal self could never achieve. And as each of us rises to our higher selves, we begin to reach each other at higher levels as well, combining our energies in more creative ways than we might have ever thought possible. Whatever is needed, our love will provide.

We will receive the "gifts of the Holy Spirit," arising to heightened dimensions of talent and intelligence. We will meet each other in magical ways. We will right the wrongs that had seemed unrightable. We will do these things through the miracles of God.

The moment the World Trade Centers fell, the complete solution to the problem that then confronted us was created fullblown within the Mind of God. The solution is a plan involving every human being, to the extent to which we make ourselves available to Him.

Everyone we meet, every situation we find ourselves in, represents a lesson that would teach us how to take our next step forward in the actualization of our selfhood. Everything that happens is part of a mysterious educational process in which we're subconsciously drawn to the people and situations that constitute our next assignment. With every lesson we're challenged to go deeper, become wiser and more loving. And whatever our next step is, the lesson awaits us wherever we are.

His work is the work of our greater becoming, and we don't have to be somewhere else, or doing something else, in order to do it. The journey to a better world isn't along a horizontal road but rather a vertical one; it's not a trip somewhere else, but only deeper into our hearts. Right in front of you, at this very moment, there are things to do and thoughts to think that would represent a higher "possible you" than the one you are manifesting now. In any given instant, there is more love we could see and more love we could express.

And as we do, we will heal the world.

Doing Our Part

As we change our perceptions, He will change who we are. When we have become who we are supposed to be, we will know what it is we're supposed to do. And when we have remembered Who is walking with us, we will have the courage to do it.

This book is a discussion of ten basic changes that each of us can make, from viewing the world through the eyes of fear to viewing it through the eyes of love. The predominance of fear-based thoughts has poisoned our psyches, creating a toxic meltdown within our minds. We seek in ways both healthy and unhealthy to escape into the sanctuary of a deeper truth. Yet it is not enough to just seek the truth or even to know the truth. We must give ourselves permission now to live the truth as we understand it, with all its myriad implications for our lives.

The miracle worker's task is this: to consider the possibility there might be another way.* There is. And He will show it to us.

You might be thinking judgmental thoughts about someone, and in this moment you could take a deep breath and pray for God to help you forgive them. You might be thinking about something you perceive to be lacking in your life, and you could choose to rethink that, concentrating instead on how much you do have. You might be worried about your ability to perform a job and then remember that God lives within you and there's nothing He cannot do. In any given moment, the greater life is available.

When we begin to *live* the greater life—not "seek" it, so much as simply *choose to participate in it*—then and only then do we find that it's all around us, all the time. God is in our mind. Wherever we go, He's there.

SOMETIMES THERE ARE ISSUES that we push to the back of a drawer, as it were. We know they belong to us and that we'll have to deal with them someday. But we keep putting them off and putting them off, and finally something happens to bring one of them to the fore. The universe makes it exceedingly clear: here, now, we're gonna deal with this one. Whatever part of our personality remains unhealed, it is time to heal it now. It might be a relationship issue, an addiction issue, a financial issue, something with our kids, or whatever. The form of the weakness is not what matters: What matters is that until we deal with it, we are limiting our availability for use in God's plan.

This is an all-hands-on-deck kind of moment on earth. It's not okay to be stuck in the smallness of our narcissism when our greatness is so needed. It is time for each of us to face once and for all whatever demons have kept us chained to our neuroses and pain; to stand up for our better selves as a way of standing up for God; and to take our places in God's plan for the salvation of the world.

This is an exciting time and a critical one. It's not a time to be a lone ranger. It is a time, despite whatever our pain or heartbreak, to reach deep into ourselves and humbly toward each other. For there we will find God, and in God there is every answer we are looking for, every solution we so desperately seek, and every joy we might have come to think was gone and gone forever. This is the time, and we are the ones.

And why are we not already functioning at a higher level of spiritual mastery? What holds many of us back is not spiritual ignorance but rather spiritual laziness. We *know* many of the principles of higher consciousness; we're just too mentally and emotionally undisciplined to apply them universally. We apply forgiveness where it's easy, faith where it seems to make rational sense, and love where it's convenient. We're serious, but not really. . . .

Now contrast that with the advocates of hate.

Do terrorists hate us just *some of the time?* Do they have a *casual commitment to their cause?* Do they take less than seriously the goal of full manifestation of *their* worldview? The only way we will triumph over hate is to become as deeply committed to love as some people are committed to hate, as deeply devoted to expressing our love as some people are devoted to expressing their hate, and as firm in our conviction that love is *our* mission as some are that hate is theirs.

A lot of us are already spiritual students; the problem is, we're "C" students. And that's what needs to change.

Living in the Light

Every moment we've deviated from our highest—bringing forth pain for ourselves and others—is a moment we deviated from love. It was a moment where we simply didn't know how to remain righteous and still get our needs met. We fall into ancient patterns of ego and fear, for no other reason than that we are subconsciously programmed to do so. And when all other efforts fail, we are likely, if only in the secret chamber of our heart, to ask God if He would please help us. And He will. He will reprogram us at the deepest levels. And then, through the alchemy of the divine curriculum, we'll meet the people we're supposed to meet, in order to go through the situations we need to go through, in order to learn the lessons that will transform us from beings of fear to beings of love. We will be given every opportunity to learn through joy, and when we deny ourselves that, we will learn through pain. But we will learn.

It isn't easy, giving birth to our spiritual potential. Spiritual labor can be very arduous—one holy instant at a time when we give it up, surrender, soften, don't care if we're right, forego our impatience, detach from the opinions and prizes of the world, and rest in the arms of God. But the end result is the love of our lives. We begin to feel more comfortable within ourselves, less laden by the chronic angst that marks the times in which we live. We begin to feel free at last of past hurts, able to fearlessly love again. We begin to exhibit the maturity and strength that were lacking in our personalities before. A new energy emanates from who we are, and others can see it too.

All of this is very simple, which is not to say it's easy. The spiritual path is not a matter of growing more metaphysically complicated; it's a process where we actually grow simpler and simpler, as we apply certain basic principles to everything we go through. We don't learn love, which is already etched on our hearts; we do, however, begin to unlearn fear.* And with every change we make from blame to blessing, we pierce the veil of illusion that separates us from the world we want.

Not every lesson will feel like fun while it's happening, and at times we will resist growth fiercely. But as long as we remain open to miracles—then we will forge ahead into a new realm of being, where love has erased the patterns of fear that have sabotaged us in the past, lifting us to unimaginable heights. Every situation comes bearing a gift: a chance to become who we really want to be and to live the lives we really want to live.

We will inhabit the world we choose to see, and that is why it is so important that we never lose sight of love. As we read about war, let's not forget the beauty of a sunset. When we think about the state of the world, let's not forget how many people fell in love today. God never loses His enthusiasm for life, and neither should we. Beneath the surface of worldly happenings, people continue to smile at each other and mean it, have babies, heal, create art, forgive each other, become more enlightened, laugh, grow wise, and love in spite of it all. In a world that seems split in two between fear and love, our greatest power lies in sharpening our own focus. Some things in the world today are very, very dark; what the world needs now is more people who are working for the light.

Seeing the light and then living in the light, we will ultimately become masters at the power it bestows.

Choosing a New Way

In the words of John Lennon, "You may say I'm a dreamer, but I'm not the only one." Dreamers must encourage each other today, as one of the ways our dreaming is suppressed is by making us think we're the only ones dreaming.

Suggesting anything close to the idea that love might actually be the Answer, we're swatted down like a fly by our contemporary thought police. We're told how naïve we are, how silly we're being, how unsophisticated our analysis of the world situation is. "She's a nut! She's New Age! He's a moonbeam!" Yeah, right. But those who build weapons systems to the tune of hundreds of billions of dollars a year and don't see a fundamental problem with that are *sane?* Those who propose building new and better nuclear bombs as the solution to global conflict are *sane?* Those who play with war like it's a little boy's new set of Legos are *sane?* The world has become like something out of Alice in Wonderland: the sane seem insane, and the insane seem sane. The entire world is completely upside down. But the good news is how many people know this; we've just been afraid to say it because we thought we were the only ones thinking it.

And we are not. A new commitment to love is rising up from the depths of our humanity, and its power is changing us on fundamental levels. Our mind has been opened to a liberating truth, and we feel this truth like an alchemical substance that bathes our cells and transforms our thinking. Though science couldn't necessarily register the change, we can feel that we're not the same. We have devoted our lives to a radical possibility: that love casts out all fear.

Externally, we don't really change. We still look the same; dress the same, play the game as the world defines it. But something has shifted in the way we see things. We sense another reality beyond the veil. The world we see is not deep enough to sustain us; we know that now and we stop pretending that it ever will be.* We are developing the eyes to see beyond the veil, and with that vision we will invoke a new world.

Every morning as we wake up, we can bless the world. We can pray to be servants today to something holy and true. We can take a deep breath and surrender ourselves to God's plan for our lives. And when we do, we will experience miracles.

What's most significant is this: *we are depressed if we do not.* For working miracles is the calling of our souls. We are literally dying to be born into the next stage of our spiritual development. The world's fear is old and dying away, and that's why it's so angry. Love has scarcely taken its first breath on this earth, and that's why it's so tender. But the meek shall inherit the earth for one reason only: their strength will literally take the place over.* Who we were is not as important as we thought, and who we're becoming is simply out of this world.

CHAPTER TWO

From *Forgetting Who We Are* to *Remembering Who We Are*

*T*o change our lives for the better, the first thing we have to do is stop projecting our ego-based sub-selves all over the place. Leading with Me the depressed, Me the insecure, Me the angry, and Me the frightened is not exactly the psychological equivalent of putting your best foot forward.

Yet these psychic splinters, as it were, are what we *do* lead with until they're subsumed into the grandeur of our true selves. Depression, insecurity, anger, and fear are not eradicated just because we have the right clothes, enough money, or the right credentials. They can be camouflaged, but only temporarily. People will almost telepathically pick up the truth of our deeper feelings and subconsciously reflect them back to us. All of us are involved in this constant interactive process, every moment, no matter what.

The only way we'll have *whole* lives is if we dwell within the *wholeness* of our true selves. And we are whole when we are one with God. The word *holy* refers to our connection to Him, and outside that connection we are dissociated from our own essence. Wouldn't it be weird to be one of Queen Elizabeth's children but somehow not know it? Wouldn't we be missing out on a pretty significant aspect of our identity? Magnify that geometrically in terms of psychological effect, and you have a sense of how bizarre it is that we've forgotten our Father is in heaven.

According to *A Course in Miracles*, what we have is an "authorship" problem.* Not recognizing our divine source, we express ourselves as creations of the world rather than as creations of spirit. The world has imprinted upon our psyches its brokenness and pain. And there is no point in trying to heal that pain until we heal our misplaced sense of heritage. We are not children of the world; we are children of God. We don't have to allow the false input of a weary world to affect us as it does.

Confusion about our divine heritage translates into confusion about ourselves: not understanding who we are or where we come from, we find it hard to understand who we are now or where we are now. And so we lack spiritual stability. In the absence of the sense of a divine creator, the mind assumes that we're our own creator and thus our own God. If God isn't the big cheese, then *I* must be the big cheese! And that thought—that we're it, we're the greatest—is not merely narcissism. It's a psychosis that permeates the human condition.

In remembering the truth of where we came from, we become more open to the truth of who we are.

The Great Awakening

In the Bible, it says Adam fell asleep—and nowhere does it say that he woke up.* It's as though the human race has been asleep for ages, not metaphorically but in a certain way literally. In our sleep, we have begun to dream. And some of our dreams have turned into nightmares.

Suffering is a nightmare. Addiction is a nightmare. Violence is a nightmare. Starvation is a nightmare. War is a nightmare. And the way we will change the world from being a place where these things happen to a place where they no longer do is not through what we *do* in a traditional sense, but because we wake up from the living nightmare in which they occur. We have been asleep without knowing it, taking part in a great forgetting—of who we are, what our power is, where we come from, and what we truly need.

But a great awakening is on the horizon, stirring like a new dawn in each of us. It's no accident that enlightened masters are called the "awakened ones." And now a species that has been asleep too long is on the verge of a mass awakening.

Resistance to this awakening, a lure to sleep, the false pleasures of numbness, are all real in our experience, but they are not as powerful as they appear to be. We are one with the Mind that thought us up, and nothing we make up separately has any meaning whatsoever.* When we remember we are one with our Source, we'll wake up to our power and our nightmares will disappear.

Ego versus Holiness

One of the exercises in the workbook of *A Course in Miracles* reads, "Love, which created me, is what I am." That statement amounts to a radical and counterintuitive evaluation of our true nature—for if I'm so good, then who is this person who keeps making mistakes, self-sabotaging, and repeating neurotic patterns?

That person is our fear-based ego. The word *ego* here means what it meant to the ancient Greeks: a small and separated self.

When we identify with the ego, it's like looking at a hangnail and thinking, "That's who I am." The ego is an impostor self, masquerading as who we really are yet in reality the embodiment of our own self-hatred. It is the power of our own minds turned against us, pretending to be our champion yet in reality undermining all our hopes and dreams. The ego is a delusional splinter that has cut itself off from our larger spiritual reality. It sets up a parallel mental kingdom in which it sees itself as different and special, always justified in keeping the rest of the world at bay. Seeing ourselves as separate, we subconsciously attract and interpret circumstances that seem to bear out that belief. That delusional kingdom is hell on earth.

When we remember who we are, when we stand firm in the light of our own true being as children of God, then the ego begins, however gradually, to recede. Darkness cannot stand when we truly embrace the light—when we consciously foster it and devote ourselves to it. That is why recognizing who we are—that we are love, that we are as God created us—is the most important thing we can do in any instant. Love is our spiritual reality, untarnished by anything that has happened in the material world.

When we forget this, thoughts of at least subtle attack and defense become a mental backdrop to our entire existence. The ego is "suspicious at best and vicious at worst."* And we should not underestimate its vengeance.* If we wish a genuine healing of our hearts—not just fixing things, not just bandaging the broken aorta of the spirit—we must question the ego's most fundamental assumptions. For only when we reject the ego's account of who we are, can we begin to discover who we *really* are.

And who we really are, is holy.

Our holiness is both the opposite of and the antidote to the ego. It is a state of being in which we have reconnected with our

Source, remembering that in fact we never left. We were created by God in a state of holiness, we were born onto the earth in a state of holiness, and we will return to this state upon our death. All of us, however, in between our infancy and death, fall asleep to our true nature and experience the hell of our self-imposed separation from God. Remembering our connection to our Source awakens us and frees us from the nightmares we create. In any Holy Instant, the ego is made null and void.

Holiness is not simply a theological construct, applicable to saints and enlightened masters but not to you and me. Keeping such a concept on a high altar, away from practical application, is simply an ego ploy to keep it at bay. To say that we are holy is not symbolic; it is to say that we are extensions of the Mind of God, and as such, our true nature is divine. When we stop to actually consider that we are children of God—not just children of this world—we begin to realize what spiritual wealth we have inherited. And it is ours to use, to cast out all darkness from ourselves and the world around us.

Through prayer we can work miracles in our lives. We have so much more power than we are using yet—to heal disease, repair relationships, reconcile nations, protect our cities, and transform our world. As long as we think that only "others" are holy, then only "others" will seem to carry miraculous authority. Yet it isn't true. In fact, all of us are holy, for all of us were created by God. As we open our hearts to Him, and to each other, our minds become conduits of the miraculous. Any and all of us can pray for miracles, and He hears any and all of us when we do.

When we have freed the inner resources of compassion that lie trapped within the maze of the ego mind, there will be an explosion of miracles that completely transforms our selves and our world. We will become reborn in spirit, free to express the creativity and passion that lie within us in a way that we never have before.

Few mortals have even scratched the surface of the potential genius we all possess and will one day realize. The great enlightened masters, from Buddha to Moses to Jesus, attained such alignment with spirit that the world around them was never again the same. They are elder brothers who demonstrated our potential. They showed us what each of us can one day become.

As the mind is permeated by the realization of the awesome power that lies within us, and as we allow ourselves to embrace the principles of higher awareness, the ego in time takes a backseat to higher truth. It cannot stand before a mind that has begun to awaken to its true reality. Eventually, accumulated spiritual knowledge pays off, and a larger life begins to emerge.

Infinite Possibilities

When I was young I didn't need a wristwatch, for at any time of day or night, you could ask me what time it was and I could tell you exactly. But something happened in my early twenties: it occurred to me that I should not be able to do that, and that it was weird that I could. And so, almost as soon as I thought that, I no longer could.

What happened to me is what happens to all of us: we are subtly and insidiously convinced that our natural powers do not exist. We become slaves to a worldview in which our human powers are diminished, seen as secondary to the astonishing powers of science, technology, and other false gods of the external planes. Modern progress seems to overrule our souls, leaving us bereft within a meaningless universe. There is no real God here, except the god of endless want.

We are trained, within this world, to see ourselves as the ego defines us. According to the ego's dictates, we are small and powerless, surrounded by an infinitely gargantuan and powerful universe. We are here but for a minute before we grow old and suffer and die. We are taught to identify with our guilt more than our innocence, and then we feel haunted by mistakes we feel will dominate the rest of our lives; we are taught to blame others more than to forgive them, and then we get stuck in feelings of victimization; we are taught that we are separate from others, and then we fall prey to grandiosity and insensitivity. We are taught that grades, credentials, past influences, mistakes, marriages, divorces, degrees, résumés, money, parents, children, or houses—whatever label or identity someone wants to stick onto us—are our essence. As a consequence, we forget who we really are.

This forgetfulness is the source of all evil, for it leaves us in personal darkness, confused about our heritage, our power, and our purpose. The mind cannot serve two masters, and when we forget the true one, we falsely bow before the other. When we mentally identify with the realm of the body, we see scarcity and death. When we mentally identify with the realm of the spirit, we see endless love, unlimited possibility, and the oneness of all things.

Look at the spokes on a bicycle wheel. At the rim, each spoke is separated from all the others. At the hub, each spoke is one with all the others. Each of us is like one of those spokes, connected with all others at the center, at our spiritual hub. Knowing ourselves as spirit is to know ourselves as one with each other, which is the esoteric meaning of the line in the Bible that "there is only one begotten Son." And that is why the Christ Mind, by whatever name we call it, is our salvation. It is a point of divine remembrance, saving us from the mistakes we make when we forget we are one with others. Spiritual renewal is the salvation of the world, because once we realize that what we do to others we are literally doing to ourselves, our thoughts and behavior simply change. To harm others, to refuse compassion, ultimately becomes unthinkable.

The Spiritual Basis of Self-Esteem

I have learned, when my life has been most painful, that the me who can be hurt is not the real me. The woman in me, the professional in me, the writer in me, the teacher in me—what do they all mean? Are they not but bricks in a spiritual prison, seeking to circumscribe my life, when in fact a life cannot be circumscribed? What difference does it make if someone betrays me when my real self, my spirit, cannot be betrayed? Is not an insult an opportunity for me to look at the part of myself that can be insulted and say, "Ha, you're not even really me"? Is not the true self beyond sickness? Then who is it that gets sick? Is not the true self unlimited? Then who is it that can be imprisoned? Is not the true self eternal? Then who is it that dies?

That is the question: who *are* we, really? For if we think we are only small and separate, mortal beings, then the world we create will reflect that belief. We will live in a world of separation and suffering and death. Yet when we change our sense of who we are—when we realize we are boundless, unified with all life—then the human experience as we know it transforms. The one exercise repeated in the workbook of *A Course in Miracles* states the following: "I am as God created me." In some essential way we still *are* who we were at the moment of our creation, and all problems derive from our forgetting that.

If you are as God created you, then no mistakes you've ever made or anyone's judgments or negative opinions about you can in any way determine who you are or change your value.* In the Holy Instant, we can remember our divine essence and choose to express it. And whatever we express will be reflected back to us. The universe is always ready to give us new beginnings that reflect our innocence, but we are not always ready to receive them. The sun can dawn, but we don't see it if the drapes are closed. No matter how much God loves us, we don't feel it if we don't believe it. As long as we think that we are less than God's perfect creation, then the experiences we attract to ourselves will be less than God's perfect creation. As we believe, so shall it seem to be.

Your value is inestimable because you are a child of God.* If you ever find yourself thinking, "I am such a loser. Time and time again I try, and I always fail," stop right there. Erase the tape by recording a new one. Say strongly to yourself, silently or verbally, "I'm the coolest person in the world because God creates only perfection. I recognize my inestimable value regardless of my mistakes, for which I ask forgiveness. I am God's creation, and in this moment I ask the universe to reflect back to me the greatness of God that is within me." (Let whoever needs to laugh at that, laugh. What kind of world are *they* creating?)

All the children of God are special, and none of the children of God are special.* You're not better than anyone else, but neither are you worse than anyone else. All of us have special gifts, all of us are born to shine in one way or another, and all of us are innocent in the eyes of God. Look at the children in kindergartens: they're all gorgeous and magnificent, and so are we.

It's not arrogant to believe that you're infinitely creative, brilliant, and potentially perfect through the grace of God. In fact, it would be arrogant to think otherwise because what God has created cannot possibly be less than perfect.* That fact applies to you and it applies to everyone. It is not arrogant, but humble, to accept God's gifts and allow them to be expressed through you.

Yet to the ego, that is not humility but arrogance, and you deserve a strong comeuppance for daring to believe in yourself.

Supporting Each Other's Greatness

We live in a world where judgments are made quickly and easily. Lies are told about people and printed by an irresponsible press; anyone can say whatever they want on their Web site and appear credible. People tear down others' reputations and assassinate people's character like it's a sport.

I've had a lot of judgment thrown my way since my public career began. For whatever reason—my womanhood, my convictions, my basic brashness—some have seemed to feel it was their duty to rain on my parade. Yet I've learned that you don't serve the world by taking on its judgments, hanging your head in shame, and saying, "Yeah, you must be right. I must be bad." Take responsibility for your part in your own disasters, yes—but take on every projection of guilt from every unhealed person? No! For whatever reason people may need to project their own anger and guilt on you, you don't have to accept it if it's not yours.

In some environments we receive basic support: "Go, girl! Fly!" And in others we get, "Who the hell do you think you are, trying to fly? Get down here, or we will force you down!" When we recognize the vengeance of the ego—how much it detests the spirit of life and love—we more easily avoid personalizing its vicious attacks. And there's learning in anything we go through. Both the challenge and the growth potential that comes from having had others judge you harshly is that it makes you have to decide for yourself what your self-esteem is based on: other people's estimation or God's.

The thinking of God is a hundred and eighty degrees away from the thinking of the world,* and one of the many areas where we have things completely upside down is in the area of arrogance and humility.* We never should apologize for seeking to actualize the greatness of God that lives in all of us. And those who refuse to support others in manifesting their dreams are only withholding support from themselves. Whatever I refuse to celebrate in your life, I will not be able to draw into mine. My thoughts about you are inseparable from my thoughts about myself. If I won't give you permission to shine, I can't give myself permission to shine either.

Today, living out our greatness takes on an urgency beyond fulfilling our individual dreams. Bringing forth our greatness is critical to the survival of the species; only if you get to live out your potential and I get to live out mine will the world be able to live out its own. Since limited thinking produces limited results, supporting others in believing in themselves helps to move the entire world forward. And becoming who we're capable of being—regardless of other people's opinions of us—is part of our responsibility both to ourselves and to God.

Unless we're supporting the emergence of greatness in the people around us, we're not doing our full part to help heal the world. A supportive smile, an e-mail, the smallest gesture can make the difference in helping another person believe in himself or herself. From a material perspective, what we give away we lose. But from a spiritual perspective, only what we give away do we get to keep.* When we're more generous with our support for others, the universe itself shows more support for us.

Surrender to Our Brighter Nature

Often we fail to develop an aspect of ourselves simply because no one modeled it for us. If a parent demonstrated "success" or "elegance," then we might have moved toward actualizing those things. But if no such model was present, either in the family or in the culture, then we simply didn't build the psychological track for that train. God, however, has built His own.

The psyche is like a giant computer with an infinite number of files. Imagine a folder called "God's Will," and inside that folder there are various files: Me the strong, Me the self-confident, Me the compassionate, Me the forgiving, etc. Everything that is God's Love is present as a file we are free to download. And none of God's files can be deleted.

Yet most of us have created some files that *should* be deleted. Me the arrogant, Me the sarcastic, Me the judgmental, and Me the cynical are all examples. They all belong in a folder called "Ego"; imagine Jesus sitting at your computer, highlighting that folder and hitting the "delete" key.

Me the angry or Me the arrogant is Nothing that has grown to seem like Something. It is part of the illusion of the world. It would be easy, however, to convince both ourselves and others that that is who we are, if we behave that way. And even if we *don't* act that way, as long as the negative file exists it acts like a seeping mental poison and has the capacity to hold us back.

Another set of imagery that reveals the truth of our eternal nature lies in fairy tales. The wicked stepmother is our Ego, and she wants to kill Snow White, who is the innocent spirit of love within us. She isn't able to, however, because what God created cannot be destroyed. What she *can* do is put Snow White into a deep sleep. It is only the kiss of the Prince—unconditional love—that awakens her.

If the prince had not kissed Snow White—if instead he had sniped at her, "What the hell are you doing, still sleeping!?!"—then she would not have awoken. It is not those who judge and condemn us, but rather those who bless and forgive us, who awaken us from our lower nature and return us to our better selves.

Someone once told me when my daughter was very little that it would always be best, when possible, to communicate with "Do this" rather than "Don't do that." I think that was some of the best parenting advice I ever received; you can see the damage done to people who are always being responded to in the negative. In their book called *Magical Parent/Magical Child*, Michael Mendozza and Joseph Chilton Pierce explain that the nature of the emotional bond between parent and child is more important than the specific information we impart to them. The tenor of our communication is as important as what we say. Our mission is to affirm the essential goodness in people even when they've made mistakes.*

I know that for me, someone constantly telling me I'm not okay is hardly what helps me improve. There is a magical power in relating to the good in people. I read in an interview where the actress Uma Thurman, daughter of renowned Buddhist philosopher Robert Thurman, said, "I guess I've surrendered to my brighter nature." She was taught well, I assume, that there *is* such a nature. The role of the parent is to see it in the child and reflect it back to her. And that nature exists in all of us.

That is a very different psychological approach to change than is normally associated with the Western mind. Usually, we think of our "negative" qualities as something we have to "get rid of." And from that comes all manner of dysfunctional parenting systems, educational systems, justice systems, etc. Imagine what the world would be if we looked at each other and thought, "I *know* there's something wonderful in there!"

In fact, our need is to *claim* and *cleave* to our spiritual potential, no matter whether it has yet been activated within our personality. That ultimate potential is our "Buddha nature" and the "Christ." To "accept Christ" is to accept that God's love is in us and in everyone. An eternal light is within us because God put it there, and invoking what we like is far more powerful than trying to destroy what we don't like. In the presence of our light, our darkness disappears.

Actors embody a character by finding its life force within their own. It is not so much another person, as it is another dimension of their own selfhood that the great actor inhabits. And most of us—whether we are actors or not—have dimensions of selfhood unexplored for no other reason than that we simply haven't chosen to explore them.

All of us can sing, though only a few of us are actually singers. All of us can paint, though only a few of us are actually painters. And all of us are actors, although usually we pretend we aren't.

In AA, it's said that it's easier to act yourself into a new way of thinking than it is to think yourself into a new way of acting. Just as children learn from playing, so do adults when we allow ourselves to. We vastly underestimate the ability of our subconscious mind to support us in creating change. "Fake it till you make it" is often good advice. When little girls play "house" or little boys play Spiderman, they are following a subconscious strategy of personality development, using their imaginations to prepare for new realms of being. And we need never stop doing this, unless we choose to.

Practice kindness, and you start to become kind. Practice discipline, and you start to become disciplined. Practice forgiveness, and you start to become forgiving. Practice charity, and you start to become charitable. Practice gentleness, and you start to become gentle.

It doesn't *matter* whether you're in the mood to be gracious to the bus driver today; do it anyway—and watch how it begins to affect your mood. Just push the button of the self you wish to be, and the file appears. It was already there, after all, just waiting to be downloaded. We become gracious when we *decide* to be gracious. We have the power to generate as well as react to feelings; to hone our personalities as we travel through life. In the words of George Eliot, "It is never too late to be what you might have been." It is never too late to become who we really are.

CHAPTER THREE

From *Negative Thinking* to *Positive Love*

A friend once told me that I'm a "sufferer." I didn't know what he meant, and at the same time I knew exactly what he meant. Things could be so good, and then I would find something really stupid to get upset about. I was simply in the emotional habit of focusing on the negative. I had yet to learn that to a very large extent, we are responsible for our own happiness. According to *A Course in Miracles,* happiness is a decision we must make. And who among us hasn't made decisions that were bound to make us suffer?

In any given moment, it's our focus that determines our emotional reality. There is rarely going to be a moment in your life when everything you look at, or think about, is absolutely perfect in your eyes. But perfection is a point of view; what becomes perfect is our ability to scan an environment and focus on it in the most helpful, loving, positive way.

There are always things to be happy about, and there are always things to be sad about. The bridge to a happier life is more an emotional decision than a change in circumstance. Life is like a piece of wet clay, and every thought we think gives it shape. A happy life can have sad days, but when you've mastered the fundamentals of a basically happy worldview, you attract more situations that prove your worldview correct.

And what could be a happier worldview than that love is real and nothing else exists?*

The trick, of course, is that it's hard to stay loving in a loveless world. And yet, with God, it's possible. When we spend more time working to view life through loving eyes, and less time trying to figure out why we're unhappy to begin with, then our lives transform much faster. The ego loves to foster the delusion that we're powerless before our suffering. For some people that is clearly true; but for most of us, that attitude is a self-defeating game we play, guaranteed to keep happiness at a distance, an always and forever "maybe someday."

Our capacity to change our minds is the greatest gift that God has given us, and it is also the most powerful.* He is present within us, in any moment, to help us return our minds to love.

We can always look at a situation and take a moment to focus on how blessed and grateful we are for the parts of it that are good. We can always invite the spirit of God to overshadow our thoughts, to lift them up to divine right order, to deliver us from the grip of the ego, and to turn us into who He would have us be. Every moment, we can invite Him to enter and purify our thoughts. And having done so, we will begin to see miracles. Some of them will seem small at first, but in time we will notice a basic shift in the tenor of our lives.

IT SEEMS TO ME THAT the key to happiness lies in getting over yourself. The happiest times of my life have been when I was more involved in something I was doing for others than in something I was doing for myself. For any perception that focuses only on our separate needs will ultimately breed fear, and any perception that focuses on our oneness with others breeds peace. Many people struggle and fail to find peace within themselves because they don't really realize who their "self" is. That is why the ego is so dangerous: it would have us believe that we are separate, when in fact we're not. We can't have inner peace unless we feel complete within ourselves, and we can't feel complete outside our connection with other people.

You cannot find yourself by only looking to yourself, because in essence *that is not where you are*. The real you is an expanded self, literally one with the entire world. And so we find ourselves in relationship to the whole. We cannot be happy unless we are wishing everyone the same.

One day I was indulging some ego-based concerns about my life, worried that this or that wasn't happening; I remember I was specifically worried I wasn't achieving enough in my career. The conversation in my head was all about me (mistake number one) and focused on what I perceived to be lacking (mistake number two). I did realize my thinking wasn't miracle-minded, and finally I told myself to snap out of it.

I was packing to leave a hotel room at the time, and shortly afterwards the bellman arrived to retrieve my bags. I started asking him about his life. Questioning others about their lives rather than rambling on about our own is a surefire way to direct our minds away from the ego. I asked him what time he came to work each morning, what else he did with his life, and so on.

And then he said to me, "Excuse me, are you Marianne Williamson?" He proceeded to tell me that he and his wife used to attend my lectures regularly in Los Angeles, that his wife listens to my tapes every day, and about how important my work has been to them. And in so doing, he perfectly assuaged the concerns I had been focused on an hour before; his comments shifted my thinking and thus my feelings. But if I had simply stayed with my self-involved line of thought, without redirecting my mind to focus on another, then I would never have received the miracle. There would have been this person ready to offer me a healing, but I wouldn't have been available to receive it. By withholding friendship from the bellman, I would have been withholding healing from myself.

Generosity, in that sense, is an act of self-interest.* And I have seen it too many times to doubt it; as long as I remember that the love I seek can only be found as I extend my love to others, then peace comes fairly easily. It's when we forget that that all hell breaks loose. Love extended is the key to happiness; love withheld is the key to pain.

A Walk with God

I used to hear the old gospel song talking about a "closer walk with Thee," and I thought the image was sweet but quaint. Taking a walk with God is actually more than that, however, because metaphysically our "walk" means our line of thinking. To pray for a closer walk with God is to pray for help in thinking more spiritual thoughts, not because we want to be a religious goody-goody but because we don't want to sabotage our lives the way we did in the past. We are asking that our thoughts and actions be guided by God, now and always.

Being distant from God means thinking whatever we're thinking without any sacred touchstone for our perception. Since we've been trained by the thinking of the world, without God's guidance we are liable to reach instinctively for thoughts that are judgmental, blaming, or unforgiving. And thus we remain in the hell of separation from the experience of God's love.

A closer walk with God means narrowing the gap between our thoughts and God's thoughts. How many times have we done things we came later to regret, for no other reason than that at that particular moment we were not in touch with our higher selves? We were allowing a fear-based impostor self to pose as who we are, while our essential, loving self lay buried and bereft beneath the illusions of our unsatisfied lives.

The thinking of the world is like a computer virus that has invaded our system. The Holy Spirit is like an antivirus program that both protects us from false thinking and dismantles fear-based thoughts once they've entered our minds.

It takes mental discipline to retrain our minds, yet such retraining is imperative if we really want our lives to change. With every inspirational reading, time taken to meditate, or act of forgiveness or charity or love, we are shrinking the influence of fear in our lives. We can't change other people's thinking, but in fact we don't need to because all minds are joined.* All we have to do is change our *own* thinking, and as we do, the world will change with us.

We're not separate from God; we just think we are. What God creates is one with Him forever, as an idea cannot leave its source.* He is love, and He is All That Is.* Therefore, when we're not thinking with love, we're actually not thinking at all.* We're hallucinating.* And that's what this world is, in fact: a vast hallucination of the mortal mind.

We're separated from our own reality by a veil of illusion, and within that illusion we feel great fear. Imagine if God were holding your hand one moment, and the next moment you couldn't find Him. He seemed to have disappeared. Wouldn't feelings of panic set in immediately? Such is our despair.

All religions propose to cure our despair by lifting the veil of illusion. Some of them say it will lift after we die; others suggest it can be lifted while we are still on earth. From a miracle-minded perspective, the glory of God lies not just in what He will reveal to us later, but in what He can and will reveal to us now.

Let's say God has given you a tremendous gift—one you feel could be very helpful right now in the transformation of the world. Yet you don't have access to the people or circumstances that could pave the way for you to express that gift. God can arrange all kinds of things, but He will not determine your choices for you. If you do not choose to deal with the personal issues that keep you from expressing yourself at your highest, then you are choosing to block your own way. God Himself will bow before that choice, because the gift of Free Will was given to you at your creation. Yet He will move heaven and earth to help you choose again. He will find a way to offer you the chance to live a different life.

All thought extends itself into the world. If it was a thought of love, then more love is on its way out there and back around to us. If it was a thought of fear, then fear is on its way out and around, as well. We cannot interfere with what happens between Cause, which is the level of consciousness, and Effect, which is the level of the world.* God himself will not intervene between Cause and Effect, as the law was set up for our protection.* But we are always free to choose another thought, and *that* is our miracle. When cause with a little "c" (the thinking of the ego) is replaced with Cause with a big "C" (the Mind of God), the world of effects changes accordingly.

God has created the Holy Spirit as a "bridge of perception," from the outer realms of anxiety and despair to the inner realms of peace and joy.* And the Holy Spirit is always on the case, empowered by God Himself to deliver us from the ego's vain imaginings. Yet just knowing that He is there, and affirming Him with whatever name we choose, does not of itself bring us peace. That miracle occurs when we truly step back and let Him lead the way; when we disconnect from the worldly realms, if only for a moment, and sink into a place of radical availability. It's only when we are empty of—or at least unimpressed by—our own thoughts, that the Holy Spirit can fill us with His.

When we "come with empty hands unto our God,"* the Light of Truth shines away the ego, not all at once but gradually, with a cumulative effect. We become more open and forgiving, more vulnerable, and less defended—and not just with people we already know and feel safe with. If we're authentic only with people we already know, then we'll experience miracles only with people we already know! We can create a new beginning with everyone. If we allow Him to, the Holy Spirit will create a cosmic reset button, and from that point on we'll move forward with a different set of options—an *infinite* set of options. He rewires the world around us as we allow Him to rewire our souls.

There is a way of being in the world that transcends the world, a way of being regular people and miracle workers at the same time. We become the lamps that shed the light that emanates from the electricity of God. No one feels deeply at home on this plane; it is not where we come from, and it is not where we are ultimately headed.* It is a place we stay but for a little while, beautiful and blessed when we allow our perceptions of it to be overshadowed by His, but a way station nonetheless. We are here because we have a mission: to be the love that is missing in a loveless world and thus reclaim this darkened world for light.

Having and Being

We can *have* in life whatever we are willing to *be*. For ultimately, being and having are the same. When we grant ourselves the emotional permission to live the life we want, there is little in the world that can stop us. As it says in the Course, we don't ask God for too much, but rather we ask Him for too little.* Our weakness is often simply a weakness of faith—believing more in the limitations of the world than in the limitlessness of God.

To God, every moment is a new beginning. *And God is held back by nothing.* God would never say, "I could help you, but you messed up badly so I don't want to." Neither does He say, "I could give you a great life, but your parents were alcoholics so my hands are tied." Limitations do not stand before the limitlessness of God, and it is the limits to our faith, not the limits of our circumstances, that keep us from experiencing miracles. Every situation provides us the chance to live with broader, more audacious hope and faith that all things are possible. God is bigger than any limited circumstance in our past; God is bigger than any limitation that the world is showing us now. Limitations exist only as a challenge to us to mature spiritually, as we realize that through the grace of God we are bigger than they are.

Bigger than financial lack? Yes, because in God you are infinitely abundant. Bigger than sickness? Yes, because in God you are in total good health. Bigger than terrorism? Yes, because in God we are infinite love, and love is the one and only force that hate and fear cannot withstand. There is no order of difficulty in miracles.*

If enough of us pray each morning, asking the Spirit of God to enter into the global mess we've created and make all things right—surrendering our own ideas and asking for His instead—all things wrong will begin to dissolve. As it is, we're treating such problems primarily on the level of effect and hardly treating the causal level at all. Our faith in the power of the problem, and the power of human solutions, far exceeds our faith in miracles.

I once went to a meeting where the leader opened by saying that the task at hand was basically impossible but of course we would do our best. The group couldn't possibly move forward confidently once the leader himself had declared the job undoable. Yet had I suggested that everyone in the group simply take a deep breath, pause for a moment of silence, and affirm that the job could be accomplished effortlessly and brilliantly through the spirit within, I would have been viewed as a flake. The power of thought is like a great gold reserve always present among us, yet the ego's resistance to our mining it is rigorous and intense.

In both the Bible and *A Course in Miracles*, we are told that moving mountains is small compared to what we can do. Through the grace of God, we can heal the sick and raise the dead; we can work miracles in relationships whether personal, social, or political. The fact that at present we are not doing such things is not to say we are incapable of doing them. The fundamental issue is our entrenched resistance to even trying—indeed, even our anger at times toward those who dare!

Why are we more afraid of being powerful than of being powerless? What is it about the notion of God's unlimited power working through us that seems so threatening? Is it not in fact that the notion is an affront to the ego's authority?

Yet what, after all, has the ego given us? Is its material kingdom as powerful as it purports to be? Is its way really working, given the state of our planet today? Can enough consumer goods buy us happiness? Can enough sex buy us love? Can four hundred billion dollars a year in military expenditure buy us peace?

"My kingdom," said Jesus, "is not of this world." The problems of the world will not be solved on the level of consciousness which is the problem. Jesus also said, "Greater works than I do will you do." He did not say we do them now; he said we *will* do them. We will do them when we have evolved to the next stage of our spiritual maturity, a process that He, among others, will lead us to. Why, in a world that proclaims so much faith in God, are we so loath to let God show us how to move to the next level of our humanity? What is our resistance to the assumption of our own greatness as children of the Light? We are His beloved children, in whom He is already well pleased. If He created us perfect and has glorious plans for us in heaven, then why are we so intent on playing small while we're still on earth? Is God withholding His greatness until we die, or are we resisting His greatness while we yet live? The ego will say anything to keep us from God, and "You'll see Him *later*" is one of its favorites.

God is a blessing that permeates our entire being, everywhere and all the time. But it is not enough that God blesses us; we have to receive the blessing gracefully to experience it fully. How we receive something is as important as what we are receiving. If we accept a gift with genuine gratitude and humility, giving praise and honor to the giver, then our bounty will increase. When we simply take a gift for granted, however, not giving thanks, then our good will shrink. How many times have we casually minimized an opportunity, not recognizing some awesome gift of life and love until it was too late? We learned the hard way how much power we have to make things less, by simply thinking they are. Who among us has never thrown away a blessing, too cocky and spoiled, perhaps, to see it for what it was?

Countless days and nights have gone by in which I have failed to even notice the sun or moon. It's so easy to take for granted the glory that is all around us.

When I was a child growing up in Texas, I used to witness the extraordinary sunsets that Texas skies are famous for. I didn't know that not every sunset was painted like this, in manifold hues of pink and purple, orange and gold. I didn't know then that not every sunset displayed voluminous clouds and glorious rays of fading sun, dramatically painted across an endless sky. I didn't know how blessed I was to see this.

Sometimes now I miss those sunsets and realize how naive I was to think they were so easy to come by. I consider what miracles I'm underestimating now, happening all around me yet unacknowledged and unpraised. It seems to me the biggest crisis that faces us—certainly that faces me—is a crisis of faith. I forget that the God who paints those sunsets and keeps the sun in the sky and turns the embryo into a baby is active in my life as well. It is because of my own mental fatigue, the failure of my own imagination, that I fail sometimes to connect the dots between the problems that beset my life and God's infinite power to solve them.

One Problem, One Answer

All of us have problems at times, even serious ones. But while we think we have many different problems, we really have only one: our separation from God.* Once we're realigned with the Truth of our being, nontruth can't remain in our presence for long.

I told my daughter recently that life isn't about not having problems; it's about becoming someone who knows how to dwell within problems in a positive way. It's about taking full responsibility for however we might have contributed to a problem, forgiving ourselves and others, praying for all concerned, and developing faith that God's miracle is always on the way.

A problem isn't necessarily something bad; if it's happening, it's part of a divine curriculum designed as a learning opportunity for everyone involved. And one of the things we learn, when we have experienced problems and then received the miracle that solves them, is faith that miracles do happen. Miracles arise from conviction,* and nothing gives us conviction like having been saved from the bottom of our own deep hole.

Every challenge is an opportunity . . . for a miracle.

God can and will disentangle the myriad lines of dysfunctional energy that pervade a situation, as long as we place it in His hands. In your mind's eye, pour light on the troubling circumstance. Loosen your attitudinal grip. See it as a lesson—a potential display of God's miraculous power to heal all things—and surrender it with thanks to God. Feel your personal self no longer holding the problem nor having to solve it. Expand into the infinity of your being, and from there approach both the problem and its solution. In this way, you gain an added dimension of power to your ability to handle anything. We are heir to the rules of the world with which we identify.* Once we identify with spirit alone, there are no rules except those of mercy and love.

> Dear God,
> I lay this problem on your altar.
> Please interpret this situation for me.

May I see only the love in others and in me.
Show me what I need to see,
Guide me to what I need to do.
Help me to forgive.
Raise me above the fear in my mind.
Thank you, God.
Amen.

The Power of Thought

It's easy to minimize the power of our thoughts, yet all thought creates form on some level.* You don't get karmic amnesty for, "Oh yeah, I thought that, but I didn't really mean it." The sub-conscious mind hears everything and simply reflects it back to us: there's no subconscious filter to leave out what we didn't really mean. Joke about how no one likes you, and pretty soon they probably won't. Affirm that you're in your power, and pretty soon you will be. The subconscious mind doesn't know how serious you are when you think something; it simply sets you up to fulfill your own expectations.

I loved the nerdy character in the movie *Love, Actually* who kept affirming he was a sex god and that women in America would adore him. His friend kept trying to tell him he was nuts, but he wouldn't believe it. And by the end of the movie he was in America being seduced by gorgeous women—several at a time!

Some people ridicule the notion that writing out fifty times, "I am smart and perform brilliantly at work," each night before you go to bed for thirty nights can be viewed as a serious agent of healing. Yet those same voices are often the first to argue that because your mother told you, "You're dumb and you'll never amount to anything," every night before you went to bed as a child you are wounded for life. So which is it? If words are dangerous, then words can also heal—at whatever age. Just as an audiotape can be erased by taping something else over it, we can begin to program our minds with thoughts that counter the ones we habitually think. For better or worse, the subconscious mind hears everything.

Remember, every thought we think takes us and others around us either straight to heaven (an awareness of our oneness) or straight to hell (the ego's state of separation). If we think good about the world, then we're liable to see it. And if we think bad, we're liable to see that too. We achieve so little because we have undisciplined minds.* We allow ourselves to wander far too easily into negative thoughts and negative words. And from both come negative experience.

Since all minds are joined, conflict between any two of us contributes to war, and reconciliation between any two of us takes us closer to world peace. Our smallest judgment adds to war, and our smallest forgiveness adds to peace. Miracles affect situations we will never even know about.* The butterfly's wings in South America affect the wind patterns at the North Pole, and thoughts of true peace in Idaho affect plans for peace in Palestine. What an extraordinary opportunity as well as responsibility we have, to try to get it right.

The Power of Language

One of the gifts we can give our children is to teach them the metaphysical power of words. "I hate school," "Everybody hates me," and "I'm not good-looking enough" are powerful statements that seem innocuous but are not. It behooves us as parents to teach our children that what we proclaim to be true will then *seem* to be true. At times I've caught myself saying negative things I don't even believe, giving in to a kind of mental self-indulgence that is the enemy of happiness. In fact, training our minds is as important as training our bodies and is just as important to our health.

Because of the work I do, I receive many letters from people around the world. There have been days when I was complaining or worrying about such meaningless things and then read a letter from a parent who had lost a child, a soldier's father asking for a prayer, or a patient battling cancer. My perspective was then radically and automatically altered. I have tried to develop the habit of gratitude and praise, as I realize how fortunate I am and affirm it with my thoughts. "Wow, what a beautiful day this is"—just a simple reminder of the beauty of life will literally make your life more beautiful.

The meaning of anything is the meaning we attach to it. I remember as a child that whenever I would complain about a rainy day, my mother would say, "Oh, no! The farmers need this rain!" What to me was a drag, to her was a relief.

A house looks so beautiful and you think if only you could live there, life would be so lovely; once you own it, however, there's the pressure of a mortgage to impinge upon all that loveliness. You think a purse isn't all that great, but then you see it on someone else and all of a sudden it looks fabulous. You think your husband isn't all that wonderful, but then someone else does, and all of a sudden he's fabulous. Everything we experience is filtered through our own thinking. How you see yourself is how you will tend to see your life, and how you see your life is how you will tend to see yourself.

I have known people who had so little and yet treated it so well. It's no surprise that what they had then increased. And I have known people who had so much and treated it so poorly. It's no wonder that what they had decreased. The world expands or contracts according to our participation in it. We are one hundred percent responsible for how we experience our experience.

I know a woman who has been through a terrible divorce and yet now glows from within. I once overheard her say, "You get bitter or better." I want to be like her in that sense; I want the negative to fall away, like a ball that has been thrown to me but that I don't have to hold onto. Even when we are victimized, we usually made some mistakes we need to take a good look at. And for that, we can thank even those who hurt us. For through the experiences they engendered, we will learn to avoid such situations. We will grow, and perhaps they will too. And life will go on, because God loves us all.

In God, there are no good guys and bad guys. There are loving choices which will be met with happiness, and unloving choices which will be met with pain. And the miracle worker interprets all that is not love as a call for love.* Regarded in this light, the closed heart of another cannot hurt us anymore. For it was not the closed heart of another that caused us to suffer but rather our instinct to close our heart in response. Pray for those who have wronged you, and the pain you have suffered will turn to peace.

It may not happen instantly, that is true. If someone lied about you, other people may believe the lies. If someone stole from you, it might take time to make your finances right. But that is the meaning of the symbolic three days between the crucifixion and the resurrection. It takes time for the light to ascend again, but it will. As long as our hearts are open while we're in the midst of a crucifixion—open to love, to forgiveness, and to what we ourselves need to learn and atone for—then resurrection is inevitable. Whatever it is, this too shall pass.

Radical Change

I've heard it said, "People don't change," but it is a principle of faith that through the radical alchemy of God's love, we can and do change. There is something in each of us that *wants* to become better, that *wants* to improve. The spirit is always seeking to rise up.

In 1999 one of my close friends adopted two young brothers, five and seven years old, from a county foster care program. Because they had been horribly abused by their parents, Carl and Dylan displayed common symptoms of severely traumatized children. As a consequence, they were not successful at transitioning into foster homes, much less an adoptive one. At one point they had even been on an adoption track with one couple and ultimately returned to the agency. They probably were on a slow track to the worst kind of life before my friend took them into his.

Many of the people around my friend, including me, worried that he had taken on too big a task. How could he, as a single man, cope with two traumatized young boys and successfully parent them? Yet as the weeks and months and years went by, all who knew them witnessed a miracle: little Carl and Dylan became model children, and no one who now meets them would ever guess that they came from troubled circumstances. My friend's love and radical care created the space for the boys to change. To grow. To become the children they were meant to be and still could be. Their adoptive father's patience and love accomplished an astonishing feat.

I read in the newspaper recently about a government study undertaken to determine what makes children learn. What was found—*after twenty-five million dollars of research*—was that the single largest determinant in making children learn is the presence of at least one adult—and this does not have to be a biological relative—who cares whether they do.

Miracles of personal transformation do occur, and they can occur in each of us.

Whenever our outer world remains stuck, it is incumbent upon us to look, not outward, but inward. It is a call to find the places in ourselves where we are holding on to old ways—where we blame others rather than taking personal responsibility for our woes; where we judge others instead of blessing them; where we are hard rather than vulnerable and open and kind. These issues hold the hidden keys to unlocking our unsolved personal mysteries. To achieve breakthroughs in the external world, we had best achieve internal ones. For the level of consciousness is the level of cause; addressing problems at their cause means addressing them inside our own selves. Addressing problems only on the level of their effects—in the outside world—is failing to address them deeply at all.

The Power of Love

When my sister was diagnosed with breast cancer in 1989, she said to her oncologist, "My sister says I should go to a spiritual support group." He responded, "And what medical school did your sister go to?"

The good news is that today such a patronizing, condescending attitude toward the physical benefits of spiritual practice is hard to find among doctors. If someone is diagnosed with a life-challenging disease, their doctor is now likely to be the first person to say, "Get over to one of those spiritual support groups." Why? Because the most prestigious academic institutions have scientifically substantiated that among people who have been diagnosed with a life-challenging illness, those who attend spiritual support groups live on average twice as long after diagnosis.

The fact we think love is a fierce and awesome power doesn't mean we're wimpy thinkers. I was once interviewed on a TV talk show, and the interviewer introduced me by making some snide comment about how I was a pacifist and thought there should be no army. I looked at him, stunned, and asked him where in the world he got that idea. "Well, I just assumed it!" he said. "You think love is the answer to everything, so I figured you think a military would be a bad thing!"

It's amazing how much ridicule the topic of love can attract when it does anything other than support the status quo. To go from "She thinks love is the answer" to "She thinks we shouldn't have a military" is to trivialize the most profound philosophical and spiritual truth ever expressed on earth.

A Course in Miracles says the world is an unhappy dream, which must become a happy dream before we can awaken from it.* That means the world must be transformed before it can be transcended. It is the *purpose* ascribed to something that determines its holiness, and there is nothing inherently unspiritual about the military. In fact, there are people at work within the U.S. military today who have more enlightened thoughts regarding future possibilities for our armed forces than one might think. Perhaps our military will manifest, in our lifetime, the ultimate fulfillment of the notion of "armed forces." They will be armed with psychological, spiritual, and emotional skills at building social and political relationships, as much as they are now armed with military hardware. Institutions evolve as consciousness evolves, and we are on the verge of a mass realization that if we want to change the world, we must become as sophisticated in the ways we wage peace as we are now sophisticated in the ways we wage war. Regardless of who ridicules us, it's important that we continue to celebrate love—not only the good feeling it brings, but also its actual power to heal all things.

On the level of true solution, love is the answer no matter what category of human experience. According to Mahatma Gandhi, love can heal all social and political as well as personal relationships. We've only scratched the surface of love's power, and when we dig deeply, we will find it to be more explosive than a nuclear bomb. We need an integrative approach to world affairs in which the emotional, psychological, and spiritual realms are given their place at the table of power. Jesus himself said, "Love your enemies, and pray for those who curse you." Martin Luther King Jr. said Mahatma Gandhi was the first person to take a love ethic and turn it into a broad-scale social force for good. And this is not just "nice"; it is imperative. King said we have come to the point where it is no longer a choice between violence and nonviolence; it is a choice between violence and nonexistence.

A few years ago, I was asked by Mrs. Coretta Scott King to speak in Atlanta at her late husband's official birthday celebration. I was one of the last speakers on the program. I sat and listened to speaker after speaker talk about Dr. King as though all he did was pour fairy dust over America. How great it was, all that l-o-o-v-e he spread! No one mentioned the fierce resistance he encountered, the struggle at the heart of his journey—a struggle for which he ultimately sacrificed his life. When it was my turn to speak, I had to mention that the love for which Dr. King both lived and died was not convenient to the status quo then and it is not convenient to the status quo now. Dr. King did not stand for sentimental love or popular love or convenient love. God's love is often none of these things. And if we are to truly honor Dr. King's memory, we must strive our best to do as he did—to take a stand for love even in the face of ridicule and hate.

The ego can destroy the body, but it cannot destroy an idea. The resurrection of both Gandhi and King lies in our willingness to stand strongly for the ideas that gave their lives meaning. Those ideas will give our lives meaning, as well. *A Course in Miracles* teaches that God is not looking for martyrs; He is looking for teachers.* Surely few among us have achieved a perfect love, an unconditional love. But the notion that a great wave of love will be the salvation of the human race is an idea whose time has come. And our willingness to be part of that wave gives a transcendent purpose to our lives. We are not naive about evil; we don't pour pink paint over it and pretend that it doesn't exist. We read the papers. We grieve the suffering. But many of us think God has a plan, and we believe—still—that its name is love. Not a silly love. Not a childish love. But a powerful love, an awesome love so aligned with God that it will change all things.

It will change all things, having changed us first.

Dr. King stressed the Gandhian concept that the end is inherent in the means: only if we try to practice peace can we truly be bringers of peace. And the universe will give us ample opportunity to try.

As I prepared to give my talk that day, I saw behind the podium a guest I had not known would be there: Mrs. Laura Bush. I had planned to speak about what Martin Luther King Jr. might have to say about President Bush's military policies, and all of a sudden I wasn't so sure about my prepared remarks!

I felt caught between a rock and a hard place. I didn't want to water down my remarks to make sure I offended no one. But I also didn't want to shame or embarrass the woman sitting near me by sharply criticizing the man she sleeps with every night. If I wasn't practicing sisterhood toward her, then I wasn't practicing peace.

I did a little editing of my speech, but not a lot. And every time I mentioned the president, I made some comment directed at Mrs. Bush about how our prayers were with her husband during this difficult time. I tried to express my disagreements with the president in a way that didn't personally dishonor him. At the end of my talk, I turned around to shake the hand of Mrs. King and then Mrs. Bush. When I got to the First Lady, I started to say I was sorry if I had sounded too hard on the president. But before I could say anything, Mrs. Bush put her finger to my lips and said, "Shhhhh . . . you did *great.*" She was a generous woman to me that day. She recognized my effort to find a middle way, and I appreciated her acknowledging it.

Over and over again, in millions of subtle and not-so-subtle ways, people are bridging the divides between us. One day we will look around, and the divides will be gone—both those in ourselves and those in the world. We will have crossed over to a much better place.

Returning to Our Right Minds

We were born with a natural desire to extend ourselves in love, yet the thinking of the world then trains us to think unnaturally. Sometimes it takes something out of the ordinary to jolt us back to our true reality.

Once I had a terrible headache while flying, and by the time we landed I was feeling nauseated. I then got very sick, apparently with food poisoning. There I was, throwing up at a public stall in an airport bathroom, and all these women who had never seen me in their lives gathered round to help me. I could hardly believe it—they were putting damp compresses on my forehead, helping me get to a place to lie down, two of them even performing a powerful hands-on healing and prayer. I started to cry, and it wasn't because I was sick—I was crying because of how touched I was, having all these complete strangers take care of me.

I was reminded that day how good people really are. Another time, I choked on a peeled almond and couldn't catch my breath. My daughter saw I was struggling and exclaimed, "My mommy can't breathe!" The driver of the car we were in pulled to the side of the road, and several highway workers on the Detroit freeway gathered round me, one of them administering the Heimlich maneuver. Those men might have saved my life.

Such spontaneous compassion occurs when situations happen so quickly that ego thoughts of fear and separation are bypassed. Ironically, dangerous situations often bring out the *natural* in people. I have a feeling that the amazing ladies who gave me the hands-on healing in the airport that day might not have approved of some of my more inclusive religious beliefs; I'm not sure the highway workers and I would have related to our common humanity so profoundly in other situations. But in the moments when we are so purely alive—when we get to see, for whatever reason, that we are life and that life itself is so precious, we give ourselves permission to see that we are all brothers and to behave that way. That is what the world will be like when our minds have been purified and our hearts released to love.

What occurred, in those instances, is that everyone showed up instinctively to contribute what was theirs to contribute. And that is how the entire world can be healed—and will be healed—when we have been *returned to our right minds*. That is the problem with the world today: we are literally not in our right minds. At least in America, we have allowed a competitive ethos that is appropriate to our economic system to dominate our social interactions as well. We have in too many cases lost our sense of community connection and larger familial relationship as children of one God. Whether someone lives in a neighboring town or a neighboring country, they are our brothers, and all of us are equally precious in the eyes of God. We know that, but do we act that way? When we do, we will return to the garden. And not before.

All of us are on a spiritual path, but some people simply don't know it. All of us, individually and collectively, are being forced by circumstances to remember who we are in relationship to love itself. And we will learn this through wisdom, or we will learn it through pain. We can embrace the truth of our oneness, or we can resist the lesson and learn it later. But the longer we wait, the more chaos we will generate.

For the sake of our children, may we learn it now.

CHAPTER FOUR

From *Anxiety* to *Atonement*

I go back and forth sometimes between thinking the world is marvelously fine and then thinking it's completely screwed up.

And that, of course, is because both are true.

According to the Bible, after God created the world, He looked at it and saw that it was good.

"Oh, He did, huh? Well, that was *then*. It's not so good now!" I blurt out as I put down the newspaper with its reports of pain and horror.

"Your eyes aren't as good as you think they are." I look around to see who's talking to me. And I know who it is. I am talking to myself.

I look down at my finger, which I accidentally cut three days ago. I take off the bandage and marvel at how the cut has almost disappeared, the skin looking almost completely healed. I look out my window and see the first buds of spring on the trees outside. I notice the sun streaming through a stained-glass window in my kitchen. I live with the same sense of disconnect that most of us feel, between the glories of love and nature and the mess we have made of this world.

Every day I have two choices: I can face the day with this conundrum raging inside me, luring me toward anger and frustration. Or I can try to deal with this now, before I leave the house. I want to rise above the news reports, not because I didn't read them but because I understand them from a higher perspective. I don't want to be hooked into all the negative energy flying around today. But no mental concept can build the bridge for me, from fear to love and anxiety to peace.

I know myself. It's time to pray.

I go into my room, close the door, and light a candle that has a picture of Mother Mary on it. I start talking to her like she's my therapist. "I don't like what it does to my personality each time I read the paper," I say. "I don't want to be that way. I want to be more like you."

And then there is silence.

My breath begins to move more slowly, my eyes begin to close by themselves, and I relax into a place where I can feel her around me. It's not that she really says anything; she just takes me back to a natural place in my mind. I know that I am going home, to a world more peaceful than the world outside. And when I'm there, I know what my job is: to become this peace, to embody it fully, and then go back into the world and take it with me. That is what she would have me do. And this is what would heal my pain.

The House of God

Things are changing quickly in the world, and there's no sense we are headed in a more serene direction anytime soon. Getting on top of things at this time has less to do with mastering particular skills or gaining specific knowledge than with mastering our own ability to find serenity and quiet in the midst of raging storms. Otherwise, we'll be thrown off our game with every drama that the world has to offer.

The dramas of life are like weather patterns: inevitable changes within the course of nature. It makes as much sense to resist those dramas as it would make to resist the weather. Dress for them, yes; avoid the dangerous parts, of course. But try to control the dance of nature? I don't think so. When it rains, you simply go indoors. And so it is with God. When life is stormy, we can retreat into the House of God.

The House of God is a figure of speech that turns out to be much more than that. On the spiritual level, there *is* a house and it *is* our shelter. "May you dwell in the House of the Lord forever" is more than a symbolic statement. It means, may your perception of what's real and what's not real be based only on God's eternal realities, every moment. For if they are, you will be emotionally sheltered during the storms of life. People are born, we get sick, we die. We get rich, we get poor, we get married, we get divorced, we have children, our children grow up, we get new jobs, we lose old jobs, people bless us, some people betray us. And every change is a challenge to remember what's true. Love is the only absolute reality, which never changes and never dies. Dwelling in that which does not change, while things around us are changing all the time, is our key to inner peace.

When I was a child, people used to build bomb shelters—a now seemingly quaint effort to defend themselves in case of nuclear disaster. Our urge to go underground when things up on top have gone haywire is an instinctive response to the ever-changing forces of the outer world. And there is a corresponding spiritual truth. We need a shelter for the heart, and the House of God is that shelter where we can go every day to find peace.

We need that peace because the world is moving very fast now, and everyone's nervous system is affected by the sheer speed of things. Almost everyone seems frazzled, like we need a vacation to get back to ourselves, a few days just lying on a beach to restore our natural balance.

We pretend the speed doesn't affect our children, but we suspect it does. We allow them to sit for hours in front of television and computer screens at such an early age that their brains would have to be affected. I saw a note written by a ten-year-old: "I'm a total f—ing nervous wreck." We clearly have a problem here.

Yet the children are simply mimicking us. We're all running so fast we can't possibly be thinking at our best or feeling our best. The mind and the body need empty space if the voice for God is ever to break through. And yet, even though we're frantic, I think we're addicted to the adrenaline of our modern lives. We keep moving as a way of not dealing with something. If we move fast enough, perhaps we'll all just forget how much we hurt.

Our existential pain becomes impacted, pushed down, and then it eats away at us from the inside. As we age, we start developing physical symptoms of early breakdown. The body can carry just so much stress before it acts like Yertle the Turtle at the bottom of the heap and cries out, "No more, no more!" Physical crisis, emotional crisis, family crisis, whatever it is . . . nature takes so much, and then it blows. Then we have the financial and every other kind of pressure that goes along with dealing with all the crises created because we had so much pressure to begin with.

If we want to, we can stop this. In God, there is a way.

The Stress of a Contracted Heart

In every moment, we either expand the heart or contract it.

When the heart is contracted, other things become contracted as well: your relationships, your career, your money, your health, your life.

We often contract as a response to stress, as though we're trying to defend against an oncoming force. But in fact, if I contract to avoid pressure, I inevitably create more of it. Why? Because my behavior when I'm contracted—tough, stressed, angry—then causes situations that add more stress.

The antidote to stress is counterintuitively to relax into it. If you have kids to raise, a job to complete, a paper to write, and two business trips to take before the end of next week, you will help yourself not by tensing up but by loosening up. Your contracting won't somehow help it all come together in time. Quite the opposite: loosen up, and time will loosen up as well. According to Einstein, time and space are illusions of consciousness. Like everything else, they take their lead from you.

Recognizing the origins of stress from a spiritual perspective, we find a key to dismantling the thoughts that produce it. Stress is simply the inevitable consequence of thinking the unreal is real. In that sense, stress is a choice.

If an issue is "of the world," then attaching to it our sense of success or failure, satisfaction or lack of satisfaction, is a setup. Nothing in the world can give us a deeper peace because the spirit is not at home in the world. To the extent that our sense of well-being is tied in any way to the things of the material world, we will be prone to worry and anxiety.

Yet we almost feel we *have* to stress when there's so much to do, so much that can happen, so much to consider all the time!

That, however, is the joke: the only reason things seem to press upon us so heavily is because we think they are so heavy.

If we ourselves had to hold all the balls in the air that we feel we're juggling all the time, then we would have every reason to feel depressed and scared. But the fact is, we're only juggling them because we think we need to—and because we think we need to, we do! Once we realize we have a choice—that the universe is as tight or as loose as we perceive it to be, that time is as limited or expanded as we perceive it to be, that things are as difficult or as easy as we perceive them to be—then stress begins to evaporate. We literally "lighten up." Every time we think, "Oh, my God, I have so much to do and I don't know how I can do it," we can change our thinking. We can place all our burdens in the hands of God, ask for a miracle, and thank Him in advance for providing it. We will stop being so tense; we will stop being so worried; we will stop living a life so devoid of joy. The lying ego will say things like, "I can't do that! I have responsibilities!" Yet that's exactly the point: once we've lightened up, we attract the people and circumstances that provide us the means to effortless accomplish a task. It's not like working miracles *isn't doing anything.*

Why are we so worried, after all, if miracles lie at our fingertips? Our very being is a space for miracles, and whatever our problem is, we can release it into the hands of God. To pray "God, please take this" is an act of empowerment, not weakness. Who in their right mind wouldn't choose miracles over stress if they truly knew they had a choice?

Sometimes people talk about the "committee" in their head, the endless chattering of the ego naysaying them throughout their day. I've learned something about that committee in my head: I've learned it's up to me to take charge of the meeting. It's up to me to think positive thoughts so there's no room for all the negative ones. When I use a miracle-minded "problem-solving repertoire"*—looking for eternal rather than worldly insight, standing in faith and asking for miracles—I stop living at the effect of worldly drama. It's my responsibility to remind myself how blessed I am and to extend that blessing to others. When I remember that God's power is unlimited, I stop stressing about how limited mine is.

It's all up to me, because it's all inside my head.

One night I was having a particularly hard time enduring one of those stretches of desperate hours that are the meaning of a spiritual wilderness. Too many things had piled up, any one of which I probably could have handled okay but the combination of which had sent me reeling. A large theft, betrayal by people I thought were honorable—a few things like that and I was reeling. It was almost five in the morning, and I hadn't been able to sleep, though I couldn't work, read, or do much of anything else either. All I could do was catalog my perceived disasters, and I remember actually saying out loud, "Dear God, I feel like such a failure."

Five minutes later I picked up a Fed Ex package sitting next to my bed. It had arrived the day before, containing the galleys of Rabbi Harold Kushner's new book. He had asked me to read it, and I figured I would get to it when I could. I picked it up in an effort to get out of myself, to do something for someone else, to try to counter the spiral of self-pity that was taking me down such a dark and painful hole.

As I began the book, my jaw dropped open. I felt I was encountering the words of God. Kushner wrote that feelings of failure occur in all our lives, and the issue is who we become as a result. Reading his words that morning, I was given the ability to completely recontextualize my experience, reframe my feelings, and grab onto some hope. The book provided a sense of transcendent meaning for my sorrow, leaving me not only able to finally fall asleep but also to wake up later with energy and enthusiasm.

I couldn't believe that that particular book, with that particular theme, just happened to be sitting next to my bed at that moment. And it wasn't lost on me that Harold is a rabbi, bringing me comfort from my own religious tradition. I knew that the shift in perception his words introduced into my mind was truly a miracle. It was not a change in what had happened to me; it was *a different way to think about* what had happened to me. God—and Rabbi Kushner—had graced me with a different point of view.

Comfort Comes

A few weeks before my father died, he was lying on his favorite bench, already gravely ill, and I was sitting on the floor next to him. He had an intense but faraway look in his eyes, and he said, "I'm not afraid. I know where I'm going." I simply looked at him and shared the moment, but I've often wished since that I had asked for more explanation. He clearly perceived an eternal reality that would carry him through death.

It shouldn't have to take death to make us so much more aware of what matters and what doesn't, what's eternal and what's not. Why can't we remember much, much sooner that love is all that matters and love is all that lasts? It's as though, when death is at the door, we're given a free dose of sacred understanding. Perhaps if we asked for it earlier, it would come.

> *Dear God,*
> *May the Holy Spirit overshadow my mind,*

And give me eyes to see.
May I perceive the love I know exists
And overlook the rest.
May I rise above the darkness of the world
and my mind be bathed in light.
May I be calm and comforted
By Truth.
Amen.

Digging Deep

Underneath the layer of our normal thinking lies a level of consciousness that is pure love and peace. Yet we cannot reach that consciousness simply by deciding to; we have to dig deep into the ground of our inner being, creating a space of listening for the "small still voice for God." The more things are happening on the outside, the more important it is to find that stillness on the inside.

Every mistake we ever made occurred because, in the moment we made it, we were not in conscious contact with our highest self. We were not centered in our spirit. That is why making that contact, and spending time each day fostering it, is the single most powerful thing we can do.

How many times have we made a mistake that affected the rest of our life simply because at the moment we made it we were moving too fast, at the effect of our stress or anger or fear? Would we have made that mistake had we remembered in that moment who we really are in a spiritual sense and who others are in relation to us? At the mercy of negative, shallow thoughts, we are bound to misperceive ourselves and others.

What happens in life depends on who we are in life. What we experience throughout the day has everything to do with who we are throughout the day. And who I am during the day has a lot to do with how I start it.

Five minutes spent with the Holy Spirit in the morning guarantees He will be in charge of our thought system throughout the day.* In every single moment, we choose between love and fear, yet the ego speaks first and the ego speaks loudest. The voice for God will not impose itself; it has to be received, made space for, and welcomed into our minds. When we reach out to God and welcome His comfort at the beginning of the day, then something happens. It's not that we become perfect, but we become more aware. And that awareness makes us miracle-ready in a way we would not otherwise be.

Every morning when I wake up, I try to remember to give praise and thanks. Thank you, God, for my life today. Thank you for my family and friends, thank you for my home, thank you for my many blessings. Thank you for Your healing power, now pouring forth upon me. I claim it now, and pray for miracles. Please bless this day, for me and everyone. Amen.

Meditation

In addition to prayer, we need quiet time with God. And that is the purpose of meditation. Meditation is like soaking a dirty pot in soapy water. Sometimes food gets stuck on the surface of a pot and the only way to clean it is to let it soak overnight. Through soaking, the dried food softens and finally rises to the surface. Quiet time with God is like a spiritual soak in which fearful thoughts that are clinging to the surface of the mind are loosened and then finally rise and depart.

Notice there's a time when the food begins to rise and the water gets dirtier, not cleaner. So it is that during meditation we might feel more agitated before we feel more peaceful. But feeling agitated is just a point in the process, to be endured until it passes.

Unless we take the time to meditate—to allow the alchemy of the Holy Spirit to transform the deepest regions of our mind— we carry fear-based, guilt-ridden thoughts around like a spiritual weight around our necks. We usually experience the effects of these thoughts as free-floating anxiety, not even sure what it is that's causing us to be nervous and depressed. Guilt and blame have permeated our thinking, causing constant discomfort and emotional chaos. Meditation is the only way to address, and eradicate, the deeper layers of our angst.

We might be walking down the most beautiful street on a gorgeous spring day, enjoying a day out with someone we love. But we won't be happy if upsetting thoughts continue to distract us. Life isn't a television commercial where if everything *looks* good then it must *be* good. You can buy the product they're selling and try to change the picture. But you can also meditate for free and change your life.

One hurried day, I had just enough time to take a quick glance into the *Course in Miracles* workbook before I left the house. I read the sentence, "My holiness envelops everything I see." As I went about my day—sitting in a cab, ordering a soy latte, waiting for an elevator—I said the sentence to myself whenever I could. I felt my sense of nervousness abate as I did so, and I wanted to kick myself for not having taken at least five minutes alone to do the exercise before leaving the house that morning. I'd had reasons, of course—I was late for a meeting, and so on. But I knew in my heart that I'd had more than reasons; I'd had resistance. As clear as I am that meditation will radically alter my day, it's amazing to me how often I still avoid it. Not like I used to, but every once in a while. And who wants their life to be less than it could be *every once in a while?*

The Indian gurus are right who say that no matter what the problem, the answer is to meditate. They're right because, as Einstein said, we won't solve the problems of the world from the level of thinking we were at when we created them. Meditation changes the level of our thinking, and that's why it changes our lives.

Particularly today, each of us carries more worry and upset than we realize. It bombards us even from halfway across the world. Much that we thought we could count on we suddenly discovered we can't count on at all. The September 11 attacks on the United States have been like a time-release capsule of collective anxiety. In a day, everything changed, and we're being forced to learn a deeply spiritual lesson: that the only real security lies in our internal strength. Anything can happen to anyone at any time. Yet our disillusionment simply means we were laboring under an illusion before—thinking external safety could be guaranteed. Now that we know which houses were built on sand, we have the opportunity to rebuild them on rock. Every time we meditate, it's like we're creating a secure underground location where we can retreat when times are rough.

In his book *The Soul's Awakening*, philosopher Rudolf Steiner wrote, "He who would create the new must be able to endure the passing of the old in full tranquillity."

When we meditate in the morning, we are placing our minds, emotions, and nervous systems at God's service. We are choosing not to be merely a jumble of nerves, stress, frantic efforts, vain imaginings, and fear, walking around in a body and pretending to be a person. The poet Lord Byron once wrote of his age, "We are living in gigantic and exaggerated times." And so are we. A huge drama is being played out on the earth today, and we're choosing to be part of it. We are signing up for prophetic duty. We are asking to be used for an effort much bigger than ourselves. We realize that the emergence of wiser, stronger, more intelligent and compassionate people is the single most important factor in the salvation of the world—and that is what we want to be. But it's hard to be any of those things if we're jumping off the walls.

Many times at my lectures I've heard a question that goes something like this: "I try so hard, but I just can't find the peace of God. Can you help me?"

I respond, "Do you do a serious prayer and meditation practice every day?"

"No," they say.

"Funny," I say. "I knew that."

Spending Time with God

The Holy Spirit responds fully to our slightest invitation.* The problem isn't that the Holy Spirit doesn't respond, the problem is how deep we sink into a problem before we bother to ask for His help. We have this ridiculous, self-defeating habit of going to God as a last resort instead of making Him our first call.

That's why constant spiritual practice matters. It takes at least a daily reminder to remember to put God first. The ego is sly and insidious; in the words of Sigmund Freud, "Intelligence will be used in the service of the neurosis." If you think you're too smart to have to worry about your ego, you have to worry about it even more.

If we meditate sometimes but not always, then it will seem to us that God helps us sometimes but not always. If we pray and meditate on some days but not all days, then we will feel the peace of God on some days but not all days. If we go to God only when we're in trouble, then of course His help seems inconsistent. Yet the inconsistency lies in us. The more time we spend with God, the more we develop our spiritual musculature and the stronger we become in dealing with life's challenges. I remember the song lyric, "Darlin', if you want me to be closer to you, get closer to me." The same applies to our relationship with God.

The form of your practice doesn't matter. It might be the workbook of *A Course in Miracles,* transcendental meditation, or Buddhist or Jewish or Christian meditation. What matters is that you practice.

Meditation rests the mind the way sleep rests the body. In Zen Buddhism there is the concept of "no mind" or "beginner's mind"; in the I Ching it is said that our mind should be like an empty rice bowl. In *A Course in Miracles* it is stated, "Forget your ideas of good and bad, forget your ideas of right or wrong, forget this Course, and come with empty hands unto your God." The idea of emptying one's mind is fundamental to all meditative practice. For once we have surrendered our extraneous thinking, then God's truth can move into the vacuum. We substitute His Mind for our mind, and thus they become one.

Five minutes in the morning is better than nothing. Thirty minutes provides serious spiritual support. Not meditating at all? Expect the stress to continue.

You can make another choice: close your eyes, breathe in the quiet, surrender it all . . .

This is from the workbook of *A Course in Miracles:*

Five minutes now becomes the least we give to preparation for a day in which salvation is the only goal we have. Ten would be better; fifteen better still. And as distraction ceases to arise to turn us from our purpose, we will find that half an hour is too short a time to spend with God.

Each hour adds to our increasing peace, as we remember to be faithful to the Will we share with God. At times, perhaps, a minute, even less, will be the most that we can offer as the hour strikes. Sometimes we will forget. At other times the business of the world will close on us, and we will be unable to withdraw a little while, and turn our thoughts to God.

. . . And we will quietly sit by and wait on Him and listen to His Voice, and learn what He would have us do the hour that is yet to come; while thanking Him for all the gifts He gave us in the one gone by.

In time, with practice, you will never cease to think of Him, and hear His loving Voice guiding your footsteps into quiet ways, where you will walk in true defenselessness. For you will know that Heaven goes with you. Nor would you keep your mind away from Him a moment. . . .

Your practicing will now begin to take the earnestness of love, to help you keep your mind from wandering from its intent. Be not afraid nor timid. There can be no doubt that you will reach your final goal.*

If You Do It, It Works

Intellectually understanding spiritual principles doesn't guarantee enlightenment, and the ego loves to use religion and spirituality as a cover.

One moment of enlightened awareness doesn't completely transform your life. The spiritual path is slow and arduous at times, as every single circumstance becomes the ground on which both ego and spirit seek to make their stand. Spiritual practice is like physical exercise: it has a cumulative effect, and if we want to enjoy its benefits, we can never stop doing it. You can't just go to the gym once and walk out with a new body, and neither can you attend one seminar, say one prayer, or sing one hallelujah and expect your life to be perfect from now on.

The mind as well as the body demands training if it's to perform at full capacity. That's why some of us go to the gym or do yoga regularly and also why we participate in religious services or spiritual practice regularly. In a world where thoughts based on fear prevail, you're going against the flow to make a true and genuine stand for love. It's not easy to walk up two flights of stairs when you're not in physical shape, and it's not easy to make an unpopular stand for faith and forgiveness when you're not in spiritual shape.

Yet if we're going to make the change from the world that is to the world that could be, it's exactly that stand that is necessary. There's nothing spiritual about avoiding the problems of the world. Our goal is not to *avoid* the world, but to heal it. Yet we can't give to the world what we ourselves don't already have; the gifts of the spirit can only be given by those who are trying to embody them. That's why, as Gandhi said, we must *be* the change we want to see happen in the world. Peace has to begin in our own lives and spread outward to heal others as we interact with them in a loving way.

The Atonement

The Atonement is the crux of spiritual practice; it is the corrective process by which our thoughts are moved by the Holy Spirit from where they have been to where they should be. But He can't enter where He's not invited, as that would be a violation of our free will. He cannot take from us what we haven't released to Him.*

To atone, we have to be willing to take an honest look at the thoughts we thought and the things we did whether or not they're fun to look at. We have to be willing to cringe, to admit where we were wrong in a thought, an action, or a word. The reason we "atone" to God rather than ask His forgiveness is because God has never judged us. We atone not because God is angry but because even He will not violate His law of Cause and Effect.

Martin Luther King Jr. used to say that while the nonviolent movement was materially passive, it was spiritually active. Since the level of consciousness is the true level of cause, then you can sometimes do more to move a mountain from sitting in your armchair than from running around the mountain or even climbing it. What we move on the level of consciousness is moved within the Mind of God.

Atonement is God's greatest gift, allowing us to get back on track when we've gotten off. Practiced by Catholics in confession and Jews on the Day of Atonement (Yom Kippur), Atonement for our sins is the act that reconciles the Creator and the created. It takes work to take full responsibility for the mistakes we've made, atone for them, and try to make things right. But it is the work God would have us do.

"The primary responsibility of the miracle worker is to accept the Atonement for himself."* The Atonement is first and foremost a correction in our thinking, a prayerful return to the love in our hearts. Then we may or may not need to take direct action; if there's something for us to do, He'll let us know.*

When we have made a mistake, the universe records it. But God would have us atone for our errors, not suffer for them. We are asked in whatever way is appropriate and possible to make amends for our wrong-minded behavior. God has sent the Holy Spirit to correct us when we need correction, and through the Atonement He provides us with the chance to begin again, no matter how far we've strayed from the truth in our hearts. Our ability to begin anew is supported by God Himself, as long as we approach Him with a contrite and humble heart. Nothing in our past diminishes the infinite possibilities inherent in our present as long as we atone for our errors and return to love.

Conscience is important, as is remorse. But they are meant to lead us to new life, not leave us drowning in a sea of guilt. When we have chosen fear instead of love—and who among us hasn't?—then the love we might have chosen "is held in trust for us by the Holy Spirit" until we are ready to receive it.* To me, that's one of the most incredible principles in *A Course in Miracles.* It's amazing when you think about it: I could have said or done the right, loving thing, and if I had, then such and such a thing would then have happened. However, I did not. I've been trained by the world to think with fear, and I did. *Yet God saved the possibility I turned down, until I'm ready to return to love and choose again!*

How much love and mercy has to be built into the structure of the universe for this to be so! As long as we atone for a mistake, we will be given the chance to correct it. That chance might not come in the form we would wish, but it will be there in a form that God determines.

One day I heard about a woman I had known many years earlier. She had suddenly stopped speaking to me, and I didn't know why.

Then I thought about it, and I did know why.

I had made a comment about her that had probably reached her ears. It wasn't a vicious or cruel comment, but it wasn't gracious either. I'd put it in the category of unconscious and unkind.

So here it was, over ten years later, and she had just done something really wonderful. I wanted to acknowledge her, and I also wanted to tell her how sorry I was for having made such a wrong-minded comment all those years earlier and ask her to forgive me. I didn't know her address or whether or not she would read my letter. But in my heart I atoned. I really got that I had been less than the person I should have been, and I was eager to make amends.

The very next day I was called by a reporter for a major European newspaper. They were writing an article about her, and they asked my opinion. I had the opportunity to go on and on about how wonderful she is, what good things she's done—in a venue where I could be fairly certain it would reach her eyes. Synchronicity is the handwriting of God: as soon as I atoned, the entire universe was programmed to catch up to my corrected perception.

When our thinking is corrected, then so is our world. We're punished not *for* our sins but *by* our sins. *And through prayer, they are transformed.*

"Prayer is the medium of miracles. . . . Through prayer love is received, and through miracles love is expressed."* If you want a miracle in your life, simply pray for one. For as long as you are willing to change your mind, then God will change your life.

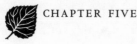

CHAPTER FIVE

From *Asking God to Change the World* to *Praying That He Change Us*

*J*esus said, "Be of good cheer," which is certainly positive. But then he added, "for I have overcome the world." He didn't say, "I have fixed the world," but rather, "I have overcome" it. The difference between fixing the world and overcoming it is huge. The problem most of us have is that we try to fix instead of overcoming, which is why we never find that fundamental good cheer.

Trying to fix the world is like trying to change a movie by manipulating the movie screen. The world as we know it is simply a screen onto which we project our thoughts. Until we change those thoughts, the movie stays the same.

If we want our lives to change, it does little good to simply move from town to town, job to job, or relationship to relationship. Wherever we go, as they say, we take ourselves with us. We manifest not so much according to geography as according to consciousness. We can travel wide, but that of itself will not fundamentally change us. For our lives to change, we must travel deep.

The truth is that our fundamental happiness stems not from anything that happens in the material world, but from love. Certainly there are some wonderful experiences to be had on the material plane, and there is nothing wrong with enjoying them to the fullest. The world itself is neutral; whether or not something of the material plane can be considered holy is determined by the purposes our mind ascribes to it.* That which is used by the Holy Spirit for purposes of genuine healing is holy; that which is used by the ego for purposes of separation is not. The body itself can be a "beautiful lesson in communion until communion is."* Wherever there is love, there is God.

But we cannot enjoy the material plane if we are overly attached to it; the secret of happiness lies in knowing that we are in the world but not of it. That understanding—keeping our thoughts on love while having our feet planted squarely on earth—is the intersection between heaven and earth. And that intersecting point is what we are. It is our mission to live on the earth while thinking only the thoughts of heaven, and when we do, the power of the intersecting point between man and God (symbolized visually in both the cross and the Star of David) overcomes all negative force. That is the overcoming to which Jesus referred and that he himself embodied.

In the Bible it is said that the Holy Spirit will give us a new mind. And who among us could not use that? It becomes fruitless to ask God to change our world once we recognize the world is merely the reflection of our thoughts. What we pray for is the healing of our minds.

It's impossible to make your life new when your mind is running old tapes. Time and time again, we've blown it at exactly the same place in a relationship or sabotaged a professional endeavor in exactly the same way. Yet we feel powerless to stop our self-defeating behavior. What's the point of attracting an opportunity if we're only going to ruin it anyway?

We pay a high price for refusing to accept the part we play in causing our problems; if I don't see I caused it, then I can't see I can change it!* But once I'm willing to take total responsibility for my own experience, I can see the value of inviting the Holy Spirit to enter my mind and fill me with His spirit. Consciousness precedes form, and the perfect form arises from a consciousness of total love.

Total love seems like a very tall order until we consider the reality that total love is what we *are*. So where's the disconnect? We ask, "If I am love, and love creates miracles, then why is my life so screwed up?"

At a certain level it's not our divine reality that's the issue— the issue is how much of that reality we allow ourselves to *experience* and *express*. In the introduction to *A Course in Miracles*, it's stated, "The course does not aim at teaching the meaning of love, for that is beyond what can be taught. It does aim, however, at removing the blocks to your awareness of love's presence, which is your natural inheritance." Love is all around us, but we're in the mental and emotional habit of deflecting it.

With every attitude of attack or defense, we send love away. With every perception of anyone's guilt, we tell love to leave. With every thought of limited possibility, we tell miracles we don't want them. And then we wonder why we're depressed.

To treat the depression, we must ask ourselves essential questions: What am I doing, or not doing, to allow fear rather than love to prevail here? Who am I attacking or not forgiving? What am I myself not giving to this situation? We indulge our fear as if we're being strong to do so, "honest" in a way that makes us more "real." But what is so real about playing weak instead of strong? Sometimes we need to tell our fear to go to hell, which is literally where it came from.

The ego is backed by the weight of an entire thought system, constantly luring us away from love and limitlessness toward fear and scarcity. It is a vicious taskmaster, and it has our hearts—indeed our entire planet—in its grip. And some people would rather die than change their minds.*

The transformation of the heart will take more than an intellectual decision. The ego is a mental addiction to the thinking of fear, and only a spiritual experience can break an addiction. If we want our lives and our world to genuinely change, then we need a spiritual experience to make it happen. And to have that experience, we must open our hearts to receive it.

Trusting the Process

If you don't know there's a force out there working for you, then why would you think to trust it? With all the millions of churches, mosques, temples, and shrines that exist in the world, how many people really think that the God who created the moon and the stars is truly looking out for *them?* Yet there is no unit of time or space, nor element of life, about which the Author of All Things is not actively concerned. He loves you because He loves everything and everyone. He who is Love cannot not love.

What an amazing thought, that ever-unfolding good is actually the natural order of the universe. And we were created to enjoy it. To the ego, that is a preposterous notion; it would have us believe that joy is something lovely to be *outgrown.* But look at small children gleefully at play; do we know something they don't know, or do they perhaps know something we've forgotten? As I listen to my teenage daughter discuss love and relationships, I remember how it was for me when I was her age. I don't look back on my earliest forays into romance and think, "Oh, but that was only puppy love." Rather, I look back and think how courageously we loved, before we knew what there was to be afraid of; how strong we were, before any other agendas stood in the way of our love; and how pure our hearts were, when they were not yet tainted by cynicism or doubt. The older we are, the more we know some things; the younger we are, the more we know others. Age only makes us smarter if we retain our bravery.

Enlightenment is not a learning but an unlearning, a letting go of all the fears we've gathered as we've walked the path of life. As taught in *A Course in Miracles*, "miracles are everyone's right, but purification is necessary first."* Purification is the process by which everything but love dissolves from our mind. As we drop the layers of fear and illusion that have hardened around our psyches, we are left with the love with which we were endowed at our creation.

Just as embryonic cells are programmed to develop into a baby, each of us is programmed to develop a more magnificent life. An invisible hand guides the embryo and guides you and me as well. But unlike the embryo, you and I can refuse it. God didn't create us as babies and then just dump us here and say, "Okay, kid, now you're on your own." But how do we know that, if we're not taught to listen to our hearts? How can we "go with the flow" if we don't know such a flow exists? And so we keep going around saying "No" to life and then wondering why life seems to be saying "No" to us.

The Divine Physician

God knows our crooked places that need to be made straight, the wounds in our hearts that fester for years unhealed, the broken pieces of our lives that seem beyond repair. And He who is the Author of miracles has infinite desire as well as power to heal them all.

So if that's the case, then why so much pain? Could it be that the doctor has the medicine but the patient refuses to take it? According to *A Course in Miracles,* God cannot take away from us what we do not release to him. It's not enough to *understand* your problem, to say, "My mother made me feel unsafe when I was a child, so that's why I react the way I do." Rather, we need to say, "Dear God, I know I react this way. Please change me." And that's an important difference.

At a certain point, it doesn't really matter so much how we got to be a certain way. Until we *admit* our character defects—and take responsibility for the fact that regardless of where we got them, *they are ours now*—God Himself has no power to heal them. We can talk to a therapist for hours about how our relationship with Mom or Dad made us develop a certain behavioral characteristic, but that of itself will not make it go away. Naming it, surrendering it to God, and asking Him to remove it—*that's* the miracle of personal transformation. It won't go away in a moment, necessarily, but its days are numbered. The medicine is in your psychic bloodstream.

Sometimes, therefore, the healing process involves our having to take a good look in the mirror before we can do anything else. You might pray for a better job situation, and the next thing you know, you experience your biggest professional disaster yet. It might seem that when you prayed things only got worse. But what actually happened is that you were moved subconsciously to create a situation in which your own weakness was on display, magnified enough for you to get a very good look at it. Things in fact did not get worse; you were simply no longer anesthetized to your own experience and the part you played in creating it.*

Let's say you finally got the dream job you had been praying for, yet within a couple of weeks of starting it, you began to display the same self-sabotaging behavior that had held you back before. At first you think, "Oh no, this isn't a miracle! It's terrible!" But then you realize, "Oh, wow, I get it. The miracle is that I have a chance, right here and now, to choose again, to stand in the same spot where I have blown it before, and do things another way. I can pray for help in becoming the person who handles this situation with ease and grace." God doesn't help us *avoid* our issues; He *transforms* our issues.

In that sense, when we're in the midst of a spiritual transformation things often seem to get worse before they get better. We usually have to look at what we hate about ourselves before we can see how much there is to love. There is a "ring of fear" around the light within us, through which the ego seeks to block our entrance into the heaven within.*

And that's why we pushed so many issues to the back of the drawer to begin with: so we wouldn't have to endure the pain of genuine self-examination. We're afraid of an ugliness we feel is lurking inside us, but in fact what we fear is an illusionary self. This illusion exudes a continuous toxicity if it remains in the dark, yet disappears the moment it's exposed to light. The ego is dispersed into nothingness when released into the hands of God.

The ego is not where we're bad but where we're wounded. Yet often we don't want to take a good look at our wounds—much less let God look with us—because we're ashamed. No one expects a wound on the body to be pretty—we're not ashamed of the blood and gore accompanying a physical wound—yet we're embarrassed that we have emotional wounds. Our emotional and psychological wounds often appear not as places where we are hurt but rather as places where we are guilty. Our spiritual wounds take the form of character defects.

While it might have been a wounded childhood that caused a negative pattern to begin with, that fact isn't necessarily obvious to others. Only to the miracle-minded does your behavior read, "I was hurt as a child. Have compassion." We're all involved in the same matrix of ego delusion—focusing not on each other's wounds, because they don't appear on the surface, but on each other's faults, because they do.

So we often try to hide who we are rather than heal who we are. We're afraid that if we show our true selves, something ugly will appear. Only when we realize Who lives within us do we see that only beauty will appear. In the meantime, our wounds fester, untended, until surrendered for divine healing. Our denial, or unwillingness to look deeply at our own issues, reflects a naive hope that if we don't look at our wounds, they'll go away by themselves. It takes emotional courage to look deeply into ourselves and face what's there. Until we do, however, God's medicine can't heal us.

Until you understand that God is your healer and not your judge, it's unlikely you will go to Him with your pain. It's understood we take our clothes off if the doctor needs to check us, but we're afraid to present ourselves naked before God. Until we make the switch from the notion of an angry, judgmental God to an all-merciful and forgiving one, we are bound to have an ambivalent relationship to Him. Why would we want to admit our mistakes to someone we think will judge us for them?

We've created a God in our own image: angry and judgmental *because we are.* God Himself is merciful and all-loving, but we have projected onto Him our fear. This separates us from His love, from His healing, and from each other. When we change our perception from a God of wrath to a God of mercy, we will realize God is a divine physician. Our pain is the pain of hell, or separation from love. It isn't God who sends us to hell for being bad, it's God who *delivers* us from hell after the ego *told* us we are bad. Hell is when you think you're a terrible person and you never do anything right; God is the One who reminds you of the innocence in which you were created and to which He will help you return. Hell is when you feel you're a complete and utter failure who will never succeed; God is the One who reminds you that He lives within you and that in Him all things are possible. Hell is when you think you can never escape your past mistakes; God is the One who makes all things new. It is the ego—not God— who casts us into the "fires of hell." It is God who lifts us out of them.

Taking Our Medicine

God knows us as He created us—perfect and innocent now and forever.* Our mistakes don't change our eternal essence, and it's that which the Father knows and loves. Our prayer for healing, for atonement, for correction, is a prayer to be healed of our own forgetfulness. We pray to be *reminded* of who we really are so our thoughts and behavior no longer reflect a dissociation from our divine self.

We can pray before every day, every meeting, every encounter that we will be our best—that we won't be thrown off our center by fear and ego. And afterward, we can surrender every aspect of what occurred—what we felt, what we did, what we're ashamed of, what we're angry about or feeling hopeful about.

We can't fix ourselves, and we don't have to. When we are willing to open ourselves completely to God, showing Him our darkness as well as our light, His spirit enters us at deeper levels than any worldly force could penetrate. Then, and only then, are we changed on causal levels of consciousness, genuinely freed of the patterns that have held us back.

We don't like it when a doctor rushes in for an appointment, spends five minutes with us, and then rushes out. How could he or she possibly understand our situation, the subtle nuances of our predicament? Yet we rush in and rush out of an appointment with the divine physician all the time. We dip in for a prayer here, a bit of meditation there. We read a book of inspirational poems or sayings. We do seminars or go to weekend retreats. But only a continuous change in the way we think is enough to guarantee a spiritual healing. It is not enough to get naked with God every once in a while. We must present ourselves authentically to Him not just sometimes but all the time: not just every hour, but every moment of every day. We can open our hearts so much that all our fear will melt away. We can live in a continuous communion with God in which every perception, every possible thing, is constantly surrendered for His blessing and review. And when we are so radically available to Him, we will find Him radically available to us.

Mercy

Sometimes we walk closely with God, and sometimes we sprint to the other side of the universe. Who among us hasn't taken a few detours into fear?*

Yet when we do, and then come back to love, we learn among other things how merciful God is. There are certain words you can't truly understand until you actually experience them. And *mercy* is one of them.

When I was young, the concept of God's mercy meant little to me; I figured it meant He was "nice." But now I have an appreciation for the concept I could never have had before; you usually have to have lived a while before you understand the meaning of real regret. But I have found that He just keeps using our mistakes, as well as our successes, to turn us into the people He has in mind for us to be.

God's mercy is an active power. His angels, both visible and invisible, are present at every step of our journey, reaching out to us as we reach out to them. Whenever we are receptive to His healing, His healing is on the way; God will do His part if we do ours. As we admit the exact nature of our wrongs, making amends wherever possible; as we atone and ask God to remove our character defects; as we open our hearts to receive His daily comfort and allow Him to use us in bringing comfort to others; as we seek through prayer and meditation to both know His will for us and *do* His will for us, a miraculous process takes place within us. We are lifted from weak to strong; we are lifted from lack to abundance; we are lifted from pain to peace; we are lifted from fear to love. None of this happens in an instant, but over time, through the daily processes of living. In every darkened corner—emotionally, psychologically, spiritually, physically—He sends His light to replace all darkness.

And thus we are redeemed. There is no situation that ties His hands. And there is no person in whom He is not interested or for whom He does not have a plan for their healing. The world as we know it can be cruel indeed, but the redemptive, all-loving power of God is present in the very nature of things.

Redemption

I once spoke at a seminar held for women on probation or parole in the federal justice system. Many had served time—some a long time—in prison. All of them were desperate to lead a new and different kind of life, and they came to the seminar in hopes of learning how. Before I spoke, a woman currently on parole and doing very well told her story. I was mesmerized by her talk, which was a profound and compelling tale of redemption.

Michelle had served five years in jail for a drug-related crime, and at the time of her sentence, her four-year-old son was taken to live with her elderly parents. When she was released from jail, she had her child and very little else. Through an anonymous fellowship and the guidance of her parole officer, she learned slowly and meticulously how to put one foot in front of the other and build a new life. Her struggles—the fact that the only kinds of jobs she could find initially were the lowest paying ones at which she was treated poorly, the initial rejection by prospective employers when they saw on her application that she was a convicted felon, her having to learn to control her anger, her difficulties with an angry young son—were all met with a deep understanding that through the grace of God, and one day at a time, she *could* stay sober, she *could* build a life for herself, and she *could* avoid ever returning to prison. In time she entered college, learned how to succeed as a student, graduated, and then earned her master's degree in social work. As she shared her hope and strength with other women who were wounded in their souls in much the same way that she had been, the light of God, which so clearly had blessed her, extended through her to touch them as well.

Michelle suffered greatly for her mistakes, but she experienced God's mercy and she can bear witness to it now in the lives of others. Sometimes He uses our suffering to hone us, as it makes us more humble, more contrite, and more open to guidance we'd rejected before. Sometimes we come out on the other side of a dark time with an inner knowledge, some sense of the soul we didn't have before. Sometimes the fire we went through becomes our purifying agent, allowing the miracle God had planned for us to seize our hearts and make us new.

And so, could it be that some of the things that hurt us the most were in fact the workings of God's love—like an operation the doctor performs in order to save you? Sometimes difficult experiences have the effect of a storm. Afterwards we see a beauty in the sky and a cleanness in the air that were not there before. What was chaotic at the time had an ultimately salutary effect. And sometimes, when we're really fortunate, we look up in the sky and see a rainbow. It could not have happened without the rain.

Becoming Teachable

Our job is not to *determine* life's meaning but to *discern* its meaning. Often we try to tell life what it means when we would be better off allowing life to *show* us what it means.* When Jesus said we should be as little children, it was because little children know that they don't know.* We go around thinking or at least pretending we know the meaning of things, when in fact the mortal mind has no basis for real knowing. Little children expect someone older and wiser to explain things to them; we can have the same relationship with God.

There's a way of relaxing into our center, working much less hard, letting other people have their say, knowing our being is even more radiant at times when we're in a space of not-doing. When the ego steps back, the power of God can step forward. He can and will, when we allow Him to. Too often we feel we're invisible unless we're making the cool comment, doing this or doing that. But we're so much more powerful when surrounded by silence. Taking a deep breath, knowing that what you don't say can be as powerful as what you do say, thinking deeply about something before making a response—such actions leave room for the spirit to flow, to harmonize your circumstances and move them in a more positive direction. How many times have we felt we've blown it simply by talking when we wish we hadn't or by showing off when we could have just sat there and seemed intriguing—because we *were?*

God's spirit will always reveal the truth to us if we simply don't block His guidance. And we block it by talking first, attitudinally walking ahead of truth. This happens when we push too hard—in a conversation or a project—trying frantically to make things happen, or keep things from happening, because we lack faith in an invisible order of things. That is why the Holy Instant matters: it is a moment of quiet when the spirit enters and makes right all things.

Often it's better to live in a question until the answer emerges; to be okay with not knowing until wisdom comes; to take a backseat and just listen until you genuinely have something to say. Sometimes it is our silence that testifies to our strength.

Our entire being—intellectual, emotional, psychological, and spiritual—can relax into a more miracle-receptive mode. When we relax into the arms of God, the mind opens to greater insight and the heart to deeper love.

When we step back with the ego and let God lead the way, we become a natural space for healing. Let's say, for instance, that you have a problem; many possibilities exist for how you could solve it. Yet if you're tense about the issue, stuck in anger or frantic searching, then the chances of one of those possibilities becoming clear are decreased.

If you have a problem but you are stuck in blaming others or trying to duck out of your own responsibility, then helpful forces are repelled. If you have a problem but you try to keep your heart open—you do your best to deal with it, take personal responsibility, remain vulnerable—then others will have a natural tendency to reach out to you and offer help. Just knowing you have a problem will not inspire others to help you; how you're handling it is what will do that.

Highest solutions don't come from you; they come *into* you and *through* you. It is not your ability to figure things out, put the blame elsewhere, or hire the right lawyers that ultimately guarantees divine right action. Rather, it is our surrender to the flow of divinity that allows divinity to flow through us.

Staying calm and trusting in the flow of the universe are hard when we can't sense a cosmic order to things. Yet once we recognize that God is everywhere, all the time, we can relax into any instant and know that healing is natural. God will exalt us if we will allow Him to. And when we feel that happening, we're liable to smile a certain kind of smile, inspiring someone around us to say, "What?" as though surely there must be something that is making us smile that way. But there is nothing that is making us smile at that moment, so much as *everything* is making us smile. We have sensed Reality and felt the peace that follows.

Strength in Our Defenselessness

The workbook of *A Course in Miracles* includes an exercise that reads, "In my defenselessness my safety lies."

It is astonishing to consider all the defenses we walk around with, emotionally and psychologically. Imagine every moment, from the time you were born, when something seemingly unsafe occurred—a spanking, or a moment of misunderstanding or invalidation. In each instance, you built a defense mechanism—an automatic closing off of the heart—and by the time you were old enough to act out these defenses, you had no conscious awareness that they even existed. Once we've reached out for love enough times and felt unloved in return, we shut down and try to defend ourselves against the blow we subconsciously have come to expect. Often our form of defense is to attack before someone else has a chance to or to intimidate in order to keep our imagined attacker at bay or to try to impress so as not to be rejected.

The problem with this is that we "create what we defend against."* If I have my dukes up, an opponent will surely appear. If I put on grandiose airs in order to impress, I will surely be rejected.

It always feels like we're protecting ourselves when we're wrapped in the ego's energies. Yet in fact, the ego is our weakness and not our strength. When we act defensive or arrogant or willful, no one will think us strong; quite the opposite. It can feel like we're exposed and vulnerable when we stand defenseless and empty before God, yet when we do is when we appear centered and in our power. Our ability to be transparent, to become an empty space through which God's love can flow, is our spiritual strength. When the ego disappears, we are hardly invisible; we're illumined. People can't take their eyes off a person who has removed his or her mask. Childlike serenity replaces childish posturing. We are gentle yet strong. The light within shines through.

As we shift our center of power from material strength to spiritual strength, we begin to change from a "go-out-and-get-'em" kind of personality to a more magnetic "be-centered-and-watch-the-world-come-to-you" kind of personality. The toughness, the intensity, and the assertiveness of the personality are second-rate powers compared to the spirit within. In any moment that we simply breathe deeply, giving up attachment to goal or outcome, living only to enjoy the instant and the love it brings, we are surrendered to God. And in losing ourselves, we find ourselves. At last.

From *A Course in Miracles*:

We will remind ourselves that He remains beside us through the day, and never leaves our weakness unsupported by His strength. We call upon His strength each time we feel the threat of our defenses undermine our certainty of purpose. We will pause a moment, as He tells us, "I am here."*

When New Life Stirs

In all the great religious teachings, there are coded messages from God. Students of enlightenment seek to understand those messages and apply them to our lives. Whether or not a particular religion is our personal path, its core mystical teachings apply to everyone.

In museums across the world there are thousands of paintings of an event described in the New Testament as the Annunciation. The angel Gabriel appeared to the maiden Mary, telling her that she would conceive a child by God, and the child would be born to be savior to the world.

Putting aside for a moment what *that* must have felt like, let's remember that all religious stories represent a deeper metaphysical truth. Angels are the thoughts of God, and Mary isn't the only one who has had angels come and talk to her. Angels are talking to all of us constantly, but most of us don't listen.

Gabriel represents a particular kind of message from God, namely that He wants to impregnate us spiritually, miraculously turn us into new people, and extend His love onto the earth through us. The difference between us and Mary is that she had the humility and grace to say, "Yes."

You and I say, "Thanks, maybe sometime," "Not now," "Be real," "Gimme a break," "No way," and a host of other things that don't exactly resonate with Mary's willingness to be used by God. But those paintings exist, as does all art, to take our minds to the place where we remember what's true. That story is not just about her; it's about us as well.

Around all of us, at every moment, there's an angel heralding a new beginning, the birth of a new being from the pieces of our scattered selves. Every situation represents a choice: do we prefer to stay with ego-based patterns of thought and behavior, or do we choose to play life in a higher, more loving way? Will we tread the path of limitation and fear, though that path has grown painful and boring and old, or do we choose to give birth to a higher mode of expression? The Christ within is a newborn self, fathered by God and mothered by our humanity, here to express the divine potential that exists inside us all.

Mary could not have said "No" to God because it would have been contrary to her nature. And at our deepest core, it's contrary to ours as well. We long to say "Yes" to Him, but we're so out of touch with who we really are, so not in conscious contact with our own souls, that we continually say "No." And there, in that rejection of love, lies the tragedy of human existence.

One day we say, "Yes, God, you can express your love through me." And on another day, in another situation, we just can't make the stretch—we say no to more forgiveness or more depth or more love. Yet Gabriel persists, and every time we say no, he simply waits around to ask us again. "I'm bringing this situation around again to give you another chance."

Slowly but surely, our hearts begin to open; we resist love less, the longer we trod the spiritual path. And ultimately we will resist no longer. If we're deeply, truly honest with ourselves, we know we're longing to be pregnant with God.

When Gabriel spoke to Mary, she was a fourteen-year-old girl, and now he speaks to each of us, no matter what our sex or how old we are. As long as we are willing to be part of God's plan, then God has a plan for us.

And that's when life begins to truly change: not when we have new things, but when we have a new spirit. The birth of God's love into the world is not just a "was," but an "is." It's important not just because of what it did to the world, but because of what it does to us. As we love each other, God lives in us. He overshadows our mind and heart. He guides our thinking, our behavior, and our words. He removes from us our thoughts of fear, miraculously replacing them with thoughts of love. In that lies our holiness, and there is literally nothing our holiness cannot do.*

When the three kings bowed down before the baby Jesus, they symbolically expressed the relative weakness of the powers of the world compared to the power of our true being when we are centered in the love of God. The radiance of the divine child is you and me transformed.

Our fears dissolve, and our energetic armor melts. As we pray constantly for an ever more open heart, the action of God's Spirit redeems our past and frees our future to be unlike it. We are spiritually reborn, as the illusions of the past fall away and we have the chance to begin again.

Sometimes someone will say to us, "You seem like a completely new person."

Sometimes we do seem like a new person. And sometimes, we actually *are* one.

The Christ

The conversion to Christ need not entail a conversion to the Christian religion. The word is a symbol for the Child of God within us, our true identity and a space of remembrance of all that is divine. To be His disciple is to take on the mantle of His ministry by refusing to acknowledge the ultimate reality of any walls that divide us. In our oneness with others lies our oneness with God, and removing those walls is His work in us and in the world. God's one begotten son is *who we are*.

So it is that we seek to see with the eyes of God's son, in which only our unity with others is seen; to hear with the ears of God's son, where only love and calls for love are heard; to walk with Him, to wherever we can be of service; and to speak for Him of our love for everyone.

Try thinking of a situation in your life where things aren't going as you wish. Now close your eyes and take a deep breath, and allow yourself to see yourself as you dwell within that experience. See how you look, your mannerisms, and your normal behavior. See how others relate to you. Feel all your feelings as they arise, even if they are painful or anxious.

Now see Jesus, as the embodiment of Christ, come up behind you and put His arms around you. He has been given by God the power to make you whole. Allow him to permeate your being and to heal every broken part of you. Allow Him to stand in the breach for you, between the you now manifest and your divine potential. He *is* that potential, and He has been given by God the power to help anyone who asks for His help to actualize it within themselves.

He is as clear in the Holy Instant as we allow him to be.* Either He's *metaphorically* there, or He's *literally* there. Which it will be in your experience is completely up to you.

The changes that spirit accomplishes within us cannot be explained to the ego mind, but looking to the ego for either approval or verification is ridiculous. We think that without the ego all would be chaos, but in truth, without the ego all would be love.* At some point, you must decide which way of looking at the world makes the most sense; you can't just kinda-sorta embrace a mystical reality. The spiritual life involves believing in an invisible reality that affects a visible one. As we change within, we change our behavior. We change our energy. We change our lives.

Creating Miracles

Centered in an attitude of blessing, we become automatic miracle workers. People feel uplifted and energized along with us, subconsciously corrected and healed in our presence. A palpably more positive atmosphere prevails. When we reach for the highest within ourselves, people around us feel called to their highest. And that is the beacon for which every soul is looking.

As we remember our spiritual heritage and stand within its power, we think, act, and then experience all of life differently. We're about to judge someone, and then we remember their eternal innocence. We're about to share an unkind story we heard about someone, and then we remember, "What I do to others I am doing to myself." We're about to reach for a win at another person's expense, and we remember that there is no such thing. We are complaining about a situation, and we stop to ask ourselves, "What am *I* not contributing here?" *This* is the birth of our better selves—a gradual and continuous process, as in any given moment we either listen to the ego or we listen to love.

Whichever we listen to is what we will become. And whatever we become is the world we will inhabit. We can live in fear, or we can live in love. And every moment, we decide. The greatest power God has given us to change the world is the power to change our thoughts about the world.* And as we do, the world transforms.

No matter how insane the world might appear, we seek to remember it's a vast illusion. We don't become more metaphysically complicated as we do this; in fact, we become simpler and simpler, trying to apply certain basic principles to everything we go through. We know there is a world of love that lies beyond what we see, and we were born to make it manifest. If we apply ourselves body and soul to the task, then one day—right here on earth—we will experience an illumined world.

CHAPTER SIX

From *Living in the Past and Future* to *Living in the Present*

*I*f we want to change worlds, then we have to change time slots.

There's no point in trying to watch *Seinfeld* at 8:00 if it's on at 7:00. And there's no point in trying to find miracles in the past or future when they only exist in the present.

I always used to wonder what my future would be like. When I was done obsessing about the future, I would be content for about five minutes, and then I would begin to obsess about the past. It's clear the ego has no intention of letting us enjoy the present.

And that's because the present is holy ground—the only place where eternity meets linear time. The past is nowhere except in your mind, and the future is nowhere except in your mind. The ego is intent on having us live in one of those two realms as a way of making sure we never *live at all*. If God dwells only in the present, then living in the past or future is bound to be painful because it leaves Him out. Living fully in the present, the Holy Instant, is literally death to the ego—and that is why we resist it. As long as we identify with the life of the ego, reality itself seems scary.

We find it easier to analyze what happened in the past and to imagine what might happen in the future than to show up fully for life in the present. Yet when we allow ourselves to fully *be*, unencumbered by past or future concerns, that moment becomes our portal to the miraculous, Harry Potter's platform no. 9³/₄. The Holy Instant *is* the miracle.

When the Bible says, "Time shall be no more," it doesn't mean the end of the world, it means the end of the illusion of linear time and the beginning of an eternal now.

The things that are most important are everlasting. *Everlasting* doesn't refer to some eternal reality that begins when this life is over and some other life begins. It refers to a moment-by-moment reality that has gone on forever, is true this instant, and will endure forever. *Everlasting* means "always true."

Eternity means a never-ending present in which God *is*. It is the dimension of His power, and to the extent that we use the present to focus on past or future, we disempower ourselves. The tennis player doesn't have time to think about the ball he or she just missed because it would take away from the effort to hit the next one. It is the same with all of us, all the time.

The past doesn't automatically blend into the future except in our minds. The past leads to the future simply because we allow it to; it is more a product of the way our brains function than of the way reality functions. By thinking about the past in the present, we simply recreate it in the future.

Yet a miracle can intercede between past and future, releasing each moment to endless new possibilities. In the Holy Instant, we can break the chain of yesterday's thought, reprogramming the future by thinking different thoughts today. A common mistake is to base our thoughts on yesterday's circumstances, not realizing that those circumstances are simply the reflection of thoughts we're now free to change.

Let's say you're thinking, "I'm broke." That might be a description of a material condition, yet material conditions change in response to a change in consciousness. To affirm "I'm broke" is to choose to extend the condition into the future by thinking it in the present. And if that is your choice, then the universe will respond, "So be it." But you might want to ask yourself why you choose to think that, considering how much power you have to change your circumstances by changing your thoughts. I heard the spiritual teacher Chalanda Sai Ma once say, "You will experience whatever you think after the words 'I am . . .'"

You could instead think, "I am infinitely abundant in spirit. I have lots of money (money is a relative concept: most Americans who think they're broke have more money than the majority of the world's population), and my fortune is growing every day." Notice how just *saying* that instructs your body as well as your mind. Saying "I'm broke" will send one kind of signal through the brain; saying "I'm wealthy" will send another. Brain chemicals, hormones, and an endless array of mental and physical functions respond to every thought. It's hard to say "I'm broke" with your spine straight and your head up; it's hard to say "I'm wealthy" in any other way. The subconscious mind is your servant, responding to your every command. And how you feel and how you present yourself will affect your material circumstances in countless ways.

Perhaps a lover or two rejected you, so now you think, "I have no luck in love; my partners leave me." But in fact, what you're probably saying is that *some* people left you while others would have overcharged their credit cards to have tea with you in Timbuktu.

But your ego just *loves* to go for that negative thought! That's the same ego that set you up to fail with the ones who left, now contextualizing the situation in such a way as to make sure it happens again. The ego's dictate in love is "Seek, but do not find."*

You could say to yourself instead, "I'm totally attractive, and the most wonderful people in the world think I'm the most wonderful person to be with." And you know why? Because the most wonderful people for you really would think that! But your thoughts that such people don't exist, or would reject you, are literally keeping them at bay. There is no magnetic force calling them toward you if you deny that they exist.

If you're thinking thoughts like, "Men reject me," then I doubt your energy is exactly reading, "Hot babe." If your energy just confirms a past condition, then expect the condition to remain. But you can inwardly prepare for what you want rather than always affirming what has been. You can *practice* the life you want. "If life *were* what I wanted it to be today, what would I think and do? Where would I go? How would I handle myself?" It's like the movie *Field of Dreams:* "If you build it, they will come." Time and space are not what they appear to be; you are not at their effect unless you choose to be. God placed you on the earth to be a master of your own destiny, not a slave to the material world.

It helps to ask ourselves why we choose to play so small when we don't have to. Belief is powerful, and whatever we believe, we will subconsciously make manifest. So why do we hold on to core beliefs about ourselves that are so demeaning? When we ask that question, the answers emerge: "My family told me it wasn't okay to think I was a big deal." "I thought people wouldn't like me if I 'had it all.'" "I thought it might hurt my father's feelings if I made more money than he did."

Yet whatever pain we might experience at others' negative reactions to our spreading our wings, is nothing compared to the pain we cause ourselves by clipping them. At this time on the planet, no one can feel good about withholding their magnificence. Expressing your full potential is not just your right; it's your responsibility.

As long as you keep thinking in limited terms, disbelieving in the possibility of infinite possibility in your life, then you will never experience the miracles God has in store for you. You will deny His gifts, taking on the ego's servitude instead. In a world such as this, fear is often the path of least resistance. If you want a miracle, you have to consciously *claim* it. And for everyone out there who might say, "How dare you?" there are at least two more who will say, "Thank you for showing me how."

Embracing the Real

Sometimes I hear people say, "I'm ready to change my thinking, but I'm afraid that others around me won't change theirs, so it won't do any good." Perhaps, but not for long. As soon as you change your mind, others will begin to change theirs, and those who do not will begin to fall away.

I was having a conversation with a young man, Andrew, who was about to reenter his hometown high school after having attended an out-of-town school for two years. He was depressed about returning home, and I asked him why.

"I was such a jerk when I lived here before. I was really insecure, and so I acted like a big know-it-all. I'm sure everyone here just thinks of me as this total loser, and going back to that is really depressing."

"But have you changed?" I asked him. "Are you different now?"

"Yeah," he said. "But *they* don't know that. They just know me as I was back then, so it doesn't matter that I've changed. No one there will like me."

"Well, actually," I told him, "from a metaphysical perspective, all minds are joined. So if *you've* changed, then *they've* got to change. The other kids might think of you a certain way at first, but if you've truly changed, then everything but who you are now will drop away. If you don't take the old stuff with you, then it won't be able to stay in their minds except for a very short time."

The universe is primed to start over again in any moment, and it is only our own thoughts to the contrary that keep it from doing so. A miracle occurs when we ask God to intervene between our past and future, cancel out all fear. and release us to new beginnings. A God who will part the seas and raise the dead has no difficulty solving your problems in high school—or anywhere else, for that matter. His is a radical power to repair and restore. When our faith is as audacious and radical as His power, we will experience that power to the fullest.

Spiritually, we are reborn in any moment we do not take the past with us.* My young friend Andrew and I prayed that day, asking God to take his relationship with his schoolmates into His hands. We asked Him to remove all walls of misunderstanding. We prayed that his relationships would be reborn, that he might start over in a different place. We asked for divine right order, in this and all things.

A few weeks later I saw Andrew again. He smiled at me and gave me a really big hug. "Had a miracle, huh?" I asked him. "Oh, yeah," he said. "*Oh*, ye-ah . . ."

Every moment is part of a divine curriculum, and if I experienced a lack of love in the past, then the present contains ways to compensate for it now. God is ever-present; His hand is on everything. Whatever situation we are in *now*, whatever person or people we are relating to *now*, contains the key to both healing the past and releasing the future. We can be someone different than we were in the past, releasing the future to be different as well.

If we release our past to God, He will change our minds about it for us.* Since only love is real and nothing else exists, the only reality about our past is the love we gave and the love we received.* Everything else is an illusion and will stay alive in our experience only if we choose to hold on to it. According to *A Course in Miracles,* "Nothing real can be threatened; nothing unreal exists." And that is the miracle: to embrace the real.

Healing the Past

When we go through difficult experiences, we have a natural tendency to want to talk about them. And to some extent, that's good; processing with counselors and friends is one of the ways we heal. Yet there is another tendency, of the ego rather than the spirit, that leads us to articulate negative experiences in a way that keeps them alive.

In a town I once visited, I had an experience that was very painful, and when my friends asked me what happened, I would tell them the story. But then I said to myself, "Enough already. It wasn't all bad; think of the wonderful people you met and all the good things that happened there too." So then when friends would ask, I would tell them the negative *and* the positive. But after a while, when I had done my forgiving and atoning and allowed my heart to heal, I found myself answering a query about that period of my life very simply: "It was a special time." The words just came out of my mouth; I didn't consciously realize I was about to say them. But at the deepest level, those words were true because only love exists. Just saying them gave comfort to my heart.

Everything that happens has a cause: either it was caused by love and offers a chance to increase that love, or it was caused by fear, and spirit is present in the situation to lead us out of it. One way or another, as people say these days, "It's all good."

Accepting Ourselves in the Present

When I was younger I wanted to be older, and when I got older I wanted to be younger. When I was living in one place I wanted to live in another, and when I was doing one thing I wanted to be doing something else. I could never just settle into who I was and what was happening at the moment. It seemed that somehow I wasn't enough, what I was doing wasn't enough, and therefore my life was never enough.

I once mentioned in a lecture that I recently looked at a picture of myself when I was thirty and said to myself, "I thought *this* was *inadequate?*" I watched the room fill up with knowing smiles from every woman who was past her youth. Who among us has not looked back on a period we thought was lacking, wishing we could go back to it now and experience the wonders we couldn't see at the time? The truth is that every stage of our lives is perfect, if we allow ourselves to really *live* in it. If we concentrate on the present, contributing and showing up for it as fully as we can, then any moment can have its blessings, and the future will unfold in the direction of ever greater good.

When we accept ourselves exactly as we are, and where we are, we have more energy to give to life. We are not wasting our time trying to make things different. Any moment that we relax into the deeper ground of our being, giving up all struggle to be anywhere else, we're in exactly the right place at exactly the right time. There is a plan for our lives—God's plan—and it oversees exactly where we are and where we need to be going. As soon as we have learned to live most brightly in our present conditions, new and better ones will arrive immediately. But until we learn the lessons of the present, they will simply reappear in new guises, and it will seem as though nothing ever changes.

It's not up to us what we learn, only whether we learn through joy or through pain.* But if we don't yet trust that every situation is a lesson, we don't bother to ask ourselves what the lesson *is*. And unless we do, our chances of learning it are nil. Then the lesson will reappear—with ever higher stakes—until we learn it. We may as well learn it the first time, when the chance to learn through joy is still available. The more times a lesson has to come around, the more pain it will generate. If you know in your heart that something is wrong, then ignoring it won't make it any less so. It will simply make fixing it even harder, when it is brought about by a louder noise than the original sound of God's whisper in your ear.

Handling Joy

Sometimes we do receive joy but then don't quite know how to handle it. At times in my life I had what it took to *attract* my good, but not what it took to *be* with it once it got here. Wonderful change was offered me, but I was too nervous to let it in. The suddenness of an opportunity, or the speed by which I was expected to make a decision about it, sort of blew my wattage and I couldn't respond. Sometimes a change presents an opportunity too at odds with our self-perception—too big, too good, too powerful. If God wants to move us in a more positive direction, but we're not yet agreeing with His positive attitude about us, then we will resist His love and resist the blessing. The days when we realize we threw away a miracle can be among the saddest days of our lives.

Once I was walking through a resort community with my fourteen-year-old daughter and her friends. The girls kept a bit ahead of me, needing a little distance and independence from Emma's mom. I didn't feel left out, as the distance felt appropriate for them and for me as well. Motherhood takes up so much of your energy for a few years; as children grow up you begin to get parts of your life back that were put on hold for a while. But as I walked behind the teenagers, I remembered the times my daughter would cling to me so tightly when she was a little girl, needing me every moment, wanting my attention to be centered on her alone. At times I subtly resisted her, feeling smothered by her overwhelming need for attention, as if I were afraid I would be swallowed up by the experience. For a while I could not surrender totally to motherhood, fully accepting that each moment of it was perfect and would transform with time into something else.

I see now that the fact it was happening meant it was exactly what I was supposed to be doing, and I wasn't losing out on anything by giving most of my attention to her. I remember she used to hate my telephone—and for good reason, because I would use it to distract myself from the intimacy of the mother-child connection. I remember once when she was a baby, she actually crawled over to the phone while I was on it, using her little finger to push the button that disconnected the call.

Now the days of her early childhood are over and will not be coming back. During those years I showed up emotionally at about 90 percent of my capacity, perhaps a little more. She may not have missed a lot, but I think I missed a few things. It's all a part of the mistakes you make when you don't recognize that the present moment is perfect.

What Will Be

Obsessing about the future, of course, is just as neurotic as obsessing about the past. It's simply another way the ego robs us of the joy of living by directing our attention away from the present. Living in the future is a way of avoiding life right now.

As miracle workers, we place the future in the hands of God.* We can release our future concerns by living fully in the present, knowing that as we do so, the future will take care of itself. God so clothed the lilies of the field; surely He will take care of us.

I remember how obsessed I used to get, wondering what my life would be like in the future. Now that my past self's future is here, I regret having wasted any time thinking about it at all when such a glorious present was available to me then. I didn't realize at the time that the present was glorious, of course; I was focused on what I perceived to be lacking. And that's the mind game that will continue forever if we allow it to. In the past I didn't realize how perfect things were, just as I don't always realize how perfect they are now. If I had simply allowed myself to *enjoy* my life more, I would have ended up better off later on. And when I allow myself to simply *enjoy* my life right now, I'm giving myself the biggest boost for the future. Every point in life's journey is inherently preparing us for our future in ways the rational mind cannot possibly comprehend.

Yet the thinking of the world is so devoid of any concept of mystery that it's no wonder we can't relax into it. We think we have to lead, when all we really have to do is follow. In whatever moment I'm deeply surrendered to what *is* in life, then what *will be* is programmed to reflect my faith and trust.

Once I was visiting New York with my daughter. We were having a wonderful time, and then she turned to me and said, "I'm so excited about going to Boston next week, I can hardly stand it!" I didn't want to rain on her parade or make her feel invalidated for wanting to go to Boston. But I did muse about how the ego works: always making us think that where we're going next week will be better, what we're doing at the next job will be more right for us, and so forth. Joy can be found only one place at one time: right here, right now. Regardless of where we're going tomorrow, it's important to bless where we are and enjoy the fruits of today. The truth is, almost any experience can be miserable if you're good enough at making yourself miserable. And almost any experience can be enjoyable if you're good enough at practicing joy.

Sometimes people think they can't relax about the future because they need to know what it will be first. I've known people who seemed to think God should send a letter, telling them exactly where to go and what to do. "Dear Gloria, this is God. I've chosen Kansas City for you, where you will live for six months starting this November and work at Carter and Associates. From there you will move to Newport Beach, where you will meet your soul mate. You'll be rich and successful and happy. And then, after a long, long time you will die." They wonder why, if God is so smart, He doesn't use Fed Ex.

But I think we're told so little about the future because there's so much more to understand about the present. God's ground, after all, is *now*. He doesn't spell out the path ahead; rather, He spells out the path within. And as we follow that path, seeking to deepen in our compassion and understanding and capacity to enjoy what is, we co-create with Him our highest future.

Past Regrets

Until you reach a certain age, the word *regret* has little meaning. It's only when you see that your mistakes *did* affect the rest of your life and realize that the bad decisions you made can't be reversed in this lifetime that you face the horror of true remorse. Therein lies the paradox: as human beings, we have such a short period of time here in which to get it right, yet as spirits living in eternity, we have opportunities unlimited. As beings with free will, we are allowed to make our own choices; as children of God, we are redeemed upon our humble and prayerful request, should those choices have been wrong-minded.

Our mistakes are not sins God wants to punish but rather errors He wants to correct. One prayer in *A Course in Miracles* suggests that we simply go back to the moment of our mistake—realizing it was a moment when, by definition, we didn't allow the Holy Spirit to make our decision for us—and allow Him to make it for us now. For miracles work retroactively. There's no need to feel guilty in such a case because the Holy Spirit will undo all the consequences of our wrong decision if we let Him.* As long as we genuinely atone for our errors, the universe will be miraculously reconfigured on our behalf. Millions of people—alcoholics, drug addicts, people who committed crimes, people who hurt others—can testify to the profound forgiveness of God. Many know they wouldn't be alive today were their God not such a merciful God.

That means so much for those of us who have lived a lot of years; for those of us who have made huge mistakes that affect ourselves and others for years or even a lifetime; for those of us who can't get over our feelings of guilt about this or that. Like prodigal sons, those of us who have deviated most from love are not relegated by God to the periphery of meaning. Quite the opposite; the Father of the prodigal son didn't reject his son but rejoiced to see him come home. Our mistakes are sometimes what it takes to make us humble, and that's when we're most of use to Him. To God we're never damaged goods. He turns our scars into beauty marks.

Stuck in the Middle

I found turning fifty harder than I expected it to be.

Somewhere around two or three months before the big day, I started to be haunted by memories of a youth now irrevocably over. As much as I told myself that fifty is the new forty, what I really wanted in my heart was to have the old forty back. I had waking nightmares of blazing memories—things I hadn't handled well, stupid choices I had made and could not make over, chances I thought were never more to be retrieved. Grieving the glory of my younger years, I had to face myself and all the pain that comes with it.

Several friends told me they had experienced the same thing, but not to worry—all of a sudden the anxiety would lift. And indeed that is the way it happened for me. Sitting at an outside café late on the night of my big five-O, looking up at the Eiffel Tower lit up against the sky, I felt the pain lift. In an instant, it was all okay. I knew the sun had set on what was no longer, but I had a sense that something new would now dawn to take its place.

Girlfriends had told me that the fifties are great because you don't care anymore what others think. I don't know if that will be true for me, but I do know that I'm not who I used to be. Fifty is as different from forty as forty is from thirty and thirty from twenty. With the coming of fifty, one makes a transition as fundamental as that of puberty. I have settled into the paradox of middle age.

On one hand, I finally have some sense of what I'm doing in the world. At last I'm convinced I have a right to be here. I'm not as frantic as I used to be, though I can't tell yet whether that's because I've evolved or just aged. On the other hand, I get tired more easily, I often can't remember things, and I'm exhausted from just looking for my glasses all the time! Most disconcerting of all, when I'm in a serious mood and I do the math, I can't garner much hope of changing things on this planet during the time I have left. Our generation's shared delusion that we would usher in paradise has been completely shattered. The older you get, the more you see how entrenched certain negatives are. There is so much cruelty in the world that you thought for years would go away; as you age, it dawns on you that it never really does.

As disillusioning as it is to realize these things—and disillusionment is actually a good thing because it means you were laboring under illusions before*—it's also the beginning of spiritual insight. Once you're deeply convinced there are no ultimate answers outside yourself, you start looking for them where they truly are: inside. And you realize that in your slowing down, you're more prepared to listen to things you were moving too fast before to hear.

So much wasted time, so many stupid mistakes. You feel you have the knowledge now, but you're not sure you have the energy left: if only you had known then what you know now. You come to understand George Bernard Shaw's comment, "Youth is wasted on the young."

Our adrenal glands decimated, our cells like fast cars beginning to show wear, the fastest generation has begun to slow down. Jack Nicholson said in a recent interview, "My generation is the new old." Our deepest burden is the accumulated sorrow, the heartbreak of one decade impinging upon the next until the heart can absorb no more. Your mind has figured so much out, but your body isn't sure that it cares anymore. When it's more depressing than joyful to wake up in the morning, then you know you have a problem.

And many do.

Most people, once they hit middle age, face a fork in the road. Which road they take, as Robert Frost wrote, will make all the difference. One road leads to gradual dissolution—a cruise (however slow) toward death; the other road becomes a birth canal, a pattern of rebirth. The older we get, the harder it is to choose rebirth. The ego's gravity seems harder to resist.

We start out so enthusiastic about life, so entertained and delighted by the very nature of things. But the newness fades; we grow jaded or exhausted, and we begin to lose some vital appreciation of the possibilities inherent in a day. As I write this, I hear teenagers in my backyard, delighting in the mud puddles produced by the afternoon's storm. I have to consciously check myself—to remind myself that the ability to have fun in the mud is what makes being young so wonderful, and not make a stink about the fact that my towels are beige and this could ruin them. My mortal truth is that I want the kids to hose off before they come back into the house, but my soul's truth is that I wish I could enjoy the mud too.

So it's completely up to me, whether I start to become an old biddy who cares too much about the towels or instead hold on to my sense of adventure. I want to focus on what's important as I grow older. So what the hell, the kids are happy and that *is* what's important! And not just for kids, but for all of us.

Choosing to See

Birth is audacious; creativity is audacious; the spiritual quest is audacious. Without audacity, we're mere cogs in the wheels of the ego's status quo. And that status quo leads to decay and death, not as a portal to greater life but as a mockery of life itself.

I was once about to throw out what I thought of as dead pink roses when a friend of mine said to me, "What are you doing? Why are you throwing those away?" I said, "They're dying!" He said, "Look at them, Marianne! They're beautiful! I think the faded pink on them today is actually more wonderful than the brighter pink they had yesterday!"

And he was right. It was not the look of the drying flowers but rather my own prejudice that led me to look at the flowers quickly, say, "They're dying," and simply throw them out. In actuality, they were not less beautiful so much as beautiful in a different way. It was not the flowers but my own eyes that needed to change.

In that situation, the flowers had had an *advocate:* my friend, a noted environmentalist, who simply had a more sophisticated eye. The more we live, the more capacity we have to see how much of life is beautiful. There are things that touch my heart now—lovers holding hands, small children laughing—that I barely noticed in days gone by.

I have a friend who worked for a middle-aged rock star, and he told me a story about an experience they once had together. I had been complaining that after a certain point in life it's hard to get excited about a lot of things that used to seem glamorous and fun. My friend said, "Let me tell you about a trip I took with John to Minneapolis.

"We were going there to see a Springsteen concert, and John rented a private jet to fly us from New York. Three of us who work for him piled into a limo and were driving to the airport when one of John's friends called on the phone.

"John exclaimed to him, 'Oh, Ben, you should be here! We're having *so much fun!* We're in a *stretch limo,* and we're going off in a *jet* to a *Springsteen* concert!' John was like an excited little boy, studying the traveler's guide to find a great restaurant in Minneapolis, excited about this trip as though it were the coolest thing in the world."

The point, of course, is that John has been in hundreds if not thousands of private jets; he has been to hundreds if not thousands of rock concerts, including his own; and a stretch limo to him is like a normal car to the rest of us. He travels the world like it's his own backyard, yet here he was studying the travel guide as though Minneapolis were some exotic destination. Apparently, everywhere John goes is exciting to him because he hasn't lost his capacity for joy. Boredom is not his frame of mind.

So then it makes more sense why he's so exciting to the rest of us: he generates fun. He's not waiting for the world to provide it;

he carries it with him. It's an emotional and mental habit he has cultivated.

My father had it. I never saw him bored. And that, I think, is because he wasn't looking for the world to entertain him. Which is precisely why it always did.

I try to remind myself, whenever I am tempted to think the world is boring, "No, Marianne, *you're* boring." And that seems to fix it. Only what we are not giving can be lacking in any situation.* The excitement isn't out there; it's in here, in all of us, when it is what we consciously choose to see.

Rebirth

A friend of mine, a man fifty-seven, said to me once, "I think I'm waiting to die." I understood what he meant, but I responded, "Well, I'm not. I took the other road. I am busy being born."

Thousands of years ago, before the earth was fully populated, there was no reason to live longer than thirty-five or forty years. When we arrived at that age, we had already served the grand purpose of human evolution, the survival of our species. Our sperm and ovaries aged, and as far as nature was concerned, there really was no further need for us to be here. That was the time when physical procreation was the highest purpose of human existence.

Women—perhaps more than men—feel nature's message within our cells: "Thanks. You can go now." Menstrual periods fade away. Doctor's reports come back: "You're done." Pregnancies we so zealously avoided seem clearly now to have been blessings we did not appreciate at the time. We grieve our unborn children, and we grieve our stupid, ungrateful youth.

Nature no longer cares whether we look good, for our attracting sexual partners is of no concern to it anymore. We silently freak. *What happened to my radiance? My voluptuousness? My breasts?* Nature no longer cares to aid our sexual adventures, for whether or not we have sex is of no concern to it anymore. We silently grieve. *What happened to my body? My libido? My juices?* When nature has clearly had its way with us on a certain level, then why are we here? Have we just entered oblivion's waiting room? To whom can we scream? With whom can we cry?

Nature is most concerned with the propagation of the species, and when we're young, our eggs and sperm are our most vital contributions to the process. Yet at this point in human history, the birth of wisdom is more critical for the survival of humanity than the birth of many more children. What we can birth from the womb of our consciousness is every bit as precious a gift to the world as what we can birth from the womb of our bodies. There are a lot of ways to be mother or father to a new world.

Our greatest contribution to the world at this time is not just what we do but who we are becoming. It's the nature of our thinking that is forging a new consciousness. Just as the beginnings of terrorism were rumbling underneath the surface, and thus below the radar, for years before they burst into view, so a new movement of love is rumbling underneath the surface today. Martin Luther King Jr. said we have a "glorious opportunity to inject a new dimension of love into the veins of our civilization." And all of us can participate in this process. Every single moment, with the nature of our thoughts, we can add to love's storehouse in a way that blesses the world.

Yet no spiritual change will ultimately matter if it doesn't reach into our cells and become a very human one as well. I recently heard from a young male colleague that he was enthusiastic about a team of humanitarian activists we had met, "except that it's four white middle-aged women."

I paused. "And the problem with that is . . . ?"

"Well, you know," he said.

And no, I did not know. I understood his political correctness, his wanting racial diversity, but I also saw something else behind this. Many people these days rush to do ceremonies "honoring the wisdom of the grandmothers" but still don't really want to deal with the real-life grandmothers in their midst. They proclaim "the rise of the feminine" but still resist and judge actual women. It's not enough to just honor an *archetype*. If the world is to change, we've got to honor each other. And those who are forging a new future for the world, at whatever age, deserve from themselves, and from those around them, all the honor in the world.

Let's forgive the past and who we were then. Let's embrace the present and who we're capable of becoming. Let's surrender the future and watch miracles unfold.

CHAPTER SEVEN

From *Focus on Guilt* to *Focus on Innocence*

*I*magine your life as a long-running movie. Now see it made by two different directors. The first movie, in the hands of one director, is a movie about fear, anger, scarcity, and anxiety. The other, in the hands of a different director, is a movie about love, peace, abundance, and happiness.

One director is your ego; the other is the Holy Spirit. And the star of the movie is you.

Because my own life has gone back and forth so much between depressing and uplifting drama, I have a good sense of the difference between the two—and how each is created. One thing I'm clear about regarding both is that when I've looked up close, I've seen these words: "Produced by Marianne Williamson; Directed by Marianne Williamson; Starring Marianne Williamson."

Which director you take your cues from depends on one thing: the thoughts you hold in your mind. To take directions from your ego, all you have to do is focus on guilt. The ego's cornerstone thought is that the child of God is guilty.* To take your direction from the Holy Spirit, focus instead on innocence. Love's cornerstone thought is that the child of God is innocent.*

Whichever focus we choose—on someone's innocence or on their guilt—determines the drama that unfolds in our lives and the part that we play in it.

The Willingness to See

It is our willingness to see the innocence in a person that allows us to see it. The ego mind is so invested in the human drama—"He did this, she said that"—that it often takes a higher power to counterbalance the ego's insistence. It helps to remember that the ego's true target is you: your ego wants you to see guilt in others mainly so you might stay convinced of all the guilt in yourself. The perception of guilt in anyone is our surefire ticket to hell. Every time we blame another, we are tightening the chains that keep our own self-hatred in place.

Forgiveness can be very hard when someone has acted horribly. But the truth, whether or not we care to admit it, is that someone did what we too might have done if we had been as freaked out by something as they were; if we had been as scared of something as they were; if we had been as limited in our understanding as they were. That doesn't mean they shouldn't be held accountable or that we shouldn't have boundaries and standards. It doesn't even mean we have to stay in contact with that person. But it does mean we can come to understand that humanity is not perfect. Just knowing that—that we all do the best we know how with the skills we have at the time—is a realization that opens the heart to more enlightened understanding. And that's what we're on the earth for, because in the presence of people with enlightened understanding, darkness ultimately turns into light.

Forgiveness isn't usually an event; it's a process. An abstract principle has to penetrate various levels of thought and feeling before arriving at the heart, and that's okay. Our hurt can be real, and our feelings matter. The only thing God is asking of us is that we be *willing* to see the innocence in another person. As long as we are willing to see a situation in another light, the Holy Spirit has room to maneuver.

With every human encounter, we either affirm for people their innocence or fortify their guilt. And whichever it is is how we ourselves will feel. We cannot escape our oneness, even if we do not acknowledge it. Do unto others what you would have them do unto you, because they will. And even if they don't, you will feel as though they did.

Because all minds are joined, whatever I choose to think about you I am in essence thinking about myself. To the extent to which I perceive your guilt, I am bound to perceive my own. It doesn't feel that way at first, of course, because the ego would have us believe that as soon as we place the blame on someone else we'll feel better. But that's just a temporary delusion—something the ego specializes in. Once we get over the temporary high of having cast the blame away from us, it will come back to us a hundredfold. An attack thought is like a sword we think we're dropping on someone else's head, when in fact it's dropping on our own.* Only if I'm willing to be easier on others will I ever learn how to be easier on myself.

Think of the things in your life you've gotten away with: things you're ashamed to think about, that you regret, or that you would do over again if you could. And now think how hard you can be on others whose mistakes are similar and sometimes even smaller than your own. Can it be that you want them to pay for what you think you haven't paid enough for? Think about how guilt is binding you to the past. Wouldn't we all want the freedom to begin again that forgiveness alone can bring? Any of us can have that freedom if we are willing to grant forgiveness to others.

Within the world, there are often very serious things we have to forgive. Forgiveness begins, as do all issues of enlightenment, as merely an intellectual concept that has yet to make its "journey without distance" from the head to the heart. It often takes a while to become integrated into our emotional nature. It seems to run counter to reason that we would choose to see the innocence in a person beyond their mistake, yet that is the visionary, as well as most powerful, aspect of faith. Our *experience* of a person might be that they mistreated us, while our *faith* is that they remain an innocent child of God.

No matter what we do to change our lives and to create new possibilities, the bridge to a new life is impossible unless we're willing to forgive. A woman might have been divorced by her husband yet left with enough money to live in a beautiful home, travel the world, and do whatever else she wants for as long as she lives. But until she finds it in her heart to forgive him and bless his path although it swerved away from her, she will live in hell although she lives in a castle. None of that is easy, ever. But unforgiveness is a poison to the soul.

Radical forgiveness is not a lack of discernment or the product of fuzzy thinking. It is a "selective remembering."* We choose to remember the love we experienced, and to let go the rest as the illusion it really was. This doesn't make us more vulnerable to manipulation or exploitation; in fact, it makes us less so. For the mind that forgives is a mind that is closer to its true nature. The fact that I forgive you doesn't mean you "won." It doesn't mean you "got away with something." It simply means I'm free to go back to the light, reclaim my inner peace, and stay there.

Sin versus Error

The world of guilt is based on one notion: the reality of "sin." Sin is an archery term that means we missed the mark. We send forth a thought, and sometimes we "miss" the loving bull's-eye. All of us miss the mark of God's love over and over and over again.

Who among us is the right-minded, love-centered, all-forgiving person we would like to be twenty-four hours a day? None of us, but we're on the earth to learn how to be.* God's desire, when we fall short, is not to punish us but to correct us and teach us how to do better. What we think of as our sins were mental miscreations, and though some of our errors are grave, even wicked, there is no end to God's forgiveness and love.

When someone makes an error, we're often tempted to focus all our attention on that person's wrongdoing, even if we previously experienced their goodness. The ego is like a scavenger dog, ever on the lookout for the slightest bit of evidence that someone has made a mistake or wronged us in any way.* *Notice how much less vigilance we apply to seeking out the good in people.* The ego mind is on an instinctive rampage to find the guilt and proclaim the guilt, in any and all, even ourselves. It is a mental attack machine. Its message to anyone, spoken or unspoken, is, "You screwed up. You're not good enough." Judgment, blame, and guilt are the ego's fuel.

The Holy Spirit, on the other hand, is the voice for love. It guides us to keep faith with the truth of God: that all of us are innocent because that is how He created us. This doesn't mean that what people do does not matter or that evil does not exist. It simply means that our task as miracle workers is to extend our perception beyond what our physical senses perceive, to what we know to be true in our hearts.*

When people do things that are not loving, it means they have lost contact with their true nature. They have fallen asleep to who they really are, dreaming the dream of an angry self or an arrogant self or a cruel self, and so forth. Our mission as miracle workers is to remain awake to the beauty in people even when they have forgotten it themselves. In that way, we subconsciously "re-mind" them who they are. As disciples of the Holy Spirit, we simultaneously see both the worldly error and the spiritual perfection in people. And in sharing God's perspective on human error—a desire to heal as opposed to a desire to punish—we become conduits of His healing power. Thus we too are healed.

To the ego, this is outrageous: how *dare* we declare the child of God innocent? Can't we *see* what a dark and sinful creature he is? Even religions that claim that God is good seem bent at times on finding His children guilty. Many point their fingers critically at other people, not realizing that the pointed finger itself is the source of all evil. It is the *concept* of enemy that is our greatest enemy of all.

What About Archie Bunker?

During one of my lectures once a man rose to ask a question. "I don't have a problem with anything you're saying," he said. "But my problem is what happens when I leave this room. What do we do about people who don't believe this way? Like my father; he's like Archie Bunker! What do I do about *him?*"

Many heads in the room started nodding, but I inwardly smiled. God doesn't let us get away with that one.

"Do you want to know?" I asked. "Do you really want to know what *A Course in Miracles* would say?"

He nodded.

"It would say you need to stop judging your father."

He and hundreds of others had a look on their faces as though to say, "Right, of course, I get it."

I continued. "Only what you are not giving can be lacking in any situation. God sent us here to work miracles, and we can only do that when we have given up our judgments. How can you help awaken your dad to his innocence if you yourself are stuck focusing on his guilt?

"And that's not to say it's always easy, either. But the primary responsibility of the miracle worker is to accept the atonement for *himself.* You're not here to monitor the spiritual progress of other people. The issues God wants us to address first are our own."

The miracle is not that his dad will become different but that he himself will become different. The irony, of course, is that he is probably judging his father for being judgmental! Only when he is no longer judging his dad, but accepting him as he is, are miracles possible.

I believe it was Martin Luther King Jr. who said that we have no morally persuasive power with someone who can feel our underlying contempt. Whose thoughts are we more likely to influence in a loving direction: someone who feels judged by us or someone who can see that all that love we *say* we believe in *applies to them as well?*

Eternal Perfection

Until we remember who we are, we are tempted to take on the shame and guilt of the ego. We see it in ourselves and project it onto others. We internalize the judgment and blame that are endemic to the world. I love the lyric from the Christmas carol "O Holy Night": "Long lay the world in sin and error pining, 'til He appeared and the soul felt its worth." If God's plan calls for us to remember our own eternal perfection, then wouldn't He be asking us to remember it in other people as well?

To the ego, the notion of eternal and unchangeable innocence is blasphemy. Guilt itself is the ego's god. But if we're to evolve beyond the ego, we have to evolve beyond our belief in the sanctity of guilt. And the place to begin is in regards to ourselves.

That doesn't mean we haven't made mistakes or that we don't need to try to make them right. But as it's often said, God's not finished with any of us yet. We're not perfect or we wouldn't have been born, but it's our mission to become perfect here.* One step at a time, one lesson after another, we're growing closer to the expression of our divine potential.

What is real is that you're a beloved child of God. You don't have to do anything to make that true; it's a Truth that was established in your creation. Your inherent perfection is a creation of God, and what God created can't be uncreated.*

Other people can think what they want to think about you, but it's only your own perceptions, not the projections of others, that program your future. It's when we *agree* with other people's projections that we get into trouble—when we give the ego power and align with its judgments. The ego is fueled by shame and loves to introduce it into any situation, directed toward ourselves or someone else; it doesn't really care. Yet we can learn to say no to shame, keeping our heads high and moving through life with the knowledge that all of us are equally blessed in God's eyes. We shouldn't have to apologize for the fact that each of us is an infinitely creative being, endowed by God with extraordinary potential that He would have us make manifest.

Sometimes we're ashamed because of something we actually did, but other times because of what other people just thought we did and seem intent on telling the world about. Either way, shame is one of the ego's most vicious weapons, sure to keep us stuck in patterns of guilt. And the purpose of the guilt is to keep us from the peace of God.

People who have the lives they want are people who have realized on some level that they deserve to have it. Many of our problems were called forth by the subconscious mind, a reflection of our own belief that on some level we deserve to be punished. That is the ego's constant message: "You are bad, you are bad, you are bad." And when the pain of that feeling gets too difficult to endure, we're tempted to think, "No, that person is bad, not me." One day we realize that there doesn't always have to be someone to blame. The terrible damage that is done in this world is less because of a few people whose hearts have actually turned to evil, and more because of the millions of basically good and decent souls whose hearts are wounded and left unhealed.

In any given moment, the universe is primed to give us new life, to begin again, to create new opportunities, to miraculously heal situations, to change all darkness to light and fear to love. God's light shines eternally clear, untarnished by our illusions. Our job is to take a deep breath, slow down, surrender all thoughts of past or future, and let the Holy Instant shine forth in our awareness. God is not daunted by our nightmares of guilt; He is ever awake to how beautiful we are. He made us that way, and so it is.

Self-Forgiveness

Sometimes you see negative patterns repeating themselves in your life and you don't know how to change them. You begin by recognizing that, as *A Course in Miracles* states, "I am not a victim of the world I see." Sometimes we can't *see* exactly how we created a disaster, but we can still take full responsibility for the fact that we did. And that is a beginning.

No matter what other people might have done to us—and there *are* people who are not nice in this world, who do terrible things—it is still our option to forgive, to rise above, to be defenseless, and also important to search our own minds and hearts for ways we might have helped create or attract their darkness. The fact that other people were bad in a situation doesn't necessarily mean you were all good.

It can be a difficult process to take that kind of brutally honest look at yourself. It can lead to painful self-condemnation, then a need for self-forgiveness that can be at least as hard as forgiving others.

Sometimes we realize some part of our personality is fear-based ego. Others might judge us for it, but that isn't even what's important. In fact, it is irrelevant because only someone's ego would feel the need to point out yours. Your ego issues don't matter because of other people's judgments of you; they matter because they are blocking your light, your joy, and your availability to God to use for His purposes. Sixty watts can't move through a thirty-watt bulb.

You're on this earth to shine your light for the sake of the entire world. The places in you where you are seemingly blocked in your ability to do that can be released to God for healing. Once you admit your defect and ask Him to take it away from you, His response to your invitation will be quick and sure. He remembers, even better than you do, the pain and suffering that led to your weakness. He was there for you when it happened, He cried tears as He watched you develop your dysfunction as a coping mechanism, and He rejoices at the invitation to heal you now.

Such are the miracles of God, and they will totally transform your life.

Whatever we refuse to look at in ourselves, we more easily project onto someone else. One of the benefits of facing our own weaknesses is that it helps us grow more compassionate toward others.

In any situation there is a focus to our perception. God would have us extend our perception beyond what the physical senses perceive, to the love that lies beyond. For when we see that love, we can *call it forth*. The physical senses reveal a veil of illusion: what people said and did on the mortal plane. But we lift the veil by seeing beyond it and invoking a truer truth. That is our purpose in each other's lives: to invoke each other's greatness and work a miracle in each other's lives.

According to *A Course in Miracles*, it's our job to tell someone they're right even when they're wrong.* That means we can affirm someone's essential innocence even when having to deal with their mistake. That distinction, however—between someone simply making a mistake you need to discuss with them and someone being "guilty" of something—is huge.

A conversation I had with a friend is an example.

My friend Ellen and I were doing a project together. A situation arose in which I was clear that I didn't want to take immediate action. She disagreed and kept pressuring me to do something.

I would say, "I don't want to do anything right now; I have to think about this," and she would come back with, "Why can't we just do it this way? Why not?"

Finally, feeling under pressure, I gave in to her. And of course, a few days later I realized I had made a mistake.

So here I was, annoyed with myself for having given in to pressure to do something that went against my own inner knowing and also annoyed at my friend for having pressured me in the first place. So the spiritual question was this: Should I say anything to her, or should I simply eat my feelings?

There is a middle way, in which we neither judge others nor suppress our feelings. We can express ourselves honestly and demonstrate compassion at the same time.

I shared with her that I wasn't happy about how I had been pressured into taking action. Ellen began to get defensive and say how much she loved me and that she would never have done that. I said, "Wait. I love you too. And I know you love me. But you *did* do that.

"It's a no-fault universe, Ellen. Our friendship is much, much bigger than a mistake that either of us made, and this situation doesn't touch the rock-bottom reality of our love for each other as friends. But *within* that love, friends have to be able to share their truth with each other. I need you to know that (1) I love you and this doesn't in any way change that, (2) I know I'm ultimately responsible for my own behavior, no matter what you did, and (3) I hope you will not pressure me like that again."

I could feel her relax, for she no longer felt the need to be defensive. And from then on, she did everything she could to rectify the problem. That one shift—from her fearing that her mistake was more important than our love to my clarity that our love was more important than her mistake—created an emotional opening that made all the difference. When we feel blamed, our defenses come up. And all defenses are a passive attack.* That cycle of emotional violence, however subtle, is the beginning of all conflicts in the world. Our shift made the difference between the situation hurting our relationship and deepening it. It did the latter because truth was present on every level.

Miracles occur when total communication is given and received.* Often we only communicate *half* the truth; we either stress our upset with someone without emphasizing the larger love surrounding the relationship, or we stress the love without honoring our need to talk about the problem. Either way is a nonmiraculous, uncreative use of the mind, and it will leave the heart unhealed.

God calls us to be both honest *and* compassionate. As He is.

Invoking the Good

Being caught in anger, judgment, and blame is disempowering; it throws us out of our center; it puts us at the effect of the love-lessness of someone else. To be there for a while is one thing; to stay there and try to justify it is wrong-minded and will not lead to peace. Spirituality challenges us to detach from the purely personal, emotional aspects of a situation—the ego's need to be right—in order to uplift ourselves to higher ground. That doesn't mean we don't feel our pain, our anger, our despair. But there is a way to *hold* such feelings in a sacred rather than chaotic way, so they heal us rather than poison us.

Whenever our lives aren't working the way we wish they would, our instinctive tendency is to blame someone else. From dysfunctional parents to corrupt society, bitter former spouses to disloyal colleagues, we carry with us a catalog of grievances: if only this or that were different, my life would be good. "I've been screwed, you see, and that's why I'm not happy."

Yet somewhere deep inside a little voice breaks through: "Maybe yes, maybe no . . ." The only way we can be happy is if we are willing to take responsibility for our own experience. Even when someone has truly wronged us, it is important to ask ourselves what part, however small, we might have unwittingly played in either creating the situation or at least allowing it to occur.

Our first work is to ask ourselves, "What did I do, or not do, to contribute to this disaster?" While others might have their own karma to clean up, we can at least try to clean up our own.

I had an experience that hurt me deeply, in which I found myself abused—not just by an individual, but by a group of people acting in a sort of psychological concert. My experience was not unique, as many people have experienced what I would call "institutional abuse."

Yet it was only when I was willing to withdraw my belief in the *ultimate reality* of what had been done to me that I could free myself from the *effects* of what had been done to me. On the level of spirit, no one had done anything to hurt me because on the level of spirit, only Love is real. Loveless behavior had certainly occurred, but if only love is real, then only love can touch me.* God could more than compensate for whatever damage had been done, for "what man intends for evil, God intends for good." As long as I held back my forgiveness, however, I held back my own healing as well.

If I could forgive what had happened to me, I would become deeper and more prepared to serve Him. It is none of my business what happens to others who were involved in this drama. The only drama that matters is the one in my own head and heart. If I can come to understand that no lies, no injustice, no transgression of any kind can begin to touch who I essentially am, then I will receive the greatest prize of all: I will *learn* who I essentially am. For the part of us that can be lied about, insulted, mistreated, or betrayed is only a fiction of our mortal mind. Marianne Williamson is a portion of a greater self, as we all are. I, Marianne Williamson, can be hurt, but the greater self in which I dwell cannot. Our opportunity, when in pain, is to remember that who we really are cannot be hurt. When we look beyond the mortal in our persecutor, we can then—and only then—experience that which is beyond the mortal in ourselves.

We can have a grievance or we can have a miracle; we cannot have both.* And I knew that I wanted a miracle. I did not want to carry any thoughts of malice or revenge. I wanted to be free of meanness shown to me, and perhaps I could do that only by rooting out any meanness within myself. If that was the lesson, I was willing to learn it. And the love I received during that time—from those who bore witness to my pain and did what they could to bring me comfort—made the cruelty of the situation bearable.

If we allow Him to, God compensates for such difficult times by using them to turn our lives into something even better than before. In the spiritual as well as the physical world, when the skies are darkest we get our best view of starlight. As the ancient Greek playwright Aeschylus wrote, "In our sleep, pain that cannot forget falls drop by drop upon the human heart and in our own despair, against our will, comes wisdom through the awful grace of God."

The Deepest Wrongs

Do you prefer to be right or to be happy?*

Clearly, people do terrible things sometimes. But if our focus is always on people's guilt, then we will find ourselves living in a dark and vicious universe. Our capacity to shift our focus from guilt to innocence is our capacity to change our world. This does not mean we should look away when bad things happen or cease the struggle for justice. It just means that there is a personal hook we don't have to sling ourselves onto—that we can always believe in the basic goodness of people even when their behavior does not reflect their goodness.

Contrary to popular opinion, this is neither a naive nor a weak position. It doesn't mean that we have illusions about the nature or the power of evil. Yet the miracle worker has a more, not a less, sophisticated view of how to deal with it. Did Gandhi never feel anger toward British imperialists? Did Martin Luther King Jr. never feel anger toward Southern bigots? Of course they did. They were human. Yet with the help of God they worked through their anger, moving past it to something much more powerful: the love that lay beyond. Their spiritual process informed their political and social process, giving them the ultimate authority to move hearts and thus move mountains.

Until we do that, we might get all kinds of people to agree with us in our position and support us in our anger. But in that way we will achieve short-term gains at best; we will not work miracles. Love is not just a feeling; it is a *force*. And it is a force that is ultimately more powerful than violence of any kind.

To forgive those who have transgressed against you is not to condone evil but rather to surrender it to a higher authority for ultimate justice. In the Bible it is said, "Vengeance is mine, sayeth the Lord." That means it's God's business, not yours. Even while prosecuting the worst crimes, we can remember that guilt in terms of humanly made law is not synonymous with guilt before God. When God parted the Red Sea in order for the Israelites to cross, the Egyptian soldiers then ran after them. At that point, God closed the waters, and the Egyptians drowned. When the Israelites began to rejoice at the destruction of their enemies, however, God commanded them to stop. They were not to rejoice at the death of other human beings, even when God's justice had deemed it necessary. So it is that we should never take pleasure in another's suffering, even if they "deserve" it. We are to hold to the light, to divine consciousness, even when we have to deal with the darkness of the world. Only in that way will the two one day be reconciled.

If you were completely victimized as the world defines it, then take heart from Dr. Martin Luther King Jr.'s notion that there is "redemptive power in unearned suffering." It's our spiritual assignment to love even those who have transgressed against us: for in the ultimate scheme of things, they are learning too.

The Miracle of Forgiveness

When I'm pondering how hard it can be to forgive, I'm reminded of people who have had infinitely more difficult things to forgive than I and who succeeded. They're like sacred role models, and the blessings they've called down upon themselves have blessed me as well.

One such inspirational example is Azim Khamisa. Azim's twenty-year-old son, Tariq, was a San Diego college student earning extra money delivering pizzas in the mid-1990s when he was gunned down by a fourteen-year-old boy in a senseless, gang-related homicide. Azim, like any parent of a murdered child, experienced trauma and grief beyond what seemed humanly endurable. Yet over the years he has demonstrated, and experienced, the miracle of forgiveness.

Azim, a religious Sufi, was told by his spiritual adviser that after forty days of grieving his son, he must turn his grief into good works. Only in that way, he was told, could he help his son move to the next stage of his soul's journey. Doing so then became Azim's mission in life: to act in such a way as to help his son even after he had died. He was told that instead of grieving the dead, he must do good, compassionate deeds for the living. For such deeds are like spiritual energy, providing high-octane fuel for the soul of the departed. In this way, Azim could serve his son although his son was no longer with him. Having felt that he had lost all reason to live, Azim came to feel new purpose in life. Channeling his grief into positive, meaningful work would benefit both Tariq and himself.

When Azim first heard that Tariq had been killed, he said it was as if "a nuclear bomb had gone off in my heart." He remembers the experience of leaving his body, and his life force, or *prana*, left with him. He went into the "loving arms of (his) maker," and when the explosion finally subsided, Azim came back into his body. When he returned, he had received a revelation: that there were victims on both sides of the gun.

That realization led Azim to reach out to the grandfather of the boy who killed his son, with whom the boy, Tony, had been living at the time of the murder. The grandfather, Ples Felix, was a Green Beret who had served two tours in Vietnam and had a master's degree in urban development. Tony had gone to live with his grandfather at the age of nine, after suffering frequent violent abuse himself as well as witnessing the murder of his cousin. By the time he was nine, Tony was already racked with anger. Reading in the papers about the boy and about his grandfather, Azim felt compassion for their story.

Azim asked the district attorney to introduce him to Ples, and they met in the office of the public defender who was representing Tony. Azim told Ples he felt no animosity toward Tony or his family, and he realized that both families had been traumatized by this tragic incident. He was concerned about Tony and all the other children who are trying to cope with such a violent world, in which the average American child has seen 100,000 images of violence on TV, movies, and video games before entering the first grade.

Azim told Ples he had started a foundation in the memory of his son, to help stop children from killing children. Ples said he would do whatever he could to help. As he extended his condolences, Ples told Azim that ever since the day of the murder, the Khamisa family had been in his daily prayers and meditations.

Azim invited Ples to the second meeting of the foundation a couple of weeks later, where Ples met the entire Khamisa family. Ples spoke passionately about his own experience, saying the foundation was an answer to his prayers. A San Diego television station filmed Tariq's grandfather shaking hands with Tony's grandfather: "Clearly," they reported, "this is a different kind of handshake."

Today, Azim is chairman of the Tariq Khamisa Foundation's board of directors, and Ples is the vice chairman. The men have grown close, and Azim says that if he were to choose ten people who are closest to him in his life, Ples would be one. The foundation has become a personal ministry for both men, and there is a job there waiting for Tony on the day he is released from prison.

The One That's Hard for All of Us

It's very difficult to talk or even think about forgiveness when confronted with the reality of September 11, 2001. Only silence—not words—can express the horror of that day.

Yet at the same time, a deeper conversation is available to us than the one now dominating our public dialogue. If we just hold to the simplistic line that "They're bad; we're good; let's kill 'em," then we're dangerously off base both spiritually and politically.

When the Twin Towers were first destroyed, the severity of the emotional blow threw America into our hearts. And with our hearts restored, our minds began working better as well. We were one nation, a true community, some of us experiencing it for the first time in our lives. And the very intelligent question on many people's lips was, "Why do those people hate us so much?" Over dinner tables and around office water coolers, we asked questions we had not been asking often enough over the last few decades: What has America been doing around the world, and how are we perceived by others? Even mainstream American television, not always known for its intellectual depth, hosted brilliant political thinkers and philosophers to educate the American people on issues we now painfully recognized were relevant to our lives.

Yet several days later it was like someone had pulled the plug. No more interesting thinkers on TV, just cheerleaders for revenge. We were to move into war mode, and quickly; that mode could not tolerate the suggestion that America had played even the tiniest part in attracting our misfortune. Anyone who even hinted such a thing was described as "blaming America." Clichés were substituted for meaningful conversation; intellectual excellence, healthy skepticism, and any discussion of spirituality or compassion as they related to the threat of terrorism were deemed the undermining machinations of unpatriotic Americans.

Yet I've noticed that it's the people who suffered the most on 9/11 who have often displayed the capacity for the highest vision of what occurred that day. From pushing for a 9/11 commission when the president himself was resisting it, to forming groups like September Eleventh Families for Peaceful Tomorrows which stand for compassion and forgiveness in the midst of this haunting darkness, those who suffered the most have taken the strongest stand for the power of truth.

One day I was watching a TV roundtable discussion with three victims of 9/11. One woman had lost her husband at the World Trade Center; one man had lost his young son, who was working at the Pentagon when it was bombed. At the end of the discussion, the news anchor asked one last question: "Do you want revenge?"

A pained expression crossed the face of each member of the roundtable at that question. I remember the woman saying, "No, because I can't imagine anyone else having to go through the pain we've been through." The man who lost his son said, "No, I think we've got to find a way to make those people over there know who we really are so they won't hate us anymore." The third panelist said something similar. And then the TV journalist, who himself had suffered no personal loss on 9/11, said this: "Well, *I* want revenge, and I want it to be fierce and swift." It was obvious that those who had suffered the most had been lifted up to a place that he had not. They didn't want to continue the violence; they just wanted the violence to end.

There are wars that the vast majority of us would call "righteous wars," such as America's involvement in World War II. Now, as then, there are people who wish our country harm and would kill us if they could; it is clearly both our right and our responsibility to defend ourselves. But the conversation should not stop there. If our first responsibility as individuals is to accept the atonement for ourselves, then America's first order of business should be getting our own actions right with God. No nation should fear deep reflection and self-examination. What we should fear is our urge to avoid them.

America has our own atonement to attend to. A humble heart, through which we admit our own errors and seek to live in more righteous relationship with the peoples of the world, is a spiritual approach to our current situation that is a healthy complement to more aggressive problem-solving options. As long as brute force is deemed the greatest power and love is deemed essentially weak, then we are mocking God and dealing dangerously with our future.

Not every cancer can be surgically removed, and when it is inoperable, we now know that spiritual practice can be efficacious in helping to heal the body. Terrorism is not an operable tumor, though perhaps we're pretending that it is. It is in fact a cancer that has already metastasized throughout the global body, and while some invasive measures might be appropriate, a holistic perspective—in which we recognize the powers of the mind and heart to help activate our social immune system—brings a more mature and effective means of dealing with it than the ego's sole reliance on retribution and revenge. If hate is more powerful than love, then we're on the right track. If love is more powerful than hate, then we're headed in a very, very wrong direction.

At the center of the American ideal are eternal values of justice and right relationship. The only way to navigate these somewhat dangerous times is to cleave to our values, not turn away from them in pursuit of short-term advantage. Nations, like individuals, emerge spiritually from the Mind of God. We will only find our safety in Him, and He is love.

In Him, we are all one. He loves every nation as much as He loves ours, and the blessing of the United States has been our stand for the equality of all people. In turning away from that stand—in building so many barriers between ourselves and others—we are literally spurning God. His greatest gift to us is not that He will give us victory in battle, but that He will lift us above the battlefield.* From there, we will see what we are not seeing now. And the power of that vision will pave the way to true peace.

CHAPTER EIGHT

From *Separation* to *Relationship*

*E*ach of us is the center of the universe. Everything we experience is happening inside us, not outside. At the deepest level, *there is no world outside us.** The world as we know it is a manifest projection of our thought forms, no more and no less. It is thought up, and it is thought up by each of us.

We are slavishly devoted to the ego's notion that we're our bodies—mere tiny specks of dust surrounded by a huge universe over which we have no control. And if that's what we think, then that will be our experience. But there is another way of viewing the world, through which we recognize that our life force is limitless because we are one with an unlimited God. No matter what we do or what we have done, now, in this moment, we are temples embodying the glory of God. Any situation seen through the light of this understanding is miraculously transformed.

Close your eyes and imagine yourself as you appear in the world. And now see a golden light that radiates from your heart, extends beyond your body, and casts a light to the entire world. Now imagine someone else standing next to you, friend or foe, and see the same light within that person. Watch the light as it grows to cover his or her body and extends beyond it. Now see the light in the other person as it merges with the light in you. On the level of spirit, there is no place where others stop and you start.

If you do this with anyone, your relationship with that person will subtly change. In the Christmas carol where we sing, "Do you see what I see?" there is a deeper question being asked than whether someone sees a physical child in a manger. "Do you see what I see?" refers to a question of consciousness, as in, do you see that spiritual reality? Do you grasp it, can you imagine it? For if you do, you can have it. The possibility exists.

When we realize we're not who we think we are—that the world has taught us a huge and unholy lie—we realize that other people aren't who *they* appear to be either. And neither are our relationships, for as spirits we are not separate, but one.

An idea does not leave its source.* You are literally an idea in the mind of God, which is why you cannot be separate from Him. And the world you experience is an idea in your mind, which is why it can't be separate from you.

We're like sunbeams thinking we're separate from the sun or waves thinking we're separate from the ocean.* But sunbeams can't *be* separate, and waves can't *be* separate of course.* The idea of our separation is nothing but a vast hallucination.* And yet that's where we live: in the illusion that you're over there and I'm over here. That illusion—that we are separate—is the source of all our pain.

The ego suggests that that space will be filled by one "special" person, rather than by a corrected sense of our relationship to everyone. Yet that is a lie. Just think about it: if in fact you're one with everybody yet you think you're not, then imagine how many people you subconsciously miss being with! No wonder we feel such a hole, such an existential emptiness inside us. What we miss is a right-minded relationship with everyone.

Feeling separate from love, we feel a panic so deep we don't even recognize it. Just as the earth is moving so fast we can't feel the speed anymore, our hysteria is so deep we don't hear our own scream anymore. Yet it permeates our being, demanding we do something, anything, to assuage the pain. And God knows we try: in ways both healthy and unhealthy, we keep trying to fill the hole that only surrendering to our love for all of life can fill. And always, there is the anger that the separation engenders: our anger at feeling separate, although we're not consciously aware from what.

In God there is escape, for He has sent the Holy Spirit to reunite our hearts by correcting our thinking. He can dismantle our thought system based on fear and replace it with a thought system based on love. He will give us a new mind.

This new mind awaits us in this next stage of our evolutionary journey. We are being challenged by the forces of history to grow into this mind, to mutate, as it were, in order for our species to survive. Jesus had the new mind, called in him the Christ Mind, as did Buddha and others. It is the mind when it is overshadowed by God, our mind when it has become one with His, when we have touched the heavenly light and been permanently altered by it. This state of enlightenment is the exaltation of our existence, the uplifting of our human consciousness to such a high place that we manifest, at last, as the children of God we truly are.

And when we do—when we realize that we are not just *like* each other, but we actually *are* each other—then we will begin to find life outside the realm of love no longer acceptable. In time, it will become literally unthinkable. And becoming unthinkable, *it will cease to exist.*

Melting the Walls

How many times have you seen a pattern in your relationships you felt powerless to change? How often have you despaired of ever breaking free of self-sabotaging behavior? How deeply have you panicked at the thought that you might never get it right?

Our despair and panic are natural responses to the relationship dramas we create in our lives. But our tears are not what we think they are because the predicament itself is not what we think it is. What separates us from others is not just codependency or neediness or any other mere psychological issue. Our barriers to love represent a cosmic force, ensconced within the human psyche in a dark and insidious way, holding dominion— temporary though wicked—over the mental functioning of the child of God. It is completely irrelevant what form the barrier takes. Our concentration on the form of fear is an ego ploy to keep us stuck in the problem, like finding a thief in your house and saying, "I have to know his name before I call the police." Who cares what his name is? Call for help immediately!

The ego is our deepest enemy masquerading as our closest friend. It is nothing we should fear, however, because the moment we recognize it as merely a mental miscreation—simply a false belief about who we are—it will disappear into the nothingness from whence it came. We ourselves, however, cannot command its departure. It has absconded with our will and confused our defenses. Like an immune system disease that attacks its own cells, the ego attacks the mind it purports to give life to. Only God can help us.

And He will. He will show us the innocence in others, that we might see it in ourselves. Through His Holy Spirit He will outwit our self-hatred and return our hearts to love.*

Most of us—all of us, in fact, except the enlightened masters—live to some extent in a state of "love withhold." We are waiting to see if a person is good enough to receive our kindness, our generosity, or our love. People hardly have dates anymore; we have *auditions*. We think we need to understand a person to see whether they are worthy of our love, but in fact, unless we love them we cannot understand them.*

Someone's religion, looks, financial status, professional position—so many things are used by the ego to dictate who is worthy or appropriate for us. Yet God would have us keep our hearts open to people as a matter of faith. And any faith that has us close our hearts to anyone is not a genuine faith in God.

God is not outside us, nor is He outside our relationship to each other. Relationships are the contesting ground between ego and spirit, which begins developing as soon as we are born.

All of us were born with a completely open heart, making no distinction between who deserves our love or not. Yet the experience of a fearful world—in which it is sad but necessary to teach our children that there are dangers of which they indeed must beware—has trained us to shut down the emotional valve from which otherwise pours forth universal compassion. Love, which is our very nature, begins to feel unnatural, and fear begins to feel natural.* Once we have lived long enough, a closed heart rather than an open one becomes our instinctive response to life.

And sometimes this happens much sooner than it should. One evening I went out with my elderly mother to a lovely restaurant, and after dinner we went to the women's room. As my mother was washing her hands, a little four- or five-year-old girl came up to the sink next to her. My mother, who grew up in what I think was in many ways a more civilized era, went over to the little girl as she struggled to reach the faucet and said, "Here, honey, I'll help you!"

At that moment, the child's mother came out of her stall, saw my mother, practically knocked her out of the way, and gave her the meanest glance you can imagine. The look of hurt on my mother's face was painful to witness. I thought to myself, "What you are teaching your daughter by making her completely distrust everyone she ever meets is more risky than the risks you are seeking to protect her from." I have a daughter, and of course I've had to teach her never to go anywhere with strangers, and so on. But not talk to them? Or be nice to them? Or be open in any way? Is that the world we want to create?

The ego would propose a world in which no one ever receives a smile unless they "earn" it. And is that where we desire to live? The love and beneficence we show each other on a daily basis—in the grocery store, standing in line at the bank, walking down the street—can be as important as any grand gesture we show to a so-called loved one. To God, we are all loved ones. And when we learn to love each other as He loves us all, we will prepare the table for the love we most want.

Even When It's Hard

One day I was thinking about my need to love the people I disagree with politically. This has been particularly difficult for me in the last few years, as it has been for many people. I was asking God to show me the innocence in some people that I couldn't quite see for myself.

In my meditation I had a vision. In it, I witnessed a terrible car accident. I was the first person to arrive on the scene, where I saw that a man was trapped in the car and the car was about to catch on fire. I immediately did everything possible to save him; all that mattered was that someone's life was in danger. I passionately worked, clawed, struggled—and ultimately succeeded. After a huge and prolonged effort, I finally freed the man and dragged him out of the car. And when I saw his face, I realized he was—Donald Rumsfeld!

So that was it. The message couldn't have been plainer. Every human being is first and foremost just that—another human being—and if I can see them that way, then I will be free. I might still disagree with people, even work for their political retirement perhaps, but I will be free of the emotional entanglements that judgment breeds. Everyone, no matter who, is a child of God. And until I get that, I'm not where I need to be to help change our damaged world. In fact, I'm just adding my own damage to it.

If I look at my judgments of you and simply lay them aside as the work of the ego, *which I do not have to obey*—then I am contributing to the work of peace on earth. And only if I am willing to give up my own judgments do I have the right to call myself a peacemaker. This is much harder than traditional peace activism because it means we're seeking the deepest change within ourselves.

The judgmental mind is a problem, then, isn't it? It's the voice that says, "You can love this one but not that one." Our job is to learn to love as God loves, which means everyone all the time. That is not to say *like* everyone; it is not to say date or marry everyone; it is not to say have lunch with everyone. It is not even to say trust everyone, on the level of personality. The love that will save us is an impersonal, not a personal love—a love that is unconditional because it's based not on what people do but on who they essentially are.

Trust

Then what are we to do about people who are genuinely not to be trusted? Are we supposed to just love people, even when they take advantage of us? At what point do we set up defenses and boundaries, keeping unsafe people at bay?

A while ago, I found out that a close associate—who at the time I thought was also a close friend—had embezzled a large amount of money from me. One week after we finally came up with a legal solution, a few former friends and associates perpetrated a vicious and dishonest campaign to undermine my work. Obviously, I was devastated. What had I done to attract such unscrupulous people? And how had I contributed to their betrayal?

Pondering the spiritual meaning of these situations, my main question regarded trust. I had trusted these people; I had expected them to behave decently. Was the lesson to be learned that I was not to trust?

Then I realized that I needed to be more trustworthy toward myself. No one could have stolen so much money if I had kept better track of it myself, and I should not have still been dealing with people who many times before had demonstrated their lack of ethical standards. In both those situations, there were ways in which I should have known better. I was blinded to what I *knew* to be true because of what I *wanted* to be true. I wasn't listening deeply to my own inner knowing, and even when its voice broke through, I didn't heed it when I didn't want to. Thus I suffered, but I also learned.

In a way, I came out of those situations not trusting people less so much as trusting myself more. I think those circumstances were important lessons for me—in choosing associates more wisely, in being more responsible toward myself, and of course in discerning between the perfection of the soul and the pernicious potential in every personality. I have now experienced other people's viciousness, as many of us have. But until I have removed every bit of it from myself, I am not a victim. I am simply standing in front of a very big mirror and seeing myself as I grow through my stuff. All that is not love is a call for love, and every situation is an opportunity to grow.

Relationships Are Laboratories

Relationships are laboratories of the Holy Spirit, but they can also be playgrounds for the ego. They can be heaven, or they can be hell. They are infused with love or infused with fear.

Most of the time, they are a little of both.

The ego speaks first and the ego speaks loudest, and it will always make a case for separation: the other peron did this or that and therefore does not deserve our love.* And in whatever moment we choose to listen to the ego—denying love to someone else—then to that extent we will be denied. Knowing that the mind works that way, we can call for help. We can pray for a power greater than our own to push back the storm of neurotic thinking.

To the ego, the purpose of a relationship is to serve our needs as we define them. *I want to get this job; I want him or her to marry me; I want this person to see things the way I do.* To the Holy Spirit, the purpose of a relationship is to serve God.

Every relationship is part of a divine curriculum designed by the Holy Spirit. It is there for a reason, but the reason might not be the one we ascribe to it. The ego and God have diametrically opposed intentions.

The only way to make sure we're not playing sick and destructive mind games in a situation—particularly in relationships where the ego has so much invested—is to invite the Holy Spirit to enter there and prevail. At the earliest moment you think to do it, place a relationship on the altar to God within your mind.

> *Dear God,*
> *I place my relationship with . . .*
> *In Your hands.*
> *May my presence be a blessing in his life.*
> *May my thoughts toward him be those of innocence and love,*
> *And may his thoughts toward me be those of innocence and love.*
> *May all else be cast out.*
> *May our relationship be lifted*
> *To divine right order,*
> *And take the form*
> *That best serves Your purposes.*
> *May all unfold,*
> *In this and all things,*
> *According to Your will.*
> *Amen.*

From Woundedness to Healing

Sometimes we try to take the paintbrush out of God's hands, under the erroneous assumption we can paint a better picture than He can. The ego will try to get a relationship to fit into our idea of how it should be rather than allowing it to organically reveal itself. We have pictures and idealizations we try to foist on others, thinking, "It should feel like this," or "They should act like that." Yet at the deepest level, we are simply souls encountering other souls, and relationships should be places where we free each other, not imprison each other. When our consciousness is simply that of one child of God honoring another—regardless of how things look in the outer world—we exude a peace and acceptance that calls people to their highest. When we're calm, people around us will be calmer; when we're kind, people around us will be kinder; when we're peaceful, people around us will be more peaceful. Once we find the love within ourselves, calling it forth in our relationships comes much more easily.

Yet even when relationships are good, the ego is always alert to ways it can drive two hearts apart. The ego directs us toward love but then sabotages it once it gets here. You think you're so in love, but then you act needy and repel it. You think you're feeling peaceful, but then love comes near and you get totally neurotic. You want to make a good impression, and then you go and act like an idiot.

The ego is always on the lookout for ways to undermine our relationships because genuine relationship means death to the ego. Where we unite with another, God *is;* and where God is, ego cannot be. To the ego, therefore, undermining our relationships is an act of self-preservation. The only way to ward off its destructiveness is to stand firm in your commitment to love—not just as a commitment to another person, who to the ego may or may not "deserve" it—but as a commitment to God and to yourself.

Loving thoughts can become a mental habit. Sometimes, when we're impatient with each other, it helps to think of the person we're dealing with as they must have been like as a child. For all of us are children in God's eyes. When children are young we know they're growing, and we take this into account in our dealings with them. We don't expect a twelve-year-old to have the maturity she or he will have at eighteen.

And as adults we're still growing too, whether or not we can always see that in each other. We're not finished once we reach a certain age; rather, we continue to grow and develop as long as we're alive. We learn, as children do. We stumble, as children do. And we sometimes fail, as children do. God sees all of us that way, no matter how old we are. He has infinite mercy upon us, and we could have mercy too.

None of us arrives in any relationship already healed, already perfect. In a holy relationship, it is understood we are all wounded but we are there to be healed together.* When the relationship is seen as a temple of healing, with mutual and proactive beneficence our daily medicine, the ego will then have far less power to snatch away our joy.

Categories of Love

There is no love but God's.*

To the ego there are different categories of love—between parent and child, between friends, between lovers, and so forth. But those categories are made up by us: in God, there is but one love. In every relationship, the fundamental things apply.

When my daughter was a little girl, I was surprised at times by how sophisticated her perceptions were. Once I said something slightly teasing about a book she was reading, and she responded by making it clear to me she felt my comments were disrespectful. And she was right; the fact that she was nine years old didn't mean she didn't have a right to her tastes and her opinions and her feelings. (Now that she's a teenager, of course, I get to remind her that I do too!)

A little respect, a little honor, can go a long way. Sometimes it's not the broad philosophic issue of cosmic innocence versus worldly guilt, but the simple ways we communicate to one another that determine whether love or fear pervades a relationship.

Someone who was working for me once said she was about to call the manager of the hotel where I had lectured the day before.

"Why?" I asked.

"I need to tell him about all the mistakes they made on Sunday."

"Whoa," I said. "Let's not do that!"

"What do you mean?" she said. "Remember all the things they forgot to take care of—the parking, the piano, the signs?"

"Sure, I remember," I said. "But this is what I've learned: if you approach that phone call just telling them what they did wrong, then that's not going to ultimately get us anywhere. They might acquiesce to our complaints, but they'll be feeling offended and hurt, and that hurt will show up in other ways down the line. When people aren't allowed to be directly aggressive, they often become passively aggressive. If people resent you, they will find a way to show it.

"So let's try another way. Didn't they do a lot of things right?"

"Sure," she said.

I continued. "I mean, the room was beautiful, the sound was great, they provided lovely refreshments, they created a homey atmosphere—they tried really hard to make us all feel welcome. Isn't that true?"

"Okay, I'll let Alex make the call. She's always really nice about things like that."

"No, Maggie," I said. "This is about more than just being nice. I'm not just talking about behavior modification; I'm talking about transformation. I'm talking about surrendering our need to focus on someone's guilt. If anyone on our team is thinking thoughts like that, it affects the whole team.

"We are all responsible not just for our behavior but for our attitudes, because our attitudes affect a situation as much as our behavior does. Everything we do, including—sometimes especially!—work, is a journey of transformation."

Later that afternoon I heard Maggie on the phone with the manager of the hotel. "Hey, I want to thank you for all the things you guys did to make it so great on Sunday!" she began. I heard them chatting nicely for the next couple of minutes. And then I heard her say, in a very kind voice, "Hey, I was wondering if I could go over a couple of things with you." She proceeded to mention, in polite and understanding ways, the issues that still needed to be addressed.

And they were.

I've had situations in my life where someone had a problem with something I'd said, and in looking back I exclaimed, "But I was right! I said the right thing!" And then I've gotten back the proverbial response: "It wasn't what you said; it was how you said it." A tone of voice can heal, and a tone of voice can hurt.

What the ego doesn't want us to realize is the practicality of love. We receive the experience of compassion to the extent to which we extend the experience of compassion. And you never know where it's most important.

Martha Stewart had her entire life brought to the brink of disaster by, as much as anything else, her personal manners. The fact that she offended her *broker's assistant* would come to affect her entire life. Here is a woman whose prodigious talents make the average person's lifetime achievements look paltry, yet she was stymied by her own personality issues. No amount of money, no professional achievements, and no external power can totally compensate for lack of people skills. At the deepest level, our relationships and personal issues define our lives.

Behind every problem is a broken relationship. And behind every miracle, there is a healed one.

Turning Issues into Miracles

Every relationship is a teaching-learning assignment. Anyone we are destined to meet, we will. We are drawn to each other for teaching and learning, as each of us is presented with the chance to learn the next lesson in the journey of our soul. Every encounter is a holy encounter if we use it to demonstrate love.* And every encounter is a setup for possible pain if we're not open to the opportunity to do that. Anyone we meet we were destined to meet, but what we do with the relationship is entirely up to us.

Sometimes someone is brought into our life to help us learn a lesson we've failed to learn before: to be accepting rather than controlling, to be approving instead of critical, or even to turn away from toxic behavior when before we would have made a beeline for it. It's no accident that certain patterns plague us, year after year, until we finally heal them. There's no point trying to go to Outer Mongolia to escape your issues; they will find you there because they live inside your head. The people you need will be brought to you; you will subconsciously attract them; there is no escaping the curriculum of the Holy Spirit.

If we have a particular problem in relationships, then we'll encounter that issue again until it's resolved. It represents a place where we become unconscious, unable to live in the fullness of our being. At that place, we break off into a fragment of ourselves, an impostor who puts a mask in front of our true face. We're lost there, not recognizing the alien environment we've created; we start grasping for emotional air, not knowing that we ourselves are the ones depriving us. This, to be sure, is the meaning of hell.

It is extremely difficult, in such moments, to use mere self-will to change ourselves. Yet if we ask for a miracle, we will receive one. For God is as clear in the Holy Instant as we would have Him be.* His mind, joined with our mind, can shine away the ego.* When lost in our illusions, His Spirit is there to bring us back.

Yet we can't just pray and meditate and expect all our personality issues to resolve themselves without any effort on our part. We have to use our prayer and meditation time to consciously *release* our relationship issues to God, that there they might be transformed. Our darkness must be brought to the light; it can't just be covered over by the light.

It's interesting to note the differences between a traditional psychotherapeutic approach to such issues and a more spiritual one. In most psychotherapy, the focus is put on the personality weakness and how to solve it. Why do we act this way? What childhood experience led to this problem? And sometimes that discussion can be very helpful. But when a more spiritual dimension is introduced to the psychotherapeutic process, we not only focus on the problem, we also pray for a divine answer.

Where our personalities are weak, we are stymied in our ability to manifest the glory of our true selves. Looking for who or what shut us down can be like looking back at the shore you just came from when you're lost in the river and can't find your way across. Better you should look toward the place you're heading (like Jesus or Buddha) and ask for guidance in crossing over. When we focus on perfection, our mind begins to head that way. We outgrow the ego as we grow closer to God.

Every time we have a problem in a relationship, we will repeat it unless we learn what we need to learn from it. This learning is part of the Atonement process, as we admit to God the mistakes we now realize we've made and pray for His help in changing us. We pray as well that He help heal whatever damage we might have done already, in our own lives or in someone else's.

Sometimes, when we have erred, there is nothing we can specifically do to make things better; it wouldn't help to make a call, send an e-mail, or whatever. But what we can change is our thinking, and the rest will follow. We might have to wait until a situation comes around again, either in this relationship or in another, and take advantage of the opportunity to act differently next time. As we do, the new behavioral pattern becomes embedded in our psychic repertoire. In time, it replaces the old.

When gemologists want to smooth out a rough sapphire or emerald, they do it by rubbing two stones up against each other. And that's often how relationships are: your rough edges rub against mine, and finally, after we suffer enough, we smooth out.

Romantic Delusions

Nowhere do we have more illusionary ideas of what love means than in the area of romance. We're trained by a world of cultural imagery to believe there is someone, one special someone, who will complete us and make us whole.

Yet what will make us whole is a deeper love for everyone. Exclusive love is not the prize it purports to be, and in truth, romantic love works far, far better when it is grounded in a larger, more inclusive love. Romance is one form that love takes—certainly a magnificent one—and yet it is content, not form, that determines love's meaning. If we are attached to that particular form of love, then we are on a slippery slope toward the fires of hell. And what are those fires? They are the anxiety we feel when that person doesn't call or acts in a way we interpret as unloving or doesn't want us anymore.

One of the biggest mistakes we make in relationships is when we get a fixed notion of what love should look like. If he loves me, he will do this. If she wants to be my friend, she will do that. But what if the feelings we want the other person to have simply don't express themselves the way we think they should? Are we going to forgo a love because it doesn't come in the package we expected it to arrive in? Relationships aren't black and white, and people aren't good or bad. We're complicated. We're trying our best. The more we live, the more we realize that the failure of others to love us the way we wish they would is as unintentional as our own such failures. Who among us isn't doing the best we're capable of, with the understanding we've got?

The ego argues that the right intimate relationship would take away all the pain of separation, yet that is delusional. Intimacy isn't a special category so much as a deeper layer of existence. When we first hold a baby in our arms, that is an intimate moment. When we sit with someone when they die, that is an intimate moment. When we share deeply from our core about our genuine feelings, that is an intimate moment. Our obsession with romantic love as the primary container for intimacy has often kept us from finding it. It is two hearts—not two bodies—that make a holy connection. When the body comes along, that's fantastic. But anyone with any experience knows that sex itself doesn't guarantee deep connection. And at times, it can obstruct it.

A Course in Miracles teaches the difference between "special" love and "holy" love. "Special" love means we are attached to another person being a certain way. We think we know what we need from a person and put our focus on trying to make it happen. Not realizing we are looking to a human relationship to fill a space that only God can fill, we are willing to go to extraordinary lengths to make the other person, or ourselves, fit into the picture our ego thinks is perfect.

The problem with this is that control and manipulation, however subtle, are not love. Love is repelled by any effort to hold onto it too tightly. God's response to the ego's "special" relationship is the creation of the "holy" relationship, in which we allow a relationship to be what it wants to be and reveal its meaning to us rather than trying to determine its meaning first.

"Holy" love allows another person to simply be who he or she is. It helps us detach from the need to control another person's behavior. Yet all of that is much easier said than done. Holy love is a pretty awesome goal for those of us stuck in our bodies in an imperfect world. Are we not to have any expectations in relationship? While it is the body that ties us to the material realm, that realm is where we are living. And we have appropriate and valid needs here.

I had an interesting lesson in nonattached love when I moved into a house with a male roommate. He's a fun person who loves excitement, traveling here and there, going off on his motorcycle. He's available when he's home, but don't even try to get him on his cell phone when he's elsewhere. I once said to him, "Casey, I understand you don't listen to your phone messages very often. But what would happen if the house burned down?"

He responded, "I guess I'd come home to a lot of ashes!"

I can appreciate Casey, even chuckle at his antics and be entertained by his dramatic entrances and exits, for one main reason: that we don't have a physical relationship. For the ego uses the body to bind us to perceptions of need and control. Whenever we're identifying with the life of the body as opposed to the life of the spirit, then the ego is in charge.

I once asked him, "But what if we were involved romantically? Your behavior would drive me nuts!" To which he responded, "If we were involved romantically, I wouldn't act this way!" That's reasonable and hopefully true, for the sake of the women in his life. But I don't know. Sex and detachment are a difficult mix and the greatest challenge within romantic love.

Several months ago I had dinner with a man I once dated but had not seen in years. The subject of politics came up, and neither of us had moved too far to the left or to the right over the last decade. We were at opposite ends of the political spectrum then, and we are at opposite ends now. What has changed, however, is that we aren't trying to change each other anymore.

We were already well into the meal when I said to him, "You realize that if this were ten years ago, both of us would be covered with scratch marks by the time the salad came!" We were saying the same things we used to say, with just as much conviction, but neither of us was reacting the same way anymore. It had finally dawned on us that other people could have different opinions, and dinner could still be good!

I remember, when I was a child, how different the reading material piled up next to my father's side of the bed was from the reading material piled up next to my mother's side of the bed. He read Goethe and Aristotle; she read Judith Krantz and Belva Plain. It never seemed odd to them that they read such different things, but I grew into an adult who wouldn't hesitate to ask, "Why are you reading *that?*" To which a man once responded to me with a sweet smile and a fabulous kiss, and then said, "None of your goddamn business!"

When I see a woman trying to control a man, even slightly, I think to myself, "Honey, it might work for you, but it sure never worked for me!"

What I've learned is that it's okay to set agreements and to share my feelings, as long as I refrain from judgment and blame. From that place—as long as I avoid the temptation to try to steer another person's behavior—miracles do occur. It's amazing how positively people respond when they feel respected for their thoughts and feelings. Learning to feel such respect—and to actually *show* it—is key to a miracle worker's power.

Levels of Teaching

There are three levels of relationship "teaching assignments."*
The first is what we would consider a casual encounter, in which it doesn't seem like anything is really happening at all.* A child accidentally drops a ball in front of us, or we share an elevator with someone. Will we throw the ball back to the child in a friendly manner, or smile at the person in the elevator? These supposedly accidental encounters are not accidental at all.*

The second level of teaching occurs when we are brought together with someone for a fairly intense learning experience, perhaps for weeks or months or years.* And we will stay together as long as physical proximity serves the highest learning opportunity for both people.*

The third level of teaching involves a "lifelong assignment";* this could be a friend, a relative, a love with whom our relationship lasts a lifetime. Sometimes it's a joyful assignment, like a brilliant lifelong love affair. And sometimes it's a painful one— relatives who cause each other grief throughout their lives. Whatever it is, however, it's part of a curriculum designed by the Holy Spirit.

Once we are joined in genuine relationship, it is never over. Whom God hath put together, no one and nothing can put asunder. While a particular form of relationship might change— through separation or through death—a relationship is never over because a relationship is of the spirit, and spirit is eternal. We are in physical connection for as long a period of time as serves the highest learning opportunity for both people, and then we merely appear to separate.* The love lives on because love cannot die.

When Yoko Ono was asked how she could bear being without John Lennon given that they had spent 90 percent of their time together, her response was, "Now we spend 100 percent of our time together." The death of the body is not the death of love.

The above is not a glib concept; it doesn't mean we don't cry, feel hurt, or grieve the loss of a love. But it does mean we have a context for transcending the loss. When our hearts remain open to the flow of Truth, the spirit can compensate for material loss. This is what happens, for instance, when people move through a divorce with loving intention, praying for God's healing of all hearts involved. Divorce is a spiritual issue with profound emotional consequences. How many children have been damaged by bitterly divorced parents? How many adults have been wounded for years, or even a lifetime, not realizing the eternal nature of a love they think they permanently lost? In delivering a divorce into the hands of God, we are asking that the relationship remain blessed in spirit though dissolved in body.

All who meet will someday meet again until their relationship becomes holy.* Whether we meet again in this lifetime or not, those who meet and love are tied together in eternity. Through the grace of God, we shall be reconciled one day. If we ever loved someone, we found them first in heaven. And it is to heaven that we will return.

Form versus Content

Someone once sent me a photograph that had been taken by a fisherman in Newfoundland. It was a picture of an iceberg, not only the part of it that protrudes above the water line, but also what's underneath the water. We all know, of course, that what is visible on top of the water is approximately 10 percent of the iceberg. Still, seeing the image was mind-blowing. It's shocking to recognize how much of life our eyes don't see.

And every situation is like that iceberg, teeming with forces that aren't visible to the physical eye. Basing our sense of reality on what the physical senses perceive as real—what people did, what people said—we base our sense of reality on a small fraction of its entirety. This means, of course, that we're hardly in touch with reality at all.

What is visible to the physical eye is the world of form, while the greater reality of a situation is not its form but its content.* Marriage is form, while love is content; age is form, while spirit is content. The only eternal reality lies in the realm of content, and content never changes. Our spiritual power lies in navigating a changing world from the perspective of that which does not change. The more we know about what's below the waterline, the more power we have above it.

We think if this or that happens in the world of form, then our lives will be fine. But while we habitually look to the material realm for something to complete us, our actual completion lies in knowing that the material realm itself is just one aspect of our greater life.

Living in the realm of body identification rather than spirit identification, we are constantly at risk for the experience of loss. We think we lose every time something in the world of form doesn't unfold the way we wish it to. Let's say I am in love with a man, we're together for a while, but then one of us decides the romantic attachment isn't working. To the ego, that means the relationship is over; to the spirit, that means the relationship simply changes form. And the spirit is correct. As much as a situation like that can bruise the heart, a higher vision of what really occurred can heal us. Love is eternal content, and it is safe and secure in the hands of God.

When We Grieve

Grief is an important healing mechanism, a way the psyche makes the transition from one situation to another. Our contemporary mania for pulling ourselves up by the bootstraps, getting back to work as soon as possible after a deep loss, and staying active no matter what is not always a perfect antidote to pain. In our modern bias for "feeling good," we often make ourselves wrong for feeling bad. Yet grief is a bad feeling without which we can never get back to the good ones.

Once I was grieving a painful situation in my life. Six weeks after the event, while talking to a friend about it, another friend walked out of the room saying, "I'm leaving. You guys can continue to obsess about this." I said, "Susan, a year from now, you can call it obsessing. After six weeks, it's still called processing." While we often bemoan the fact that people don't feel their emotions deeply enough, we're still tempted to blame them when they do.

And so, instead of allowing ourselves to grieve, we often force ourselves to suppress the grief, mistaking it for negativity or self-indulgence. Yet it is dangerous to shut out or suppress our pain because events we don't process we are doomed to repeat, or at least act out in dysfunctional ways. The time to cry is when we need to cry. Only then will we ultimately not need to cry anymore.

When a relationship is over, whether through separation or death, our center of emotional gravity shifts. We view life from a different spot on the mountain when someone who used to be next to us is no longer there. It is a good idea to do a thirty-day prayer vigil for the person who is no longer physically present with us, whether our conscious feelings for that person are loving or not. Prayer will neutralize the feelings, lifting them to serenity and peace. Going out shopping will not do this; dating or getting married again as fast as possible will not do this. Only being with yourself, your loved ones, and God will do this. You will internalize the change, your internal scars will heal, and you will, you will, be better than before.

The Spaces in Between

There is a mystery to the spaces in between relationships, when we have the opportunity to understand more deeply, to correct our course, and to redirect our ship if necessary. When a relationship is over, we can look back at it honestly, assess our part in it, and forgive ourselves and others if necessary. Did I or did I not show up for the relationship as authentically and honorably as I might have? Was I in it for the right reasons? Did I stay too long? Did I leave too quickly? Did I allow God to guide its course?

It can be helpful to make a list of every person and situation associated with the situation now passing. Silently bless them all. Ask forgiveness, and grant forgiveness. Place the situation in the hands of God, and know that He is there.

Love Is Everywhere

God's love will always find a way to express itself. One of the reasons we grasp at good things is because we think if we don't, we'll be left out of the joy in life. But of course the controlling and needy behavior that results from such a belief is sure to keep our good at bay. It's when we settle into the depths of who we are, knowing that's enough, and let other people be whoever they need to be and go wherever they need to go that the universe delivers our optimal good in a way we can receive it.

Love is everywhere, but if our eyes aren't open to see it, we miss out. Who among us hasn't missed out on love because we were looking for it in one package and it came in another? Our problem is rarely a lack of love so much as a mental block to our awareness of its presence.*

Once I was speaking to a teenager about her problems with her friends at school. She was sad because a group of girls who had been so close the year before were no longer so, and Hayley felt left out of the new group. She felt rejected and bereft, thinking she no longer had good friends.

"Hey, Hayley!" I said. "You've got to diversify!"

"What do you mean?" she asked, looking at me through adorable, tear-filled eyes.

"I mean love is everywhere! I mean there are other relationships to experience—not just those! It means you're more tied to those particular kids being the source of love in your life than you need to be. People are free, and you want to let them go when they're not moved to be close to you. But that doesn't lessen the amount of love that's available to you. Release them, bless them, feel your loss, and release it to God. I promise you—there's a miracle up ahead."

We said a prayer in which we surrendered to God her relationship with those girlfriends and asked that her heart be opened to receive the love that God intended for her. A couple of months later I saw Hayley as she ran into her house, chatting away, obviously happy. She was talking with her mother about going to a movie with a couple of friends. I asked if there had been some changes on the friendship front.

"Well, kinda!" she said. "But mainly, I have these new friends! It's fantastic!" I spoke with her for a moment about how the first situation, an apparent loss, led to something good. She had learned to release what was apparently no longer hers so that something new and wonderful could make its way into her life.

She agreed and then said to me, "I think I had a miracle."

I know she did.

Relationships That Mend the Heart

The Holy Spirit has many ways of paving a path for us, saving us from the pain of our own delusions. Sometimes it's a teacher or a book. And often it's simply another human being.

I'm often grateful for how much help I receive from people around me who can see something I can't see at a time when I most need to see it. Someone will just happen to call, and I'll just happen to tell them what's going on, and they'll just happen to share their thoughts in a way that brings the clarity my mind was seeking or the peace my soul was longing for.

The closer we grow to God, the closer we grow to our natural talent at protecting our brothers.* The more aligned we are with the love of God, the better we are at being true friends. We know how to be there, to say the right things, to give casual counsel to the people we love.

There are three people I often talk to on the telephone late at night. If someone were to ask me to write down on a piece of paper my most significant activities, I probably wouldn't write, "Talking to Richard, Victoria, and Suzannah and telling them everything." Yet it *is* one of my most important activities because it clears my head for everything else. In fact, I think such phone calls are more important than they appear.

Sociologists have now amended a traditional theory about how people respond to stress. As it turns out, the "fight or flight" syndrome that had been taken as gospel for the last few decades was derived from research based on the reactions of men only. When women were added to the research, researchers found another kind of reaction: "tend or mend." In other words, women tend to build relationships as our primary response to stress.

All of us have male and female aspects to our psyche; all of us fight or flee sometimes, and all of us tend or mend sometimes. But when we call each other to process our thoughts and feelings, it's no accident that those calls often happen late at night, when a deeper quiet is available to the soul. From the earliest days of recorded history, people told stories around nighttime campfires. We share stories as a way of holding our psyches, indeed our cultures, together. It is difficult to feel the love of God when the love of others is unavailable. The times when we bring His comfort to each other is hardly a less important time of day.

Where We Are Now

We are at a place where few of us can move forward without the help of another. Not because we are not whole but finally—at last—because we are. We are no longer fractions of ourselves looking for others to complete us. We are fairly whole—and now what?

Now we must conceive new life from deep inside ourselves. For that to occur, we must be in relationship. To cocreate life, we need each other—and God's help.

The miracle of love draws us to each other. And into that union God pours forth Himself. We will become, in each other's arms and in His as well, a new humanity. We will conceive something new. We will grow wings of divine compassion and intelligence, and the entire world will change. God Himself will rejoice.

And life will go on.

CHAPTER NINE

From *Spiritual Death* to *Rebirth*

When I was in junior high school, I really liked chemistry. On the other hand, I was a terrible chemistry student. My teacher had no place in her thinking for someone who was a terrible student but really liked chemistry anyway. In her mind, there was either "good chemistry student" or "bad chemistry student." And she let me know which one I was.

Pow! Any belief in myself as a science student died right there.

Perhaps a parent told you that you would never be pretty, and any belief in your beauty died right there. Perhaps someone told you that you were dumb and would never amount to anything, and your self-confidence died right there. Or someone told you that you had no talent and would never be able to play in an orchestra, and your belief in your musical ability died right there.

For most of us, there's not a tomb big enough to hold the bones of the parts of ourselves that died along the way.

The you that has been invalidated, put down, suppressed, violated, hurt, endangered, smeared, humiliated, mocked, brutalized, abandoned, lied about, stolen from—on and on goes the list of ego delight—such is your crucified self.

The crucifixion is not specifically a Christian concept; metaphysically, it is a pattern of energy, demonstrated physically in the life of Jesus but experienced psychically in the life of everyone. Energetically, it symbolizes a pattern of thought. Death is its mission and life its enemy, for it is the mind at work against God.

Thus the drama of every human life, as love is born into the world and then crucified by fear. But the story does not stop there. Resurrection, like crucifixion, is a metaphysical truth: it is God's response to the ego, or the ultimate triumph of love. All that is ever going on, in any situation, is that love appears, it is crucified, and ultimately love holds sway.

One night I was watching *Dances with Wolves* on television with my daughter. Both of us were deeply moved by the lives of the Sioux Indians—their harmony with nature and spirit, the way they allowed the ways of true, essential being to order their lives and bless their world. They treated life itself as a sacred treasure. Yet the collective ego of the Western world tried to destroy, and ultimately succeeded in destroying, their civilization of that time.

Such are the tragedies of human history. There *is* a dark force, not outside us but within us, always at work to destroy the love that God creates. That force, or ego, is held in place by our belief that we are separate from God and from each other; it expresses itself constantly through judgment and blame. It is every unkind word, attack, thought, or violent action. Sometimes it whispers, as in a mean glance; sometimes it shouts, as in the genocide of a people. But it is always active, as long as it has fear to fuel it. And today it has its eye on the biggest prize of all—the prospect of global annihilation.

Sometimes it's other people who string us up on the cross, and at other times we do it all by ourselves. Frequently, it seems to be a combination of both. The ego does not discriminate so much as it seeks to harm whoever it can reach. But the part of us that can be crucified is not the part of us that is who we actually are. The ego can destroy the body, but it cannot destroy the spirit.

Crucifixion takes many forms: material, mental, emotional, and spiritual. Mentally, it is a progressive disease at work within all our minds. It is sometimes called the second force, the anti-Christ, the devil. It is the destructive, anti-life element in the human experience.

All forms of ego have ultimate destruction as their goal. Alcoholism and drug addiction don't want to merely inconvenience you; they want to kill you. A terminal disease doesn't want to inconvenience you; it wants to kill you. Escalating violence doesn't want to inconvenience you; it wants to kill you. God knows this, and He has answered: He has sent His holiness to save us from ourselves. And as we embrace our holiness and the changes it engenders within us, He has a plan for what comes next.

The resurrection is God's answer to the crucifixion; it is His uplifting of our consciousness to the point where the effects of fear are canceled. Our holiness—God's love within us—is the only way humankind has ever transcended darkness, and it is the only way we ever will.

"Jesus wept," as we all do, challenged in our various ways by the lies and projections of the ego. Jesus's crucifixion—the torture and murder of an innocent man—is a radical teaching example, a demonstration of the strength of fear and then the power of love to overcome it. Jesus died, then lay in his tomb for three days. And for that period of time, of course, it seemed to those who loved him as if all hope were lost. Yet hope is of God, and what is of God is never lost.

Jesus transcended the crucifixion by taking it on, as it were. Confronted with the murderous projections of others, he continued to love with an open heart. And by allowing his heart to be as big as the universe, he became a vortex of the miraculous. Just as in the presence of Moses the laws of time and space were suspended in the parting of the Red Sea, in the presence of Jesus, the laws of death were suspended as well.

What did Jesus have that we don't have? Nothing. The issue is not that he had something we don't have, but that he didn't have anything else.* His love of God had cast out all else, leaving only the eternally true.

Collective Darkness

Today our personal crucifixions are particularly intense, as we take on the individual pieces of a huge and cosmic darkness. It's a universal pattern that the darkness seeks to destroy the light, and no one ever said, "Except in your case." And the darkness is most intense when it senses encroachment by the light. If you're doing good things and extending loving energies, then the second force is on its way to you. But that doesn't mean it's *about* you.

In today's world, to truly make a stand for holiness, for universal love, is in most situations so far from the status quo that you have to decide how much you're willing to compromise your heart in order to get along. The world as we know it is dominated by fear, and some of our major institutions are its unwitting headquarters. Think this way, don't think that way. Go in this direction, not in that one. Yet the spirit isn't known for conformity. Where there is no room for the ecstatic impulse, there is no real room for the revelation of love.

If you can rise above the fear in your life and live the love within you, and if I can rise above my fear and live the love in me—if that drama is reenacted enough times by enough of the world's people—then we will pierce the cosmic darkness and tip the world in the direction of light. Every one of us counts, and there is no such thing as a neutral thought.* Every perception leads to more fear or more love, for us and the world around us. With every prayer, every act of kindness, and every thought of forgiveness, we are building a wave of love that will turn back fear.

But we cannot take on the fear of the world until first we have taken it on within ourselves. And that we cannot do alone. We can't heal ourselves of a deep neurosis simply by intellectually deciding to change. Many of us have tried and failed.

God can do for us, however, what we cannot do for ourselves. When His spirit comes upon us, fear is silenced. It is nullified. It is gone. Once we have embraced the fullness of our spirit, then the effects of our former brokenness disappear. From physical disorders to painful relationships, from world hunger to world conflict, once we have risen to our divine potential, we will become people with the courage and intelligence to cast out darkness. With God in charge, we will rise above the thoughts that keep us bound. And thus the world will be changed. We can forego a collective Armageddon if we learn the lessons from our personal ones.

Tomb Time

There is metaphysical meaning to the three days between the crucifixion and the resurrection. It symbolizes the time it takes for the physical world to catch up with a change in consciousness, for light to ascend again after darkness has overwhelmed us. Resurrection occurs when we hold to love despite appearances and thus invoke a miracle.

Sometimes when we have been deeply wounded, there's a time during which we have to let our souls bleed, take the pain, and wait till the cycle completes itself. You can't rush a river or a heartbreak. Just know that "this too shall pass."

The three days is referred to by a friend of mine as "tomb time," during which it might seem that all hope is lost, when in fact the miracle is just around the corner. Every night is followed by a new day. The ego has its way with us in cruel and vicious ways, to be sure, yet we are delivered by God each day to a new morning—the "promised land" of inner peace.

We have all known crucifixion and then lived through a tomb time when it seemed as though the light in our lives might never return. Yet the movement of the universe is always in the direction of ultimate love; in the words of Martin Luther King Jr., "The arc of the moral universe is long, but it bends toward justice." The ego roars, but God will always have the final say.

Our crucifixions deal us a material blow, but in the hands of God the blow can become a spiritual gift. No matter what occurs in our lives, we can become better people because of it. If we had not stumbled, we could not have gotten back up. And now that we have gotten up, our backbones are a little straighter and our heads a little higher. There is nothing more beautiful than the mantle of survivor. There is nothing more illuminated than the resurrected body, the new personality that emerges when the old one has been laid to rest.

In the words of Charles Swindoll, a pastor and radio Bible teacher in the mid-twentieth century, "I have tried and I cannot find, either in scripture or history, a strong-willed individual whom God used greatly until He allowed them to be hurt deeply."

I remember once watching Richard Nixon in a television interview years after he had left the White House. He spoke with a wisdom and compassion I had never seen him exhibit during his time in politics. A president for whom I had previously felt such disdain had become a different person. And how could he have not? Given the crucifixion he endured—brought entirely upon himself—how could he have done other than to have either died or broken through to another place? Clearly, he had done the latter. A failure that in worldly terms is almost impossible to fathom had led to a spiritual success.

Crucifixions take us into the darkness of the soul, where we wrestle with the demons of shame and loathing, anger and hatred. We are asked to die to so many parts of ourselves—to lay down both sword and shield, to give up judgment and willfulness and hate. Yet when we stand there naked, having forgiven so much, we can feel a sense of lightness return to our hearts, and we know we have made it to another place. Crucifixion is never the end; in a way, it is just the beginning.

With every scar, we become carriers of the universal wound as well as transmitters of a universal healing. When we have suffered and transcended our suffering, we emerge with sacred knowledge embedded in our cells. In our life at least, some darkness has been overcome. And we will be led to others who have similarly overcome, as well as to those who have not yet but will be inspired to in our presence. Together, we will form a unified field of resurrective possibility, an opening that does not just bless our own lives but the entire world. And that is what is occurring on the planet today. People are feeling the pain of the world, almost like an inoculation. We are hurrying to rise up so we can create a higher field for everyone.

The women around Jesus waited and prayed at his feet while he was crucified. These women symbolize the friends who bear witness to our crucifixions and care about our suffering. When they go to the tomb to claim the body—that is, when they have empathized with our pain and now accompany us on our psychic journey back to wholeness—they often find that the person we were before no longer exists.

They find, when the spirit of God has moved in us, that we were not defeated but rather we became our better selves. We died to who we used to be, that's true, but who we will be now is a spirit reborn and refreshed. The fever has broken, the tears have dried, and we emerge again into the light of our true being. Such is the resurrection, the light of God upon our souls.

Rebirth

There is passion to the crucifixion, but there is passion to the resurrection as well. It cannot be seen with physical eyes, however, for the emergence of a reborn self is not a material occurrence. You have the same eyes, but there is a new light in them. You have the same brain, but it operates differently. You have the same heart, but it is beating with His now. And the resurrection is not a moment but a pattern. For every two steps into the light, we might fall one step back into darkness. But once we are on the way up, once we have glimpsed the One who has promised to take us there, there is no real going back.

It doesn't matter what anyone says or does to try to stop you. You're on your way to a brand-new life, not just for yourself but for others as well. You are not a martyr; you're a teacher of love. You have seen the light, and you are walking toward it.

Just know who you are and Who lives within you. He is risen, and so are you.

The Power of Faith

In both the Bible and *A Course in Miracles* it is stated, "Blessed are those who have faith who cannot see." It's easy to believe in love when you're surrounded by kindness; it's not so easy when you're confronted with the judgments and the attacks of the world.

Faith is an aspect of consciousness. We either have faith in the love that is eternally true or faith in the illusions of the ego. In that sense, there is no such thing as a faithless person. If you have faith in the reality of disaster, then disaster will be real for you. If you have faith in a reality of love that lies beyond a disaster, then you become an opening for its transformation. The miracle worker does not look *away* from darkness, but *through* it to the light beyond. Faith is a kind of positive denial: we don't deny that something is happening in the physical world. We simply have faith that this reality is but mere illusion before the love of God. We deny the ultimate reality of the world itself.

Does your faith lie in the reality of the crucifixion or in the reality of the resurrection?

We tend to have greater faith in the limitations of the world than in the limitlessness of God's power. When the disciples of Jesus thought they were going to drown, their faith lay in the power of the storm. When Jesus came out and walked on water, He didn't say to His disciples, "O ye of little walking-on-water proficiency; didn't you read the brochure?" He said, "O ye of little faith."

Faith means we're open to the possibility of miracles, knowing that when we stand on the ground of love, within the space of holiness, then all material forces are automatically programmed to work on our behalf. We don't have to *do* anything new so much as *become* someone new in order to fundamentally change our lives. And then we do not just believe in the resurrection; we *share* the resurrection. As we humble ourselves and step back with our ego, allowing God to lead the way, miracles occur naturally. No stress, no strain.

A Change of Heart

While traveling in Amsterdam several months ago, I noticed that something about myself had changed. I have traveled extensively since I was a child and visited scores of museums throughout the world. I have always delighted in portraits, landscapes, sculpture, Oriental screens, decorative arts, jewelry design, and all the other visual treats that are offered in such places. But one particular category of painting never moved me, and I always passed it by without giving much attention. That was nautical art: ships in the harbor, ships on the sea, ships wherever. It simply wasn't my thing.

But if you're visiting museums in Holland, you're going to see pictures of boats. And this time, for whatever reason, they touched me in a different way. This time, when I saw a painting of a ship on a rough sea, facing the clear possibility of shipwreck, my mind went to the sailors who were on the ship, the reasons they were there, the terror they were feeling, and whether or not they survived. I thought about their loved ones on land and what they felt when they heard there was a storm at sea. I thought about whether the painter had ever seen such a roiling ocean, and if he hadn't, how did he know what it looked like? I realized that for many years I had looked at those paintings, yet I hadn't really seen them at all. For I had brought nothing of my heart to the experience.

On the same trip, I visited the house of Anne Frank. It's been years since I read *The Diary of Anne Frank,* and I thought I had internalized her story and its meaning. Yet visiting the Anne Frank museum with my daughter on this trip, I could barely stop crying—in fact, I couldn't stop crying—as I walked through the rooms of her family's house. Seeing where she slept, unable to run outside and play or even look at sunlight through the window; seeing the places on her wall where her father pasted pictures from magazines so it wouldn't seem quite so dreary; thinking of the extraordinary, daily tension and fear that were experienced by those hiding in those rooms as well as by their friends who were hiding them; thinking of all the years they survived that way, only to have their hiding place betrayed a year before the end of the war; and thinking of Anne's horrifying days at Bergen-Belsen concentration camp, only to die one month before the liberation of the camps—I could hardly bear the weight of such sorrow, mixed with Anne's profound and compassionate insights into the nature of the human heart. I thought about her father's survival, his learning of his family's death, his publishing Anne's diaries—and always with the realization that this same tale of suffering was experienced not once but six million times.

As we walked through the rooms and read the exhibits, I told my daughter how important it is to bear witness to the suffering of others. For such pain as the Frank family's is experienced still, all over the world, by people as unfortunate today as they were then. And only if we allow ourselves to grieve for them all will we devote ourselves, as God would have us do, to creating a different kind of world.

At one point my daughter said to me sweetly, "Oh, Mommy, please don't cry." And I thought to myself, "Oh, Emma, please do."

There are those who would not visit such a museum, who would rather shut themselves off and not feel the agony or face the horror of all the suffering in the world. We do whatever we can to distance ourselves from it. But when Jesus said to the disciples who were falling asleep in the Garden of Gethsemane, "What, can you not remain awake with me one hour?" I think he was referring to our need to remain awake when others suffer. If nothing else, doing so reminds us how extraordinarily fortunate we are—and I do mean extraordinarily fortunate—to have a roof over our heads, food in our stomachs, and the right to simply see sunlight each day. As long as that is not true for everyone, there is much, much work for us to do on this earth. And if we will not do it, who will?

Even when there is nothing we can specifically do to help those who suffer, remaining awake to their predicament exudes its own kind of moral force. There are those in the world—imprisoned, in pain—for whom the difference between choosing life and choosing death lies simply in knowing that someone cares.

After visiting the Anne Frank house, I sat drinking coffee at a café right across the canal. On the same street where she so longed to run and play but could not, I was free to wander and shop and sip coffee and laugh out loud. By what gift of fate am I so fortunate?

There is a building in Amsterdam where all Jews were rounded up by the Nazis for deportation to the concentration camps, where many of them would be gassed immediately upon arrival. A plaque on the building says we should take a moment and remember them. In that moment, I think the departed souls feel our blessing; hopefully, in some way, it helps bring them peace.

As for us, may it bring us depth. May our hearts explode from the sheer size of it all. For therein lies the only real hope for humankind.

Resurrection

It is the consciousness of peace, not the behavior of war, that will ultimately turn back the tides of fear. And it is incumbent upon each of us to foster that consciousness. I am not referring to just making things better; I am referring to transcending all physical laws, bending the rules of time and space, and coming alive where we were previously dead. It's time to see miracles in our own lives, to be resurrected from the littleness of our former selves. Through God, these things are possible. These miracles are available, and they are necessary now.

It doesn't matter what someone said when you were a child; you know now that you're smart and attractive. It doesn't matter what happened before; you can rise up now and start over. It doesn't matter what they did to you; forgiveness has washed you clean.

Boys who have become men will now become great men; girls who have become women will now become great women. We will give birth to our better selves. Those who rise to the heights of their potential will not be the exception; they will be the rule. Through them—and by *them*, I mean *us*—a plan will emerge for the salvation of the world.

A new world awaits all of us, as our minds are healed by love.

CHAPTER TEN

From *Your Plan* to *God's Plan*

*A*n underground revolution is sweeping the hearts and minds of the people of the world, and it is happening despite the wars and terror that confront us. This revolution is a fundamental change of worldview, and it carries with it the potential to reorganize the structure of human civilization. It brings a basic shift in the thoughts that dominate the world. It wages a peace that will end all war. It is a global phenomenon that will change the cellular structure of the human race. To those who are part of it, who feel called to it, its reality is a growing if not obvious truth. To still others, it's a lofty but ridiculous notion, a preposterous and silly idea.

Yet no social revolution of any import emerged because everybody woke up one day saying, "I get it! I get it!" Such revolutions emerged instead from what anthropologist Margaret Mead described as "a small group of concerned citizens." Not only are such groups capable of changing the world, according to Mead, but in fact, they're the only thing that ever has. And they are doing it now.

A spiritually attuned counterculture is already in our midst. It is marked not by clothes or music, drugs or sex, as was the counterculture of the sixties, but by the internal attitudes of those who perceive it. They make suggestions and comments that are just a little bit wiser; they bring new insights into areas previously locked down by the status quo. They see some star in the sky that not everyone is seeing. And in their presence, we start to see it too.

Signing Up for Duty

We sign up for duty, for participation in this revolution, through a sincere desire to be used by something larger than ourselves, for the purpose of healing the world. It doesn't even matter if we don't call that "something larger" by the name of God. For some people conspire with God who do not yet believe in Him.* It is ultimately not our belief but our experience that matters.* God has no ego by which to be insulted if we do not get His name right.

But whatever name we call Him, we come to realize that we are the army, but He is in charge. He cannot use us to change the world deeply until first we have been changed by Him. To surrender the world to Him, first we must surrender ourselves.

The change begins with a shift in the lens through which we perceive the world. It grows within us to affect not only our own lives, but also the lives of those around us. It leads us to connect with others who are similarly undergoing a transformation of their ego structures, from an old perspective to something new. And through our individual and collective efforts, divinely inspired, we will turn the world around in time. Just when we thought all hope was ended, hope will reappear.

For those of us who are cynical; for those of us who are too tired now; for those of us who are weary of the way things always go; for those of us who used to care but are too busy now just trying to get by, there is a change afoot. It begins in the heart. And as it rises to the surface, it will change all things.

IMAGINE THAT GOD HAS ASKED YOU if He could use your hands and feet, to go where He would have you go and do what He would have you do.

Imagine that God has asked you if He could use your mouth, to say what He would have you say and to whom.

Imagine these things because He has.

"Many are called, but few are chosen" means that everyone is called but few care to listen.* The call goes out to all of us, all the time. None of us has more or less capacity for contributing to the salvation of the world.

Choosing to serve God, we are choosing the path toward God's greatness within us. When we see people who are clearly letting the spirit work through them—who have found their genius, their power, their passion—we are not seeing some special force at work that chose them over others. The power did not choose them so much as they chose *it*.

Those among us who have achieved the most have achieved only a fraction of what all of us are capable of.* The "gifts of the Holy Spirit" are waiting for all of us, when our lives are dedicated to God's plan.

Every morning, we have a choice: Will I seek out God's plan today, or will I go about my day as a slave to my ego's agenda? To choose God's plan is to choose the option with the best opportunity for turning your life into a conduit for the miraculous. As soon as we start asking Him how we can help with His plan, rather than just asking Him to help with *our* plans, everything will be better for everyone.

We're here to be teachers of God—that is, those who demonstrate love. God has a plan for the salvation of the world, called "the plan for the teachers of God."* His teachers come from all religions and no religion.* There is nothing to sign up for, no worldly organization or institution to belong to. It simply refers to a stirring in the heart, which then activates an internal guidance system already present within us. If we *ask* how to help, He will show us how to help.

While there are hate-filled people planning ways to sow violence and destruction on earth, God has a blueprint for creating peace on earth. It's not a physical blueprint, but rather a plan that exists in His Mind, pieces of it ready to be downloaded into the mind of anyone who asks to receive his or her part. Each of us carries maximal potential to be used by God to heal the world.

He has a plan. And it cannot not work.

Our Father's Business

Sometimes, going about "our Father's business" involves something we *don't* do as much as something we do. It can be our passive resistance, even more than a direct challenge, that subverts an unjust influence.

I knew a minister whose job was terminated unjustly, and the board of directors at his church chose to assassinate his character to avoid any challenge from his congregation. He was understandably upset, yet the actions of many friends who supported him touched his heart.

One was a woman who cut his hair every month. After the minister's dismissal from the church, one of the board members, a man who had been largely responsible for the campaign against him, began going to her to have his hair cut as well. Every month the man would come in, sit in her salon chair, and repeat the same mischaracterization of the facts, steeped in self-serving untruths and denial.

After a couple of months, the woman simply didn't wish to cut the board member's hair anymore. She no longer felt good about doing business with him. Her loyalty to her friend, and standing firm in a principle of righteousness as she understood it, mattered more to her than business. She couldn't understand, she said, how a place could abuse people and still call itself a church. She called the board member to say she no longer wished to cut his hair.

The woman's action was a demonstration of Mahatma Gandhi's principle of nonviolence, which declares that *moral force emanates from righteous action.* While such force might not have observable effects, it indeed has effects on an invisible plane. By simply standing in Truth—not only in our words but through our behavior as well—we help create a wave of power that will heal the world.

In 1955 Rosa Parks sparked the civil rights movement by simply saying no to the white bus driver who told her to give up her seat for a white man. When Dr. Martin Luther King Jr. called for a boycott of the Montgomery bus company, he was calling for a huge sacrifice on the part of hundreds of people. For 381 days, people walked miles to work, sometimes enduring terrorism and harassment, rather than continue to participate in a system of segregated busing. By simply saying no to what she knew to be unjust, Mrs. Parks demonstrated the tremendous powers such action sets in motion.

We never know what effect our simply standing on truth might have. We think, "I'm just one person; what difference can I make?" But none of us is "just one person." All minds are joined, and each of us has a chance every day to say yes to something that could make the world a better place and no to something that degrades it. We're sometimes looking for the big plan that will save the world, while not recognizing our own part in it. The plan that will save us involves little ways that each of us becomes more righteous every day. And enough tiny droplets, in time, make up an ocean.

The woman who refused to cut the hair of someone she knew had wronged her friend did not just help her friend. She helped herself as well. By fueling the forces of loyalty and integrity, she generated moral power that added to her own spiritual stature.

No action goes unregistered by the universe. The political philosopher Edmund Burke wrote, "The only thing necessary for evil to triumph is for enough good people to do nothing." And the only thing that will triumph over evil is for enough good people to actually *do good.*

It's not enough to simply talk about goodness. The fact that I say I love you means little unless it's acted on. The fact that I say I love you means little unless you experience me as a loyal and ethical friend. The fact that I say I love you does not make everything all right if my behavior argues otherwise. That is often the problem with a so-called spiritual worldview: there are those who act as though the use of the *L* word renders an authentic effort at ethics, integrity, loyalty, or even honesty unnecessary. But surely God is less impressed by our words than by our deeds.

In the movie *Meet Joe Black*, there is a scene where Death tells a woman's father that he plans to take her with him when he leaves the earth, as he has fallen in love with her and doesn't want to be without her. At that point, her father argues that real love is more than just appetite or even need: it's an active caring for the ultimate well-being of another human being.

Love isn't always easy; and if it doesn't stretch you personally, then it probably isn't love.

The Goal of God's Will

For many of us, the problem is not that we don't believe in God or don't want to be conduits of His love. The problem is simply that we have quite a few other goals as well.* We don't recognize how our separate, individual goals can actually get in the way of God's.

The miracle worker is asked to do two things: see forgiveness as our function, and relinquish all other goals we have invented for ourselves.

Sometimes people ask me about my early years lecturing on *A Course in Miracles* and the interesting ride I've had professionally. Twenty years have passed since I gave my first talk, and from this vantage point I can see clearly why my early accomplishments came effortlessly: I had very little and wanted little more. I was delighted with my apartment, my work, my friends, my life. I was so completely naive to concepts like best-seller status, royalty statements, lecture dates, house payments, public perception, and everything else in the material world that I gave total energy to the work I felt moved to do. My naïveté was an asset.

Walking through a fancy store never used to cause me stress. I couldn't buy anything, and I knew it, so it was like walking through a museum. It's when you can buy one good dress but no more—*that's* when the stress kicks in!

Now, when I read that as a miracle worker I'm supposed to relinquish *any goals I have invented for myself,* I am definitely stopped short. Lecture dates, nest egg, enough for Emma, book contracts—and the list goes on. The world has both rewarded me and imprisoned me. Like many of us, I built a prison around myself and now have the audacity to complain.

So we get caught in a loop: we're trying to escape the pain of a world that *is* the pain. The innocence of ignorance—when we were pure of heart because we simply didn't know anything else—surely must be beautiful to God. But there is another kind of innocence as well: an innocence lost and then regained, having been consciously chosen by one who *does* know something else. It's one thing not to covet because we wouldn't even know what there is to covet, and another thing not to covet because we've been there, done that, and it didn't fix us anyway. Think how useful we are to God then, when our goals have been superseded by His.

Often we try to get clear about what our goals are, figuring out a five- or ten-year plan, making treasure maps, identifying those we wish to emulate. But we should think about our spiritual goals as well. The question shouldn't just be, "Where do I want to be in five or ten years?" It should also be, "*Who* do I want to be in five or ten years?" How long until I move beyond judgment and blame? How long until I stop playing victim? How long until I forgive myself and make the most of the life I have?

Our goal in any situation should be that God's will be done.*

We will be told exactly what we need to know in every instant that our hearts are open.* God speaks to us through what is called "the small still voice for God." Through forgiveness, prayer, and meditation, we can quiet the mind enough to be able to hear it.

One of my favorite prayers in *A Course in Miracles* is the following:

> *Where would you have me go?*
> *What would you have me do?*
> *What would you have me say, and to whom?*

With that prayer, we are asking God to use us—to use our hands and feet and thoughts and feelings. And once we have surrendered ourselves to be used for a higher purpose, we give up the obsession with planning that dominates so much of Western civilization. We know we can't know what's on the other side of a particular turn in the road. We choose to walk across the Holy Spirit's bridge of perception instead, knowing that the destination is not as important as who we are while we are walking.

Inner peace brings more positive experiences into our lives because it aligns us with superior aspects of our own personality. We shift from grandiosity to grandeur and from littleness to magnitude.* We attract rather than repel affection and trust, and—just as important—we develop the power to retain them. It does little good to attract our good if we are too frantic or uncentered to hold onto it once it gets here.

Our Spiritual Magnitude

What will happen as we grow into our spiritual magnitude? In each of our lives, it will look different. Every moment holds infinite possibilities, and how much magnificence we allow to move into us and through us is determined by our willingness and receptivity. To whatever extent the blocks are removed to the awareness of our divine nature, to that extent we are magnetized to the events and situations—and they are magnetized to us—that resonate with our grandeur. If we're vibrating at a low energy, we'll attract low-energy situations (how many times have we stubbed a toe or banged a finger when we were angry?); if we're vibrating at a high energy, we'll attract miracles.

People will call out of nowhere; situations will just seem to improve; abundance of all kinds will just appear. And when they do, it is good to acknowledge them. We often build an altar to our disasters, giving them so much time and attention and energy. But do we do the same for our blessings? Are our minds truly disciplined to call forth and accept the good?

We're living during a "celestial speed-up" in which everything is moving more quickly—including us!* Our issues aren't coming through in slow gentle breezes anymore, but in huge torrential storms! And that's not because we're failing; it's because we're available, God knows it, and *this is it.* I remember watching television one night about the D-Day invasion, how the Allied forces had rehearsed it for months, and then one morning things were different: *this was real.*

This is a critical time in all our lives because it's a critical time on earth. Each of us has the opportunity now to grow into the fullness of our divine potential in order to take our place in God's plan. The plan exists in the Mind of God, and to the extent to which we surrender our thinking to Him, we take our part. Our primary function is to stand in the light of who we are and become the people we are capable of being. From that, all good will follow.

And we step into that light in any moment we choose. When our hearts are closed to love—when we're judgmental, withholding, unforgiving—we are literally *not being ourselves*. We are, in those moments, choosing to be hostage to the ego rather than host to God.

Our function, our happiness, and our purpose all emanate from the same point of power: our capacity to embody love in any given instant. And love is more than "being nice." It is the surrender of a separate sense of self, a claim to the totality of life as part of ourselves. Knowing that we are part of the whole, we shift our perspective from a sense of individual identity to a sense of universal connection. It becomes impossible to act only for yourself when you know that your self includes everyone.

If someone suffers on the other side of the world, he or she is no less a part of ourselves.

And when a critical mass of humanity realizes this, then obstacles to world peace will fade. In the realm of spirit, we see our goal fully accomplished: we want a world remade in the image of love. In the realm of the body, we achieve it gradually: we will do what we can to make the world a better place. Yet the power of the vision keeps the process on track. We know that through our individual efforts, we are contributing to a larger one. Our goal is not just to create a world in which loveless things are outlawed: our vision is a world in which such things have become literally *unthinkable*. That is the role of the miracle worker: to think with so much love that fear begins to lose the false authority by which it rules the world. *Think* of a world in which there is only love, and hold that thought for several minutes each day. The day will come when our thinking will lead to our believing, which will lead to our acting to make it so.

Are We Really Trying?

Everyone I know wants the world to change. All of us want to be part of the solution. We find the thought of the complete revolution of human values a very attractive idea. Everyone's all ready to sign up. Let's go!

But wait. You start to hear a few little complaints. "Can we do this when *The West Wing* isn't on?" "Could I sign up for a slot between two and four on Saturday, when the kids are at soccer?" "Couldn't we meet in a nicer place?" We're the only generation in the history of the world that wants to reinvent society over white wine and brie.

Only in America would someone expect changing the world to be *convenient!* Hello. Reality check: The suffragettes had no cell phones. The abolitionists had no faxes.

They did have love in their hearts, however. And so do you and I.

I asked a friend what I should speak about at a talk I was to give in his bookshop, and he said, "Speak about the challenges of living a spiritual life today—I mean, we all try so hard!"

And I thought to myself, "No, we don't!"

For whatever reason, however, we keep telling ourselves we do. We're all revisionists these days, and we're not content to just revise our past—we even revise the present. We seem to have a magical belief that if we describe ourselves a certain way, then it must be true.

We talk about how hard it is to live a spiritual life when we're not even meditating regularly or making the deepest effort to forgive those who have hurt us. Perhaps we have spent so many years in the classroom that "student mode" has become a habit.

It's time to graduate. Enough of us know spiritual principles now; we've read the same books and listened to the same tapes. It's time to *become* the principles now, to embody them and demonstrate them in our daily lives. Until we do, we will not really learn them at the deepest level. They will not inform our souls or transform the world.

And if that's the case, we will go down in history as the generation that knew what we needed to know yet didn't do what we needed to do. I can't imagine how it would feel, to die with that realization.

We've subscribed to a kind of ivory tower notion of spiritual education: keep it abstract and intellectual and safe. Yet the spoils of history usually go to those willing to get dirt underneath their fingernails.

I heard a woman talking recently about her frustration with politics: "We've tried so hard, and nothing ever seems to change!" I thought she must be joking.

"Uh, no, we haven't. How many of us even vote?" I asked her. "And if we do, what does that mean—we go to the voting booth every two or four years? Where do we get off thinking that we've *tried so hard?*" Are we thinking we made some supreme and noble effort to change the world, and it didn't *work?!* We've been so trained by thirty-minute sitcoms that if we don't get what we want in half an hour, it's like, uh-oh, we tried but failed. Too bad. It's over. Next.

Mother Teresa made a supreme and noble effort. Martin Luther King Jr. made a supreme and noble effort. Susan B. Anthony made a supreme and noble effort. We have not made a supreme and noble effort. In fact, most of us make very little effort to change the world. But then we feel frustrated when we see that it's not changing!

Usually, when people say, "We've tried so hard!" they're not really talking about themselves. It's more like, "Well, there are other people I know who have!" It's laughable when you think about it. Perhaps we don't realize the big secret in our midst— which isn't how *little* power we have to change things, but rather how *much* power we have that we aren't using! We're like birds who were never informed, or have forgotten, we have wings.

But a great remembering is reverberating among us, and whatever we've done or haven't done, succeeded at or failed at; whatever time we've used well or time we've wasted; we are here, we are available, we are present to the moment and up to the challenge.

All we need remember is this: if God has given us a job to do, He will provide for us the means by which to accomplish it.* All we have to do is ask Him what He wants us to do and then be willing to do it.

Goals

Before a spiritual awakening, we live our lives pretty much on our own. We go into situations with our worldly thought forms usually centered around our own agenda, our individual goals, and our needs as we define them. Yet once we're on the miracle worker's path, we start to surrender our goals to God.

Sometimes I have found myself being fairly surrendered in deciding what to do, yet grab the controls when it comes to how I go about doing it. It's not enough to allow God to decide what action to take. We have to also allow the Spirit of God to deeply influence who we are within the action.

You might feel guided to a certain meeting. But if your thoughts during the meeting are arrogant or judgmental, if your behavior is controlling or immature, then even if you're where you "should" be, you still blow it once you're there! Our personal energy both attracts and repels our good. People telepathically feel the tenor of our thoughts, and very few people jump up and down to be with a negative person.

If I walk into a room and silently bless everyone in it, no one will know exactly why they feel more peaceful, but they will. When our thoughts are aligned with God's, we are lifted into a greater realm of possibility than our ego-based thinking can provide. It is not enough to pray, "Dear God, should I go to this meeting?" It's also helpful to remember, before walking into it, to pray, "Dear God, now that I'm here, I surrender this meeting to you. May I be an instrument of your peace. Amen."

We often ignore the amazing power of prayer, and for an equally amazing reason: *we don't believe it could be that easy.* Yet is it difficult for the rosebud to blossom? Is it difficult for the stars to shine? Part of God's genius is that He makes it all look so easy. We keep looking for the wings of a sparrow when the wings of an eagle have already been given us.* We keep clinging to our weakness while our true strength is huge.

Trading Ambition for Inspiration

The point is not to do something or not do it. The point is to do something if we're internally guided to do so and not to do something if we're not guided to do so. Sometimes people think they have a great idea, and then it falls apart. Yet if the plan was self-initiated rather than divinely inspired, then it might not have reflected the best use of your talents in a particular area.

Miracle workers are warned to "avoid self-initiated plans."* What this means is that ideas we come up with ourselves— ideas that come not from a sense of deeper guidance and inspiration but rather from a sense of ambition and a desire for control—come from the ego self and are not backed by the heavens. Quite simply, they are not blessed. They might be good ideas, and very well intentioned, but if they do not emanate from the Holy Spirit, then they represent "my will" and not "Your will." Our good intentions are not enough; our willingness is everything.*

Often I've heard people complain about a plan that failed. "But it was a good idea! I don't know why it didn't succeed!" But though we might have thought something was a good idea, the mortal mind has a limited perspective on "good ideas." By what criteria can we discern a truly good idea, given our inability to know what will happen in the future, what lessons need to be learned by whom, and how our actions fit into God's larger plan? A blessed idea does not come from the mortal mind, which has no idea how our talents and abilities would work best within a larger unfolding good. And from a spiritual perspective, there *is* a larger plan of unfolding good, a will-to-healing that is built into the workings of the universe. We will be told everything we need to know and shown everything we need to see. The Whole (Holy) Mind (Spirit) of God impresses itself upon us when we pray and meditate and seek to follow spiritual principles. As we open ourselves to receive His guidance, our thoughts and feelings fall into patterns that lead all things within and around us to realms of divine right order.

Ministry Is Not Just for Ministers

When I was a young woman, I remember being overwhelmed with the thought that I didn't know what I should do with my life. I had no inkling that there might already be a divinely ordained plan, some track I simply had to ride my train along. I thought I was responsible for the train *and* the track. No wonder they were both so poorly built at times.

Following God's way is not so difficult as it is different.* What's difficult is retraining our minds, getting over our resistance to thinking in such a different way than we've been taught. If in fact our only function is love and forgiveness, then the entire world as we know it is wrong. And it is. The thinking of the world is 180 degrees away from the thinking of God.*

It takes a certain humility to present ourselves truly empty and available to God. But when we do, we become filled with information we don't otherwise possess. Like what to do with our lives—which is significant information to be lacking.

We're always wondering whether we should do this or that when from a spiritual perspective what's most important is not what we *do* so much as who we *become.* Some things God indeed would have us do, but first we must become different people in order to know how to or to be able to. God can't work for us until He can work through us.

Once I was taking a vacation and had been working with a travel agent named Connie. At the last minute, because of a work commitment, I needed to change my date of departure. When Connie looked into it, however, she found that she had sold me a completely nonrefundable and unchangeable ticket.

I was upset because I would not have bought the ticket had I known that. But I also knew that this was a great opportunity for me to strike the balance between asserting appropriate displeasure regarding someone's professional performance and showing grace and compassion toward someone who had simply made a mistake. As my fourteen-year-old daughter said to me after listening to my end of the phone call, "You did great, Mom. You let her know she had done it wrong, but you didn't *shame* her."

From a purely mortal perspective, God's plan might have been that I take a vacation. But on a deeper level, God's plan had to do with what Connie and I both learned from that experience: she, to be more careful in the work she was doing for her clients, and I, to handle such a situation without being either too easy or too hard on someone around me.

No matter what greatness might otherwise unfold in Connie's life, it's blocked if she's not performing at her best. And no matter what greatness might unfold in my life, it's blocked by whatever issues I might have in dealing with people. And *that* is God's plan—that the blocks to our inner light be removed, that His light might then shine through.

The *Course in Miracles* workbook exercise "I am among the ministers of God" says, "It is not our part to judge our worth, nor can we know what role is best for us; what we can do within a larger plan we cannot see in its entirety. . . ." It continues,

Whatever your appointed role may be, it was selected by the Voice for God, Whose function is to speak for you as well. Seeing your strengths exactly as they are, and equally aware of where they can be best applied, for what, to whom and when, He chooses and accepts your part for you. He does not work without your own consent.

. . . You become aware at last there is one Voice in you.

And that one Voice appoints your function, and relays it to you, giving you the strength to understand it, do what it entails, and succeed in everything you do that is related to it.

Sometimes someone says, "Well, I'd love to be off doing God's work, but I've got three kids at home—I can't go anywhere!" Yet ministry is determined by its content, not its form. There is certainly no ministry more important than parenting. Being conscious and attentive in your dealings with a fifteen-year-old trying to figure out how to get through high school is as important as feeding AIDS patients in Africa. If more people running the world today had been raised with greater spiritual awareness when they were fifteen years old, perhaps the world wouldn't be in the mess it's in now.

The Holy Spirit assigns each of us to the place our talents and abilities can best be put to use and our lessons most powerfully learned.* Don't doubt the plan; just make yourself available to it.

A while ago, I was visiting my mother, talking to her and her nurse. Years ago I would have been impatient, thinking I needed to be out in the world trying to do something important. What I know now is that the world is wherever I am, and my lessons for both teaching and learning are right here, right now, in this case with my mom and her nurse. For I might have things to teach them, but even more importantly, they most certainly have things to teach me. Like getting over myself. Like being more patient. Like showing gratitude to the woman who gave me my life. Just little things like that, ha ha . . .

MY HOUSEMATE (the one with the motorcycles, who rarely checks his messages) once called from a vacation and told me he had met a woman he liked very much, and he was bringing her home for a visit. I was happy he had met someone, but I felt some fear regarding our living arrangement. Was she going to live in the house with us? Would she like my daughter, and would she like me? Would I still feel comfortable in my home? What if she didn't like us and wanted us to move out?

I allowed my monkey mind to do what it needed to do, yet I remembered that my only mission is to love. For hours before I met her, I simply prayed that our meeting would be blessed. I asked to be an instrument of love in her life. I asked that my heart be opened to her, that our relationship reach its highest possibility. I knew that if I put my heart and mind in the right place, the future would reach its highest expression. I am not here to design God's universe but to allow Him to show me the design He has already created. It was created in total love, for me and all living things. My mission is to trust that.

Love is infinite, and infinitely creative. If that woman is coming into the house, then that is my blessing for the day. It is part of my spiritual curriculum. It's what's up, and that's how I know it's important. Reality now is the reality that matters. Whatever is happening is our opportunity to heal our wounded parts, should our hearts and minds be open to God's love.

It was going to be a lesson no matter what: either a lesson in being open to a new situation or a lesson in setting boundaries with compassion. But the key to learning the lesson lay in opening my heart. Only in that way was I doing my part to move the universe and myself toward divine right order.

Running my mind along that track, I prepared the way for higher things to unfold. And they did. We were friends by the end of the evening.

God Is Not Your Gofer

Sometimes we talk to God as though we're giving Him our shopping list. *Please do this for me, and that. Amen.*

Which is not to say we shouldn't ask for what we want, but even more important, we should ask God what *He* wants. Placing ourselves in service to God is the single most important key to finding right relationship with everyone and everything.

We can't save the world without God, but God can't save the world without us. In making ourselves available to His plan, we can't always see how our part fits into the overall scheme of things. But we don't need to. What we need, perhaps more than anything else, is enough faith in ourselves to appreciate His faith in us. He doesn't create small spirits, and He doesn't have small plans. He created us in greatness, and He has greatness in Mind for us. Mediocrity has no place in God's creation.

There have been times in my life when I backed away from something extraordinary, thinking, "Who am I to do such a thing?" But in reality, who was I not to do something if God had placed it in front of me? Like everything else, we have humility and arrogance completely upside down. It's not humble to think you can't do what God is asking you to do; it's arrogant to think you know yourself better than the One who thought you up.*

Whatever it is you are guided to do, don't be concerned about your own readiness; just be consistently aware of His.* Once you've asked to be the conduit through which God operates, your only job is to relax into the Holy Instant and allow the Holy Spirit to guide your thoughts and actions. We're only the faucet; God is the water.

The presence of fear is a sure sign that we're trusting in our own strength.* Once again, it's making ourselves the big deal that throws us into fear. You're not the big deal; God within you is the big deal.

Once you know that, you are so far ahead of the game.

Making Decisions

The world tells us all kinds of ways to make intelligent decisions, but there is no intelligence like Divine Intelligence. It emanates from a place in which all things past, present, and future are known and blessed. It makes decisions based on the highest good for all living things. Surrendering all decisions into the hands of God is not a giving up of personal responsibility; it is the highest form of *taking* responsibility.

When we decide things for ourselves, not only are we driving blind—unable to see around the next bend in the road—we are also trying to compensate for whatever we thought we lacked in the past. The past is a poor navigational tool. You can't steer your car forward when you're staring in the rearview mirror. Since the perception of lack then forms our core belief, we inevitably and subconsciously repeat it. Making decisions with the ego mind will only result in more ego, tightening its grip even more on our minds and on our lives.

When we place an issue in the hands of the Holy Spirit, however, He uplifts and rearranges our perceptions. When we place an issue on the altar, He alters our thinking.

I've often received direct guidance after prayerfully requesting it before going to sleep at night. If we pray at that time—"Should I do this?" or "Should I do that?"—often relevant dreams appear during our sleep, guidance may wake us during the night, or we may wake in the morning with a sense of knowing.

Those moments can be important because the ego hasn't had a chance yet to put up its mental filter and muffle the voice of God. It's odd that we teach children to say their prayers at night but somehow think that once we're adults we don't need to. Like what, once we're grown up, we know everything already so we don't need any help?

When my daughter was born, I put the name India on her birth certificate; it was the name we had decided on months before. Yet when I brought her home from the hospital, I wasn't so sure. Several names kept popping up. So the first night we were home, I prayed before I went to sleep and asked God what her name should be. I awoke the next morning with a vivid image in mind, like a clear dream just as I was waking, in which a blond little girl was holding up a white poster board with very big, clear, black letters: E M M A. I was startled, and the little girl said, "Mommy, my name is Emma." Hardly subtle.

The voice for God is like a spiritual radio signal, and late at night and first thing in the morning are when it's easiest to get clear reception—then and when we meditate. Those are the times when the world isn't so much with us, when the obfuscation of worldly plans isn't burdening our minds.

Whatever time of day it is, we can become attuned to receiving guidance that we know comes from beyond our mortal mind.

In early 1984 I was working as a temporary secretary at the World Savings Building in Los Angeles, and I had just begun lecturing on *A Course in Miracles* at the Philosophical Research Society. While a few people were coming to my lectures, I had no inkling that this would become a full-time career. As I stood at the elevator bank at work one day, I heard a voice, inside my head yet as clear as a bell, say, "This will be your last secretarial job." And other, very personal guidance has lit my way at other times. The same is true for many others I know. There are more dimensions of consciousness than the ego's worldview deems possible or real.

The voice for God doesn't ignore the realities of practical existence. The Holy Spirit understands the world yet understands its place in God's scheme of things as well. He is like an ambassador from God, entering the worldly illusion with the function of guiding us beyond it.* He shows us how to dwell on the earth while still holding on to the principles of heaven. He doesn't teach us to ignore the world or our worldly responsibilities. He simply teaches us how to live our lives with deeper meaning and in a way that serves the world best. In that way, we participate in a collective effort to reclaim this realm for love.

Many times we do hear God's guidance but we simply can't square it with what our mortal minds believe. "Why would spirit direct me to go to Chicago if Seattle is where that job is?" Only a year later will you know, and you'll feel bitterly disappointed if you missed out on something great in Chicago and find yourself saying, "I had a *feeling* I should go there!" Once you've messed up enough times because you didn't follow your inner guidance, you become much more obedient. God has only our happiness in mind—and the happiness of every living thing. Once we realize that, His path becomes much easier to follow.

Following Love

Obedience to God means a willingness to follow the dictates of love: thoughts and behavior prescribed for us by a force that wants only our happiness and good, as opposed to thoughts and behavior masquerading as our self-interest but that are in fact our own self-destructiveness.

This makes for a radical departure from a traditional notion of God as stern, frowning, judgmental, or narrow. The purpose of our lives is to be happy; God wants us to be happy, far more than we seem to want it for ourselves. It's contrary to much of traditional religious teaching to believe that surrender to God is surrender to something with only our highest good in mind. To the ego, suffering looks somehow more important, more substantial than happiness. The ego realizes that suffering changes things, but the Holy Spirit realizes that joy changes things too. Watching babies at play, are we not moved to smile? Being loved by our mate, are we not moved to smile? Achieving a creative task, are we not moved to smile? What could be more natural than joy?

Under the ego's spell, we are tempted to think, "Do I want to do God's will, or do I want to be happy?"* As long as we doubt that happiness and God's will *are the same thing*, we tend to decide against ourselves. How easy can it be to surrender if we're not convinced that what we're surrendering to really wants us to be happy?

Basing our decisions on the matters of the world should be balanced with weighing them against the matters of the heart. Once legalities, medical opinions, accounting, and other people's perspectives have been factored in; once all options have been researched and analyzed; then all decisions should be placed in the hands of God. The most powerful way to make a decision is to ask God to make it for you.*

> *Dear God,*
> *Please make this decision for me.*
> *I do not see the future,*

But You do.
I do not know what's best for everyone,
But You do.
I cannot make sense of this,
But You can.
Dear God,
Please decide this for me.
Amen.

Such a prayer authorizes spiritual forces to move mountains on your behalf. And they will.

Sometimes I feel I've asked and asked and the answer still hasn't come. At such times I know what the answer really is: as it's often said in AA, "More will be revealed." Sometimes the answer isn't as simple as "Do this" or "Do that." Sometimes it's about becoming more patient—knowing that as we continue to grow in depth and understanding, we'll either know what to do or the question will take care of itself. Only infinite patience produces immediate results.* When our faith is strong enough, we're not worried that God didn't hear us or that He might not get back to us.

And there's another issue that can tempt us to make decisions that only God should be making: our false belief that we know what is best for others. Such thoughts as "I can't leave him because he needs me" or "I have to stay in this job because the people here wouldn't be able to make it without me" are examples.

In fact, it's a win-win universe—when the Holy Spirit enters into a situation, it will be an automatic "win" for all concerned.* We are afraid to make a decision that might hurt someone, and we go around with the best of intentions trying to avoid that. Yet if we simply ask God to make our decision for us, then He who knows what is *ultimately best for everyone* will decide from a vantage point much wiser than our mortal mind could muster.

In truth, whatever God's guidance is for *you* is what would be best for others in the long run as well.

Allowing God to make our decisions is just another form of deep surrender. When God is invited to choose, more insight becomes available to us. More dimensions of knowing begin to blossom. We become so full once we make ourselves empty; we become so smart once we realize we're not; and we become so powerful once we understand we're powerless.

Exchanging our mortal intelligence for divine intelligence, we will begin to see beyond appearances. And nothing will be the same.

CHAPTER ELEVEN

From *Who We Were* to *Who We Are Becoming*

I've often heard people say they're afraid of change. But I'm someone who grows nervous when things *don't* change. I think at times I thrive on it.

People are always walking into my house and saying, "Wait, didn't that picture used to hang in the other room?" I'm so obsessive about moving furniture (particularly pillows) around that once I actually lifted up a chair while my friend was still sitting in it!

But I have also been done in by change, overwhelmed by changes I myself set in motion, casually releasing energies that were not casual at all. I've judged certain changes to be light spring showers that turned out to be hurricanes. I have underestimated the force of change. And so I've been humbled on the subject, having learned the hard way how important it is to move slowly on the inside when things on the outside are moving fast. While I don't fear change in and of itself, I fear myself when I'm not slow and conscious and prayerful while it's happening.

In 1992 my first book, *A Return to Love,* was published. Thanks to Oprah Winfrey and her generous enthusiasm for the book, my world changed. Money came that I had never had before, along with press attention and a slight celebrity status. I didn't think of it as incredible; I just thought of it as lots to do! I became a chicken with my head chopped off, no longer taking as much time to listen, to reflect, to meditate, to think. At a time when I most needed to repair to my inner room, to ask God to enter and explain things to me, I was beginning to forget. I was moving too fast. I put some second things first and some first things second in ways I would come to regret.

I remember receiving my first royalty check, more money than I had ever seen. And perhaps particularly because I was living in Los Angeles at the time, I bought into the notion that if you have the good fortune to have money, you must buy a house. But I remember praying about this, and my guidance was clear though it seemed odd to me: "Redecorate your condo."

I kept having that thought: "Redecorate your condo." But people around me laughed at such a thought. Why would I redecorate my condo when I could afford a house? *A Course in Miracles* states that the Holy Spirit often gives guidance that sounds startling at the time, but I guess I forgot that part. I went with the voices of the world instead of the voices of my heart.

In the greater scheme of things, whether or not you purchase a house is not what matters. But it matters indeed when the voice in your heart loses volume in your head. Why was the Holy Spirit directing me to redecorate my condo? Because I needed time to adjust to the new turn my life had taken. I needed time to grow into my new circumstances, to inhabit emotionally the space I was already inhabiting materially. I needed time to think about what things meant and how to deal with new situations in the most mature way. Sometimes change lifts you up like a tornado and puts you down someplace you've never been before. Tornadoes are fast, and they are also destructive. Speed can be the enemy of constructive change.

Another reason I was being inwardly directed to remain in my condo, I think, was in order to say good-bye. I needed to say good-bye to parts of myself that were being called to transform into something new, and I needed to say hello to parts of myself that were being born. The biggest mistakes I have made in my life I would not have made had I taken more time. Time to think. And meditate. And pray.

Perhaps you were one thing and now you're another: perhaps you were in high school and now you're entering college; perhaps you were single and now you're getting married; maybe you were married and now you're single; perhaps you were childless and now you're a parent; perhaps you had a child at home and now you no longer do. Whatever door you've walked through, your life won't be quite the same as it was before. The room you were in is behind you now.

The emotional ground underneath your feet is different, and you need time to reorient yourself. Rushing through change is an unconscious move, and it's a setup for mistakes.

Navigating Change

When one stage of life gives way to another, it's the end of an era and the beginning of a new one. How we navigate such transitions spiritually will determine the joy or despair that comes next. In navigating any change, we may be tempted toward either of two extremes—resisting the change, on the one hand, or being reckless toward it, on the other. These extremes are really the flip sides of an ego-based response to change. The deeper spiritual task is to achieve moderation by avoiding both extremes.

Moderation is emotional sobriety, bringing a deep and considered awareness of both the pitfalls and the opportunities inherent in any situation. It implies a capacity for reflection, an ability to stay aware and act responsibly no matter what's occurring. Without moderation, change can be more damaging than miraculous. But no matter whether a change is happy or sad, it can be a sacred experience if we're spiritually awake.

If a change is happy, you remain awake by being grateful to God and to the people who have helped you make this happen, by remembering those who haven't been quite this lucky lately, and by not allowing yourself to get cocky or giddy. If you do, you're liable to blow it. You remain awake by praying to be worthy of your good fortune, now and always.

When a positive change is occurring in our lives, it's a good idea to take the time to sit quietly and breathe it in, literally and figuratively. In your mind's eye, see a picture of the new situation, and imagine yourself functioning at your best within it. Now with your eyes closed, breathe deeply and feel yourself inwardly expanding into that possibility within yourself. Such exercises are not idle fantasies but actual powers of the mind.

If you don't make such efforts, the ego will do everything it can to sabotage you. That, after all, is its raison d'être. Unless you firmly establish your emotional center in the midst of a new condition, you remain psychologically outside it although within it. If you're not yet dwelling within it from your own spiritual center, you'll neither take full advantage of the situation nor behave in the most centered and powerful ways. Psychic space is every bit as real—and, on a certain level, more real—than physical space. If you're *here*, and psychologically a condition is *over there*, then the split between the two will be reflected in the circumstances of your life.

Using Ritual

One of the ways to powerfully align a material circumstance with an internal reality is through ritual. We can use simple ceremony to imbue any transition with enlightened understanding.

We can do more than simply give birth to our children; we can uplift the experience of their childhood and our relationship to them through baptism, bris, a baby-naming ceremony, and so forth.

We can do more than simply watch our children grow into adolescence; we can prayerfully bid farewell to their childhood and welcome them into adulthood, uplifting this new phase of their lives through coming-of-age ceremonies, bar and bat mitzvahs, and so forth.

With ritual, we do more than simply begin a new job; we prayerfully ask that it serve God's purposes and invoke spiritual forces to support us in the effort. We do more than simply get married; we pray for God to unite our hearts, to enter the marriage and make it a blessing on the world. We do more than simply get divorced; we ask for God's help in healing our hearts, filling us with forgiveness, and paving the way for new beginnings. We do more than lose a job; we perform a ritual to ask God's help in turning this situation into a blessing, providing a higher form of abundance and service. We do more than bury our loved ones; we perform a memorial service to bring their souls, and ours, to comfort and peace in the arms of God.

In the summer of 2004, the United States officially unveiled our World War II Memorial, honoring men and women who fought valiantly for freedom in that war. A Washington memorial has more than symbolic significance; it becomes part of the psychic landscape of a nation, as we permanently enshrine the memory of those who sacrificed so much for us. Still, to have its greatest power, a memorial must be emotionally and spiritually *met* by those who visit there. In visiting the Lincoln, Jefferson, or Washington Memorials, you can feel that some people are visiting with a tourist mentality, but you can also feel the presence of those who bring with them a depth of spirit that makes their visit a civic pilgrimage. Their hearts and minds are open to sacred contact with great beings who lived before us, whom we will never meet, and yet who profoundly affected the lives we live. You can read the quotes from Jefferson or Lincoln on the sides of their memorials with mere historic interest or with a soulful immersion in the power and meaning and blessing of their lives.

Travel has great ritualistic potential. If you visit the Sphinx and the pyramids in Egypt or the Parthenon in Greece, the Mother Temple in Bali or the Glastonbury Cathedral, who you are when you go there—what consciousness you bring to the experience—will determine the depth at which the visit will affect your life.

Ritual is so instinctive within human beings that we spontaneously create it when it's needed. From people leaving millions of flowers at Kensington Palace after the death of Princess Diana to flowers and teddy bears and pictures left at the door of the late John F. Kennedy Jr.'s apartment; from the picture- and prayer- and poem-strewn fence around the Oklahoma City Murrah Federal Building bomb site to the candle-lit gathering in

New York City at which thousands prayed for the victims of the World Trade Center disaster, people know we need a vessel for our feelings—to order them, give them meaning, and spiritually lift them up.

Some rituals are collective, such as the inauguration of a president or the coronation of a monarch. The psychic rite of passage is as important as the legal one, in that it touches the heart not only of the leader but also of the people who will be led.

If someone whom I did not vote for wins an election, then my heart might not as easily acquiesce to his or her leadership. An inauguration, however, calls forth the psychological, emotional, and spiritual affirmation that I might otherwise withhold. The relationship of a people to their leader is an ancient, archetypal connection imprinted on the human psyche; a ritualistic beginning summons the heart's goodwill.

If things are good, perform a ritual to praise and thank God. If things are sad, perform a ritual to call the angels to help you endure. Either way, a ritual will envelop you in a light that no material force has the power to bestow. It is an outer event that realigns internal forces, lifting them back up to where they came from and where they belong. Holy ritual joins heaven and earth together.

Then a fractured world becomes whole again because we do.

Preparing the Heart for Change

Before I knew I was pregnant with my daughter, I walked around for days with a strong sense that everything was about to change. That's all I knew. It was only with time that the realization of just *what* was about to change made its way into my conscious awareness; when it did, there was no way for me to know—never having given birth before—what a profound and fundamental transition was under way.

When my daughter was born, I loved her, of course. But my psyche was as thrown by the experience as it was exalted. I see now that pregnancy and childbirth are rife with psychological and emotional changes just as significant as the changes occurring inside a woman's body. In a materialistically oriented culture, of course, we tend to give more credence to physical changes than to emotional ones, and that is to our detriment. "She's pregnant, so she's a little nuts right now" is hardly a profound description of a pregnant woman's psychological condition. I wish I had prepared myself inwardly for motherhood as well as I prepared my life externally. There should have been a room for her inside myself as carefully designed as the darling baby's room for her inside my apartment. Her room was painted with precious pink and white clouds, with bluebirds holding up yellow ribbons near the ceiling. But looking back, I wish I had paid more attention to the room inside my heart, where the inner dynamics of motherhood had just begun to reverberate.

How would I have done it differently? I remember a big baby shower that was held for me at the home of my girlfriend Victoria. I have a photograph of me—with those forty additional pounds of pregnancy—sitting on Victoria's couch (if you can call what you're doing at that point "sitting"), surrounded by my girlfriends just a week or so before Emma was born. The gifts they brought to me were wonderful, and I felt a lot of love. But I see now that far more serious business was at hand at that time of my life, and had I known then what I know now, I would have held a ceremony, a woman's circle, some ritualistic process to mark this extraordinary moment in the life of two females—my daughter and me. Motherhood is a mystery, neither aided nor revealed by the registry at Toys "R" Us.

When a woman gives birth, two are born: a baby is born from the womb of its mother, and a woman is born from the womb of her former existence. Physical birth more or less takes care of itself, while spiritual rebirth is an experience we must consciously cultivate.

Postpartum depression, I suspect, is an experience that does not emerge in a society devoted to the sacred. In fact, what society regards as postpartum depression is the emotional consequence of unfinished business: a woman not yet having cut the umbilical cord with the woman she used to be. The transition into motherhood involves grieving a life that must now be psychically set aside, not just to make room for a child, but to make room for a new dimension of the woman's consciousness and life experience. With every new stage of life, there are things to grieve as well as things to celebrate.

By the time my daughter reached adolescence, I was clearer about a lot of this. I made sure that both she and I held her bat mitzvah in the highest light possible. This was a transition from life as a Jewish girl to life as a Jewish woman, and I knew that, as in everything else, we could play it deep or we could play it shallow. I wanted to lay down a carpet of roses for her, leading her out of childhood and into maidenhood, then into the womanhood that lay beyond. Many women, and men as well, would be so much less wounded had someone done that for us.

I told her I would give her the fun and fancy party, but only if she did the real work. None of this memorizing a few lines of Hebrew and pretending that's the real deal.

One day she asked me what I thought the theme should be for her bat mitzvah. I said, "What do you mean, theme?"

"Oh, kids have a theme," she said. "Like, for the party. Some people have a Detroit Pistons theme or a Britney Spears theme. . . ." I thought I would faint. I said very clearly and distinctly, "The theme of your bat mitzvah is that you are becoming a woman in the eyes of God. *Period.*"

Much to her credit, my daughter understood. She studied assiduously for months with a great cantor who taught her well, and as the bat mitzvah approached, we had marvelous conversations about what this transition would mean for both of us. For her, it meant she would no longer be a child. She wouldn't be a woman either but would rather be entering a phase of her life undervalued by contemporary culture: becoming what those before us called a maiden (or for boys, a master). Without consciously honoring this period, young people often play it out like a psychic circus, with belly button rings replacing prayer beads and casual sex replacing a connection to the divine. I wanted Emma to have a sacred context for these extraordinary years. I wanted her to appropriately separate from her childhood bond to me, and for both of us to move gracefully into new dimensions of ourselves and of our relationship to each other.

During the bat mitzvah, I ceremonially gave my daughter up to God and to the world. After saying prayers on the *bima* with her, I then, like millions of Jewish women before me, took my place in the congregation and watched my child lead the rest of the service by herself. As she read from the Torah in Hebrew, the presence of God was like a glow that filled the room. And after she carried the Torah on her shoulders and placed it back in the ark, the cantor led her to me and said, "You brought her here a child. I return her to you a woman."

I never felt more power, or more love, in my life.

Torches Pass

Sometimes we perform ritual without even knowing that we're doing so. When I was an eighteen-year-old college student, I went to hear a lecture by the late author Norman O. Brown, whose book *Love's Body* had inspired me greatly. After his talk, I stood in line to ask him very earnestly if he had any advice for me. He told me the Talmudic principle that in the midst of the darkest night, we should act as if the morning has already come. And then he kissed my forehead. A feeling of complete bliss came over me that lasted for hours.

A kiss on the forehead is a power-filled gesture: someone kisses (gives love to) your forehead (your third eye, or seat of the soul). What more profound ritual could there be for sending someone off with your blessing?

During that same period I received another, equally wonderful, blast of energy. I was walking with one of my professors—now jazz critic Stanley Crouch—to attend a lecture by Jane Fonda. This was 1970 or '71, and Fonda was visiting college campuses to discuss her antiwar activism. She was gorgeous, very thin in jeans and work shirt, wearing the layered haircut she made famous in the movie *Klute*. And she looked like she was lit from within. The combination of her stunning physical beauty and her almost spiritual radiance blew me away then and still does when I think about it. And while she was walking to the lecture, she did something that changed my life.

Crouch, who is African American, and I were walking down a sidewalk perpendicular to the one she was strolling on. As she crossed our sidewalk, she turned her head and glanced at us. I don't know what made her face light up—young white female walking with black professor? (remember, this was 1970)—but she then shot a smile in my direction that rivaled in power the transmissions of energy I received years later from a spiritual master. She seemed to project some wonderfulness onto Stanley's and my merely walking together, and her approval hit me like a tidal wave of positive energy. From that point forward, it felt like I had been blessed by Jane Fonda.

I wanted to mention this incident when I met Fonda almost thirty years later, but I didn't. I would have felt stupid. What was I supposed to say: "I saw you thirty years ago, and there was light pouring out of your head, and when you smiled at me I felt like a thunderbolt had hit my chest and I knew I was okay"? That moment had clearly passed. But I had been given a gift that would stay with me forever because my choices—or at least one of my choices, on some level symbolizing many others—had been validated by a woman of power.

Today many young women come up to me at my lectures, and I see in them the young woman I once was. They tell me they want to do what I do, and I'm sure they will—only better. A torch is always being passed from one generation to the next. My speaking might have lit some star in their sky the way other women have lit stars in mine. All of us are passing from one state to another all the time, and God sends guides and angels, inspirers and mentors, to light our way. He is always, always preparing new life.

The In-between Times

Sometimes we are living in the in-between times: when we're no longer who we used to be, but we haven't yet arrived at our next stage either.

In January 2004, I took my daughter to see Bette Midler perform; for me, this was the third time. I remembered seeing her perform in New York City in the seventies and then again in Los Angeles in the early nineties. The years had passed and so much had changed. Taking my daughter to see the show, I felt like I was passing on to her a beautiful gift that had meant a lot to me. Midler's music had stirred my soul, and now it would perhaps stir hers.

It was interesting to see how Bette had changed and how she had not changed. On one hand, jokes that played well ten or twenty-five years ago do not play the same way now: the world is entirely different, and so are we. But the change that I noticed most was in Midler herself. She clearly cares deeply about people and is herself a very serious person; her commentary on the state of the world, and in particular American politics, was searing and real. (It was courageous even, given that some in her audience would surely not have agreed with her!) Yet I could sense an angst in her that seemed to me a poignant reflection of the state of our generation. We're still telling jokes, but nothing seems all that funny anymore.

What the evening impressed upon me was that we can't go home again. The seventies, eighties, and nineties of the divine Miss M no longer exist. They were a fun point in time, like a really cool party. But the party has ended, and the world, as she pointed out, is no longer safe for any of us. We were like children in those days, and we are children no more. I sensed she was not entirely kidding when she said she had taken a couple of years off to suffer through her menopause in silence.

Midler really didn't seem able to throw herself heart and soul into the old jokes. How could she? I could imagine her arguing with someone on her production team: "Oh come on, Bette. Those jokes are still funny! That routine still works! There's a whole new audience out there that hasn't heard this stuff yet, and they'll love it!" Her response—at least in my imagination—would be that she's too sick about the state of the world to do those jokes anymore. How can we laugh like that when the world is so messed up? Bette Midler lit up only two times during the night: When she was dead serious about politics and the state of the world and when she was singing songs that were musically profound.

I could see her conundrum, because she—like so many of us—is neither here nor there. She is no longer who she was (though she can mimic it brilliantly)—but she is not yet who she is becoming. She can *do* the other things still—Delores the Fish and Clementine and Ernie—but I sensed they weren't quite as true to her soul anymore. Perhaps this is all my projection, but it was how I felt. She, like so many of us, now seems in a middle zone, where real change happens. We are spiritually too big at this point to fit into the attitudinal clothes we used to wear, yet the new ones are still hanging in the closet.

When you take off one set of clothes, you are naked for a minute before you put on another. When age is seen in a purely material context, you sort of wonder if there *is* another set of clothes. Yet in a spiritual context, there is no phase of life—because there is no point in the universe—where God is not. We are always on the road to the next stage, whether we are days old or decades old. The spirit of life is not diminished by time. In the present moment, our task is to let go of what was, with love or even sorrow, and embrace what emerges next from the Mind of God. When we have seen the world and understood the world and felt our souls grow sick of the world, it's time for us to become children again. We look to God to give us new life when the old one has begun to die.

I'd go see Midler's brilliance anytime, but I have a distinct impression that the next time I see her, Clementine and Ernie might have morphed into something new. She has already demonstrated theatrical greatness and now seems headed toward our generational destiny: a greatness that will be the crowning glory of all her achievements up until this point, paving the way for the transformation of our world. Shakespeare said all the world's a stage, and all of us players on it. Today—whether we are famous entertainers or just regular folks—it feels like years of rehearsal are finally over, and the greatest performance of our lives is about to begin.

Playing Our Part

There was a time when the thought of changing the world didn't really seem all that hard.

When you're young, it's fairly easy to embrace the notion that we will someday cast away all problems from the world. Our bodies are young and voluptuous, our energy endless, our opportunities seemingly infinite; we think it's only a matter of time before all problems will bow before the power of our efforts (which are, after all, so impressive). Yet life has a way of wearing you down. You learn through often painful means that in the face of your prodigious intellect and energy, evil does not just step aside. It's tempting to succumb to the cynicism of age when you see how often things do not change. Especially when the most recalcitrant factors, the most immovable mountains, seem to be within yourself.

How can I believe the whole world will change its neurotic patterns when I keep marrying the same person over and over again? How can I believe two nations that keep murdering each other's citizens are going to find peace anytime soon when I'm still not talking to my parents?

Our attitudinal, not just our physical, muscles become less flexible with age. It's amazing how much fatigue enough disappointments can cause. It takes energy to change, and sometimes our energy is in short supply. You can feel the pressure, once you reach middle age, to simply go along with a status quo that is hardly what you hoped for but is here, so what the hell.

Jesus said of Lazarus, "He is not dead. He is only sleeping." And so are we. There lies in most of us the accumulated frustration of our unlived dreams and the squelched desire to spread our wings and fly above the worldly limitations that hold us back. These painful energies are not automatically transmuted except through prayer and surrender and holy relationships. They attach themselves to our spiritual organs of faith and hope, taunting us with lines like "You're too old" or "You blew it" or "You're washed up." And at times they seem to be backed by evidence.

To say to those voices, "Satan, get thee behind me," is not mumbo jumbo or wishful thinking. Spiritually, it's our power and our strength.

Angels and Demons

During the wee hours of the morning, both angels and demons take shape. The glories of a life as well as its terrors are clearer before dawn has broken. Once the light of day casts its spell upon us, deeper meanings—sometimes obvious only hours before—are easily forgotten. We fall prey to the mind-set of the world.

How unnatural our modern Western relationship to nature's clock. Did Edison realize the havoc that lay hidden in his gift to humanity? The electric lightbulb would change the world. In service to the industrial era and its demands for productivity, we trained ourselves to sleep when the system needed us to sleep and to wake when it needed us to awaken. How often, then, we miss the sunrise and its simple blessings. These blessings are not metaphorical. They are more than merely beautiful; they are a reminder from God: "Look what I bring forth out of every dark night; such is the work I shall do within you."

Growing older is a form of night, full of angels and demons as well. We are closer to wisdom, yet we are closer to death. It takes a lot of climbing to get a clear perspective: climbing above the thoughts and feelings that would keep us tied to the ground we have trod before. The ground of yesterday is barren now. Its drama is over. Only the present, lived in fullness and intensity, holds the promise of a new tomorrow.

Night after night, I have lain awake, my eyes having popped open for no apparent reason, my body unwilling to fall back asleep, my hormones not feeling like they are mine anymore. For a while, I said the usual things to myself: "I hate this; I must have my estrogen checked again; I need to buy more melatonin; this will feel so awful tomorrow." Yet finally I noticed that more was going on: "I'm that age, so I'm having a hard time sleeping" was such a hand-me-down notion, so devoid of dimension, so superficial in its interpretation of my own experience. From a spiritual perspective, these hours were not tired; they were deeply awake. The rest we seek we will find not from sleeping but from waking.*

In those hours that I've lain so inconveniently awake, I think I've begun at last to know what awakened means. Noting the witching hour—4:15—at which I awake more often than not, stealing outside to look at the stars and marvel at the moon, I return again to my ancient self. In those hours, I am not a menopausal nutcase. I'm a magical witch, and I can feel it in my bones.

WHEN ASPECTS OF YOU that used to work have peaked now; when situations that used to seem exciting have lost their edge, and so have you; when a phrase like "over the hill" suddenly means something after all, then you are ready for rebirth. It is time to face the terrifying void—not in resignation but in faith. For this void is the womb for a new emerging self. From the acid of regrets over things that did and did not happen to our tenacious hopes for what might yet still occur, a profound, transformative alchemy is at work within us. We are not done—not until God rings the bell.

And that bell, as we know, might be far, far off. A television interviewer once asked Clint Eastwood about his marriage to a woman decades younger than he. I loved his wry answer: "If she dies, she dies!" Indeed, who knows who is leaving when? In 1994, my sister died at the age of forty-four. The next year, my father died at eighty-five. Go figure.

So what are we to do with the rest of our lives should we choose a path of spiritual rebirth? First, we must *consciously choose to live them.* Hidden beliefs are dangerous, and the belief that "the best years of my life are behind me" is a powerful agent—not of change, but of inertia. Whether or not we consciously embrace the thought, many of us do think it. And thoughts like that can be changed.

If we primarily identify with external realities, as we've been trained to do by the ego's thought system, then it's hard to look forward to better years after a certain number of them have passed. Yet this is our challenge: to see beyond the world and thus invoke new beginnings. A child grows whether or not he or she chooses to. At a certain point in life, however, we grow *only* if we choose to. And in that choice lies a choice not only for ourselves but indeed for everyone.

Deeper with the Years

Visiting London in the fall of 2003, I went to the Royal Academy of Arts to view Andrew Lloyd Webber's collection of Pre-Raphaelite paintings. One of them, a picture called *Silver and Gold*, shows a beautiful young woman walking with an elderly lady. I stared at the painting for quite a while, remembering what it was like to be the young woman in the picture, like a part I had acted in a play that had closed and would not be opening again. I'm certainly not yet the elderly woman but rather I'm perched somewhere between the two. I can now relate to the older woman I will hopefully be someday as much as to the younger woman I no longer am. And what is striking about the picture, to me, is the seriousness with which the older woman is listening to the younger one. Is the younger one her granddaughter? Her charge? One doesn't know. But she clearly cares about the younger woman, who seems to be drinking in her attention. It is part of the younger woman's initiation into the mysteries, that she experiences the goodwill of a woman who has passed through her own youth and now cares about someone else's.

My mother once said to me, "You know, Marianne, whatever age you are, you experienced all the ages before it." She had probably said that in response to something I had patronizingly said, indicating that youth was something she couldn't possibly understand! And my father, at around the age of eighty, said to me, "It's funny. When you're old, you don't *feel* old." My conclusion is that age, while in an eternal sense is truly nothing, in a material sense is truly something. And I honor both, since both are mine.

I had a personal assistant who was twenty years younger than me, and sometimes when I would see her coming down the hall I would swear I was looking at a younger version of myself. I enjoyed her joy at things I hardly even noticed anymore—her amazement that Cameron Diaz makes more than *two million dollars!* to star in a movie, and her excitement about going to Paris for the first time. Watching her was like a chance to say hello to a me I no longer was. And I knew she too was staring down a hall toward a woman she might one day be.

I once had a friend who was dying of cancer, and after her death I began dating her boyfriend. He told me that during the last few months of her life her sessions in therapy often centered on her intuitive sense that one day he and I would be together. She had to deal with the fact that the arc of her life was winding down while on a certain level mine was just starting up. It pained me to think of what she must have felt. And now, having entered the last half of my life, I realize more and more what she was letting go.

None of us has control of the parts we're cast in during the ever-changing drama of life. You're the young Turk when you're the young Turk; you're the aging crone when you're the aging crone; you're the innocent in love when you're the innocent in love; and you're jaded when you're jaded. Yet something in us is none of those things; who we truly are is changeless in the Mind of God. We're just experiencing different corners of the universe, to learn its dimensions, its lessons, before going on to another. I don't think death is the end of our lives, for as surely as we're headed out of here we're heading toward some new adventure. I assume the wheel of karma keeps turning until every point God wanted to make He's had a chance to make, and He can see we got them all.

It's important to give up yesteryear when yesteryear is gone. I remember complaining to my best friend that when I lecture, I'm not as fast as I once was, not as snap-crackle-and-pop in my delivery. His response was helpful: that many in my audience aren't as fast now either, that they too are no longer as snap-crackle-and-pop, and it would seem disingenuous if I tried to be. Age slows us down, but it takes us deeper, into realms no less fertile, spiritually, than those we inhabited before. As the years go by, we lose some of the outer sparkle that so gloriously infused our youth—but an inner sparkle emerges that we never before had. Ralph Waldo Emerson wrote, "As I age, my beauty steals inward."

And it's more than just our beauty that steals inward. The entire richness of life begins to burrow underground as we age; no less magical, just not as visible to the physical eye. In fact, in a way, life becomes more magical. For magic is of the invisible planes.

Thinking about my young assistant's excitement about going to Paris for the first time, I thought about my history with that city vis-à-vis the men I've known. The years that take a woman from youth to maturity are marked emotionally by her history in love. There are phases of Paris, like there are phases of certain relationships: getting ready for it, being there, and remembering what it was like.

When I was young, I once went to Paris with a man who enchanted me as much as the city did. Our efforts to make the trip happen and the times we had there once we did are memories I'll hold dear forever. But decades later, there was another man. And when the subject of Paris came up between us, one quick glance said it all.

Both of us had been there, I could tell, and both of us had loved there; I could feel it. Both of us had had dreams come true there, and both of us had dreams that died there. We didn't even have to have the discussion, so clear it was in that one split-second glance that both of us knew all sides of it. I realized then that where we had gone in that moment—not in spite of the years we'd lived but clearly because of them—was a place more enchanting than Paris.

A New Future Begins

And what of those who say, "Well, maybe we could change the world—but not in my lifetime. So why should I try?"

According to Buddhism, it is not what we achieve in our lives but what we at least die *trying* to achieve that gives meaning to our existence. Susan B. Anthony never lived to see the passage of the Nineteenth Amendment. Yet millions of women live infinitely more empowered lives because of her. Her tireless efforts for generations of women she would never know provided half of all Americans—and I think the other half as well—with a greater capacity to express themselves fully. Surely, on some heavenly level, her soul receives the blessing she gave.

And now, in our time and through our efforts, we too are called to a great vision: to think the thoughts of a world at peace, infused with total love. For until we think the thoughts of peace, peace will not be ours. We will end war not because we hate it so much; we will end it by loving peace so much more. We will love it enough to try to live it in our own lives. We can wage a preemptive peace, in our hearts and in our politics. And then one day we will notice that war has disappeared.

Years from now, when we ourselves are no longer remembered, people will live on a peaceful planet, not knowing whom to bless, not knowing whom to thank. Children will ask their parents, "Is it true that there was once a time when people had wars?" And the parents will say, "Yes, there was such a time. But a very long time ago. Wars don't happen anymore."

And when that happens, surely on some level our souls will receive the blessing we gave. We will lift our glasses to the heaven we are already in, and with both tears and laughter we will howl, "We did it!"

NO MATTER WHO YOU ARE or what you have done, God is aware if you are willing to work on His behalf. If you have stumbled and then gotten back up—whether you stumbled through your own doing or someone else's intent to harm you or both—you will arise now with new power. You will speak with deeper credibility and carry a deeper compassion for those who suffer. You will have gained wisdom and humility and will never again be as easily tricked by the ego. You are further prepared for service to God.

This is a time in all our lives to deal with those issues that we have pushed into the back of a drawer, that keep us from performing at less than 100 percent. This is the time for us to make a radical break from our weaker selves, devoting each day to the total elimination of whatever ego energies remain attached to our psyches to ruin our lives. This cannot be done without prayer. It cannot be done without work. It cannot be done without brutal self-honesty. It cannot be done without forgiving self and others. It cannot be done without love. But when it is done, we achieve spiritual mastery. The rock in front of our tomb is removed. Our spirit resurrects, and we are ready for the light. We are ready in the sense that we can contain it now: We have come at last to live in the comfort of our own skin.

We realize the huge calling of history at this time. We have been called to a collective genius, and each of us is being prepared to play our part. Our world needs spiritual giants, and it takes not ego but humility to sign up for the effort. Many of our problems arose because we chose to play small, thinking there we would find safety. But we were born with wings, and we are meant to spread them. Anything less will hurt us, will deny love to ourselves and others, and will mean that we end our lives not having flown the flight of spiritual glory.

Let us fly.

> Dear God,
> If left to my own devices,
> my perceptions will be skewed.
> I surrender to You everything I think and feel.
> Please take my past, and plan my future.
> Send Your Spirit to redeem my mind,
> that I might be set free.

May I be Your vessel
And serve the world.
May I become who You would have me be,
that I might do what You would have me do.
And I will, dear God.
Amen.

Now imagine yourself as you would like to be. Close your eyes and see yourself as elegant, dignified, and calm. See yourself as smart, insightful, humble, and kind. Imagine all your weaknesses replaced by strength. And do not stop. Remain in stillness with your eyes closed for as long as you can, for you are conceiving new life. Ask the Spirit of God to come into you and give you birth into the fullness of your possible self. Whatever the portal through which you enter the house of God, know that His house is where you are truly at home. It is where you will find who you are, receive repair of your soul, heal from the world, and begin again. You will go back into the darkness of the world and bring to it your light. You will have experienced a miracle, and through you others will experience miracles too.

God so loves you, and loves the world, that He is sending it the person He has created you to be.

Remember that in any situation, only what you are not giving can be lacking. Bring the love of God, and you will bless all things. He will be at your left, and He will be at your right. He will be in front of you, and He will be behind you. Wherever you go, He will be there with you.

And together, you will change the world.

For information about my books, lectures, and classes,
please check my Web site, *www.marianne.com.*
You will also find my audio recordings, which can be
downloaded to your iPod or MP3 player.

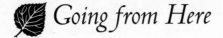 *Going from Here*

*F*or those of you who would like to follow up on studying *A Course in Miracles,* you might appreciate the following resources:

1. My book *A Return to Love* is like a primer on *A Course in Miracles.*

2. *The Circle of Atonement* offers a wide range of teaching materials designed to help the student walk this transformative path. Headed up by Robert Perry, author of *Path of Light: Stepping into Peace with* A Course in Miracles, the Circle is one of the most internationally respected voices among Course students. It offers a vision of *A Course in Miracles* that is both faithful to the Course and practical for the student. Visit the Circle's Web site at *www.circleofa.com* to access a wealth of free materials.

Contact:
The Circle of Atonement
P.O. Box 4238
W. Sedona, AZ 86340
Phone: 928-282-0790
E-mail: info@circleofa.com
www.circleofa.com

3. Since 1978, Miracle Distribution Center has been the world-wide contact point for students of *A Course in Miracles*, supporting their understanding and integration of the Course's principles into daily life. President Beverly Hutchinson is a gracious presence within the Course community. Services include *The Holy Encounter,* a free bimonthly magazine with inspirational and educational articles on the Course; international Course study group listings; weekly recorded classes on the Course; worldwide prayer ministry; international Course conferences and retreats; mail-order and online catalog service; counseling referral service; and an interactive Web site that includes chat and live monthly webcasts. Most importantly, the center can fill you in on other Course activities going on throughout the world.

Contact:
Miracle Distribution Center
3947 E. La Palma Ave.
Anaheim, CA 92807
Phone: 800-359-2246
www.miraclecenter.org

4. Any work by Dr. Gerald Jampolsky is wonderful. He and his wife, Diane Cirincione, founded the Center for Attitudinal Healing in 1975. Attitudinal healing is a process based on *A Course in Miracles,* teaching that in every moment we can choose love over fear, peace rather than conflict, and experience the peace that forgiveness brings. The Centers for Attitudinal Healing are an international network dealing with illness and dying, loss and grief, but also with anyone who wishes to heal a relationship and live life to the fullest.

Contact:
The Center for Attitudinal Healing
33 Buchanan Dr.
Sausalito, CA 94965
Phone: 415-331-6161
E-mail: home123@aol.com
www.healingcenter.org or *www.attitudinalhealing.org*

5. Aeesha and Kokomon Clottey do marvelous work applying the principles of *A Course in Miracles* to racial healing. They are coauthors of a book called *Beyond Fear: Twelve Spiritual Keys to Racial Healing,* and their Racial Healing groups take place at the Attitudinal Healing Connection in Oakland, California, the last Wednesday of every month.

Contact:
The Attitudinal Healing Connection
3278 West St.
Oakland, CA 94608
Phone: 510-652-7901
www.ahc-oakland.org